# A MUSLIM VIEW
# OF CHRISTIANITY

# FAITH MEETS FAITH

*An Orbis Series in Interreligious Dialogue*
Paul F. Knitter & William R. Burrows, General Editors
*Editorial Advisors*
John Berthrong
Diana Eck
Karl-Josef Kuschel
Lamin Sanneh
George E. Tinker
Felix Wilfred

In the contemporary world, the many religions and spiritualities stand in need of greater communication and cooperation. More than ever before, they must speak to, learn from, and work with each other in order to maintain their vital identities and to contribute to fashioning a better world.

The FAITH MEETS FAITH Series seeks to promote interreligious dialogue by providing an open forum for exchange among followers of different religious paths. While the Series wants to encourage creative and bold responses to questions arising from contemporary appreciations of religious plurality, it also recognizes the multiplicity of basic perspectives concerning the methods and content of interreligious dialogue.

Although rooted in a Christian theological perspective, the Series does not limit itself to endorsing any single school of thought or approach. By making available to both the scholarly community and the general public works that represent a variety of religious and methodological viewpoints, FAITH MEETS FAITH seeks to foster an encounter among followers of the religions of the world on matters of common concern.

FAITH MEETS FAITH SERIES

# A MUSLIM VIEW OF CHRISTIANITY

## Essays on Dialogue
## by Mahmoud Ayoub

*Edited by*
## Irfan A. Omar

ORBIS BOOKS

Maryknoll, New York 10545

Founded in 1970, Orbis Books endeavors to publish works that enlighten the mind, nourish the spirit, and challenge the conscience. The publishing arm of the Maryknoll Fathers and Brothers, Orbis seeks to explore the global dimensions of the Christian faith and mission, to invite dialogue with diverse cultures and religious traditions, and to serve the cause of reconciliation and peace. The books published reflect the views of their authors and do not represent the official position of the Maryknoll Society. To learn more about Maryknoll and Orbis Books, please visit our website at www.maryknoll.org.

Copyright © 2007 by Mahmoud Mustafa Ayoub.

Published by Orbis Books, Maryknoll, New York 10545-0308.
Manufactured in the United States of America.

Library of Congress Cataloging-in-Publication Data

Ayoub, Mahmoud.
    A Muslim view of Christianity : essays on dialogue / by Mahmoud Ayoub ; edited by Irfan A. Omar.
        p. cm. — (Faith meets faith)
    ISBN 978-1-57075-690-0 (pbk.)
1. Islam—Relations—Christianity. 2. Christianity and other religions—Islam. I. Omar, Irfan A. II. Title.
    BP172.A878 2007
    297.2'83—dc22
                            2006103207

To all those who,
through sincere and patient dialogue,
have sought to make peace on God's earth

# Contents

*Part I*
## THE NEED FOR DIALOGUE
*Setting the Context*

## *Part IV*
## *MUSLIM-CHRISTIAN DIALOGUE IN THE MODERN WORLD*
### *Comparative Studies*

# Preface

Since the beginning of formal dialogue between Christians and Muslims in the latter half of the twentieth century, numerous Muslims have participated in meetings, conferences, symposia, and the like. Many of these Muslims were also scholars of Islam. Few among them, however, can be said to have been so much at home with both Islam and Christianity as Mahmoud Ayoub.

Professor Ayoub is one of the pioneering Muslim scholars who have invested heavily in interreligious dialogue. His familiarity with and expertise in the Jewish and Christian as well as Muslim textual sources allow him to approach these religions with a sense of grounding that is necessary for any authentic dialogue and comparison.

As a historian of religion, he has written on Islamic theological, historical, and cultural issues with deeper insight and a broader perspective than many of his contemporaries. As a scholar, Professor Ayoub writes from within a historical-critical framework, and yet his writings carry an appreciation of and sensitivity toward the issues he addresses. As a practicing Muslim, he does not shy away from criticism where it is due in his own religious tradition. As an honest partner in dialogue, he seldom holds back his appreciation and praise for aspects in other traditions that he regards as conducive to human spiritual and social progress.

This volume is a result of more than three decades of research and scholarly effort. Even though these studies have been previously published in various scholarly venues, their increasing relevance in the twenty-first century merits their renewed presentation. Professor Ayoub has devoted considerable energy to a scholarly investigation of Qur'anic directives for pluralist living. He has, by example and through his writings, shown the way that may prove to be a model for other Muslims to emulate.

Many Muslims will agree with the conclusions Professor Ayoub has drawn from his analyses of the texts he has explored. While the purpose of his writings was to show convincingly what he as a Muslim scholar finds in his sources, he remains open to further dialogue and discussion. This is consistent with Muslim scholarship since the beginning of Islam where different schools of thought argued and debated their respective theological positions vis-à-vis other positions while being open to new ideas. Thus, in the end, an important point of this book is not necessarily to convince others of its conclusions but mainly to invite them to continue the dialogue in the service of learning and greater understanding.

The essays included in this selection are not exhaustive of Professor Ayoub's writings on interreligious dialogue. He has published more than twenty-five essays that deal with Islam's relationship with other religions; a vast majority of them are concerned with Christianity. Twenty-one of these were published in Arabic as *Dirasat fi al-'Alaqat al-Masihiyyah al-Islamiyyah* (Studies in Christian-Muslim Relations).[1] The sixteen essays included here were selected based on the following criteria: (1) their relevance to contemporary Muslim-Christian dialogue, and (2) their comparative theological and/or historical content.

Many of the essays in this volume have been regarded as essential materials for any study of Islamic and Christian historical issues. They have been widely cited in scholarly studies related to the larger theme of Christian-Muslim relations. While the relevance of these essays remains, access to some of these has become harder. Some of the essays were published in periodicals and books that have become inaccessible. Therefore it was deemed necessary to present them here collectively so as to add to the already growing library of studies in relations between Christians and Muslims. This particular volume is unique because it is a product of both the intellectual and experiential effort over a period of several decades and provides insights that are sensitive and timely; and it is the result of a Muslim scholar's effort. While other studies on themes in Christianity and Islam do exist, very few are authored solely by Muslims. Fewer yet among them deal with deeper theological perspectives that are brought to bear on a host of historical and contemporary issues relevant to both Muslims and Christians. What makes this volume important for a student of interreligious dialogue is that throughout these essays, Ayoub has maintained a standard of theological discourse that is the hallmark of a seasoned and passionate scholar.

The work of publishing these essays would not have been possible without the help and support of Susan Perry at Orbis Books. I am very grateful for her helpful suggestions and for her assistance at every level of the process. It is also gratifying to know that this project has the blessing of Professor Paul Knitter, himself an internationally recognized authority in interreligious dialogue, who offered valuable suggestions toward making the final selection of essays. Thanks also to Carol Bebawi at the Center for the Study of Islam and Christian-Muslim Relations in Birmingham, U.K., who always responded to my queries with diligence and compassion. I am equally grateful for the help given to me by James Schultz, Ahmad Fuad Rahmat, Etin Anwar, and Shalahudin Kafrawi in looking over the draft for diacritical errors and other omissions. For me, this entire process gives hope for a continued discussion and dialogue between various groups engaged in improving relations between Muslims and Christians. It is vital to have examples of individuals that inspire such prospects, and I am deeply grateful to Mahmoud Ayoub for agreeing to have these essays published here and, of course, for writing the introduction which helps situate the essays in their proper context.

Finally, I owe a debt of gratitude to my wife, Farah Chen (Xue Zhu), who has been a constant source of support and inspiration in this and all of my other projects. Her dedication and help in providing a workable format of the printed essays made it possible for a timely completion of the editing and proofreading of the manuscript.

# Notes

1. *Dirasat fi al-ʿAlaqat al-Masihiyyah al-Islamiyyah*, 2 vols. (Beirut: Markaz al-Dirasat al-Masihiyyah al-Islamiyyah, 2000 [vol. 1]; 2001 [vol. 2]).

# Note on Transliteration and Style

For the sake of the general reader Arabic words (names and titles in notes) have not been transliterated with diacritical marks such as overbars and underdots. However, Islamic terms relevant to the subject matter of the text (both within the body of the text as well as in notes) are italicized and have been rendered with complete diacritical marks because these facilitate their correct pronunciation. A glossary of such terms appears on pages 251-53. Islamic terms commonly used in English such as the Qur'an, hadith, surah, and jihad are not italicized and are free of diacritical marks.

The Arabic letter *'ayn* has been retained in most Islamic words and is represented by an open single quote mark ('), while the closing single quote mark (') denotes the *hamza* consonant.

To indicate the feminine, the final *h* (*ta' marbuta*) has been retained in terms such as *shahadah* and *jannah*. The *h* becomes a *t* in *idafa* elisions, as in *jannat al-firdaws*.

The short vowel mark (') is retained in words such as *sama'* (heaven), *'ulamā'* (religious scholars), and *hunafā'* (pl. of *hanīf*, a generic monotheist).

Unless otherwise noted, dates are given in A.H./C.E. format. A.H. refers to *Anno Hegira,* the Islamic Hijri calendar. The year A.H. 1 corresponds to the 622 C.E., which was the year when Prophet Muhammad migrated from Makkah to Madinah.

All translations are by the author unless otherwise noted.

# Biography of
# Mahmoud Mustafa Ayoub

Mahmoud Mustafa Ayoub was born in 1935 in South Lebanon. He received his education at the American University of Beirut (B.A., Philosophy, 1964), the University of Pennsylvania (M.A., Religious Thought, 1966), and Harvard University, where he received his Ph.D. in History of Religions in 1975 under the supervision of Annemarie Schimmel. Since 1988 he has been Professor of Islamic Studies in the Department of Religion, Temple University in Philadelphia.

Professor Ayoub is an adjunct professor at the Duncan Black Macdonald Center, Hartford Seminary, Connecticut, and a research fellow at the Middle East Center, University of Pennsylvania. From 1997 till 2001, he taught at the Reconstructionist Rabbinical College, Wyncote, Pennsylvania. Previously he was a lecturer in Religious Studies at the University of Alberta; assistant professor of Religious Studies at San Diego State University; visiting professor at the Institute for Islamic Studies at McGill University; visiting professor at Balamand Greek Orthodox Seminary in Koura, Lebanon; and research associate at the Center for Religious Studies at the University of Toronto.

In 1998, Professor Ayoub helped create and launch a graduate level (Master of Arts) program in Christian-Muslim Relations and Comparative Religion at the Centre for Christian-Muslim Studies, University of Balamand, Koura, Lebanon. He has been part of a major consultation for the program since 1996, and since the spring of 1999 he has been a visiting professor at the Centre.

Professor Ayoub was also involved in the formulation and establishment of the joint Temple-Gajah Mahda Universities' Comparative Religion Program in Yogjakarta, Indonesia. He has lectured at that Indonesian university on several occasions over the years since the start of the graduate program in 1999.

Professor Ayoub has received many distinguished awards and scholarships, both for his community work as well as for his academic achievements. Among others, he was a recipient of the Kent Doctoral Fellowship and the Canada Council Fellowship. In 1994-95, he was awarded the Fulbright Fellowship for lecturing in Malaysia. In the spring and summer of 2000 he traveled to Egypt and Lebanon, also on a Fulbright Research Fellowship. In recent years, at the request of the United States Department of State, Professor Ayoub has served as an ambassador to various parts of the Middle

East lecturing on American society and institutions, interreligious dialogue, and Islam in America.

He has decades of experience in interreligious dialogue and has given more than sixty addresses on the subject. He has served on the advisory board of the Jewish Chautauqua Society, New York. His recently published two-volume work on Christian-Muslim dialogue, *Dirasat fi al-'Alaqat al-Masihiyyah al-Islamiyyah* (Studies in Christian-Muslim Relations), is a testament to his extensive research and involvement in interreligious issues.

Professor Ayoub has authored several books in the area of Islam and interreligious dialogue. The most notable are *Redemptive Suffering in Islam* and *The Qur'an and Its Interpreters* (2 volumes to date). He has published over fifty scholarly articles, both as chapters in edited works as well as in well-known academic refereed journals such as *The Muslim World, Journal of the American Oriental Society, Bulletin of the Institute of Middle Eastern Studies*, and *Islamochristiana*. Two of his recent works are *The Crisis of Muslim History: Religion and Politics in Early Islam* (2003), and *Islam: Faith and History* (2004). Currently he is working on the third volume of *The Qur'an and Its Interpreters*. Professor Ayoub has also contributed to a number of encyclopedias and serves on several advisory and editorial boards including those of *The Muslim World* and *Islam and Christian-Muslim Relations*.

# A MUSLIM VIEW
# OF CHRISTIANITY

# Introduction

MAHMOUD MUSTAFA AYOUB

Muslim-Christian dialogue is as old as Islam itself. It began when the Prophet Muhammad sought confirmation of the authenticity of his message in the witness of the Christian savant Waraqah b. Nawfal,[1] the cousin of his wife Khadijah, who may have herself been a Christian. Furthermore, tradition reports that while still a youth, Muhammad met a Syrian monk called Bahirah who recognized him as the "prophet of the end of time."[2] The Syrian monk is said to have recognized Muhammad by the seal of prophethood, which he saw between his shoulders.[3]

The Qur'an affirms more than once the special importance of this Christian witness to the truth of its own message.[4] It tells Muhammad, while still uncertain of the veracity of his prophetic experience, "If you are in doubt concerning what We have sent down to you, ask those who read the Scriptures before you" (10:94). The Qur'an likewise attributes to Jesus the prediction of a messenger who would come after him, "whose name is Ahmad," that is, Muhammad (Q. 61:6). This led Muslim traditionists and historians to seek confirmation of the truth of Muhammad's prophetic mission in the books of both the Old and the New Testaments.[5]

The view that Muhammad may have often met desert monks, in or around Makkah, even before the beginning of his prophetic career, is not implausible. But such encounters, if indeed they took place at all, could only have left a generally positive personal impression on him. Both the possibility of such an impression and also its lack of decisive impact on his message find some support in the Qur'an, as will become apparent in the course of this discussion. But they could not have influenced the making of the Qur'an itself or the general tenor of Muhammad's message. Therefore, the well-known Swedish scholar Tor Andrae, in my view, goes much further in assessing the psychological and spiritual effects of such hypothetical encounters on the Prophet's thought and mission than either the Qur'an or earliest sources of prophetic biography and tradition could bear out.[6]

The Qur'an is ambivalent in its treatment of the people of the Book—Jews and Christians—and their beliefs, as well as their moral and spiritual conduct. While it cannot be denied that the Prophet's attitudes toward the two faith communities were to a considerable extent determined by the social, political, and theological realities of the time, the Qur'an always dealt with these realities within the logic of its own faith and worldview. This ambivalent approach can be discerned in the Qur'an's warm and sympa-

1

thetic appreciation of Christian piety,[7] on the one hand, and the brief allusion to a well-documented positive but disputatious meeting between Muhammad and a delegation of the Christian community of the valley of Najran of South Arabia, on the other.[8]

Two points concern us in this meeting. The first is that the Prophet first challenged the Christians of Najran to the well-known context of imprecation (*mubāhalah*)[9] to prove the truth of his new faith against the Christian claim of his divine sonship. Then he concluded a peace treaty with the Christians, which they themselves had wisely proposed, instead of forcing a confrontation in which they would at all events have been the losers. The second, and more important, point in my view is that when the time for their afternoon prayers came, the Prophet allowed them to pray in his mosque. This he did in spite of the loud protestations of some of his companions.[10]

This significant report is fully consonant with the Qur'anic view of the inviolability of and open access to houses of worship. Mosques, monastic cells, churches, and synagogues are houses of God in which "His name is mentioned, and where He is glorified evenings and mornings" (Q. 24:36). God, the Qur'an further asserts, in His wisdom protects such houses of worship by repelling their would-be destroyers by others who would defend them: "Had God not restrained some people by others, monastic cells, churches, synagogues and mosques in which God's name is remembered much would have been demolished" (Q. 22:40). Furthermore, the Qur'an emphatically condemns those who hinder God's worshipful servants from frequenting His houses and who seek their destruction. It accuses such evil perpetrators of wrongdoing (*ẓulm*) and predicts for them a grievous punishment (Q. 2:114).

Coming after both the Torah of Moses and Gospel of Jesus Christ, the Qur'an saw itself not as contradicting or replacing these Scriptures, but as confirming them. It asserts, "He [God] sent down the Book to you [Muhammad] with the truth, confirming (the scriptures) that were before it, and He sent down the Torah and the Gospel aforetime, a guidance for humankind . . ." (Q. 3:3-4). This means that the Qur'an came to confirm not only the Jewish and Christian Scriptures but every "Book" that God had, or may have, revealed before it.[11]

The Qur'an lays down four basic rules or principles that it considers to be necessary for the truth claim of any religion. The first is that a true religion must be enshrined in a divinely revealed scripture or sacred law (*sharī'ah*). Second, it must acknowledge and proclaim God's absolute Oneness (*tawḥīd*). Third, it must enjoin dynamic faith in God and the last day. Fourth, it should foster righteous living (*iḥsān*). On the basis of these four principles, the Qur'an affirms the truth of the faith of Muslims, Jews, Christians, and Sabaeans.[12]

It must be observed that, based on these principles, the Qur'an's view of the truth or untruth of any religion is both particularistic and universal. It is particularistic in that it demands of other religious traditions conformity to its own criteria in upholding or denying their truth and authenticity. It is universal in that it sees these principles as perennial truths on which not only Islam but all revealed religions and philosophies are based. In fact, in themselves these principles constitute the universal and primordial *islām* to which the Qur'an came to call all of humankind.

Moreover, in accordance with the principle of the Oneness of God the Qur'an calls on all the people of the Book, Jews, Christians, and Muslims, to come together to a unity of faith in and worship of God alone. It calls on them to repudiate all forms of idolatry, and particularly the idolatry of elevating other human beings to a level of equality with God (Q. 3:64). Within this unity of faith and worship, the Qur'an calls for a community of Scriptures, revealed by God, the Lord of all the people of faith in Him. Thus, in quest of this interreligious unity of faith, the Qur'an commands the Muslims to engage the people of the Book in the "fairest dialogue," and to say to them, "we accept faith in that which was sent down to us and that which was sent down to you. Our God and your God is One, and to Him we are Submitters" (Q. 29:46).

To this end, the Qur'an categorically condemns the arrogant boasting by any of the followers of all three monotheistic religions of the superiority of their faith over that of either of the two other communities. It states, "It is not in accordance with your [Muslims] wishes, nor the wishes of the people of the Book; rather, whoever does evil, s/he will be recompensed for it, nor will s/he find any friend or helper against God. And, anyone who performs righteous deeds—male or female—and is a person of faith, those will enter the garden [of paradise] and they will not be wronged in the least" (Q. 4:123-24). Thus we see that the criterion for acceptance with God is neither religious identity nor class or gender but faith and good deeds.

I have dwelt on the Qur'an at some length in this brief introductory essay for three reasons. First, while the Islamic tradition with all its richness has always been open to much debate and controversy, the Qur'an remains the only foundational source on which all Muslims agree, and to which they all turn for guidance and support. Second, as can be deduced from our cursory discussion so far, the Qur'an accepts with approval both religious pluralism and diversity. The centrality of the Qur'an in Muslim life and piety needs no argument or explanation. The Qur'an's attitude to religious pluralism and diversity, however, remains a challenge and source of much debate and contention for Muslims and non-Muslims alike. It will, therefore, constitute one of my main concerns in these essays.

Third, one of the central theses of this book is that the Qur'an came not to establish an Islamic empire but a community of faiths that would include Muslims, Jews, Christians, Sabaeans, and any other faith community that claims to live by the four principles outlined above. In other words, I am convinced that neither the Qur'an nor Muhammad demanded that Jews and Christians abandon their faiths for Islam in return for living in peace and harmony with Muslims.

Sad to say, neither Muslims nor Jews nor Christians have so far heeded this Qur'anic summons. In spite of disagreements with, and even polemics against, specific Jewish and Christian beliefs and practices, the Qur'an repeatedly calls for peace and harmony among all the peoples of the Book, based on the mutual acceptance of all God's Books and Prophets, including Muhammad and the Qur'an. In short, for almost fourteen hundred years the Qur'an has been calling Muslims, Jews, and Christians to what we have still in vain been trying to achieve for the last half century or so, namely, inter-religious ecumenism based on a sincere dialogue of faith. One of the primary aims of this book is to echo this call.

The present volume is a collection of sixteen essays that deal with a wide variety of topics and that have been written over a period of four decades. They thus mirror my spiritual and intellectual growth and maturity. Dr. Irfan A. Omar, the editor of this book, and I have, however, attempted to give the book a semblance of coherent presentation by grouping the materials thematically.

The book is divided topically into four sections. In the first section are essays that reflect on both the context and the need for genuine Muslim-Christian dialogue and on some of our commonly held values and beliefs. The second section deals comparatively with important theological and juridical issues. In the third section, I offer some Islamic and personal reflections on christology, which remains one of the richest and most difficult areas in Muslim-Christian dialogue. One of the central arguments of the essays in this section of the book is the need to recognize the reality of a genuine Islamic christology and to take it seriously both in our dialogue and in our study of the Qur'an and its message. It is hoped that this small contribution will be a good step toward that goal.

No one can deny the goodwill both Christians and Muslims have been showing around the world, and especially in North America, in tackling such difficult issues as the September 11, 2001 tragedy and its aftermath and the recent infamous Danish cartoons, caricaturing the Muslims and their Prophet. In the fourth and final section, I turn to some specific issues of dialogue in the modern world. Here too, I offer some comparative perspectives on issues of common concern. The first essay deals with an important Qur'anic expression of amity and appreciation of the piety of the desert monks who played a crucial role in the formation of both Eastern Christian and Islamic spirituality. Here I deal with some contemporary interpretations of the Qur'anic verses expressing this attitude. The next article deals with modern Muslim views of Christianity, and discusses the views of four Egyptian scholars. The final essay looks at the specific Christian approach to Islam, that of his holiness the late Pope John Paul II.

It remains for me to thank a few institutions and individuals that helped these scattered articles to come together in one volume. I have over the years enjoyed with gratitude much help and encouragement from the World Islamic Call Society, which has kindly helped both morally and materially in the production of this book. I likewise acknowledge gratefully the continued help and encouragement of the Alavi Foundation. The present publication would have not been possible without the kind permission of the previous publishers of the articles who are too many to list here. But to them all, I am most thankful.

This book is the fruit of the patient and dedicated labors of my former student and present colleague and friend, Irfan Omar. He has been urging me for years to agree to such a project; I am glad I finally agreed. To his meticulous editing this book owes its attractive presentation and value.

Finally, I acknowledge with thanks and deep appreciation the encouragement and willingness of Susan Perry of Orbis Books to republish these studies in one volume. To her and all those who helped this book to appear in print I express my deep indebtedness. I hope that this effort will contribute in a small way to a better understanding among the Christians and Muslims of our troubled world.

# Notes

1. See Alfred Guillaume, *The Life of Muhammad* (London: Oxford University Press, 1955), 107.
2. For a traditional account of this encounter, see ibid., 79-81.
3. Ibid., 80. Western scholars have questioned the veracity of this tradition on the grounds that the Qur'an makes no reference to any trade journeys of Muhammad, and that the Syriac word *bhira* means simply monk, which renders the entire account, in their view, a tale of pious fiction. See W. M. Watt, *Muhammad at Mecca* (London: Oxford University Press, 1953), 33-38.
4. See Q. 16:43, where the people of the Book are called "the people of the remembrance," that is, the scripture; see also Q. 21:7.
5. For an early claim that the Holy Spirit (*paraclitus*), which Jesus promised his disciples to come after him (John 14:16; 16:7), referred to Muhammad, see Guillaume, *Life of Muhammad*, 655-66. For a sustained effort to find support for the truth of Muhammad's prophethood in the Bible, see Ali ibn Rabban al-Tabari, *al-Din wa'l-dawlah fi ithbat nubuwwat Muhammad,* translated by A. Mingana under the title, *The Book of Religion and Empire* (Manchester: Manchester University Press, 1923).
6. See Tor Andrae, *Muhammad: The Man and his Faith*, trans. Theophil Menzel (New York: Barnes & Noble, 1935), 90-93.
7. See Jane McAuliffe, *Qur'anic Christians: An Analysis of Classical and Modern Exegesis* (Cambridge: Cambridge University Press, 1991), 204-39 (chap. 7), and my essay "Nearest in Amity: Christians in the Qur'an and Contemporary Exegetical Tradition," chap. 14 in the present volume.
8. See Mahmoud M. Ayoub, *The Qur'an and Its Interpreters* (Albany: State University of New York Press, 1992), 2:183-93.
9. The *mubāhalah* is an old pre-Islamic Arab custom, whereby two opposing parties each makes an oath affirming their standpoint on an issue of conflict and invokes God's curse on the lying party.

10. The Qur'an makes no direct reference to such a delegation, but exegetical tradition has generally linked Q. 3:61 to the Christians of Najran. See M. Ayoub, *The Qur'an and Its Interpreters*, 2:5ff., 188-91.

11. See Fazlur Rahman, *Major Themes of the Qur'an,* 2nd ed. (Minneapolis: Bibliotheca Islamica, 1994), 162-70; and, for examples, Q. 2:171 and 2:285. See also 5:46-47, where the Qur'an declares that in the Gospel there is "Guidance and light," and calls on the people of the two scriptures (Jews and Christians) to judge in accordance with what God has revealed in them.

12. See Q. 2:62 and 5:69. For further discussion on this, see my essay "Islam and the Challenge of Religious Pluralism," in *Global Dialogue* 2, no. 1 (Winter 2000): 53-64.

# PART I

# The Need for Dialogue

## Setting the Context

# 1

# The Need for Harmony and Collaboration between Muslims and Christians

A distinction is usually made in Christian circles between ecumenism and interfaith dialogue. Ecumenism is taken to mean dialogue among Christians—between Catholics, Protestants, and Orthodox—while interfaith dialogue means dialogue with people of other faiths. I would like to suggest that, as Christians and Muslims, we should re-examine what the term "revelation in faith," or the trust which God has laid upon us, really means.

The old Greek use of *oikoumenē* (ecumenical) meant the inhabited earth, which was not inhabited only by Christians or Muslims. The *oikoumenē* was a religious civilized society. I look forward, therefore, to the time when "ecumenical" is used in its proper sense.

Whether we like it or not, we live today in a pluralistic world. Yet, we are not and cannot be an undifferentiated mass of humankind. Yes, we are one humanity, but we are also different peoples, cultures, and religious communities. The Qur'an repeats many times the idea that God created us all from one soul, and from that soul created its mate; and from the two He scattered many men and women. The other important and often-quoted verse related to this is the following Qur'anic challenge: "humankind we have created you from one male and one female and made you into different nations and tribes that you may know one another, surely the noblest view in God's sight is the most righteous." Humanity is one in essence and substance but diverse in culture and race, that is, ethnic composition. Moreover, humanity is one in its quest to comprehend and do the will of God, for "surely the noblest in God's sight is one who is the most righteous" (Q. 49:13).

For us to make sense of our two traditions today, we have to trace some of the important outlines of our history and our relationships. The first thing that we must understand is that both traditions were born in seclusion and

Previously published in *Information and Formation* (Kuala Lumpur: Catholic Research Centre, 1994), 109-19. Reprinted by permission.

9

in public. Christ, before embarking upon his ministry, spent forty days in the wilderness, alone with God but also with Satan. The Prophet Muhammad spent months of seclusion, one month every year, the month of Ramadan, when he contemplated God's creation and the plight of his own people. Islam was born not in the humdrum of a crowded city, the city of Makkah, but in the meditative solitude of one man with his Lord in the cave of Mount Hira.

This private and public character of our two faiths continues to dominate their development. Christianity arose at the time when religions proliferated in the Mediterranean basin, and the quest for the truth was clear indeed. Not everything written by early Christian polemicists about these religions is true. People were seeking a noble ideal by which to live. They sought this ideal in the mystery religions and in ancient Greek philosophies. Christianity came with a call to morality and with a synthesis of the truth that people were looking for. We see this searching very clearly in the career of St. Augustine, who moved from the ideal of his Latin culture to the Manichean religion of Iran and then to Christianity. Even then, St. Augustine was disillusioned with the treatment of the problem of evil "in the books of the Platonists."

In the same way, Islam was born at the time when many Arabs were convinced of the futility of their ancient religious practices and many were looking for meaning and truth. A whole class of people, the *ḥunafā'* (the pious ones), to which the Prophet Muhammad may have belonged, was thoroughly influenced by Jewish and Christian ideas and moral principles. The "pious ones," however, did not join either of the two communities because they thought that the Christians and the Jews were always at odds, accusing each other of infidelity. This is attested to by the Qur'an in the following words: "The Jews say the Christians have nothing on which to stand and the Christians say the Jews have nothing on which to stand, yet both of them read the scriptures" (Q. 2:113).

Islam remolded, as it were, aspects of Arab culture, such as the pilgrimage and animal sacrifices, and ideas from Jewish and Christian sources, into a new religious worldview. This worldview is both personal and universal. The Qur'an presents Islam as the first and primordial religion, the Islam of all the prophets, of all those who believe in the one and only God, creator and sustainer of all creation. Those who have that faith and obey God are Muslims in the broadest and most essential sense of the word. Yet the Qur'an, and this we see clearly in the career of the Prophet Muhammad, was also aiming at establishing a new world order (Q. 26:214). The earliest commands to the Prophet were to preach the faith to his nearest of kin. Then he was ordered to warn the mother of cities, Makkah (Q. 6:92).

The Qur'an declares in two interesting verses both the spiritual dimension of Muhammad's message and the historical dimension. Spiritually, Muhammad, the Prophet of Islam, was told, "we have not sent you except as a Mercy to humankind" (Q. 21:107). Muhammad as Mercy is a new spiritual guide to humankind, one sent to guard and to do good. In another verse the Prophet declares, "O humankind I am the Messenger of God to you all" (Q. 7:158; see also Q. 34:28); here, then, we see a move from the most particular to the most universal in Islam. Muhammad as a messenger to humankind is also a lawgiver and maker of civilization.

Christianity and Islam came with the claim that they are universal faiths, meant for all of humanity, and both claimed that all human beings are equal. This is an ideal that I believe was held both by the early church and also by the Muslim community. To be sure, it was often violated, but the ideal remains an ideal.

Two principles distinguish Islam and Christianity and serve as principles on which we can find a theological basis of harmony. But we can also recognize a basis of difference. The challenge for us is to listen to the way God has spoken to each of our two communities, to respect what God has said to them, and to recognize that it may be different and sometimes vastly different from what was said to us. (1) The scriptures of both communities state that God has always spoken to people. The beginning of the Epistle to the Hebrews declares, "At various times in the past and in various different ways, God spoke to our ancestors through the prophets; but in our own time, the last days, he has spoken to us through his Son [Jesus Christ] . . ." (Heb 1:1).

The Qur'an even more universally declares that there is not a nation but that God has sent to it a warner or a prophet speaking its language and calling it to God within its own historical context. Thus, Muslims are required by the Qur'an to believe in all the prophets of God, all 124,000 of them, even though the Qur'an names only twenty-one.

The two traditions also give prominence to community and revelation. But here comes the difference. The Muslim *ummah* was shaped by the Qur'an, while the New Testament is a product of the church. Where, then, is revelation in the two communities? For Islam, God revealed himself and His will in human words. Hence, the transcendent became human, that is to say, the transcendent and eternal word of God, preserved with Him in the well-guarded tablet, took on human words which we recite and we write in a book. Yet it is the Muslims themselves who shaped the Book when it was collected during the rule of the third caliph, Uthman. But the authority of the Qur'an was supreme, even at the time of the Prophet. We see this in the fact that the Qur'an often went against Muhammad's decisions. In that sense, only during the life of Muhammad can we speak of the Islamic state as a true theocracy. Thereafter, the Islamic state becomes, what I would call, a nomocracy, a state or an order based on Islam or on commitments to obey the divine law.

Revelation in Islam is therefore a Book. To explain my point, let me read the first verses of the Fourth Gospel, both from an Islamic and from a Christian perspective, which will highlight the differences between the two traditions. John writes, "In the beginning was the Word." So far Islam would agree. "The Word was with God." Yes, but Islam would not go on to say, "And the Word was God." God transcends his revelation.

Then the Fourth Gospel affirms the Word to be the agent of creation. The Qur'an, however, is not the agent of creation, but rather of human history. Revelation is in history, and through it history is made. Revelation and creation go hand in hand, but the word of God, that is, the word of creation, is not the Qur'an. It is rather the word of command (*amr*) or the divine *fiat*. When God wishes to create something, He says to it, "Be," and it is.

The crucial difference comes later in the prologue to the Fourth Gospel. John writes, "And the Word became Flesh and dwelt among us." If we were to read this verse Islamically, we would read, "And the Word became Book and entered our history," to be shaped by it and to shape it.

A parallel has often been made by both Western and Muslim scholars between Christ in Christianity and the Qur'an in Islam—both the Word of God. The parallel is useful if it is not carried too far. Muslims also say that Christ is the Word of God, but they do not mean it in the sense of the *Logos* of the Fourth Gospel or of any *Logos* christology of the church. Christ is, according to the Qur'an, a direct creation of God through His word of command, "Be" (Q. 3:59).

In Islam, revelation as scripture comes from an original heavenly source. The heavenly Book is an idea that goes back to the Babylonians. The Qur'an calls this heavenly source "Mother of the Book," or the "well-guarded tablet."

The essence or the truth of revelation is the Trust (*amānah*) that God offered to the heavens and the earth, to the mountains and the hills. But they all honored it, cowered before it, and refused to bear it. But humankind accepted it. Humankind is foolish and self-destructive.

This Islamic understanding of revelation came to be superimposed on all revelations; thus Muslims could not, in the Qur'an or later, understand or accept the idea that God could reveal himself in a human person, that is to say, Jesus Christ. Rather, God revealed His will to Christ, in the Gospel. The Gospel becomes not the good news of the kerygma of faith that "Jesus is risen," but rather a sacred text of moral and quasi-legal principles, in many ways resembling the Qur'an. Therefore, if a Muslim were to be asked, "Where is the Gospel of Jesus Christ?" he would say, "It is the parables of Jesus and the Sermon on the Mount and whatever in the Gospel that can be isolated as the teaching of Jesus, but it is not the story of the life, ministry, and passion of Christ." We cannot, therefore, agree on the concept of revelation in either Islam or Christianity.

The expression "people of the Book" (*ahl al-kitāb*) can, in my view, be used as a unifying idea. In the Qur'an it is limited to Jews, Christians, and Muslims. The Muslims are "people of the Book" in the strictest possible sense. This concept was eventually broadened so as to include all communities possessing scriptures, for example, Hindus and Zoroastrians. In the Qur'an, however, this concept is limited to the family of Abraham.

Rarely does the Qur'an use the word *ahl* to characterize a community of people; rather, the Qur'an and the Arabic language in general use the word *ahl* to mean a person's husband or wife and children and so on. That is to say, *ahl* is one family. I am justified then in interpreting the Qur'anic expression *ahl al-kitāb* to mean "family of the Book." This concept too is one that can unite us. All the people of the Book are the spiritual and physical descendents of the monotheistic faith of Abraham, whose faith is basic to all our faiths and whose faith, as the Qur'an says, predates the Torah and the Gospel. In that sense, the Prophet Muhammad in the Qur'an insisted on calling people to the faith of Abraham.

In choosing Abraham, the Qur'an makes a good choice. He not only represents the father of faith of all the monotheistic peoples, but he also represents the rational person who spends much time and energy in quest of the knowledge of God.

This brings me to yet another basic principle that Islam formulates and presents in the Qur'an which is common to all humankind. It is the principle of the *fiṭrah*, or the original state of creation of all human beings. The Qur'an says, "Set your faith, that is to say, 'your person,' straight in the religion as a man of pure faith" (Q. 30:30). "Pure faith" is the faith of Abraham, who is often called in the Qur'an the "man of pure faith." The verse goes on to say, "This is the original creation upon which God fashioned all of humankind. There is no altering of God's creation."

A prophetic hadith explains this verse as follows: "There is not a child that he or she is born upon this *fiṭrah*, this original state of the knowledge of God. And his parents make him a Jew, a Christian, or a Zoroastrian." The hadith continues, "and if they are Muslims, a Muslim."

Here we come to an interesting distinction between Islam as an institution and Islam as inner submission to God, or, if you wish, between Islam and *īmān*, "faith." I have already mentioned Islam as a universal and primordial principle—God's way for all creation. But Islam is also on one level an institutionalized religion that was to distinguish one particular community from all other communities. We see this clearly in the *shahādah*, or witness, of Islam: "I bear witness that there is no God but God and I bear witness that Muhammad is the Messenger of God." The first part is universal, and, if we are open, we can understand it and even adopt it through our own unaided reason. But when a Muslim goes on to say, "I bear witness that Muhammad is the Messenger of God," he or she is affirming his or her commitment to follow the religion or law that God reveals to Muhammad—in other words, to be a Muslim in the institutionalized sense.

Here we come to a very important legal distinction between Muslims and non-Muslims that cannot be ignored. It is interesting to note that in one very important prophetic hadith the minimum that is expected from people is an affirmation of God. The Prophet says, "I have been commanded to fight with people until they say 'there is no God but God.' When they say this they protect from me their lives and their possessions. Accept what is due from them in the *zakāh*, 'legal almsgiving,' and their final reckoning is with God."

This is perhaps an early and very significant stage, and this is in total agreement with the Qur'anic challenge to Muslims and non-Muslims to "come to a word of common agreement to worship no other but God."

I am convinced that the Prophet Muhammad and the Qur'an did not expect Jews and Christians to give up their religion and to become Muslims unless they wanted to but only to observe God's continuous care for humankind and acknowledge that the revelation he gave to the Prophet Muhammad is a genuine revelation and that Muhammad is a genuine prophet. This is something that can be done. Once in an interfaith meeting, for example, the non-Muslim organizers wished to incorporate elements of the Islamic call to prayer in their final prayer service. "God is greatest, come to prayers, come to the good," were the words they chose. They omitted the phrase, "I bear witness that Muhammad is the Messenger of God." Had they included the reference to Muhammad, it would have meant a commitment to Islam. The original demand that the Qur'an made of Jews and Christians is simply to accept Muhammad as a Prophet and Islam as an authentic religion, without necessarily having to give up their faith.

The following verse occurs twice in the Qur'an in exactly the same way: "Surely those who have faith, those who are Jews and those who are Christians, and the Sabeans, whoever has faith in God, and the last day, and does good works, will have his reward with his Lord. No fear shall come upon them, nor will they grieve" (Q. 2:62; 5:69). Muslims have written much about the identity of the Sabeans. I would say that they represent all people who have no Book—that is, people who are not Jews and Christians but who have an idea of, and in some way worship, a transcendent Supreme Being, or God. There are few religious traditions, if any, that do not have some idea of a supreme being.

The early church always saw herself as an *ecclesia semper reformanda*, a church that is always in a state of reforming itself. This also characterizes Islam. Islam is a continuously self-reforming religion. In a commentary in the Qur'an on the meaning of animal sacrifices, we are told, "God does not receive either the fat or the blood of these animals, but what reaches Him from you is righteousness (*taqwā*)" (Q. 22: 37). It is not the sacrifices we offer but our intention behind them that eventually matters. Islam always tries to go beyond the institutionalization of religion in law and custom. We see this clearly in an important verse of the Qur'an, which in part reads as follows:

> It is not righteousness that you turn your faces toward the East and the West [that is, in prayer]. True righteousness is this: to have faith in God and the last day, the angels, the scriptures, and the prophets; to give of one's wealth, though it may be cherished, to the next of kin and the orphans, the destitute and the wayfarer, to the needy

and for the redemption of slaves; to observe regular worship and to give the obligatory alms. Those who fulfill their covenant having bound themselves by it and those who are patient in misfortune and adversity and in times of strife: these are true in their faith; these are God fearing. (Q. 2:177)

The essence of faith in both traditions is expressed in the Sermon on the Mount and in the parables of Jesus, in particular, the parable of the Good Samaritan and the apocalyptic parable in Matthew 25. Those who will be on God's right hand, the sheep as it were, will not be people who went to church every Sunday or prayed five times a day or who were bishops or popes; rather, it will be those who consoled the sorrowful, visited the sick, cared for prisoners, clothed the naked, and fed the hungry. Martin Luther may not like this, but this is what Jesus said.

In other sayings of Jesus, care for others is placed next to love of God. This, according to him, is the essence of the law and the prophets. Jesus, of course, was referring to the book of Leviticus. The idea that the best way to obey God is through care for our fellow human beings is essential to all three monotheistic faiths. Caring for the wayfarer in Islam, for example, can be translated in modern times into caring for those who have no home, who are always on the move, either as refugees or as homeless in our big cities, helping those who are in dire poverty, or who are sick. Obeying God means to clothe the naked, to care for the children, to do social work, in short, to work together toward achieving a just society.

On this we can all agree. This is work in God's cause, to which the Qur'an is calling Muslims, Jews, Christians, and all human beings. It is a call to worship God alone and to realize that part of the worship of God is to do good to His creatures.

As for the theological points, such as the question of revelation, the mystery of the Trinity, the divinity of Christ, the prophethood of Muhammad, these are points that need much patience and prayer. We cannot create harmony on the basis of these points. Perhaps in time Christians and Muslims will be able to relate to the ideas of the other without having to resort to a supermarket religion, where one can pick and choose the concepts one likes, or to compromise one's faith in any way. We must obey God as Muslims and as Christians, not as Muslims who are also Christians or Christians who are also Muslims. We are different, and it is God's will that we be different. God says in the Qur'an, "surely in the diversity of your languages and your colors [and that would include cultures as well], there is a divine sign if you can only understand" (Q. 30:22). Diversity is not bad; it is an act of divine mercy that we are different, that we can have a rich spirituality that takes different forms and different traditions.

We are also one humanity under God. Theological doctrines may divide us, but faith unites us. In faith, as Muslims and Christians trying to understand the will of God for our lives, we are all challenged by God to be Muslims and Christians in the deepest possible sense. We are strangers in this world; in this we are together. We are together as strangers in faith, in a world that is dominated by brute power, materialism, and disunity. In Europe, in the Middle East, in South Asia, in South America, even in the American cities there is much poverty and pain.

What faith teaches us most, in my view, is humility before God. He is the king, and we are all His creatures. This is where the Islamic declaration *Allahu Akbar*, "Greater than all things is God," is a declaration that can have profound meaning for all of us, Muslims and Christians.

If we cannot be united on the basis of faith and liturgy or devotion, then we can at least try to understand why it is that our doctrines are different. We are different and we are what we are because it is God's wish. The Qur'an again states, "Had your Lord so wished he would have made all of humanity one *ummah*" (Q. 11:118). The challenge is this: "Vie with one another in the performance of good works. To God shall be your return and He will inform you of the things concerning which you have differed." Let us be grateful for our differences as they enrich our lives. But also, let us be humbly grateful for our similarities as members of one humanity. Faith itself is a stranger in the world. When wars that began while the Prophet Muhammad lay unburied tore the community apart, and when Christians killed one another during the centuries of the Inquisition and the period following the Reformation, faith was a stranger. We can perhaps find solace in the words of the Prophet Muhammad: "Islam came to the world stranger and it will return a stranger as it began. Blessed are the strangers."

# 2

# The Islamic Context of Muslim-Christian Relations

From its inception, Islam was nourished by the piety, lore, and spirituality of the people of the Book, Jews and Christians. In ancient Arabia, it was the desert monks who provided healing and hope, faith and fulfillment for generations of men and women. From Jesus and St. Paul to Muhammad, Christian spirituality, learning, and culture possessed an air of fascination and mystery for Arabs. This fascination is clearly evident in Islamic lore, the Qur'an, and poetry before and after Islam. In fact, Christianity alone provided religion, properly speaking, to the Arabs before Islam. Apart from the *hajj* pilgrimage rites, the religion of the Arabs lacked liturgy and ritual. More importantly, it lacked a proper perspective or philosophy of history. Arabic was a private language, and Christian Arabs worshiped in Aramaic, the lingua franca of Syro-Aramaean culture.[1] Likewise, beyond the starkly pessimistic and rudimentary notion that Time (*al-dahr*) was an agent of death and misfortune, not to be trusted, pre-Islamic Arab religion was crude and primitive (Q. 45:24).[2] It was natural, therefore, that the religious experience of Jews and Christians should provide both the witness and frame of reference for the new faith, at least in its formative stages.

This special relationship between Islam and Christianity did not imply that the Prophet Muhammad, Islam's scripture, and early community were not aware of their own distinctive identity and the originality of their new faith. It was rather that the awareness of a continuation with, and even dependence of, the Islamic message on its Jewish and Christian predecessors, together with Islam's sharp differences with both of them, led Islam and Muslims to adopt an ambivalent attitude toward Christians and Jews. To be sure, this attitude was less ambivalent and more hostile toward the Jews. That, however, was due to certain political and economic circumstances in the new Muslim state of Madinah with its influential and generally well-organized

Previously published in *Conversion and Continuity: Indigenous Christian Communities in Islamic Lands Eighth to Eighteenth Centuries*, ed. Michael Gervers and Ramzi Jibran Bikhazi (Toronto: Pontifical Institute of Mediaeval Studies, 1990), 461-77. Reprinted by permission of the publisher. © 1990 by the Pontifical Institute of Mediaeval Studies, Toronto.

Jewish community. It must be further noted that the confident assertion of absolute originality, primordiality, and supersessionism of Islam over Christianity and Judaism was only a later development in Muslim law and theology that was read back into the Qur'an and hadith tradition.

Islam saw itself from the beginning as yet another expression of the Abrahamic faith and obedient submission (*islām*) to God. This faith, moreover, was not limited to Abraham; rather, it was the faith of all the prophets before and after him, including Moses and Jesus. The early Islam of the Prophet and his immediate successors did not, in my view, require the people of the Book to abandon their religion as a price for living in amity and interacting positively with Muslims. Nor does the Qur'an claim that Islamic sacred law, the *sharī'ah*, has abrogated the sacred law of Moses and Christ. Why, then, it must be asked, did Muslims insist on these and other exclusivist and supersessionist principles, and how were such principles made to abrogate all that was irenic and conciliatory in the Qur'an and early tradition? There are many and diverse answers to this important question. Among them is the fact that neither Christians nor Jews were prepared to accept a genuine religious tradition after their own final communication with heaven. Equally significant were the political and military circumstances that dominated the history of the Near and Middle East before Islam and during the formative years of Muslim history.

Muhammad preached his new message after Jesus and Mani. Thus, Islam was heir to the universalism which they preached and which characterized the crucial period of Near Eastern history between Alexander and Muhammad. But while Manichaeism failed to establish its legitimacy as a universal faith, Christianity and Islam succeeded. They did so, however, through a long struggle, rivalry, and competition. Had not Islam imposed limits on its own universalistic ideal, it would have lost its raison d'être as a distinctive faith and culture. Thus, while it did impose such limits on itself, it sought to do so without losing its universal character. The result has been a tension between exclusivistic confrontation with, and open accommodation of, the faith and community of its main rival, Christianity. This, I believe, is the true context in which the historical relations between the two communities must be studied. It is within this framework that alternating periods of interaction and conflict, creative symbiosis and devastating warfare can be explained. The purpose of this discussion is to present this Islamic dimension which, it is hoped, will serve as a useful background to the rest of this volume.

## Confrontation and Accommodation:
## The Case of the Qur'an

That the Prophet of Islam regarded his message to be consonant with, and complementary to, that of the Torah and Gospel is clear from the Qur'an's frequent reference to the witness of the people of the Book to its own truth and authenticity. Thus, the Qur'an reassured Muhammad in the face of the Makkan detractors of the new faith: "If you are in doubt concerning that which we have sent to you then enquire of those who have been reading the scriptures before you" (Q. 10:94). The Qur'an even directs its own wavering followers to the people of earlier scriptures for knowledge and reassurance: "Enquire of the people of remembrance (*ahl al-dhikr*) if you do not know" (Q. 16:43). In yet another instance where the Prophet, during the initial period of his preaching in Makkah, was maligned by the men of the Quraysh (the tribe to which Muhammad belonged and that led the Makkan opposition to Muhammad's new faith) for declaring that Hell is guarded by nineteen angels, he found consolation in the fact that the people of the Book and the people of faith are certain of the truth of God's revelation (Q. 74:31). These few examples demonstrate clearly the unity of faith and purpose which, according to the Qur'an, should exist among the three communities of faith.

Recognition of the priority of Judaism and Christianity as bearers of divine truth was actualized in the Qur'an and early prophetic tradition in accommodation and appreciation of the people of the Book and their scriptures. In a late surah, revealed toward the end of the Prophet's career in Madinah, the Qur'an removes the two most important social barriers separating the people of the three communities, namely, dietary and marriage restrictions. "The food of the people of the Book is lawful for you and your food is lawful for them, and the chaste women of the people of the Book are [lawful for you to marry]" (Q. 5:5). Free from the quibblings of later jurists, this verse clearly allows unrestricted social intercourse among the people of the three faiths. Accommodation, moreover, was not limited to social interaction but included intellectual and theological debate. The Qur'an enjoins Muslims to be fair in their debate with the people of the Book. "Do not dispute with the people of the Book except in the fairest manner, save with those of them who have committed wrong. Say, 'We have faith in that which was sent down to us and that which was sent down to you. Our God and your God is one God; to Him we are submitters (*muslims*)'" (Q. 29:46).

It has already been argued that the Islamic attitude toward the people of the Book was from the start one of both accommodation and confrontation. It must be added here that the Qur'an at times presents these two aspects in the same breath. Furthermore, confrontation did not, generally speaking, revolve around political or social but rather strictly theological issues. Two noteworthy theological issues have figured prominently in both the Qur'an and later hadith and exegetical tradition. The first, which has already been mentioned, is the Qur'anic call for mutual recognition and acceptance. With regard to the Jews, this was a call to abandon what the Qur'an perceives as their pride in being the chosen people of God, and hence their smug rejection of Islam and its prophet (see, e.g., Q. 2:80; 2:142; and 62:7). The second issue, which continues to divide Muslims and Christians, is the nature and mission of Christ.

The first major and direct confrontation between the Prophet and Christians was his alleged debate with the Christians of Najran, a Christian district in the Yaman. This debate is alluded to in the Qur'an in the famous verse of the *mubāhalah,* the "invocation of God's curse" (Q. 3:61). The *mubāhalah* was an old Arab custom in which two parties making conflicting claims would pray with an oath that God's curse be upon the liars of either party. In this case, the *mubāhalah* concerned the humanity and divinity of Christ. The question as to whether such a debate ever took place does not concern us here. It is sufficient to observe that the men of Najran prudently opted for peace, albeit at a price, instead of the challenge of the *mubāhalah* with its political and military consequences. Of greater importance, for our purpose, is the fact that the verses relating to this debate conclude with the following conciliatory call to the people of the Book: "O people of the Book, come to a just word common between us and you: that we worship none other than God, that we associate nothing with Him, and that we do not take one another as lords instead of God." The verse concludes: "But if they turn their backs, say, 'Bear witness then that we are *muslims*'" (Q. 3:64).

The ideal relation envisioned by the Qur'an between Muslims and Christians is not only one of accommodation and co-existence but of amity and mutual respect. This ideal hearkens back to the desert monks, who were motivated not by theological arguments and doctrinal formulations in their dealings with nonbelievers but by holiness and compassion. The Qur'an declares: "You shall find the nearest in amity to those who have faith to be those who say we are Christians. This is because there are among them learned men and monks, and they are not arrogant. When they listen to that which was sent down to the Messenger, you see their eyes well up with tears as they recognize the truth. They say, 'Our Lord, we do have faith! Inscribe us, therefore, among the witnesses'" (Q. 5:82-83; see also Q. 5:84-85).

The Qur'an recognizes the good intentions of the Christians even where it considers their actions to be in error. A clear example of this is the assertion that Christians have themselves invented monasticism, desiring by this God's good pleasure (Q. 57:27). This Qur'anic acceptance of difference, and acknowledgement of its value, is the clearest sign of tolerance and accommodation.

This call for mutual acceptance is based on the Qur'anic notion of the unity of scriptures. The Qur'an regards both the Torah and Gospel as sources of guidance and light. As expressions of the one and primordial truth, they must be the sole arbiters in any disagreements or conflicts among the people of faith (see, e.g., Q. 5:46-47). Yet in spite of this essential unity of revelation, the Qur'an does take notice of the deep conflict between the two communities: "The Jews say Christians have nothing upon which to stand, and the Christians say the Jews have nothing upon which to stand, although they both recite the same scriptures" (Q. 2:113).[3] Thus, the hope for mutual recognition, which the Qur'an presents as an ideal goal and a challenge, and which many Muslims and Christians continue to cherish, turned into mutual exclusivism and rejection, rivalry and competition. In what appears to be a clear instance of reaction to the negative Jewish attitude toward the new faith and its adherents, the Qur'an cautions Muhammad not to follow the whims of the Jews and Christians who would never be pleased with him "unless he follows their religion" (Q. 2:120). In this hardening situation of reaction and counterreaction, many in all three traditions were soon to ignore the real meaning of their faith and insist that their opponents follow their religion, if they were to have peace with them. Despairing of ever arriving at a just word of common consent with the people of the Book, the Prophet addressed his followers in the words of the Qur'an, saying, "O you who have faith do not take the Jews and Christians as allies. They are allies of one another. Whosoever amongst you takes them as his allies, he shall be one of them" (Q. 5:31). These words, which in fact referred to political alliances in a specific time of war, became normative for many Muslims, in spite of numerous other Qur'anic injunctions of amity and cooperation between Muslims and the people of the Book.

The Qur'an, far more than Muslims have ever done, accepts the pluralism of religions and affirms the unity of faith. The only common elements it insists on are sincere faith in God and works of righteousness. In a rare instance where a verse occurs twice almost verbatim, this basic principle is unequivocally stated. The verse in question occurs in Surah 2, the first major surah revealed in Madinah, and in Surah 5, one of the last major surahs before the end of Muhammad's prophetic career. "Surely those who have faith, the Jews, Christians and Sabaeans: those [among them] who have faith in God and the last day and perform works of righteousness, will have their reward with their Lord. No fear shall come upon them, nor will they grieve" (Q. 2:62, 3:69).[4] Two points in this verse deserve special attention. The first is that faith here is more than a mere religious label. The second point, which in fact reinforces the first, is that the Sabaeans, who, according to most Muslim historians, Qur'an commentators, and heresiographers were star worshipers, are included among the people of the Book. As star worshipers, they ought to have been classed with the "associators" (*mushrikūn*) of Makkah, and thus be subject to the choice "between Islam or the sword." Yet because, in the view of commentators, the Sabaeans were akin to the Jews, in that they accepted some of their ancient prophets and adopted the Psalms (*zabūr*) of David as their scripture, they were numbered among the communities of faith.

The Qur'an claims to be a universal message addressed to all of humanity at all times. It was necessary, therefore, that this message be presented to others who then must be left to choose whether or not to accept it. Convincing one's opponent through debate is a time-honored custom among theologians and philosophers. The Qur'an thus calls upon its people to invite others to God through wisdom and good counsel. It enjoins them to "debate with them [the people of the Book] in the fairest manner" (Q. 16:125). But the Qur'an had in view only theological and not political and economic issues and conflicts. Only toward the end of the Prophet's life, after the whole of Arabia was brought into the domain of Islam, did he begin to look beyond the Arabian peninsula and its environs. The two expeditions of Mu'tah and Tabuk in 629 and 630 respectively, into what was still Christian territory, were tentative but significant. The Qur'an, likewise, dealt with such tentative episodes in a tentative way. With the exception of the Sword Verse,[5] the Qur'an had little to say by way of ordering the relations between Muslim authorities and their non-Muslim subjects. And even this controversial verse is placed in the context of the rules governing the relations of Muslims with the unbelievers of Makkah before they too joined the new faith.

Islam and Christianity as religions of the Book have far more in common than the theologians of either tradition have been willing to recognize or admit. This fact was recognized early in the contact between living Christians and Muslims. Long before St. John of Damascus declared Islam to be a Christian heresy, the Qur'an regarded Christians as extremists in their faith. Extremism (*ghuluw*) is the Islamic equivalent of heresy. The Qur'an says: "O people of the Book, do not go to extremes in your religion, nor should you say about God except the truth. Christ Jesus son of Mary is only the messenger of God, His word which He cast into Mary, and a spirit of Him. Accept faith, therefore, in God and His messengers, and do not say three. Desist! It shall be better for you. God is surely One God, glorified is He over having a child. To Him belongs all that is in the heavens and earth; sufficient indeed is God as guardian" (Q. 4:171). This reproach is not directed against Christianity but against Christians who may mistakenly think of God as three independent deities. The Qur'an does not offer theological arguments against the Trinity but counters anthropomorphism with absolute divine transcendence. Nor would Christian theologians, then or now, have disagreed with this Qur'anic assertion. Christians clearly do not believe the Trinity to be three gods. The appreciation of this point requires much patience, sensitivity, and openness on the part of Christians who would explain the Trinity as a mystery of faith, and of Muslims who would try to appreciate it as an expression of God's infinite compassion *(rahmah)*, and not a divine exercise in obscurantist mathematics.

The Qur'an has a great deal more to say about Christ and Christians, but if this brief survey has demonstrated that the matter is far more complex than the analysis of any Qur'anic verse or any event of Muslim history would suggest, then the purpose of this discussion has been well served.

As we have seen, the Qur'an deals not so much with specific rules regulating Muslim-Christian relations but rather presents principles and general guidelines for such rules and regulations. The Qur'an could be used by later Muslim jurists, rulers, and even theologians only as a primary source to be supplemented by other and more specific sources. The most immediate source after the Qur'an, in this as in all other spheres of Muslim life, has been the *sunnah*: the sayings, actions, and silent approbation of the Prophet.

To complete our presentation of this broad and complex Islamic context within which Muslim relations with other communities, particularly with the Christian community, must be studied, we shall turn briefly to the *sunnah* of the Prophet and its interpretation and interiorization by his Companions. The situation here is even more complex, but equally instructive.

## Confrontation and Accommodation:
## The Hadith Tradition

The Qur'an views true religion to be that which is based only on revelation. That the Islamic concept of revelation placed great obstacles in the way of meaningful Muslim-Christian dialogue is an undeniable fact. This complex problem, however, lies outside the scope of this discussion. On the positive side, this unity of scriptures, from the Islamic point of view, could and did foster a unity of faith and destiny. The term *ahl al-kitāb* (people of the Book) expressed an all-inclusive identity not only among Jews, Christians, and Muslims. The list grew as more religious communities, such as the Zoroastrians and Hindus, advanced the claim that sacred scriptures were the basis of their faith.[6]

This unity of faith and destiny between Muslims and Christians is touchingly demonstrated in the Qur'an and tradition. Before the Prophet's migration to Madinah, the Byzantines were defeated by the Persians. The small band of Muslims felt disappointment at the defeat of a people of the Book like them. The Qur'an refers to this defeat and its eventual reversal thus: "The Byzantine Empire (*al-Rūm*) has been defeated in the nearest regions of the land, but after their defeat they shall achieve victory in a few years. . . . On that day the people of the faith shall rejoice in God's support. God assists whomever He wills; He is the Almighty, the Compassionate" (Q. 30:2-5). Traditionists report that when the Byzantines were defeated, the unbelieving men of the Quraysh were glad because, like the Persians, they had no scriptures. But when this verse was revealed, the Muslims were happy because they and the Christians were people of the Book. In joyous anticipation, Abu Bakr, a close friend of Muhammad and later his first successor (caliph), went around the streets of Makkah proclaiming the verse. The men of the Quraysh challenged him to a wager on a Byzantine victory within five or six years. But they achieved victory over the Persians seven years later, and Abu Bakr lost his bet.[7]

It was argued earlier that the Qur'an did not require the people of the Book to convert to Islam as a condition for religious recognition and peaceful co-existence in Muslim domains. In fact the Qur'an's ideal is that faith in God must include assent to all His prophets and scriptures. It is in this universal faith, manifested in good deeds, that true righteousness lies (Q. 2:177). This view finds concrete support in prophetic tradition as well. The prophet is said to have declared, "Any man of the people of the Book who believes in his own prophet and in Muhammad shall have a double reward."[8] It was also argued that the Qur'an regards faith alone and not religion as a decisive factor in establishing good relations among the people of faith. Not even a common ritual need deprive a person of his or her religio-cultural identity. The famous traditionalist Ibn 'Abbas reported that when the Prophet sent his well-known companion Mu'adh bin Jabal as his representative over the people of the Book of the Yaman, he gave him the following instructions: "You shall come to a people of the Book. Invite them to bear witness that there is no God but God and that I am the messenger of God. If they submit to this, then inform them that God has prescribed for them a free-will gift (*sadaqah*) which must be taken from the rich among them and distributed among the poor. If they obey you in all this, then beware that you touch their principal wealth. Beware the prayer of the oppressed for between it and God there is no veil."[9]

It may be argued that this is a call to conversion. This, however, would be the case only when later jurists and theologians reduced this and other such prophetic hadiths (*ḥadīth qudsī*) to a system that defined and delimited faith communities. Faith and ritual in the Semitic milieu of the Qur'an, the Torah, and Eastern Christian piety were not an affirmation of a theological doctrine, but of a sanctified life before God. In this milieu, affirming the prophethood of Moses, Jesus, or Muhammad did not imply membership in the community of that prophet. Not long after Muhammad, a number of Jewish sects, such as the "Isawiyah," accepted Moses, Jesus, and Muhammad as true prophets of God.[10]

The term "people of the Book" as used in the Qur'an is a neutral term of faith identity. Even when used in a hostile context, it did not—again with the exception of the Sword Verse—denote a legal status. Although Muslim jurists applied the Sword Verse indiscriminately to all Jews and Christians, the text clearly refers to those among the people of the Book who are not bound by the imperatives of their own faith and morality. What jurists implied, in obvious contradiction of the general Qur'anic view and especially of this verse, was that all the people of the Book, simply because they were not Muslims, are subject to the harsh judgment of this verse. Indeed, this kind of generalization from the Qur'an and hadith became the dominant pattern for later Muslim jurists and theologians in their dealings with Christians and Jews. Generally, moreover, the neutral epithet "people of the Book" was replaced with the legal identification, *ahl al-dhimmah*, the people under the protection or covenant (*dhimmah*) of God, His Prophet, and the Muslims.

The most distinctive mark of humble subjugation of the people of the *dhimmah*, in accordance with the Sword Verse, is their payment of the *jizyah* (poll tax), which they must "give with their own hand while being humbled" (Q. 9:298). As things developed, the *jizyah* became a public service tax in return for which Christians and Jews were protected without having to render military service to the Muslim state. Socially, it did imply a status inferior to that of Muslims. It was, therefore, more of a social stigma than a financial burden.

Malik bin Anas, the founder of the Madinan school of jurisprudence which bears his name, observes in his hadith collection *al-Muwatta'* that the *jizyah* was taken only from males who had reached the age of majority, that is, who were able to bear arms, while women and young children were exempted. The economic nature of this arrangement may be seen in the further stipulation that when Jews or Christians engaged in trade outside their own city of residence, they had to pay a tenth of their earnings in return for protection away from the land where they were subject to the protection of the Muslims as part of their universal covenant (*dhimmah*) with them.[11]

The word *dhimmah* means a binding commitment, pact, or covenant between two persons or communities. It is a sacred trust or responsibility that cannot be violated. When a *dhimmah*, or pact of protection, is established between Muslims and others, it is established on behalf of God and His Prophet. Thus *ahl al-dhimmah* are in reality God's people.[12] Therefore, they must be shown mercy and kindness, trust and constancy, as these are God's characteristic dealings with His creatures. It is widely reported that the Prophet declared, "Assuredly anyone who kills a soul with whom Muslims have a pact—having the protection (*dhimmah*) of God and His Messenger—would have violated God's *dhimmah*. He shall, therefore, not smell the fragrance of paradise, although its fragrance may be sensed from the distance of a seventy years journey."[13]

This divine protection did not confer on the people of the Book only an inviolable right to life and property under Muslim rule. It also gave them an aura of sanctity and right conduct even in the manner of their dress and general deportment. The Prophet, we are told, used to emulate the people of the Book in letting his hair down instead of parting it, as the people of Makkah used to do. This he did because he wished to agree with the people of the Book in all things, "unless he was commanded to do otherwise."[14] Between this attitude of fraternal sympathy and the girdle (*zunnar*) and other distinctive marks of humility that the people of the Book had to endure under Muslim rule, there is an incomprehensible world of difference.

The special spiritual status of the people of the Book is vividly contrasted with that of all other peoples in the following eschatological prophetic tradition. The Prophet begins by describing the great bliss of paradise and its special characteristics. The purpose of this long pedagogic hadith is to encourage the people in their faith and good works. The Prophet was imparting to the people "what God had taught him." Thus God says, "I created all my servants with pure faith (*hunafā'*). Then devils came to them and caused them to stray far from their faith. They made lawful for them things which I had made unlawful, and commanded them to associate with me things concerning which I revealed no authority." The Prophet continued, "God looked at the inhabitants of the earth and despised them all, Arabs and non-Arabs, except for small remnants of the people of the Book."[15] These are the same "people of the Book" whom later jurists regarded as impure and unholy.

Unlike Christianity in its formative period before it became the state religion under Constantine, Islam was from the start conceived as a socio-economic and religio-political order. These aspects had their foundation in the congregational prayers, the *hajj* pilgrimage, and the *zakāh* or obligatory religious alms. In Madinah, these rights were translated into an all-inclusive Islamic polity buttressed by a state structure that was soon to become the most international domain in human history.

Muhammad was neither a political theorist nor an author of a universal code of law. He was a prophet who received and transmitted a revealed scripture. This scripture, along with the Prophet's *sunnah,* does not constitute a coherent body of law but a decisive source of law and morality for Muslims. Many groups and individuals have claimed to have the correct interpretation of the "Book of God and *sunnah* of His Prophet."

The earliest and most venerated of such men were the Prophet's Companions, whose high status derived from the fact that they lived with the Prophet and were spiritually and morally nurtured by the Qur'an and *sunnah*. They thus acted as moral guardians of the community and its normative guides. One of them, we are told, passed by a group of the people of the Book in Syria who had been made to stand in the hot sun as a form of punishment. He asked, "Who are these," and was told that they had not paid their land tax (*kharaj*) in full. He said, "I bear witness that I heard the Messenger of God say, 'God will punish on the Day of Resurrection those who torture People.'" He then went and related this hadith of the Prophet to the governor of Syria, who ordered that the men be set free.[16]

One of the most venerated and admired of the Prophet's Companions has been 'Umar bin al-Khattab, the second caliph. In his last will, 'Umar enjoined the caliph after him, "I enjoin him concerning the people of the *dhimmah* of God and His Messenger that he fulfill their covenant. He should fight in their defense [literally: behind them]. Nor should they be charged beyond their capacity."[17]

In times of war, the Prophet sought to regulate fighting and gave it a purpose. Above all as both prophet and statesman, he legislated a code of conduct intended to minimize the human tragedy that is a part of every war, however noble may be its purpose. In one of his raids against a neighboring Arab tribe before it accepted Islam, the Prophet's men killed some children. When he was told of this, he angrily reproached the men saying, "Why is it that some people could not restrain themselves today from killing, so that they even killed children?" One of the men answered, "O Apostle of God, they are children of Associators." The Prophet countered, "Certainly the best of you are sons of Associators." He then ordered: "Never kill children," repeating it twice.[18]

It is widely reported that whenever the prophet dispatched an army of detachment, he enjoined its commander to fear God and deal kindly with the men under his command. He then addressed the men saying, "Fight in the name of God and in the way of God. Fight those who reject faith in God. But do not transgress. Do not commit treachery, mutilate [a slain fighter], or kill a child."[19] Of course, Muslims have not always heeded this injunction, as history clearly testifies. Yet to say that this and other rules governing the conduct of Muslims in war were always ignored would be equally contrary to historical facts. The fact that Islam accepted war as a human reality and laid down strict moral principles regulating it contributed substantially, in my view, to the tolerance and accommodation that Muslims have shown toward the "people of the Book" in their midst.

It was earlier observed that toward the end of his life, the Prophet began to sense the far-reaching significance of his new community with its faith and discipline. His first expedition into Syria was a failure. It did not, however, deter Muslim armies—especially after Islam was consolidated in Arabia—to venture beyond the confines of the Hijaz. Thus, shortly before he died, the Prophet began preparations for a fresh military expedition into Byzantine territory. He died, however, before the plan was implemented. Soon after his death, a large army set out under the leadership of Usamah bin Zayd against the Syrian frontier. Abu Bakr, then newly installed as the first caliph, accompanied the army to the outskirts of Madinah and delivered the following instructions regarding the conduct of Muslims in war. The Prophet said, "Do not betray one another [in war]. Do not commit acts of treachery. Do not mutilate [an army fighter], or kill a young child, an old man or woman. Do not cut down trees bearing fruits. Do not slaughter a sheep, a cow or camel, except if you need it for food. You shall pass by people [i.e., monks] who have dedicated themselves to acts of worship in their cells. Let them be and that to which they have dedicated themselves."[20] These ethical rules were often infringed by Muslims not only in their wars with non-Muslims but in their own internal conflicts as well.

The purpose of this discussion is not to justify Muslim conquests or to apologize for them. Nor do I wish to exonerate Muslims from the wrong they committed against their Jewish and Christian subjects. My aim is rather to emphasize the fact that Islam, like Christianity, is first and foremost a religious system, whose fundamental purpose is to reform society, to extirpate wrongdoing, oppression, and immorality. Its purpose is to establish God's kingdom here on earth. While it cannot be denied that Muslims and Christians have collectively failed to realize this goal, an honest historian must not lose sight of its significance in analyzing the history of the two communities. We can no more study Muslim history without the Islamic context of the Qur'an, the *sunnah,* and the lives of the first generation of Muslims than we can look at Christian history without the framework of the life and teachings of Christ. The actions of Muslim jurists and politicians must not be simply judged on face value but on the degree to which they have or have not conformed with the ideals and values of their faith.

History is not a meaningless flow of events which, once documented, can explain everything. No "conversion stories," exegetical opinions, or account of what happened during the reign of this or that ruler can fully explain the complex relations of communities belonging to rich and multi-faceted faith traditions. A serious historian must take cognizance of the the-ological, moral, and, in the case of Islam, legal dimensions of his subjects. In other words, a historian, if he or she is to preserve the intellectual integrity that serious scholarship demands, must be sensitive to the dimension of faith in the life of human society. It is in the end this dimension that gave both the Muslim and Christian communities the impetus and drive toward a rich and universal civilization. It is faith that has served and will continue to serve as judge and nourisher of their respective cultures as long as they continue to play their role on the stage of human history. It is in this context of faith and moral responsibility that conversion and continuity in both the Muslim and Christian communities must be studied.

## Conversion and the Freedom of Faith

There is an underlying assumption in most studies of Muslim-Christian rela-tions that conversion from Christianity to Islam is never the free choice of the convert. This is because, it is assumed, Islam lacks the spirituality of the Christian faith. It lacks the spiritual and moral example of Christ. Islam, it is claimed, is at best a Christian heresy, or to use the words of a more recent Christian savant, it is "the bastard offspring of the Gospel and the Mosaic law."[21] Hence, what is good and beautiful in Islam must be originally Chris-tian; the rest it not worth bothering about. Conversions must therefore have been made by force or for ulterior motives. Christians flocked to Islam, it is argued, either to avoid paying the *jizyah*, to avoid the humility and incon-venience of a second-class status, or to secure a lucrative military or admin-istrative post in the Islamic state.

Historians have provided ample documentation of many such cases. Because such isolated cases do not tell the whole story, all other conversions, and especially large-scale conversions, are often explained as conversions of simple-minded peasants, too ignorant to know the truth. Often these unknown masses are presented as crypto-Christians because they were part of a society dominated by superstition and a primitive culture.

This assumption has several serious implications. First, it assumes that knowledge of Christian truths was limited to a small elite of theologians and ecclesiastics. Second, it ignores the fact that not all those who converted to Islam were "simple-minded peasants" or opportunists. Third, and perhaps most important, it is an insult to Islam and Christianity, as well as to Mus-lims and Christians, to dismiss the faith commitment of millions of people as a manifestation of simple-mindedness, enticement, or brute force. The "simple-mindedness" explanation is at best a hypothesis that can neither be proven or disproved for lack of concrete evidence. Of course, if religious piety as such is to be regarded as simple-mindedness, then there have been very few sophisticated people in human history. As for coercion, it can take many forms. Be that as it may, many cases of forcible conversion to both religions have been documented. But in discussing the case of Islam, the principles of religious freedom and its role in Muslim history cannot be ignored.

This principal is clearly expressed in the Qur'anic dictum, "Let there be no compulsion in religion" (Q. 2:256). This verse has been both crucial and most controversial in the history of Muslim thought, law, and theology. It is crucial because it has been invoked by both apologists and jurists to argue for Islamic tolerance, and to safeguard the integrity of the Qur'anic basis of *sharīʿah*. It is controversial because, in times of crisis in the relations of Muslims with their neighbors, jurists exerted much effort to circumvent it without appearing to go against the dictates of their sacred scripture.

Classical Qur'an commentators generally agree that this verse was revealed in answer to a specific situation. A man had two sons who converted to Christianity under the influence of Syrian Christian oil merchants who carried their trade to Madinah. Trying in vain to dissuade the youths, their father went to the Prophet and complained, "Should I let a part of me enter the Fire while I look on?" The Prophet had no answer until this verse was revealed. He then insisted that the youths be not compelled to return to Islam. The youths migrated with the merchants to Syria.[22]

There are still other verses in the Qur'an that clearly affirm this religious freedom without limiting it to the people of the Book. The Qur'an calls Muhammad a "Warner" (i.e., a bearer of warning). His task is to convey the truth, but as to who accepts or rejects faith is God's not the Prophet's responsibility. Thus we read: "Had your Lord so wished, all the people of the earth would have accepted faith. Would you [Muhammad] then compel people to be people of faith?" (Q. 10:99). In still another verse, faith is declared to be a personal choice, since the truth is made known by God: "Truth is of your Lord. Let him then who so wills have faith, and let him who so wills reject faith" (Q. 18:29).

The idea of divine revelation of the truth and the human freedom to accept or reject it is fundamental to the Islamic view of revelation and human responsibility. It is the basis of the primordial divine covenant with humanity (Q. 7:172), and hence the basis of obligation (*taklīf*) and its consequences for reward and punishment in the hereafter. The verse forbidding compulsion in religion goes on to declare: "right guidance has become distinguished from manifest error." It concludes with the assertion that those who choose faith in God over faith in idols (*ṭāghūt*) have grasped a "firm handle" which can never be broken.

This verse, it must be further argued, played a crucial role in checking the excesses of immoral tyrants or naïve and bigoted religious zealots. It was on the basis of this verse that Christians who were forcibly converted to Islam were often allowed to return to their faith. There is no doubt but that this principle of freedom of faith has helped preserve Eastern Christianity in a predominantly Muslim society.

Conversion is never a simple exchange of one set of beliefs and rituals for another. It often involves a complete change of national and cultural loyalty. This was the case in Spain and North Africa, in Egypt and Syria, and in almost all areas where Islam and Christianity competed in the unhappy task of winning souls, not for God or Christ but for religion. This religious idolatry in the name of God and faith has been the cause of untold suffering, misery, and bloodshed. Whether it is the martyrs' movement in Spain, the Inquisition, or the crusades, the result has been the same: lives were lost and noble principles violated to no purpose. The crusades ended leaving scars that have yet to be healed. The Muslims were expelled from Spain, and Islam was washed away with blood. But with the Muslims and Jews went a rich and unique experiment in cultural and religious symbiosis. Did the pious monk and his fellow martyrs achieve their purpose?

Muslims have been equally guilty of this religious idolatry in the name of God and Islam. They too contributed to the collapse of the Hispano-Arabic experiment. Had they sought to realize the moral imperatives of the Qur'an instead of reducing them to lifeless and often bigoted laws, the history of Muslim-Christian relations would have been more humane, and no doubt, more promising.

Much of the credit for the good in that history, and for the peaceful spread of Islam, goes not to brilliant jurists or even to enlightened rulers but to pious traders and sufis. It was this long and imperceptible interaction of pious Muslims with the masses of pious Christians, Jews, Hindus, and others that was responsible for widespread conversion into Islam. This quiet and unorganized missionary activity was carried out not so much among "simple-minded peasants" but among highly sophisticated urban populations. What Muslims won through conquest and war was lost. But what was achieved through "wisdom and fair exhortation" continues to grow and prosper.

# Notes

1. J. Spencer Trimingham, *Christianity among the Arabs in Pre-Islamic Times* (London: Longman, 1979), 18-19, 54, and passim.
2. See also Toshihiko Izutsu, *God and Man in the Koran: Semantics of the Koranic Weltanschauung* (Tokyo: Keio Institute of Cultural and Linguistic Studies, 1964), 124-27.
3. For the interpretation of this verse, see Mahmoud M. Ayoub, *The Qur'an and Its Interpreters* (Albany: State University of New York Press, 1984), 1:141-43.
4. For the interpretation of Q. 2:62, see Ayoub, *The Qur'an and Its Interpreters*, 1:109-12.
5. See the essay by Jane Dammen McAuliffe, "Fakhr al-Din al-Razi on *ayat al-jizyah* and *ayat al-sayf*," in *Conversion and Continuity: Indigenous Christian Communities in Islamic Lands, Eighth to Eighteenth Centuries*, ed. M. Gervers and R. Bihkazi (Toronto: Pontifical Institute of Mediaeval Studies, 1990).

6. Although the Qur'an includes the Zoroastrians among the people of the Book (Q. 5:69), they nevertheless sought to strengthen their claim by producing a canon of scripture during the Abbasid period. On the treatment of Hindus as "people of the Book," see Aziz Ahmad, *Studies in Islamic Culture in the Indian Environment* (Oxford: Oxford University Press, 1964), 79-80.

7. Muhammad ibn 'Isa al-Tirmidhi, *Sunan al-Tirmidhi*, ed. 'Izzat 'Ubayd al-Da'as. 10 vols. (Hims, Syria: n.p., 1965-1969), 8:335-36.

8. Muhammad ibn Yazid ibn Majah, *Sunan ibn Majah*, 2 vols., ed. M. F. 'Abd al-Baqi (Cairo: 'Isa al-Babi al-Halabi, 1952-53), 1:629.

9. Ibn Majah, *Sunan ibn Majah*, 1:568.

10. For a discussion of these sects, see Mark Wasserstrom, "Species of Misbelief: A History of Muslim Heresiography of the Jews" (Ph.D. diss., University of Toronto, 1985).

11. Malik bin Anas, *al-Muwatta'*, 3 vols., ed. M. F. 'Abd al-Baqi (Cairo: Dar Ihya' al-Kutub al-'Arabiyya, 1951), 1:16, 270.

12. For the evolution of the term *ahl al-dhimmah* and its application to Jews and Christians, see the essay, "*Dhimmah* in the Qur'an and the Hadith," chap. 9 in the present volume.

13. Tirmidhi, *Sunan al-Tirmidhi*, 5:88.

14. Ahmad ibn Muhammad ibn Hanbal, *Musnad al-Imam Ahmad ibn Hanbal*, 6 vols. 2nd ed. (Beirut: al-Maktab al-Islami li'l Taba'ah wa-al-Nashr, 1978), 1:245, 47.

15. Muslim Ibn al-Hajjaj al-Qushayri, *al-Jami' al-sahih* (Cairo: Dar al-'Amirah, 1343 A.H.), 299-300.

16. Ibn Hanbal, *Musnad al-Imam Ahmad ibn Hanbal*, 3:403.

17. Muhammad ibn Isma'il al-Bukhari, *al-Jami' al-sahih*, 4 vols. (Cairo: n.p., A.H. 1343), 1:185.

18. Ibn Hanbal, *Musnad al-Imam Ahmad ibn Hanbal*, 3:435; see also 4:24.

19. Tirmidhi, *Sunan al-Tirmidhi*, 5:338.

20. 'Ali ibn 'Abd al-Malik al-Muttaqi, *Kanz al 'ummal fi sunan al-aqwal wa al-af'al*, 16 vols., ed. B. al-Hayyani (Beirut: Mu'assasat al-Risalah, 1977), 10:579.

21. Miguel Asin Palacius, *Islam and the Divine Comedy*, trans. H. Sunderland (London: J. Murray, 1926), 277.

22. For this and other traditions regarding the verse 2:256, see Ayoub, *The Qur'an and Its Interpreters*, 1:252-56.

# 3

# Islam and Christianity

## Between Tolerance and Acceptance

Basic to the understanding of Christianity and Islam as faith identities are their principles of ultimate power or authority. For both, ultimate power belongs to God alone, and human authority must reflect this divine power. In both, a tension exists between these two powers which determined the course of their respective histories and interaction with each other. While in both religions tolerance is a fundamental principle based on the imperative of love and respect for human life and dignity, the Qur'an clearly advocates mutual acceptance and cooperation among the people of the Book: Jews, Christians, and Muslims. This is evidenced in the term *ahl al-kitāb*, the family of the Book, which includes all the children of Abraham.

The dictum *cuius regio eius religio* (whose rule, his religion), so well recognized in medieval Christendom as a general but unalterable rule of sociopolitical and state relations, exists also in Arabic, and some have even claimed for it Prophetic authority in the famous saying *al-nās-u ʿalā dīn-i mulūkihim* (people adhere to the religion of their monarchs).[1] The significance of this principle in Islam can be clearly discerned in the title and methodological structure of the most important classical world history by the great historian Tabari, who called his ambitious work *The History of Apostles and Kings*.[2]

The two great powers here meant, and which provide the context for both the Christian and Islamic view of the world and of human history, are the divine and temporal powers. These two powers are represented in Islam by the prophetic history, which is the framework within which human history moves, and the temporal power, represented by the ruler. In Christianity they are the "city of God," represented here on earth by the church, and human secular power. The first is eternal and immutable; the second ephemeral and transient.[3] Both concepts, moreover, are based in the scriptures of the two communities: "the Kingdom of God" in the Gospel and God's absolute dominion (*mulk*) in the Qur'an.[4]

Previously published in *Islam and Christian Muslim Relations* 2, no. 2 (December 1991): 171-81. Reprinted by permission.

In classical Muslim piety these two powers were seen as reflecting each other. When the ruler is just and good, nature is good as well. But nature becomes less giving and harsher when the ruler is harsh and unjust.[5] Therefore, it may be argued that in Islam the temporal and religious powers are closely intertwined. They are two dimensions of one absolute divine power without which no power, be it good or evil, can exist. This is to say, power in human society ultimately belongs to God alone.

This principle and its implementation have, since the death of the Prophet, been the issue that split the Muslim community into warring factions. They are the challenge to the legitimacy of any authority in Muslim society. This challenge was proclaimed early in Muslim history in the uncompromising dictum "no authority or judgment except God's judgment or authority."[6] This principle, moreover, which is common to all three monotheistic traditions, has been a source of strength and moral cohesion for the pious but also a justification for exclusiveness, conflict, and bloodshed.

From the preceding it may be concluded that religion in the Middle East has always been, and remains to this day, not merely a set of beliefs or even a theological system. It is rather the framework of a socio-political identity: a culture and way of life, a communion of worship and liturgy. Therefore, the ultimate aim of religion is not orthodoxy or right belief, but holiness and healing. This phenomenon has been well investigated and need not occupy us further in this discussion.[7]

The Qur'an did introduce a new element, or at least a new emphasis, to this religious identity. This is the challenge of active and responsible faith, which the Qur'an presents not only to the Muslims at the time of the Prophet Muhammad but to all those who believe in God throughout human history. Here again, faith is not simply right belief, but true *islām*, or the total surrender of the human will and destiny to God. Faith, moreover, is a source of blessing, healing, and salvation not only for those who live by it but, through them, for the whole society.

For instance, in narrating the story of Lot and God's judgment over his wicked people, the Qur'an concludes, "We brought out of it [that is, Lot's city] those in it who had faith, but We found in it only one house of the *muslims*" (Q. 51:36). As in the Genesis account of the same story (Gen 9:1-29), the implication is that there was not a sufficient number of people of faith living in the wicked city for God to spare it. Faith can become not only a source of blessing and salvation but also a cause of judgment and chastisement.

Thus, in discussing the fate of the martyrs of Najran,[8] the Qur'an asserts that they were martyred for their faith and thus lays God's curse on those who subjected them to martyrdom by fire, only because "they had faith in God." In the same context, the Qur'an further threatens with the punishment of hell fire in the hereafter those who seek to tempt people away from their faith by means of coercion, torture, or death (Q. 85:4-10).

It may be further concluded from the above discussion that the Qur'an posits a two-level faith identity. The first is an identity that is legal, cultural, and social, expressed in the individual's membership of the Muslim community. The framework of this identity is Islam as an institutionalized religion and legal system.

The second is a deeper identity that is based on faith, or *īmān*. It belongs to God alone to decide as to the truth or falsity of this identity. The Qur'an speaks of the nomadic Arabs (*al-a'rāb*) who said, "We have faith." The Qur'an counters, "Rather say, 'We have become Muslims,' for true faith has not yet entered your hearts" (Q. 49:148).

This point is again brought home with graphic irony in the following exchange between the Prophet and a young and enthusiastic fighter for the new faith, Usama bin Zayd:

> In battle with the polytheistic tribe of the Bani Murrah, Usama killed a man after he pronounced the *shahādah*, "there is no god but God," adding, "Do not kill me, I am a Muslim." The Prophet reproached Usama for killing another Muslim. But Usama protested, "He declared the *shahādah* under my sword." The Prophet ironically retorted, "Then you did not of course neglect to split open his heart," to determine whether the man had indeed accepted faith or not.[9]

These two levels of identity stood side by side in the formative years of the Muslim community, and their legal and theological legitimacy is clearly affirmed in the Qur'an and early hadith tradition. Faith as a universal and primordial basis of true religious identity was not limited to the Muslims alone. Rather, it was extended to the Jews and Christians, as people of the Book, and to all those who have true faith in God.

In a rare case where a Qur'anic verse is repeated, almost verbatim, once near the beginning of the Prophet's mission in Madinah and again toward its end (Q. 2:62; 5:69), we read, "Surely those who have faith, the Jews, the Christians, and the Sabaeans, whoever accepts faith in God and the Last Day, and performs good deeds; they shall have their reward with their Lord, no fear shall come upon them nor will they grieve" (Q. 2:62).[10] This verse presents again two criteria whereby a genuine religious identity can be ascertained: possession of a divine revelation, or scripture (*kitāb*), and faith in God. Faith, to be more precise, is the primary, universal, and overarching principle within which scriptures are a concomitant but not absolutely necessary criterion.

The Jews and Christians here represent the first criterion as people of the Book (*ahl al-kitāb*). This criterion, however, could be extended to include all other faiths based on scriptures. This, in fact, the Muslims soon did as they treated first the Zoroastrians (*majūs*) and later the Hindus as "people of the Book." The Sabaeans may be taken to represent all those who had faith in God, other than the Jews and the Christians. This is because classical Qur'an commentators and traditionists generally differed as to whether the Sabaeans actually possessed a sacred book.[11]

As for the legal religious identity that determined the status of an individual or group in Muslim society, it was more often than not subject to cultural and political considerations. For example, the Christian Arab tribes in early Islam were torn between their own faith identity as Christians and an ethnic and cultural affinity with the Muslims. They therefore decided to fight alongside the Muslims rather than pay the poll tax, which they regarded as a humiliation for true Arabs. They were not only exempted from the poll tax but were also allowed to share in the booty.[12] Eventually, I believe, more on cultural than religious grounds, these people were largely assimilated into Muslim society.

In yet another example of Christian-Muslim relations we see reflected the principles of religious tolerance and even mutual acceptance, on the one hand, and of polemical debate, repudiation, and subjugation on the other. In Makkah, the Qur'an presents the Christians of Najran to the oppressed Muslims as an example of faith martyrs to be emulated. In Madinah, however, the Christians of Najran become the model community of *dhimmis* living under Islamic protection with all the positive and negative elements that this status entailed.[13]

When, under the leadership of the Prophet, the Muslim commonwealth of Madinah became increasingly recognized as the principal religio-political power in Arabia, a number of delegations from neighboring tribes and communities were sent to the Prophet to pledge allegiance or to make peace with Madinah. The delegation of Najran came to the Prophet, according to tradition,[14] with two aims in view: to share their faith in hope of winning Muhammad to Christianity and, failing this, to establish a peace covenant with the Muslim state that would insure for them religious freedom and social independence. The men, who included religious and political leaders, were allowed to offer their prayers in the Prophet's mosque in spite of the protestations of some of the Companions.

The Qur'an clearly indicates that a sharp debate concerning the divinity and humanity of Christ took place between the Prophet and the men of Najran but does not report the actual disputation. Accounts of this debate are late and appear to reflect an already developed legal system governing the social, religious, and political status of non-Muslims in a vast Islamic state (Q. 3:59-63).[15] The two elements that are of interest to us in this encounter are, first, the fact that the men of Najran were allowed to worship in the Prophet's mosque and, second, that while the Prophet and the Christians of Najran did not agree theologically, they worked out a mutually acceptable relationship.

The first of these two elements indicates, in my view, an acceptance by both faith communities of the essential truth of each other's faith, and hence the legitimacy of both Christian and Islamic worship. The second demonstrates an attitude of mutual tolerance in spite of profound and irreconcilable theological differences. This tolerance unfortunately had within it the seeds of intolerance and hostility, nurtured by a long history of conflict, rivalry, and domination. This is because it was a tolerance dictated by military rather than moral strength, and by political exigencies rather than the imperatives of a common faith in God.

This encounter, moreover, along with the ongoing interaction of the first generation of Muslims with their Jewish and Christian neighbors, raises another important question. What is the Qur'anic demand of non-Muslims, particularly the people of the Book, as far as their relationship with Islam goes? This question is important because it bears directly on Muslim-Christian relations today. I am convinced that the Qur'an and early prophetic tradition generally demanded from Jews and Christians no more than what we are struggling to come to terms with today. It is the recognition that Muhammad is one of the prophets of God, that the Qur'an is the Book of God, and that Islam must exist alongside the two previous religions as an authentic religion based on an authentic revelation from heaven. In support of this view may be cited the Qur'an's repeated claim to be "a Book confirming the scriptures that were before it" (Q. 2:97; 3:3; 3:50; 4:47; 5:46).

To be sure, there are verses in the Qur'an that appear to evince not harmony and concord but discord and conflict between Muslims and the other people of the Book. Most notable among these is the famous *jizyah* verse, which reads, "Fight those among the people of the Book who do not have faith in God and the Last Day, and do not prohibit what God and His Messenger had prohibited, and do not abide by the true faith, until they give the *jizyah* with their own hand, humbled" (Q. 9:29). The verse, however, lays down three important conditions for fighting, two of which are unverifiable: "not having faith in God and the Last Day" and "not abiding by the true faith." It may be argued that these, and the third condition, namely, not abiding by the sanctions of the Qur'an and the Prophet, apply to Muslims as well. Conversely, all three conditions may, at least from the Islamic point of view, equally apply to all faith communities.

Like all legislative verses of the Qur'an, the ultimate purpose of this verse is not legislation but moral and religious guidance. This may be inferred from the many conditions and qualifiers that the Qur'an attaches to its legal sanctions and prohibitions. Often this purpose is obscured by the juristic purely legal or political rules formulated on the basis of moral and religious precepts. Who is therefore to decide that such and such Jews and Christians do not have faith in God or do not abide by the true religion? Obviously, if the judgment concerning the true *islām* of Muslims ultimately belongs to God, then should not the sincerity and truth of faith of Jews and Christians also be left to God to decide?

This question raises yet another problem. If we cannot decide who of the people of the Book have true faith in God and who do or do not follow the true religion, how are we to apply the Islamic law of the *jizyah* to these people? Yet, jurists legislated not for the exception but for the rule. Furthermore, jurists often broadened the applications of Qur'anic sanctions far beyond their apparent sense to include Jews and Christians within their purview.

I believe that only after the Qur'an was codified and there were no longer any "associators" (*mushrikūn*) of other gods with God in Arabia that terms such as associators, previously restricted to non-Muslim Arab tribes, came to designate Christians and even Jews.[16] The Qur'an consistently refers to Jews and Christians as people of the Book. In the hadith tradition, which is the second source of Islamic sacred law, after the Qur'an, the word *dhimmah* was used to designate the people of the Book as people with a special covenant of protection with the Muslims, but the term did not imply a second-class status. Rather, the word *dhimmah* was used as an expression of the responsibility of the Muslims for their non-Muslim subjects.

The people of *dhimmah* were sometimes referred to as the "people of the *dhimmah* of the Messenger of God." At other times they were called the "people of the *dhimmah* of God." This is to say, the charge for the well-being of these people rested primarily with God. The entire community is to represent God and His Messenger in safeguarding their covenant of protection with the people of *dhimmah*. Thus did the protection and well-being of Christians and Jews in Muslim lands become the sacred charge of all Muslims.

With the development of the schools of jurisprudence (*fiqh*) and the deepening conflict between Christendom and the world of Islam, the people of *dhimmah* came to be regarded as a special category, not only different from but also inferior to the Muslims. This development may be contrasted with the original Muslim attitude, illustrated by the following anecdote:

> Hizam bin Hakim, one of the Prophet's Companions, saw one day in Syria a group of Christians standing out in the hot sun. He was told that they were being punished because they had not paid their land taxes in full. Hizam went to the governor of Syria-Palestine 'Umayr bin Sa'd and reproached him saying, "I heard the Messenger of God, peace and blessings be upon him, say, 'He who torments men in this world, God will torment him on the Day of Resurrection.'" Hearing this, the governor ordered that the men be set free.[17]

The development of a legal system and the institutions to implement it, however necessary for the survival of Islam as a faith and civilization, resulted in the reification of *islām* into a closed religion. It rendered Islam the final religion and Muhammad the final Prophet. Theologically and juristically, this finality meant that Islam superseded all previous religions, and the Qur'an abrogated all previous scriptures. These exclusivist ideas and the exclusivist attitudes that they engendered belonged to the development of Islamic religious disciplines such as theology, jurisprudence, and the Qur'anic sciences.

It must again, however, be stressed that religious exclusivism does not accord with the spirit and worldview of the Qur'an. The Qur'an states, "To everyone have we appointed a way and a course to follow" (Q. 5:48), and, "For each there is a direction toward which he turns; vie therefore with one another in the performance of good works. Wherever you may be, God shall bring you all together [on the Day of Judgment]. Surely God has power over all things" (Q. 2:148).

By the end of the eleventh century, both the Christian and the Muslim communities had different concerns: the Muslims had established an Arabo-Islamic culture in Spain, hence the Catholic *reconquista,* and the Christians embarked on two centuries of crusades in the name of Christ. Thus, the voice of God in the Qur'an and the Gospel was completely drowned by the clamor of human folly and the cries of victims of war and oppression.

In such circumstances, the ideals of love, universalism, and openness which are basic to both faiths gave way to ideas of exclusivism and hostility on both sides. Motivated by the affirmation that salvation is by Christ alone, Christians sent both missionaries and armies to colonize and convert the Muslims. For Muslims, the people of the Book became the rejecters of faith (*kuffār*) who obstinately refused to accept God's final revelation; that is, they refused to become Muslims. Thus, they took the place of the Makkan "associators" as legitimate objects of religious warfare and domination.

Muslim and Christian men and women have lived together in the Middle East for the most part as good neighbors. Given the mosaic character of Middle Eastern societies throughout their long history, Muslims, Christians, and Jews lived with a good measure of concord and harmony. This was due, at least in part, to social courtesy, which is a common characteristic of Eastern peoples, regardless of their religious affiliations. There were, of course, outbreaks of conflict, but often these were incited either by a particular group of people for particular political ends or by outside influences.

Within the framework of this common courtesy, dialogue between Muslims and Christians in the Middle East has not been a dialogue about religious beliefs and theological doctrines. It is rather a neighborly relationship of sharing in each other's festivals and other joyous celebrations, and in sad occasions of death and calamity. In short, they shared a daily life as one community of different but mutually respected faiths.

Among the many things Middle Eastern Christians and Muslims have learned from the West is to dialogue, Western style. This kind of dialogue, however, is too foreign to the whole culture and mentality of the people. It is therefore not going very far, and many people are suspicious of both the form and purpose of this dialogue. Communities which have long taken for granted that everyone must have a socio-religious identity naturally live the ideal of religious pluralism.

The cultural courtesy of which I have made so much in this discussion is based on an old Arab adage that is, in turn, inspired by the Qur'an. The Qur'an says, "To you your religion, and to me my religion" (Q. 109:6). The adage goes, "To each his religion, and may God help him," that is, to live by it.

The Qur'an speaks to us today as directly as it did to the people of its time of revelation more than fourteen centuries ago. It enjoins all the people of the Book, Jews, Christians, and Muslims, mutually to accept one another on one basis alone, "that we worship no one except God, and that we do not take one another as lords besides God" (Q. 3:64). This invitation to the people of the Book to come to one word of common purpose remains a challenge for all of us today as it was for the Prophet and his people.

It may be further argued that the Qur'an legislates for a pluralistic society in which diverse religious communities can live side by side in mutual and creative acceptance that would far transcend mere tolerance. No doubt, in both Christianity and Islam, this ideal exists. Both the Catholic and Orthodox Churches have long had a historical and philosophical tradition of interfaith relations, and many Protestant churches and other religious and civic organizations are playing a major role in the effort to realize this ideal.

The challenge of the Qur'an, I believe, and more to Muslims than to Christians, is to regard the people of the Book as a large family of faith, speaking different languages, but worshiping the One God. The Qur'an employs two terms to denote people bound by a common faith or destiny: *aṣḥāb* and *ahl*. It calls *aṣḥāb* the inhabitants of paradise (*aṣḥāb al-jannah*) and hell (*aṣḥāb al-nār*), and people with a shared destiny, such as the "people of the Cave" (*aṣḥāb al-kahf*) (Q. 2:39; 2:257; 7:42; 10:26; 18:9), while the immediate family of such prophets as Noah, Abraham, Moses, and Muhammad, it calls *ahl* (Q. 3:33; 11:45; 3:121).

Consistently, the people of the Book are referred to in the Qur'an as *ahl al-kitāb*. The word *ahl* always signifies a family relationship. The *ahl* of a person are his or her family, wife, husband, and children. Therefore, the phrase *ahl al-kitāb* may properly be translated as "the family of the Book." The Qur'an, furthermore, enjoins Muslims and all the people of faith to show kindness to their near relations.

Muslims, certainly more than Christians if not Jews, are in the strict literal sense people of the Book. For Muslims, therefore, "a true religion" is faith in a revealer God and His revelations. Islam to a large extent shares a deep reverence for the sacred word with Eastern Christianity and all the ancient Semitic cultures of the Middle East. The Christian concept of the incarnate divine word notwithstanding, it still cannot be argued that Islam has imposed on Christianity a concept or idea that it did not already have. The church had, until Martin Luther, argued for the equality, if not primacy, of tradition over scriptures. This is because the New Testament is a product of the church and a record of its early history and witness. But with Luther's proclamation *sola scriptura*, Islam and Christianity again came closer together in the recognition of the centrality of the scriptures as a source of moral, legal, and spiritual authority. The centrality of the "revealed Divine Word" in the life and worship of the church has been specially emphasized by Vatican II in its eucharistic theology wherein the faithful are urged to turn for spiritual nourishment to "the divine Scriptures," "since from the table of both the word of God and of the body of Christ she unceasingly receives and offers to the faithful the bread of life, especially in the sacred liturgy."[18]

Thus, the "revealed Word of God" (*al-kitāb*) may once more become the common bond that binds all the people of faith together. The Qur'anic emphasis on the centrality of the Book could help Jews, Christians, and Muslims become for the first time the reconciled children of Abraham, one happy family.

# Notes

1. This saying has no basis in the hadith tradition. It is, however, reported in the Prophetic tradition as a moral indictment of the community's laxity: *kama takunu yuwalla 'alaykum* (just as you are, so will be those in authority over you). See *Mishkat al-masabih*, trans. James Robson (Lahore: Sh. Muhammad Ashraf, 1975), 789.

2. Muhammad bin Jarir al-Tabari (d. 310/923), *Ta'rikh al-rusul wa'l-muluk*. For the life of the author and his methodology, see *The History of Tabari*, vol. 1, *General Introduction and From Creation to the Flood*, translated and annotated by Franz Rosenthal (Albany: State University of New York Press, 1989), 5-140.

3. The classical expression of this idea is St. Augustine's *The City of God*, which is the first major attempt at presenting a Christian philosophy of history.

4. See the Lord's Prayer in Matt 6:9-13 where the addition to v. 13 in some manuscripts, "For yours is the kingdom and the power and the glory for ever. Amen," stresses this idea further. In the Qur'an this idea provides the framework of God's role in human history; see Q. 3:26, as well as 2:107; 3:189.

5. See Geo Widengren, *Muhammad, the Apostle of God, and His Ascension* (Uppsala: Lundequistska Bokhandeln, 1955), and also Nizam al-Mulk, *Siyar al-muluk* or *siyasat-namah*, trans. Hubert Drake as *The Book of Government* or *Rules for Kings* (London, Henley, and Boston: Routledge & Kegan Paul, 1978), pt. 1, chap. 5, 32-42.

6. "*Lā ḥukma illā li-llāh*" (cf. Q. 6:57; 12:40) was the slogan raised by the Kharijites against 'Ali bin Abi Talib, the fourth of the "rightly guided caliphs," first Shi'i imam and one of the most venerated personalities in Muslim history.

7. See J. Spencer Trimingham, *Christianity among the Arabs in Pre-Islamic Times* (London and New York: Longman/Librairie du Liban, 1979), 100-116, and passim.

8. See the illuminating study of this pre-Islamic South Arabian Christian community by Irfan Shahid, *The Martyrs of Najran: New Documents* (Brussels: Soc. des Bollandistes, 1971).

9. Ibn Qayyim al-Jawziyyah, *Zad al-Ma'ad*, ed. Shu'ayb 'Abd al-Qadir al-Arma'ut, 6th ed. (Beirut: Mu'assasat al-Risalah, 1304/1984) 3:361.

10. For a comprehensive discussion of the major interpretations of this verse, see Mahmoud M. Ayoub, *The Qur'an and Its Interpreters* (Albany: State University of New York, 1984), 1:108 ff.

11. Ibid.

12. Marshall G. S. Hodgson, *The Venture of Islam* (Chicago and London: University of Chicago Press, 1974), 1:199, 229.

13. For a discussion of the term *dhimmah* in the Qur'an and its legal signifi-

cance for Jews and Christians under Muslim rule, see *"Dhimmah* in the Qur'an and Hadith," chap. 9 in the present volume. For a very useful presentation of translations into English of numerous primary texts on the status of *dhimmis*, see Bat Ye'or, *The Dhimmi: Jews and Christians under Islam* (Rutherford, Madison, Teaneck, N.J.: Farleigh Dickinson University Press/London and Toronto: Associated University Presses, 1985), passim.

14. For a discussion of this event and the traditions concerning it, see Mahmoud M. Ayoub, *The Qur'an and Its Interpreters* (Albany: State University of New York, 1992), vol. 2, Introduction: Occasion of revelation of Sura 3 (*Āl ʿImrān*) and commentaries on the *mubāhalah* verse (Q. 3:61).

15. Ibid.

16. See Q. 9:30. See also *"Dhimmah* in the Qur'an and Hadith," chapter 9 below; and Mahmoud Ayoub, "'Uzayr in the Qur'an and Muslim Tradition," in *Studies in Islamic and Judaic Studies: Papers Presented in the Institute for Islamic and Judaic Studies* (Atlanta: Scholars Press, 1986), 3-18.

17. Ahmad Ibn Hanbal, *Musnad Ibn Hanbal* (Beirut: Dar Sadir, n.d.), 3:403.

18. Cf. chap. 6 ("Sacred Scripture in the Life of the Church") of the "Dogmatic Constitution on Divine Revelation" of Vatican Council II, in *The Documents of Vatican II*, ed. Walter M. Abbott (New York: Guild Press, 1966), 125ff.

# 4

# Roots of Muslim-Christian Conflict

Islam and Christianity have from the beginning had an ambivalent relationship which, at one and the same time, has held possibilities of deep and violent conflict as well as of constructive and meaningful dialogue. The Qur'an calls for dialogue with the people of the Book (Jews and Christians) in a fair manner. It requires of Muslims to declare, "our God and your God is one God . . ." (Q. 29:46). Yet the Qur'an categorically condemns belief in the Trinity and the divinity of Jesus. It considers Christians to be nearest in amity to Muslims (Q. 5:82), yet commands its followers to wage war against people of the Book who reject faith in God and the Last Day, until they humbly remit the *jizyah*, or poll tax (Q. 9:29).

Both the negative and positive aspects of this relationship may be observed in the long history of interaction of the two communities. The Qur'an provides only the basis for the attitude of Muslims at any given time toward Christians and Christianity. It was not theology but concrete political, economic, and social considerations that determined the form and outcome of such an attitude. However, because the Qur'an recognizes Christianity as genuinely a true faith and Christians as a legitimate faith community, Christianity has survived in the Muslim world in a variety of forms and expressions that the West could not tolerate.

Early Christian theology had to find a place in its view of history as salvation history for previous religious and philosophical systems. Judaism presented a great problem which began to receive serious attention only after a long and tragic history. The church has reluctantly come to accept Judaism as a legitimate religious tradition independent of Christianity.

Islam is a post-Christian religion. Thus, while pre-Christian philosophies and religious dispensations might be regarded as a prelude to the Gospel, or *preparatio evangelica*, Islam could not be fitted into this schema. Hence, Islam required a new theology which is only now, after fourteen centuries of struggle and conflict, beginning to be tentatively formulated.

In the following pages an attempt will be made to study the roots of this conflict from a Muslim point of view and to point to new and hopeful hori-

Previously published in *The Muslim World* 79, no. 1 (January 1989): 25-45. Reprinted by permission.

zons in relations between the two communities. I shall first examine the claims of supersessionism and finality in the two traditions. This will be briefly contrasted with the view of the universality of truth which is basic to the theology of both faiths. In the light of this claim it will be possible to discuss the Christian justification of the Crusades against Muslims and the role the Crusades played in determining even contemporary Muslim views of the Christian West. In close conjunction with the Crusades, three important elements of more recent developments in Western relations with Islam will be studied. These are colonialism, evangelization, and orientalism.

My task will be mainly to present coherently and as objectively as possible the Muslim view of the attitude of the Christian West toward Islam. The history of Muslim-Christian relations has largely been a story of mistrust, misgiving, and misunderstanding. A new and genuine beginning based on mutual goodwill and patient dialogue is needed. Because I believe this to be imperative for the peace and survival of both communities of faith and of the world, I present this study as a small contribution toward this goal.

## Supersessionism and the Universality of Truth

Like Islam, Christianity was born at a time and in an area of intense cultural and religious activity. It was natural, therefore, for the early fathers of the church to recognize the place of previous manifestations of the truth, and to see Christianity as heir to and final expression of this truth. Thus, early in the history of the church, Saint Cyprian (d. 258) argued that nothing less than full membership in the Catholic Church would avail a heretic of salvation, not the baptism of blood.[1] Saint Cyprian argued further, and more forcefully, that, "he cannot have God as a father who does not have the Church as a mother. If whoever was outside the ark of Noah was able to escape, he too who is outside the Church escapes." Cyprian then quotes the well-known words of Christ (Matt 12:30), "He who is not with me is against me, and he who does not gather with me, scatters." He then comments, "he who gathers somewhere outside the Church, scatters the Church of Christ. He who does not hold this unity [that is, of the Church] does not hold the law of God, does not hold the faith of the Father and the Son, does not hold life and salvation."[2]

The doctrine of the church as the exclusive source of salvation, expressed in the well-known formula *extra ecclesiam nulla salus*, had many and often tragic ramifications even within the Christian community.[3] According to Saint Augustine, "what is now called the Christian religion existed even among the ancients and was not lacking from the beginning of the human race until 'Christ came in the flesh.' From that time, true religion, which already existed, began to be called Christian."[4] A thousand years later the Council of Florence (1438-1445) reiterated the same doctrine in much stronger language:

The holy Roman Church believes, professes, and preaches that no one remaining outside the Catholic Church, not just pagans, but also Jews or heretics or schismatics, can become partakers of eternal life; but they will go to the "everlasting fire which was prepared for the devil and his angels," unless before the end of life they are joined to the Church.[5]

It must be observed that this doctrine has had its political and military repercussions in Christian history since the time when God favored the Emperor Constantine with victory under the sign of the cross. In the thirteenth century, Pope Boniface VIII (1294-1303) declared with clear political intent that there is only one Catholic Church and that "outside this Church there is no salvation and no remission of sins." This is because, the pope went on, "It is absolutely necessary for the salvation of every human creature to be subject to the Roman Pontiff."[6] Pope Urban II (1088-1099) had invoked the same doctrine at the Council of Clermont in 1095 to justify the First Crusade. Here again, the real motives were far more political than religious. It must be noted that this doctrine, or perhaps problem, continued to occupy theologians and church authorities alike, also and even particularly after Vatican II.[7]

Islam also has its exclusivist doctrine. The Qur'an asserts that "surely the (true) religion with God is Islam . . ." and, "whoever seeks a religion other than Islam, it shall not be accepted from him, and in the hereafter he shall be among the losers" (Q. 3:19; 3:95). Later Muslim traditionalists, and even contemporary thinkers, have affirmed this position in spite of other verses in the Qur'an that clearly present a far more universalistic and inclusive view of faith and salvation.

The Qur'an frequently uses the term *islām* in its essential meaning of submission of all things to God (Q. 3:83). Yet the prevalent view in Muslim tradition has been that any given religious dispensation remains valid until the coming of the one to succeed it; then the new dispensation abrogates and supersedes the previous one. Thus, until the coming of Jesus, the Torah of Moses was binding on anyone who had heard of it. Thereafter his book, the Gospel, superseded the Torah. Islam is regarded by Muslims as the last religious system given to humankind; the Qur'an is the final revelation and Muhammad is the seal of the prophets. The Prophet is said to have declared, "whoever died in the faith of Jesus, and died in Islam before he heard of me, his lot shall be good. But whoever hears of me today and yet does not assent to me, he shall surely perish."[8]

Since the middle of the last century a number of intellectual movements arose in various parts of the Muslim world in opposition to Western colonial domination and missionary activity. New ideas and interpretations of Islam that assert its vitality, universality, and finality constitute the main thrust of such movements.[9] For example, the late Egyptian thinker and prominent member of the Society of Muslim Brothers (an Islamic revivalist movement originating in early twentieth-century Egypt) Sayyid Qutb (executed by President Nasser in 1966) argues that Christianity had from the beginning a limited role to play in the life of human society. Its purpose was to revivify the stagnant Jewish law. Thus, Christianity came for a limited period of time between Judaism and Islam.[10] It is clear then that in Islam as in Christianity the doctrine of supersessionist exclusiveness was motivated more by political than religious considerations.

Christianity and Islam: each claimed from the beginning to be a universal message intended for humankind. Yet each also claimed to be the final and universal expression of the Truth. This latter claim made any recognition by either one of the other impossible. Moreover, it contradicted the basic tenet of both, namely, that God created all human beings and that He is a God of love who wishes the guidance and salvation of all His creatures. God is the Truth, Islam insists; if we truly know Him, He will, Christ assured us, "set us free" (John 8:32).

The New Testament asserts in many places the universality of truth. Thus, St. Paul declared to the seeking but misguided Athenians that "God never left Himself without a witness" (Acts 14:17). Furthermore, the writer of the Epistle to the Hebrews opens his discourse with the reassuring proclamation that God had spoken to men at sundry times and in sundry ways; in the fullness of time, the writer to the Hebrews asserts, God spoke through His son, Jesus Christ. Does this necessarily mean that henceforth God should forevermore hold His peace? The early church lived in the anticipation of Christ's second coming, the Parousia. This did not mean, however, that after Christ's earthly sojourn God could no more call His human children to Him, but rather that the end was at hand. Time had reached its fullness. Soon, however, the church did realize that the kingdom of God was not at hand, and that the church must, therefore, live in the world and find its place in history.

As the early church fathers encountered the truth in ancient philosophical and religious systems, they heard the voice of God speaking in them. This they called the "seminal divine word." Thus, "according to the Christian theology of the second century (especially Justin) and the third (especially the Alexandrians, Clement and Origen), the divine Logos (*logos spermatikos*, 'seminal word') was active everywhere from the beginning." Hans Küng, who makes this observation, rightly asks, "but if the pagans Plato, Aristotle and Plotinus, or later—for others—even Marx and Freud could be 'pedagogues' leading men to Christ, why not also the philosophers and religious thinkers of other nations?"[11]

This universalist view of divine guidance in history was soon to be obscured by the theological wranglings within the church, as well as political, economic, and military rivalries within the Christian community and between it and other communities of faith. Truth has therefore been denied its universality and, according to Küng, has become Catholic or Protestant, European or American. The Christian message has become the religion of the

West. Thus, not only were other faiths denied access to the truth, but other Christians were also lost because they were not Latin, European, Catholic, American, or Protestant.[12]

Islam as well demands a universalist view of the truth operating through divine revelation in human history. The Qur'an insists that "there is not a community but that a warner [that is, a messenger] has come to it" (Q. 24:35). The Qur'an further argues for divine wisdom in human diversity of culture, language, and religion. The purpose in this diversity is for men and women to cooperate in a life of righteousness and vie with one another in the performance of righteous deeds. Goodness must not be judged, therefore, by ethnic, racial, or even religious identity; "surely," the Qur'an asserts, "the most noble of you in the sight of God is he who is most pious" (Q. 49:13).

Guided not always by this and similar passages of the Qur'an but by theological, political, and other worldly ambitions, Muslims also sacrificed the universality of truth on the altar of religion. Yet while the Christian attitude of triumphal supersessionist finality was born in the church and nurtured by its theology, that of Islam, although having its seeds in early tradition, evolved out of the long history of hostility and conflict between the two communities. It is to some aspects of this history that I shall now turn.

## The Crusades Old and New

Jerusalem, the city of David, home of the Temple and Holy Sepulcher, is also the Holy House and home of the "furthest place of worship" (al-Aqsa), whose precincts God blessed (Q. 17:1). Jerusalem was the first *qiblah* (direction of prayer) for Muslims and a place of pilgrimage. It is the bridge between earth and heaven whose sacred rock served as a stepping stone for the Prophet Muhammad's celestial journey (*mi'rāj*) to God. Yet Jerusalem, the "city of peace," became a powerful symbol for Muslims, as it is for Jews and Christians, not only of religious loyalties but also of their historic identity and political power. It is God's holy mountain, the hill of Golgotha, and the goal of Islam's sacred *hijrah* (migration).[13]

Jerusalem has been, in many important respects, the focus of Muslim-Christian relations. It is what happened in Jerusalem during the period of the Latin kingdom (July 1099 to October 1187) that determined the subsequent history of Muslim-Christian relations. The Crusades in themselves were not a very important chapter in Muslim history. They have been, however, crucial in providing the pattern for and spirit of the long history of conflict and mistrust between Muslims and Christians. Important in this tragic history was the conquest of Jerusalem, as recorded with gory details by eyewitnesses and other chroniclers.[14]

During the eleventh century, Europe was torn by internal strife and warfare. This made it necessary for both civil and ecclesiastical authorities to find other avenues to channel the energies of their warring subjects. A crusade ostensibly to free the Holy Land from the hands of the "pagans," that is, the Muslims, provided such an avenue. The Crusades had other important objectives, not least among which was to reunite the church after the schism of 1054. Instead, however, the Crusades helped to deepen this division.

On November 27, 1095, Pope Urban II proclaimed a crusade in a fiery speech delivered before a large audience assembled for that purpose at the Council of Clermont. According to the famous chronicler of the First Crusade, Fulcher of Chartres, the pope exhorted his subjects in the name of Christ to "hasten to exterminate this vile race from our lands and to aid the Christian inhabitants in time." To add greater stress to this exhortation, the pope declared that "Christ commands it."[15] It was natural for the fighters to cry out *"Deus le volt"* (God wills it) in their merciless assault on Muslim cities. The holy pontiff then granted absolution to all those who would join in this "holy war." No doubt papal absolution contributed to the ruthless savagery with which the crusading armies carried out their mission. In the initial stages of the Crusades, the cities that were captured were virtually depopulated.[16]

For a better understanding of Muslim perceptions of the Crusades and their aftermath, a brief look at the Islamic rules of war and interreligious social relations is necessary. Only then will we be able to see the contrast between the treatment of Muslims by the Crusaders and the way Muslims treated their non-Muslim subjects. It is on the basis of this contrast that Muslims have argued for the tolerance of Islam and Muslims against the intolerance of Christians.

The Qur'an clearly states as a general principle that "God does not forbid you concerning those who do not fight against you on account of your faith, or seek to drive you out of your dwellings, that you act justly towards them; for God surely loves those who are just" (Q. 60:8). Just treatment of neighbors implies social intercourse between two different groups of people. This the Qur'an recognizes and encourages, at least between Muslims and the people of the Book: "The food of those who were given the Book is lawful for you, and your food is lawful for them. Likewise, the chaste women of the people of the Book [are lawful for you to marry]" (Q. 5:5). This means that in times of peace and security, Muslims and non-Muslims must live as one society, each of these two communities of faith being subject to its own special socio-religious laws. Thus the general juristic principle has been "to them belong whatever [privileges] belong to us, and incumbent upon them is whatever is incumbent upon us."[17] This principle must be upheld in times of war as in times of peace.

The Qur'an distinguishes between those of the people of the Book who live in accordance with their own faith and scriptures and those who exchange their faith and God's revelations for worthless personal gains. The former recognize the truth in their own scriptures and in the Qur'an. This recognition, moreover, creates between them and the Muslims a bond of amity and friendship:

> You shall surely find the nearest of men in amity to those who have
> faith, these who say: "We are Christians." This is because there are
> among them devout men and monks; nor do they act arrogantly.
> When they hear that which was sent down to the Messenger
> [Muhammad], you see their eyes well up with tears for what they
> recognize of the truth. They say "Our Lord we have faith; inscribe
> us, therefore, among those who are witnesses [to the truth]." (Q.
> 5:82)

The Qur'an recognizes further that there are strong differences in belief
between the two communities of faith that would necessarily lead to debate
and argumentation. It stipulates, therefore, that Muslims "do not dispute
with the people of the Book except in the best manner, save those among
them who do wrong. Say: 'We believe in that which was sent down to us
and that which was sent down to you. Our God and your God is One, to
Him we are submitters [that is, Muslims]'" (Q. 29:46). This is ecumenism in
its widest sense. In times of prosperity and of security from external dan-
gers, this tolerant attitude was the hallmark of Muslim-Christian relations.
Yet even in times of conflict and hostility, Muslims could be reminded of
such principles as a restraint against the all-too-common human tendency in
times of war to cruel revenge against the enemy.

The application of these principles in the time of the Prophet became
*sunnah*, an example binding on all later generations. We are told that when
the Prophet sent out an army, he instructed them (as related on the authority of Abu Bakr, the first caliph) as follows:

> Do not betray [one another in war]. Do not commit acts of treach-
> ery. Do not mutilate or kill a young child, an old man or woman. Do
> not cut down trees bearing fruits. Do not slaughter a sheep, a cow
> or a camel except if you need it for food. You shall pass by people
> who have dedicated themselves to acts of devotion in their her-
> mitages. Let them be, and that to which they have dedicated them-
> selves.[18]

It is important to observe that these injunctions, which were to remain the
Islamic rules for war, were communicated by Abu Bakr to Muslim fighters
on their way to their first engagement after the Prophet's death. It is also
noteworthy that this was the first major battle with the Byzantine Christians.[19]

Fighting, in Islam, is only one aspect of jihad. In its basic sense, jihad is
striving against evil, whether in one's own life or that of society. Sayyid Qutb,
one of the most influential Muslim thinkers of the twentieth century, sees
jihad as a struggle against oppression wherever it may be. Jihad must not be
used to compel people to embrace Islam but to free them from oppression,
regardless of their religious affiliation. Another end of jihad is the protec-

tion of the Muslim community, and especially its youth, from being lured away from their faith. Sayyid Qutb seeks to reassure Christians that they have nothing to fear under Muslim rule because it will not oblige them to accept Islam or to perform any of its acts of worship. For all this, Sayyid Qutb finds support in the Qur'an, prophetic tradition, and Muslim history.[20]

Like Sayyid Qutb, other Muslim apologists have tirelessly invoked Muslim and Christian history to demonstrate the tolerance and humaneness of Islam and its adherents and their opposites in the West. This, they argue, is in spite of the teaching of Christ and the Gospel. In fact, Sayyid Qutb argues that Christianity came as a life-giving force to the Jewish law. Europeans, he believes, soon found that Christianity could not be applied as a cure to the ills of society because of their hard life and harsh climate. Instead, religion was reduced to a private relationship between a person and his Lord. Thus, the author concludes, "Europe was never for one day Christian. Rather, from the day religion penetrated Europe to our own time, it has remained in total isolation from the conditions of life and its institutions."[21] Since the West has been, as many Muslim thinkers claim, deprived of the spirit and values of Christianity, then Western civilization has nothing of value to offer to Muslims. It follows in their view that Western society is dominated solely by materialistic interests. In fact, it is precisely this which has been seen as the root cause of Western aggressive colonialism in all its aspects.

In a small pamphlet entitled "Western Leaders Say: 'Destroy Islam and Exterminate its People,'"[22] the author asserts that the Crusades continue and that the conflicts which caused them in the first place still stand today. He sees the creation of Israel as part of the West's long-term plan to destroy Islam as a faith and civilization. As proof of his argument, the author observes that the conquest of Jerusalem by General Allenby during World War I was seen by European powers as "the eighth and final Crusade." Allenby is said to have declared after his victory, "today the wars of the Crusades have came to an end."[23] Likewise, when the French general Gouraud quelled Syrian uprisings against the French mandate, in 1919 and 1920, he went to the tomb of Salah al-Din (Saladin) in Damascus, kicked it with his foot, exclaiming, "we have returned, O Saladin!"[24]

Muslims see a sinister alliance between modern Western colonialism, or the "new world crusadism" (*al-salībiyya al-'ālamiya al-jadīda*) as they call it, and "world Zionism." They see the struggle between the West and the Arab world not as a struggle between two peoples but between two civilizations, two religions, and two worldviews. Thus Randolph Churchill, the grandson of Winston Churchill, writing after the Six Day War of June 1967, exults in the final return of Jerusalem to Western domination through Israeli power.[25]

In view of this, the question of the motives behind the Western Crusades against Muslims must be raised. Were these the results of long and bitter wars between Muslims and Christians, wars that led to Muslim domination of some of the fairest lands of Christendom, or were there other and stronger motives? The real motive, as Muslims see it, has been colonial domination. The only formidable obstacle in the way of achieving this goal is Islam. This is the view of Western missionaries, one of whom, Lawrence Browne, is said to have declared, "Islam is the only barrier in the face of western colonialism."[26]

Muslims believe that Islam and it alone is still capable of uniting so many millions the world over into a world power, across all racial, ethnic, and cultural differences. It is for this reason that they believe Islam is greatly feared in the West. This fear was vividly demonstrated at the start of the Iranian Islamic revolution. The West has always striven to prevent Muslim unity at all cost, Muslims maintain. Three important forces were mustered for this purpose: colonialism, missionary activity, and orientalism.

Still, the glorious days of the Crusades continue to provide, at least for some, a nostalgic dream of past grandeur. This dream is eloquently voiced by a French missionary priest who is said to have spent many years as head of the Jesuit university in Beirut, Lebanon. He said:

> The missionary comes under the banner of the Cross dreaming of the past, and looking forward to the future as he listens to the wind whistling from afar, from the shores of Rome and France. No one can prevent that spirit from repeating to our ears in its words of yesterday, the cry of our crusading forebears: "God wills it."[27]

Muslims have unfortunately detected this spirit in every sphere of Western activity in their society. The three areas of Western activity in the Muslim world already mentioned—colonization, evangelization, and orientalism—have always occupied the minds of Muslim thinkers particularly since the Second World War and the establishment of the state of Israel. It has already been observed that at the root of Muslim-Christian conflict stood centuries of mistrust. Nowhere can this be more clearly discerned than in the way Muslims have interpreted their relations with the Western world in light of these three areas. They must be examined frankly and candidly if we are to move from a relationship of conflict and confrontation to one of meaningful dialogue based on mutual trust and goodwill. This is because we can seek to build a better future only if we understand our past history.

## Colonialization, Evangelization, and Orientalism

When Christ commissioned his disciples to "go therefore and make disciples of all nations" (Matt 28:19), he did not wish them to achieve this with the help of secular authority. Nor did he intend this sacred mission of love to be carried out in the spirit of triumphal superiority and sectarian competition. Yet it was this spirit that dominated missionary activity for most of its long history. This has been especially the case since the Protestant Reformation and the beginning of European colonial history.

My concern in this study is not Western colonialism as such, but rather the spirit that nurtured it along with missionary work and orientalist schol-

arship. More precisely, I shall be concerned with the ways Muslims have per-
ceived these three activities and the attitudes that inspired them. In a recent
work on modern Islamic thought and its relation to Western colonialism,[28]
the author observes that by the middle of the nineteenth century, India, which
for centuries had been permeated by Islamic Timurid culture, Iran, Indonesia, and North Africa fell prey to British, Dutch, and French colonialism. By
the end of the First World War, the entire Muslim world was parceled out
among European colonialist powers. Throughout its colonial history, Europe
was inspired by the same spirit of mission that inspired Christian missionaries. Thus the author quotes the well-known French historian Gabriel Han-
otaux, who asserted that "France carried to the Semitic Muslims the salt and
spirit of civilization."[29]

For many orientalists, Islamic civilization is an imperfect residue of
Byzantine civilization. This idea was born out of nationalistic and ethnic ideologies of the nineteenth century. Among these, Aryanism, or the "master
race" theory as applied to white Europeans, has played a major role in shap-
ing Western attitudes toward Islam as a faith and a civilization. Thus, Islamic
mysticism, or Sufism, which had a great appeal to Western thinkers, was
seen as the expression of a primitive Aryan religious phenomenon that is foreign to Islam.[30] This meant that Islam, as an impoverished Semitic religion,
would be incapable of developing such a spiritual heritage. Sufism was, therefore, mistakenly considered to be a purely Iranian phenomenon. This implied
that Islam was spiritually and ethically lacking, and that it was therefore the
mission of the West to save Muslims from Islam.

Based on this and other notions, the attitude of Western colonizers, missionaries, and orientalists toward Muslims and their faith was one of dis-
dain and insensitive paternalism. It is this attitude that continues to occupy
the minds and pens of educated Muslims. One of these, Omar Farrukh, who
was educated first at the American University of Beirut and later in Europe,
has made this problem one of his lifelong occupations. His book *Evangelization and Colonialism in Arab Lands*[31] has set the tone and provided the
themes for all subsequent works in Arabic on the subject. It is, therefore,
important that we examine this seminal work in some detail. Farrukh makes
a distinction between what he calls "official colonialism" and "actual colonialism." The former is political; the latter intellectual, social, and economic.
Although official political colonialism has largely come to an end, neocolo-
nialism or actual colonialism in many of its forms is still with us.

Missionary work has had a long history of cooperation with colonialism,
with which it enjoyed a symbiotic relationship. Farrukh regards missionary
work as "of greater harm to our countries than colonialism, because colonialism penetrated into our lands only under the cover of missionary activity."[32] He further states:

> We believe missionary work to be altogether evil. This is because
> American, British, French and Dutch [missionaries] speak good with

their tongues, but the effects of their actions are clearly visible to us in Palestine, North Africa, Indochina, Cyprus, Kashmir, South Africa and even in the United States. All these people must, at least, first wash their hands of the blood of their victims before they can play on the stage of humanity the role of the magnanimous do-gooder.[33]

In the view of Omar Farrukh, the motives behind missionary activity are not in the least religious. This is because, he argues, Western society is itself atheistic. It is a materialistic society that knows no meaning of the spirit. Then, quoting the words of a Lebanese Arab Christian, he continues, "America, which worships gold, iron and petrol, has nonetheless covered half the earth with missionaries claiming to call others to a spiritual life and religious peace."[34] Likewise, he argues, France is a secular state at home, yet abroad it protects missionaries. The Jesuits, who have been expelled from France as enemies, are its reliable agents and friends in its colonies. Italy also, while showing hostility to the church in its struggle for independent statehood, had nonetheless built its imperialist policy on the efforts of monks and missionaries. Even Soviet Russia, which in its own domains has called for a war against all religions, nevertheless pretended to support religious leaders calling for an ecumenical council in Moscow when after the Second World War it sought to enlarge its economic and political sphere of influence.[35]

Farrukh continues: in recent Western colonial history the word has preceded the sword. Because of the close cooperation between missionaries and their home governments, most Third World peoples have become quite suspicious of all missionary work, regardless of its motives. Muslim thinkers may, at times, have exaggerated what they considered to be the evil alliance between missionaries and colonialist powers. Omar Farrukh, for example, sees the real and primary aim of missionaries to be the total abolition of all religions other than Christianity as a means of enslaving their followers. He writes, "The battle between the missionaries and other religions is not one of religion; rather, it is one whose aim is political and economic domination."[36] The author then lists the means by which missionaries often sought to win converts. These are, first, education; second, medical services; and third, monetary gifts and bribes. This, the author asserts, often took the form of outright brokerage of souls.

Among those just listed, education was and continues to be the most effective. In schools and universities founded by missionaries, both curriculum and subject matter were those of the mission's homeland. Textbooks, even those dealing with Muslim history and culture, are written by often hostile orientalists. Omar Farrukh gives the example of a textbook used in French schools in Lebanon. Discussing Islam in the seventh century, the book in question calls the new religion the "new enemy." Yet in the end, "the power of the crescent was overcome by that of the cross, and the Gospel gained victory over the Qur'an. . . ."[37] Farrukh observed that Pope Leo XIII highly approved of the book.

The political implications of Western education in the Middle East are easy to see. Muslim as well as Christian Arab students who could learn more about the history, geography, and culture of France, Britain, or the United States than their own heritage, of course lost their national identity. This conditioned such students, who often became leaders of their countries, to tolerate and even sympathize with the colonialists or neocolonialists of their own country and people.

Since the seventeenth century, European powers have championed the cause of Christian minorities in the Middle East. In Syria and Lebanon, these minorities have always held divided loyalties. Today's Middle East problems, and especially those of Lebanon, are in large measure the outcome of such colonialist machinations.

The most serious problem by far has been the Zionist presence. Farrukh observes that very early in the nineteenth century a number of missionary organizations were formed in Europe expressly for the evangelization of the Jews. The plan was that the Jews would return to Palestine where the process of evangelization would begin. At that time, the whole area of Syria-Palestine was occupied by Muhammad Ali of Egypt. Muhammad Ali embarked on an extensive plan of Westernization of his domains. Missionary societies therefore counted on the good relations between Muhammad Ali and the West. But when in 1840 Muhammad Ali withdrew from Palestine, the Ottoman authorities did not favor this plan, which was soon abandoned. Nonetheless, the ideas of the Jewish return to Palestine lived on and bore fruit a century later.

Muslims have generally considered all this to be part of an overall plan to destroy any central authority in the Muslim world. Thus, the aim of the return of the Jews to Palestine was seen not as the will to create a Jewish state but to introduce a destabilizing factor into the Arab world.[38]

Another contemporary Muslim writer has characterized colonialism, evangelization, and orientalism and their agents in the Muslim world as "the three wings of cunning and their pinfeathers."[39] Expressing the mistrust and frustration of Muslims in the aftermath of three Arab-Israeli Western-supported wars, the author describes the points of common interest among the three wings as "hatred and malice." He protests, "we can see no noble humane principles that would justify such hostility and hatred."[40] He then argues that these feelings cannot be prompted by Islam, because it respects the divine message that came before it. Islam calls for harmony and amity among people of different faiths through "the best manner of debate." The Qur'an leaves open even the question of truth and error in religious belief: "surely we and you are either upon right guidance or in manifest error" (Q. 34:24). This leniency, the author bemoans, has always met with hostility and hatred. But why, he asks, have European Christians been for so long conditioned to hate and mistrust Islam and Muslims? The author thinks that "politicians and military men, as well as missionaries, have, because of the failure of the Crusades, inherited this hatred and malice from their forebears

who for two centuries incited the crusading armies to attack Muslim lands."
He continues:

> were these causes to be humanely and fairly analyzed, they would be
> seen as the worst prejudice arising from the narrowest psychologi-
> cal horizons and extreme egotism. All these must be rejected by fair-
> minded people of high character who seek the truth wherever it may
> be, and desire good for themselves and for all of humanity.[41]

It should be clear from the discussion so far that Muslims have come to
suspect everything Western. Behind every Western activity they see a colonialist or neocolonialist plot. There are, no doubt, Western scholars who are
genuinely interested in Islam as a rich civilization and spiritual heritage worthy of their lifelong occupation. Some indeed have contributed greatly to
Islamic scholarship and hence to a greater appreciation of Islam in all its
aspects. There are missionaries as well who are genuinely and sincerely interested in sharing their faith with others without any coercion or ulterior
motives. Yet so many Muslims thinkers have been unable—or unwilling—to
distinguish between the objective and profound Western orientalists and missionaries and the biased, sympathetic, hostile, and superficial ones. They
rather have regarded them all as an evil scourge upon Islam and Muslims.
The reasons for this are obvious from what has been said so far. They will
become even more apparent as we examine later in this discussion some of
the attitudes of well-known missionaries and scholars toward Islam.

In a large encyclopedic work on Arabic and Islamic thought, an entire
volume is dedicated to "dangerous ideological influences."[42] The author considers the aim of orientalists and missionary schools on all levels as a well-
planned and executed process of Westernizing educated Muslims. He argues
that the rigorous and comprehensive treatment of modern Islam by orientalists is a concrete proof of this aim. The long-term method used to realize
this aim is the production of anti-Islamic literature containing facts and theories based on misrepresentations, errors, and distortions. These are then
propagated by missionary organizations and the media, and become
implanted and grow in the minds of Muslims. This process would secure the
goal of the colonialist powers, "which is the melting of Muslims and Arabs
in the pot of western universalistic intellectualism." The author goes on to
define this process of Westernization more specifically:

> Westernization in its simplest conception, is the conditioning of
> Muslims and Arabs to willingly accept the western mentality and
> reject the fundamentals [of Islam] which impose [on Muslim society]
> a particular identity and a specific Islamic character. In addition, it
> seeks to raise doubts concerning Islam's educational, social, intel-
> lectual and legislative principles.[43]

The reason for this determined effort, in the view of the author, is
Europe's failure to dominate the Muslim world through the Crusades. While

the West has given up the strategy of confrontation, it is only the means that have changed. The end remains the same. This is to destroy Islam—its legislative, social, and economic character—by reducing it in the minds of Western-educated Muslims to abstract theological principles divorced from the reality of the daily life of Muslim society. Through missionary work and orientalist Islamic studies, the West has endeavored to kill the spirit of jihad in Muslims, which was one of the most important principles in the preservation and growth of the Muslim community. This general aim was, the author asserts, clearly and succinctly stated by Samuel Zwemer when he said, "The aim of missionary work is not to bring a Muslim into another religion; it is to bring him out of Islam, so that he may become its opponent and staunch enemy."[44]

There are, according to the writer under discussion, other strategies in the realization of this aim. The first is spreading promiscuity and atheism among young, educated Muslims. Second, modern European scientific and educational methodologies in the study of Islam have led to the compartmentalization and fragmentation of an otherwise unified and well-integrated system. The third element is the fostering of a feeling of inferiority among Muslims.

The latest stage of the colonialist plot, as the author sees it, has been for orientalists to lay aside their ecclesiastical vestments and hide behind a thin veil of academic integrity. The author decries the fact that orientalists have often concentrated on side issues—religious and legal differences, esotericisms, and foreign ideas—seeking by all this to recreate in the Muslim society of today old divisive ethnicisms and nationalisms. To sum up, "Orientalists have concentrated on borrowed ideas, imported philosophies and vulnerable positions; all of which they sought to bring into the pure heritage of Islam."[45]

The mission of Christ was a mission of love which transcends all political and religious considerations. However, the history of missions, especially since the Reformation, has sacrificed love for sectarian competition. Writing early in this century, the well-known British missionary scholar Temple Gairdner describes the scope of missionary work thus: "Whether by the tens of thousands of Bibles and religious works distributed yearly from Assuan to Alexandria, or by itinerant or village missions, or preachings, visitings, disputations in the capital, or medical missions in several centers, or the steady work of the education of boys and girls, the work goes on, and success is sure."[46] Gairdner was writing in the wake of the British occupation of Egypt and the protection consequent upon this occupation. The disputations to which he refers often took place at al-Azhar, the most important center of Islamic learning. Students from all parts of Africa and Asia flocked to this ancient institution, and that, of course, provided enthusiastic missionaries with a rare opportunity. It was the opportunity of carrying the Gospel to the far corners of the earth in one convenient location. Gairdner, therefore, exults in the fact that "In the memory of living men no Christians could so much as enter that place; now they enter unmolested." As a result, the author goes on, "Students and ex-students have been converted to Christ, and not a few students have, as they paced or sat apart, studied there, not the Koran, but the Gospel of Jesus Christ."[47]

The attitude of insensitive superiority, already noted, is concisely and poignantly expressed in these words: "As ignorance is the Church's greatest stronghold of Mohammedanism, so education is the Church's greatest weapon in meeting it."[48] With this observation, a list of proposals to combat Islam is presented. The strategic proposals themselves do not concern us. What concerns us is the attitude of belligerent confrontation that they reveal. The author first proposes that "as Mohammedanism claims to be a larger revelation, and to supersede Christianity, it is imperative that this bold challenge should be met, and not passed over in silence, and that every mission pupil should learn not only the Christian truths, but also their position with regard to attacks on these truths." Another proposal is that a special effort be made to occupy strong Muslim centers in order to quell any Islamic influence on non-Muslims, especially the pagans of sub-Saharan Africa.[49] This, of course, is possible only with the help of the colonizing power.

To missionaries like Gairdner, as to many Western Christians and Jews, Islam is a menace. From a work of that title, Gairdner quotes a few phrases that powerfully characterize the long history of conflict and competition that has existed between the two traditions and their communities of faith.

> Islam is the only one of the great religions to come after Christianity; the only one that definitely claims to correct, complete and supersede Christianity; the only one that categorically denies the truth of Christianity; the only one that has in the past signally defeated Christianity; the only one that seriously disputes the world with Christianity; the only one which, in several parts of the world, is today forestalling and gaining on Christianity.[50]

Islam is seen as a baffling problem, baffling because it directly challenges the basic beliefs of Christianity and competes with it in the claim to be the final universal message to humankind. The political success of Islam for so many centuries only added credibility to an otherwise, from a Christian point of view, vast and incredible error. Yet in the end, the most important source of mistrust and conflict between Islam and Christianity revolves around places like the "Church-mosque at Damascus . . . where a Cross once stood, and where there stands a Crescent today."[51] It is the fear that Islam would once more make great incursions into Christian lands.

Islam, according to Gairdner and many Western thinkers even today, spreads not because it has anything of value to offer but because it makes no moral demands on its people or converts. "Where little is expected," Gairdner consoles his readers, "there is no disappointment." Thus, murderers, fornicators, and bad men, that is, orientals, can be staunch defenders of Islam.[52]

Two world wars within half a century have changed the exuberance of the nineteenth century into a realistic sobriety. Lawrence Browne, writing during the Second World War, while still insisting that Islam is a "lacking religion," concedes nevertheless that there are some things in Islam that must be preserved.[53] These are worship of One Exalted God, the sense of brotherhood among Muslims, and their zeal in the observance of religious rites.[54] His well-known Dutch contemporary, the missionary scholar Hendrik Kraemer, is far less compassionate. For Kraemer, Islam is altogether superficial, having nothing of value to offer to the rest of humanity. Kraemer calls Islam a "riddle," because even though it is lacking in depth and originality, it nonetheless "excels all other religions in creating in its adherents a feeling of absolute religious superiority."[55] But of this feeling is "born that stubborn refusal to open the mind towards another spiritual world, as a result of which Islam is such an enigmatic missionary object."[56]

The three elements which, according to Browne, are worth preserving, Kraemer considers negative and dangerous. Islamic worship he sees as part of a process of "super-heating" in Islam. He writes, "Islam is theocentric, but in a super-heated state. Allah in Islam becomes white-hot Majesty, white-hot Omnipotence, white-hot Uniqueness. His personality evaporates and vanishes in the burning heat of His aspects."[57] Had Kraemer himself not been blinded by his own frustration with a community so tenaciously bound to its faith, he would have called this "divine transcendence." The comprehensiveness of the Islamic system as a way of life and worship Kraemer calls, "secularized theocracy," or "religious imperialism."[58] As such, Islam is a problem for missionary work. It is so, Kraemer believes, because of the stubbornness of its adherents and their unity or group solidarity and religious cohesion. Thus, it is this sense of brotherhood, or group solidarity, that presents the most serious danger for European powers and their missionaries. Kraemer defines Islam as "a mediaeval and radically religious form of that national-socialism which we know at present in Europe in its pseudo-religious form."[59] This is, from a European point of view, the greatest insult that can be leveled against Islam. It is Nazism.

The situation of Muslim-Christian relations has changed little through centuries. What Kraemer, Gairdner, Browne, and other Christian writers considered in this study have said has become familiar to students of Islam and Muslim-Christian relations. It was said already in the eighth century when St. John of Damascus, an official of the Muslim state, declared Islam to be a Christian heresy. It was repeated by the Crusaders along with the *chanson* extolling the chivalry of Saladin. More recently, it and much more has been said in works such as *The Arab Mind* by Raphael Patai and in the media, especially following the Islamic revolution in Iran. The Crusader image of Islam, although further romanticized and elaborated by orientalists from the time of Peter the Venerable to the present, remains virtually the same. Yet to despair is to die. A new beginning can and must be made. New horizons in Muslim-Christian relations are slowly but firmly being discovered. I shall end this study with a brief glance at these glimmers of hope for a better future of understanding and acceptance of the many common challenges of our two faiths.

## New Horizons

Muslims and Christians have so far lived in two separate worlds. *Dār al-Islām* and the Church Militant have not only been two distinct geographical domains competing for domination and world hegemony, they have also been interiorized by millions of men and women across the centuries. They have thus shaped the lives of individuals as well as of world history. The stage on which this violent tragedy has been played is the Middle East, where the three monotheistic faiths were born and nurtured. The Middle East, and particularly Jerusalem, remains the center of both realms: of the hopes and fears, peace and war, and all the good and evil of both communities.

The holy city of Jerusalem has become an integral part of the narrow exclusivism of all three religions. As a consequence, this city (and indeed the Middle East as a whole) has lost its interreligious character. It can therefore no longer serve as a meeting place for dialogue.

The purpose of dialogue ought to be better understanding, peaceful coexistence, and the establishment of a fellowship of faith among people of faith. This is only possible among people enjoying the same standard of security, economic well-being, and social equality in all respects. This ideal cannot be achieved between the rich and technologically advanced West and the Muslims of the so-called Third World. It must begin in Europe and North America where Muslims and Christians share the factory workbench, the school, community center, and even the cemetery.

New and promising beginnings are being made both in Europe and in North America. Speaking on behalf of the British Council of Churches and the Conference of Missionary Societies in Great Britain and Ireland, David Brown observes that "to build relationships with Muslims is a novel experience for many Christians in Britain today."[60] This is true for most Muslims and Christians anywhere outside the Middle East. But even there, when relations are cordial and productive, they have been socio-cultural rather than religious relations. The main obstacle in the way of a meaningful sharing of spiritual ideals and experiences between Christians and Muslims has been the exclusive claim to truth on both sides. This has often included the truth that gives one community the right to the other's life, dignity, and home. It is here that change is most urgently needed.

Important first steps toward this goal have already been taken. One of the most significant has been the "Declaration on Non-Christian Religions" of the Second Vatican Council. This declaration is important because it speaks for so many Catholic Christians and represents a clear departure from the church's classical stance with regard to people of other faiths. The earlier attitude is recognized and rejected. A Catholic interpretation of the declaration states "Catholic missions formerly took an almost purely negative stand against the world religions. They were seen only from the viewpoint of conversion. The stand was even stronger in the case of the Muslims who were considered militant enemies of the Church." Regarding the church's future attitude, this interpreter goes on: "The activity of God in all religions is recognized, notwithstanding that the Church was given the fullness of truth by and in Christ. Moreover, the Church is linked to the Muslims inasmuch as Muslims honor Jesus and the prophets."[61] To be sure, this is an absolute minimum. Muslims do much more than merely venerate Jesus, but they do so not to please the church or show a spirit of ecumenism, but because God in the Qur'an demands of Muslims to accept all the prophets and messengers of God who came before Muhammad.[62] The declaration is nevertheless exceedingly important in that it lays a firm foundation, without setting any limits, for the development of fruitful dialogue between Catholics and Muslims.

With regard to the Jews, the declaration categorically states, "The Jews were and are God's chosen people."[63] That the declaration then goes on to repudiate anti-Semitism and exonerate the Jews as a people from the guilt of killing Jesus Christ is a laudable and long-overdue act of redemption of the church itself from its own human folly. The assertion of divine chosenness of the Jews, however, carries with it many dangerous political implications. History has, during the last three decades, proven that this is far from being simply a theological doctrine.

Islam and even Christ have repudiated any doctrine of chosenness on the basis of ethnic or racial identity. "Not through your desires," the Qur'an declares, "nor the desires of the people of the Book; rather whoever does evil will be punished for it: nor will he find for himself friend or protector against God. But whoever performs good deeds, be it male or female and has faith: these shall enter paradise, nor will they be wronged in the least" (Q. 4:122 and 123). Christ cautioned his people not to pride themselves on being children of Abraham, for "God is able from these stones to raise up children to Abraham" (Matt 3:9). God turns in His mercy toward those who turn to Him in humility and thanksgiving, whatever their ethnic or religious identity.

In Christian history, this doctrine of election often led to un-Christian behavior. Admittedly, Christianity is a universal message. This has often meant, however, universality of mission but exclusivity of salvation (Acts 4:12). Contemporary Christians have, for the most part, rejected the doctrine of *extra ecclesiam nulla salus* in its narrowest form. Instead, many have come to accept universal salvation on the basis of a divine cosmic covenant. But even this idea has not been accepted as the only universal basis of salvation. Rather, "the purpose of calling a special people by God is not for their salvation and everyone else's damnation, but for their establishment as a witness people to God so that through them 'all families of the earth will bless themselves.'"[64]

We now know that no religion can claim an exclusive monopoly on salvation and truth. We must accept the fact that our forebears knew far less about world religions than we know. Hence, we must see our faith in global perspective as one among many, each having its own spiritual heritage and civilization. In light of this, no religious community or religio-ethnic group can claim a special and exclusive mission to humankind.

The problem of today's world is no longer one of disparity of belief or theological disagreement. It is rather the disparity among nations in wealth and in technological and industrial development, and the exploitation of the resources and markets of poor nations by the rich ones. In the Middle East especially, the incessant strife and warfare is not over God, revelation, Moses, Jesus, or Muhammad; it is rather over land, oil, and the destiny of peoples. To be sure, the old religious issues and deep-seated prejudices and hostilities that they engendered lie at the root of today's conflicts. Yet these issues are now far easier to resolve than the conflicts arising from them. This fact is already attested to by the noticeable change in approach and attitude of current Islamic scholarship in the West. There is now far greater objectivity, sensitivity, and appreciation of Islam among purely academic Western scholars than among their predecessors, who were mostly civil servants, missionaries, or both.

People of faith today are one people, regardless of their religious affiliation. They are in the same predicament, in a world dominated by materialistic and selfish interests. We, all of us, live in the exile of faith in a world torn by civil strife, competition for power, and demonic ideologies. Diagnosing this world situation, Sayyid Qutb argues that after two world wars, the world is divided into two power blocs: the communist bloc in the East and the capitalist in the West. Yet, Qutb writes, "This is a superficial division, not a real one. It is a division over interests not principles. It is a struggle over goods and markets, not beliefs and ideas."[65]

Sayyid Qutb argues further that the materialist basis of both ideologies could lead either of the two blocs either way. What prevents America from becoming communist is not its belief in God, or communist atheism, but rather purely economic considerations. The struggle is in reality over world markets and, Qutb says, "we are these markets." He sees the struggle as one between Islam and both blocs. The truth, he further asserts, is that all spiritual value systems, Christianity not excluded, reject the materialism of both the communist and capitalist worlds.

Both Europe and America are, in the view of Sayyid Qutb, inevitably headed for communism. Because, as the author sees it, Christianity can no longer play a positive and totally revolutionary role in the real life of today's world, Islam alone, he is confident, is capable of giving the world a complete system for living. It is a system of worship and prayers, of economics and commerce, of family and international relations, and of war and peace.

Islam may be able to help humanity in its quest for a way out of its predicament of destruction and alienation, but only when Muslims live equally seriously the piety of their faith and its social, political, ethical, and economic demands. In the end, the challenge of Islam as an institutionalized religion is the inner Islam, or surrender of all things to God. It is the courage to let God be God in our individual lives, society, and world affairs. This is a challenge not for Muslims alone but for all the people of God. If domestic politics and foreign policy in the West could be truly Christianized and the world of Islam in all its aspects Islamized, then *dār al-Islām* could include the church, and the church would see the entire world as the "mystical body of Christ." Then will the righteous servant of God and the meek "inherit the earth" (Q. 21:105 and Matt 5:5).

# Notes

1. St. Cyprian, *Letters 1-81*, trans. Rose Bernard Donna, The Fathers of the Church 51 (Washington, D.C.: Catholic University of America Press, 1964), 281-82 (letter #73).

2. St. Cyprian, *Treatises*, ed. and trans. Roy J. Deferrari, The Fathers of the Church 36 (Washington, D.C.: Catholic University of America Press, 1958), "Unity of the Church," 91.

3. Note, for example, the problems resulting from the Augustinian doctrine of the damnation of unbaptized children.

4. St. Augustine, *The Retractions*, trans. Mary Inez Bogan; ed. Roy J. Deferrari, The Fathers of the Church 60 (Washington, D.C.: Catholic University of America Press, 1968), 52.

5. "Council of Florence (1438-45), 'Decree for the Jacobites,'" in *The Church Teaches: Documents of the Church in English Translations*, ed. and trans. John F. Clarkson, John H. Edwards, William J. Kelley, and John J. Welch (St. Louis: B. Herder Book Co., 1955), 78 (#165).

6. "Unam Sanctam" (1302), in *The Church Teaches*, 73-75 (nos. 153-54).

7. For a comprehensive analysis of this doctrine throughout the history of the Catholic Church, see Karl Rahner, *Theological Investigations, II*, trans. Karl-H. Kruger (London: Darton, Longman & Todd, 1963).

8. Mahmoud M. Ayoub, *The Qur'an and Its Interpreters* (Albany: State University of New York Press, 1984), 1:112.

9. For a survey of these movements, see Albert Hourani, *Arab Thought in the Liberal Age, 1798-1939* (Oxford: Oxford University Press, 1962).

10. See Sayyid Qutb, *al-'Adala al-ijtima'iyyah fi al-Islam* (Cairo: al-Babi, 1958), 6-12.

11. Hans Küng, *On Being a Christian*, trans. Edward Quinn (New York: Doubleday, 1968), 113.

12. Ibid.

13. See al-Katib al-Isfahani, *al-Fath al-Qissi fi al-fath al-Qudsi*, ed. Muhammad Mahmud Subh (Cairo: Dar al-Qawmiyah, 1965), 48-53.

14. For a vivid account of the conquest of Jerusalem, see Fulcher of Chartres, *A History of the Expedition to Jerusalem: 1095-1127*, trans. Frances Rita Ryan; ed. Harold S. Fink (Knoxville: University of Tennessee Press, 1969).

15. Ibid., 66.

16. Ibid., 112.

17. Muhammad Qutb, *Shubuhat hawl al-Islam* (n.p., 1968), 210.

18. 'Ali ibn Husam al-Din 'Abd al-Malik al-Muttaqi al-Hindi, *Kanz al-'ummal fi Sunan al-aqwal wa al-af'al,* ed. Bakri Hayyani (Beirut: Mu'assasat al-Risalah, 1979), 10:579.

19. See Philip K. Hitti, *History of the Arabs from the Earliest Times to the Present,* 10th ed. (London: Macmillan and Co., 1970; 1st ed., 1937), 147-54.

20. Sayyid Qutb, *al-Salam al-'alami wa al-Islam* (n.p., n.d), 129ff.

21. Sayyid Qutb, *al-'Adala al-ijtima'iyyah fi al-Islam,* 10.

22. This pamphlet is an extreme expression of Muslim polemics against the West. Its author, Jalal al-'Alim, is little known. Its title in Arabic reads *Qadat al-Gharb yaqulun damirru al-Islam abidu ahlahu* (2nd ed., 1395/1975).

23. Ibid., 25-26.

24. Ibid., 26.

25. Randolph S. Churchill and Winston S. Churchill, *The Six Day War* (Boston: Houghton Mifflin, 1967), 190.

26. Jalal al-'Alim, *Qadat al-Gharb* ("Western Leaders Say. . ."), 30.

27. I have not been able to establish the identity of this priest. I found this statement in Omar Farrukh and Mustafa Khalidi, *al-Tabshir wa al-isti'mar fi al-bilad al-'Arabiyya,* 3rd ed. (Sayda, Lebanon: al-Maktabah al-'Asriyah, 1982), 38.

28. Muhammad al-Bahi, *al-Fikr al-Islami al-hadith wa silatuhu bi al-isti'mar al-Gharbi* (Beirut: Dar al-Fikr, 1970).

29. Ibid., 31.

30. See Annamarie Schimmel, *Mystical Dimensions of Islam* (Chapel Hill: University of North Carolina Press, 1975), 64-70.

31. Farrukh and Khalidi, *al-Tabshir.*

32. Ibid., 6.

33. Ibid., 11.

34. Ibid., 34.

35. Ibid., 34-35.

36. Ibid., 35.

37. The book in question is *Recherche de la vraie religion,* by E. Cauly (Paris: C. Poussielgue, 1898 and reprints). See Farrukh and Khalidi, *al-Tabshir,* 72-73.

38. For a discussion of this problem, see Farrukh and Khalidi, *al-Tabshir,* 179-82.

39. The Arabic title of this book is *Ajnihat al-makr al-thalatha wa khawafiha.* The author is 'Abd al-Rahman Habannakah al-Midani, a well-known Syrian educator (Damascus and Beirut: Dar al-Qalam, 1395/1971).

40. Ibid., 119.

41. Ibid., 121-27.

42. Anwar al-Jundi, *Mawsu'ah al-Islamiyah al-'Arabiyah,* 1st ed. (Beirut: Dar al-Kitab al-Lubnani, 1974), vol. 3, which is used in this study, is entitled *Islam wa al-da'awat al-haddamah,* literally, "destructive ideological influences."

43. Ibid., 245; see also 243-45

44. Ibid., 245.

45. Ibid., 254.

46. W. H. T. Gairdner, *The Reproach of Islam* (London: Student Volunteer Missionary Union, 1909), 267.

47. Ibid., 269.

48. Ibid., 255.

49. Ibid., 255-66.

50. Ibid., 310-11.

51. Ibid., 313.

52. Ibid., 318.

53. Laurence E. Browne, *Prospects of Islam* (London: SCM, 1944); see chap. 8.

54. Ibid., 117-19.

55. Hendrik Kraemer, *The Christian Message in a Non-Christian World* (Grand Rapids: Kregell, 1963 [1st ed., 1938]), 220.

56. Ibid., 220.

57. Ibid., 221.

58. Ibid., 223.

59. Ibid., 353.

60. David Brown, *A New Threshold: Guidelines for the Churches in Their Relations with Muslim Communities* (London: British Council of Churches, 1976), 4.

61. "Declaration on Non-Christian Religions," in Mario Von Galli, *The Council and the Future* (New York: McGraw-Hill, 1966), 297-98.

62. See, for example, Q. 2:285.

63. "Declaration on Non-Christian Religions," 298.

64. John Carman and Donald Dawe, eds., *Christian Faith in a Religiously Plural World* (Maryknoll, N.Y.: Orbis Books, 1978), 19. See also Gen 12:3.

65. Sayyid Qutb, *al-'Adala al-ijtima'iyyah*, 285.

# 5

# Christian-Muslim Dialogue

## Goals and Obstacles

Christianity may have come to Arabia with St. Paul when he retired to the desert east of the Jordan River for several mysterious years. From the Syrian desert, Christianity was carried into South Arabia, perhaps by wandering monks, where it played a significant role in the rise of a rich civilization. From there, Christianity came to northern Arabia, where it helped prepare the moral and spiritual grounds for Islam.

From its inception, Islam grew in an environment permeated with Eastern Christian spiritual and moral values. It is likely that it was to this spiritual heritage of Eastern Christianity that the Prophet Muhammad referred when he declared, "I sense the breath of the All-merciful (*nafas al-Raḥmān*) from the Yaman." The breath of the All-merciful is the divine spirit of holiness which Jesus manifested as the victorious savior over demonic powers. Thus, the Christianity that the Qur'an extols is not the official Christianity of Rome and Byzantium with its elaborate theology but the popular piety of desert monks who carried on the work of healing and purification that Jesus began during his earthly sojourn.

The Qur'an speaks tenderly of the spirituality of the humble monks and learned priests of the Christians, ". . . for there are among them monks and learned priests, and they are not proud" (Q. 5:82). The Qur'anic passage just cited goes on to make two significant assertions, which can still serve as a good motivation for constructive dialogue between the two faith communities. The first is that the Christians are the nearest people in amity to the Muslims. The second is that Christian monks and learned priests recognize the truth when they hear it and shed tears of humble gratitude for God's guidance. Furthermore, like the people of faith among the Muslims, these humble monks and learned priests covet God's grace and pray that they be accounted among the witnesses to God's oneness and guidance to the truth. Therefore, dialogue between them ought to be a dynamic and creative engagement among friends, not enemies, to which the Qur'an (3:64) invites

Previously published in *The Muslim World* 94, no. 3 (July 2004): 313-19. Reprinted by permission.

the people of the Book. Even when the Qur'an reproaches the Christians for their deification of Jesus, it considers this to be extremism (*ghuluw*) in their religion rather than outright *kufr*, or rejection of faith. It then affirms, as the Christians do, the absolute truth that "God is One" (Q. 4:171).

There is, however, another side to this positive Qur'anic view of the Christians and particularly with regard to their status in the Islamic state. The Qur'an is not only a book of moral and pious precepts but is also the primary source of the sacred law (*sharī'ah*) of God, which must guide the Muslim *ummah* and regulate its relations to other faith communities. The Qur'an did not legislate the *jizyah* poll tax for the people of the Book in return for protection or exemption from military service alone, nor was it simply meant to buy Jewish and Christian subjects security and safe conduct in *dār al-Islām*, as many Muslims have apologetically argued. Rather, it was to humble them because of their lack of faith in God, failure to follow the true religion, and failure to consider unlawful what God and His Messenger had made unlawful. Either the veracity of these accusations must be deemed impossible for anyone but God alone to judge, or the verse is meant to punish the people of the Book only because they refuse to embrace Islam.

I believe that this difficult verse of the Qur'an (9:29) presents an ideal of faith and piety that only God can judge. But on a practical level, it seeks to regulate the socio-political and economic relations of Jewish and Christian subjects to the Islamic state. This is the reason why the *jizyah* law that this verse legislates was for a long time legally considered and applied by Muslim jurists and rulers alike, with little attention to its moral and theological implications. Since, however, the verse in question cannot be implemented in contemporary Muslim nation states, where citizenship rather than religious affiliation is supposed to determine the equal rights and responsibilities of all citizens, it has been employed as an effective anti-Christian polemical tool by Islamist ideologues. Be that as it may, the language of this verse rendered the Qur'anic attitude to the people of the Book, and particularly the Christians, an ambivalent one, to say the least. This set the stage for an even greater ambivalence in subsequent Muslim history, and hence for the conflicts and hostilities that have tainted Christian-Muslim relations forever after.

## Immediate and Long-term Goals

Christianity and Islam are both universal faiths meant not for any particular race or ethnicity but for all of humanity. This important principle encapsulates the goals and opportunities for constructive dialogue as well as the obstacles that make it difficult, if not virtually impossible, to achieve. Both traditions recognize God's love for all of humankind and His providential acts in human history, but both claim to be God's final message of salvation and eternal bliss for the world. Thus, in spite of the call for tolerance and respect toward the people of the Book, which the Qur'an frequently makes,

Muslims have generally condemned Christians as polytheists. Since Islam came after Christianity and challenged some of its fundamental doctrines, Christians have likewise often condemned Islam as a religion inspired by the devil, and Muslims as barbaric people without any moral or spiritual values.

The most urgent goal toward which both communities ought to strive is, therefore, the mutual acceptance of the legitimacy and authenticity of the religious tradition of the other as a divinely inspired faith. This fundamental requirement for honest and constructive dialogue remains an ideal hope, not a reality. This is because the most that Muslim-Christian dialogue has so far been able to achieve is the formal recognition of the common Abrahamic ancestry of the two faiths, and hence their historical and theological kinship. This is not to deny the immense significance of this recognition as a positive step toward a true existential acceptance of the faith of the other, but more is needed if dialogue is to progress beyond mere formal courtesy or polite indifference.

Despite its urgency, the need for mutual recognition and acceptance is a long-term goal that should always guide our efforts towards fruitful spiritual, moral, theological, and social dialogue. Mutual acceptance must not stop at recognizing, and even accepting, the existence of the other as a fellow human being and a good neighbor. Rather, Muslims and Christians must accept each other as friends and partners in the quest for social and political justice, theological harmony, and spiritual progress on the way to God, who is their ultimate goal.

This noble effort demands the genuine and sincere respect of the faith of the other, including their beliefs, ethical principles, social values, and political aspirations. This ought to be the second goal of Christian-Muslim dialogue. Within this framework of mutual respect and acceptance, interreligious dialogue can develop into a genuine and creative intercultural dialogue. In fact, without meaningful intercultural dialogue, mutual understanding and respect are not possible.

A third goal is the acceptance by both Christians and Muslims of the other as an equal partner—and not an opponent—in dialogue. This equality should be equality in humanity and dignity, and equality in the claim for religious authenticity. In all its aspects, this implies the admission by the faithful of both communities that both Christianity and Islam have in themselves the moral and spiritual resources to guide their followers to the way of salvation.

Christ taught us all to seek the truth, and that the truth shall set us free. The Qur'an teaches that the truth is God. Therefore, freedom in the truth is freedom in God, which is the freedom of faith. Within this freedom in God, Muslims and Christians can and should freely share their faith experiences with each other, but without making this an occasion for *da'wah* or mission.

Another important goal is to let the two traditions speak for themselves, that is, to represent themselves in dialogue. This means for Christians and Muslims not to engage in dialogical activities on the basis of what they think they know or understand of what the religion of the other is all about. In other words, they should not remake the other in their own image, as a precondition for acceptance. Rather, they should listen and learn before they venture into the sacred precincts of each other's faith.

More practically speaking, Muslims must not seek to explain Christianity solely on the basis of what the Qur'an and subsequent Islamic tradition have said about it but should seek to understand Christianity from its own sources and on its own terms. Similarly, Christians must not interpret Islam, especially its sacred scripture, in accordance with their own understanding of the divine economy of salvation, however enlightened and universally attractive such a divine schema may be, but should take seriously the Islamic worldview and its divine plan for the attainment of forgiveness, salvation, and bliss in the hereafter.

A final goal is to strive for absolute fairness and objectivity in drawing any comparisons between the two traditions. Several guidelines must be strictly observed in this regard. The first is that the ideals of the two traditions should be compared with ideals and the realities with realities. Second, all attempts at scoring points for one tradition over the other by contrasting the good things in it with the bad things in the other must be strictly avoided. Rather, the good should be compared with the good and the bad with the bad. Conversely, the misbehavior of the followers of one tradition at any given point of its history must not be covered up or excused by wrongly imputing similar behavior to the followers of the other. Nor should such misbehavior be dismissed or excused on the grounds of human sinfulness or frailty.

Third, the scriptures or traditions of one religion should not be used as criteria to judge the truth or errors of the other. Islam and Christianity have their distinct worldviews that must guide and inform Muslim-Christian dialogue on all levels.

## Types of Dialogue

Christianity and Islam are two world religions whose adherents comprise over half of the world's population. While the *oikomenē*, or Christian realm, and *dār al-Islām*, Muslim realm, were limited historically to specific geographical areas of the world, both realms have geographically and politically long since disappeared. Now the sphere or abode of Islam is the homes and hearts of the people of the *ummah*. Similarly, the house of the Christian faith is the church and the hearts and minds of its members.

Millions of Muslims are now citizens of Western Christian countries and many Muslim countries have an equal number of Christian citizens. In the West in particular, Islam is no longer the religion of strangers, but the religion of next-door neighbors. Muslims share with Christians the neighborhood, school, workplace, hospital ward, and even burial ground. They share all the moral and social problems as well as the amenities of modern urban living. They also share the sacred space of their houses of worship—the churches and mosques, where meaningful and sustained dialogue is nurtured.

The most concrete, widespread, and basic type of dialogue is the dialogue of life. It is the dialogue of concerned neighbors with their adjacent churches and mosques, who work together and live on the same street. This type of dialogue is concerned with issues of social justice, pollution problems, and teenage children in mixed public schools with their problems of sex and drugs and a host of other issues. Here the common Abrahamic prophetic moral and spiritual heritage can help the children of all three families of Abraham to come together to face the problems of the modern world. Through their synagogues, churches, and mosques they should strive together for the common good of society.

The dialogue of life is the active concern of citizens with the problems of life together in one free and democratic country. One of the most important changes in the Muslim *ummah* is the rise of the nation-state. The modern state has both strengthened the bond of faith and also fragmented the *ummah*. Thanks to the nation-state model, the *ummah* can now, more than ever before, transcend all ethnic, cultural, geographical, and national boundaries. Moreover, where Muslims live as minorities in developed Western countries, they are far more free to experiment with new ideas and actions than their confreres in their countries of origin. Thus, they can help the *ummah* find its rightful place in the modern world.

A second type of dialogue is the dialogue of beliefs, theological doctrines, and philosophical ideas. This type tends to be restricted to the academy. It is often technical and abstract. For these and other reasons, it is often avoided. It is nonetheless vitally important, as it engages the minds and hearts of the people of faith of both traditions in their common search for the truth.

Another type of dialogue may be euphemistically called the dialogue of witnessing to one's faith. It, however, often becomes an invitation to conversion through methods of *da'wah* and mission. Here the name dialogue is used to cover up a nondialogical agenda. However well-intentioned participants in such dialogue may be, their ultimate aim is not to understand and accept the other but to absorb and assimilate them.

A final type is what I wish to call the dialogue of faith. It uses the ideas and methods of the second type but on a deeper and more personal level. Its aim is to deepen the faith of Muslim and Christian women and men by sharing the personal faith of the other. The ultimate purpose of this dialogue is to create a fellowship of faith among the followers of Islam and Christianity. This goal may be achieved by sharing one's faith with the other through worship, spiritual exercises, and the existential struggle in God. The Qur'an promises those who strive in God that He will guide them to His ways. His ways are the "ways of peace" (Q. 29:69 and Q. 5:16).

## Insurmountable Obstacles?

It was observed above that all that Muslim-Christian dialogue has so far achieved is the recognition of the Abrahamic roots of the faith of the two communities. This recognition has, since the last quarter of the twentieth century, led to genuine appreciation of the commitment of Muslims to their faith by many liberal Christians and equal admiration of Christian charity and openness by liberal Muslims. It may be thus argued that Christians have come to accept Muslims as people of faith but are not so far able to accept Islam as an authentic post-Christian religious tradition. Muslims have conversely from the beginning accepted Christianity as a revealed faith, but have been unable to accept the Christians and their faith in the triune God, the church as a source of guidance, and the books of the New Testament as authentic scriptures.

Here the problem lies in our inability to accept each other's faiths on their own terms. Muslims have acknowledged an Islamized Christianity and Christians have often Christianized Islam. Thus, with all good intentions, both communities have sought to negate, or at least neutralize, the individuality and integrity of the faith of the other in order to find room for it in their own tradition and worldview.

The main obstacle to true Christian-Muslim dialogue on both sides is, I believe, their unwillingness to truly admit that God's love and providence extend equally to all human beings, regardless of religious identity. This is tantamount to denying that God could and in fact did reveal His will in Hebrew, Greek, Arabic, and in every sacred language of the world. Therefore, the ultimate goal of all interfaith dialogue ought to be the ability of all women and men of faith to listen to and obey the voice of God as it speaks to all communities through their own faith traditions and humbly listen to the same voice speaking to each individual through her own faith tradition:

> To every one of you We have appointed a way and a course to follow, for had God so willed, He would have made you all one single community. Rather He would test you by means of that which He had bestowed upon you, who of you is of better deeds. Vie therefore with one another in works of righteousness. For, to God shall be your return and He will inform you of all that in which you had differed. (Q. 5:48)

> Beloved, we are God's children now; it does not yet appear what we shall be, but we know that when he appears we shall be like him, for we shall see him as he is. (1 John 3:2)

# PART II

## Critical Theological
## and
## Juridical Issues

*A Comparative Perspective*

# 6

# A Muslim Appreciation of Christian Holiness

Holiness (is) "the state or character a thing has by being set apart and specially dedicated to God and His service."[1]

Holiness is not, therefore, an inherent quality in a person or thing, but an acquired state or character. The attainment of this state has constituted one of the most important quests in the religious history of humankind. The ways of attaining a life or state of holiness show a remarkable similarity among the Semitic religious traditions. Thus, to offer a meaningful and genuine "Muslim" critique of this concept or quest in Christianity would, to say the least, be presumptuous. Islam and Christianity share a common moral and spiritual heritage which places their respective communities of faith in closely analogous positions of moral and existential responsibility before God's demand "be holy as I the Lord your God am holy" (Lev 19:2). I see my task, therefore, and indeed the task of all of us gathered here in this holy city, as not to criticize, but to understand; not to judge, but to listen to the voice of God calling us to dedicate our lives and talents to His service.

## The Basis of Holiness in Christianity

The concept of holiness in Christianity has its basis in the Hebrew Bible and the first Christian church, in which the New Testament was formed. Holiness, for both the ancient Hebrew society of the biblical age and the early church was conceived in two important spheres. These were moral and cultic, or the life of the individual within a community of faith and worship in all its aspects. The source and model of holiness for both the individual and society are God, who alone is absolutely holy. God's holiness is His absolute transcendence, or otherness. It is also His absolute power and majesty which fascinate and frighten us. This numinous quality of God, to use Otto's famous term,[2] could also be manifested to a much lesser degree in objects, places, and people.

Previously published in *Islamochristiana* 11 (1985): 91-98. Reprinted by permission.

The cultic, or ritualistic, dimension of holiness becomes the basis of a moral order reflecting the moral, or relational dimension of God's holiness to human society. Nowhere are these two dimensions presented with as great a harmony and dramatic power as in the Temple vision of the prophet Isaiah (Isaiah 6). This marvelous and awesome theophany was not a mere manifestation of irrational or dread-inspiring majesty but also a sanctifying call to service. Only after the prophet's lips were touched by the divine fire, and thus made clean, could he go forth and speak on behalf of God to the people.

Yet in the Hebrew Bible, or the Old Testament, we see a great tension between cultic holiness and moral sanctity. This tension is vividly presented by prophets like Amos, Jeremiah, Hosea, and others (e.g., Amos 5:21ff.). After the fall of the Temple, cultic holiness assumed a rigidly legalistic character. Rabbinic Judaism, which developed as an answer to the disappearance of the Temple ritual, was clearly responsible for this shift. This important change, however, had little if any effect on the early church, and need not detain us here.

## At the Center of Christian Holiness: Baptism and Eucharist

The Christian church regarded itself from the beginning as "the communion of saints," a fellowship of the faithful, made holy through faith in Christ.[3] Holiness in the church is redemption from sin. This redemption has been concretized and interiorized by the faithful in the sacraments, chief among which were those of baptism and the eucharist, or the mass. These two sacraments, however, have important moral implications without which they become empty mechanical rituals. It may be best for the sake of greater clarity and coherence that the rest of this discussion be centered around these two important elements of holiness in the life of the Christian individual and community. Because the mass, however, consists of the eucharist and the liturgical hymns or prayers, we shall discuss these two elements separately.

### Baptism as a Sign of Sanctification

Baptism was an ancient rite of purification and initiation practiced in many widely diverse religious communities.[4] It was taken over by Christians from Judaism and transformed into a sign of sanctification and salvation. It signifies a new identity, initiation, or birth into a new community and a new life of holiness.[5] Baptism meant for the early church, and especially for St. Paul, freedom from the Law, or the "old covenant."

The early church did not, in our view, theologize baptism, so as to reduce it to a rigid and narrow rite subject to specific rules and regulations with regard both to its efficacy and performance. It was, rather, freely performed on all those who accepted the new faith and joined its community, regardless of age.[6] Soon, however, baptism went beyond its symbolic and ritualistic significance and was seen as a necessary condition for salvation. Theologizing what was a dynamic sign of faith and purification inevitably led to the unfortunate practice of fetus baptism with all the suffering, both physical and emotional, that this entailed.[7] Since the Reformation, furthermore, the question of the age at which this rite is to be administered led to more conflict, persecution, and even bloodshed.

## Eucharist as a Ritual of Sanctification

The eucharist likewise was an ancient meal of fellowship and initiation. It is a transformation of the ancient Hebrew ritual of the Passover; both rituals are expressions of thanks to God for His salvation. But while the Passover was a feast of thanksgiving for deliverance from Egypt, the eucharist is a memorial feast of thanksgiving for the deliverance from sin. Like baptism, it was meant to be a symbolic act of renewal or reaffirmation of faith in God's salvific love.

When the eucharist was sometimes reduced to violent theological controversy, it too lost its sanctifying power and became a badge of identity, or membership in one or another Christian church or denomination. The theology of transubstantiation, whatever its dogmatic significance may have been, deprived this rite of its sacramental character and reduced it to a quasi-cannibalistic doctrine.[8]

Another important development in the theology of the eucharist in the Middle Ages was withholding the cup from the laity.[9] This practice resulted in making both the bread and wine, which was an actual meal that the Lord shared with his disciples, too sacred for anyone but the priest to touch. All this finally led to the eucharist losing its character as "a feast of thanksgiving," as the bread was reduced to a little sacred wafer and the cup to a mystery hidden from the faithful for whom it was instituted. It had become a ritual subject to theological and ecclesiastical rules, rather than the fellowship meal of the early church.

This is not to deny, of course, the profound meaning of the eucharist to Christian faith and holiness, but to argue for the restoration of this meaning for Christians today. This fact has been clearly recognized by the Second Vatican Council in its recommendations toward a new understanding of the mass. The faithful, the council recommended, should be not mere spectators at God's holy banquet but full participants.[10]

God's holiness is an expression of God's transcendence and absolute otherness. Human beings can share most effectively in divine holiness or transcendence through the fellowship of prayer. The liturgical prayers of the mass become a link between ephemeral humanity and the Transcendent.

The mass is essentially a ritual of sanctification. The significance of the mass as a form of prayer is in its structure as a dramatic re-enactment of a redemptive moment. Yet should the mass be repeated as sacred words and acts or should it not be a personal prayer of sanctification and affirmation of the ultimate gift of grace?

## Mystery, Dogma, and Piety in Western Christianity

The element of mystery is necessary because God is the ultimate mystery. Yet prayer, be it the mass or the *ṣalāh*, must be an act of worship, thanksgiving, and supplication. Prayers become means of purification and sanctification because God's word becomes our word. We pray to Him and through Him with His own words, "Lord, grant us peace."

Reference has already been made to the tension in the church between dogma and piety and between symbolic and literal meaning. This tension led different people in the church in different ways, depending on their religious temperament. Sacramental theology led in the West to medieval scholasticism, which, while helping to safeguard the basic creed of Christianity from error, nonetheless resulted in an arid legalism that often stifled the spirit of the sacraments.

The culmination of this process was the rationalism of the Reformation. Protestantism has often reduced Christian holiness to biblicism or a shallow liberalism. The result has been not a living faith but rational and emotional systems.

It is not fortuitous that the Reformation has not produced a true mystical tradition with its particular spiritual discipline and philosophical outlook. Holiness is a divine gift of grace mediated by the people of God. The lack of a mystical tradition in Protestantism may be due to the fact that there are no saints to mediate this gift of sanctifying grace to the people. It is for this reason that so many young Christians who are earnestly seeking have been obliged to look outside their churches for spiritual guidance.

Holiness as a quest in Christianity has been the obverse side of sin. This is clearly manifested in yet another sacrament, the sacrament of penance, which depicts both sin and its expiation. The value of penance, confession, and absolution and their abuse have been always recognized in the church, as they have been in different ways also recognized by other spiritual traditions and associations. But in a cosmic sense the obverse of sin is redemption. Yet redemption has remained in the church a perceptual process in history rather than a conceptual theological doctrine. Still, theories of redemption have often led to legalistic theological constructs antithetical to the spirit of redemption as a manifestation of God's mercy and love. This legalistic approach is typified by the theology of merit of St. Anselm, Luther's understanding of the Pauline doctrine of salvation by faith, and Calvin's theology of predestination.

## Mystical Theology of Deification in Eastern Christianity

The other major trend in the Christian understanding of redemption has been the mystical theology of deification in Orthodox and Eastern Christianity. The mystical theology of Orthodox Christianity has been largely enshrined in the liturgy. It has thus become a veritable source of holiness and spiritual nourishment. It seeks to sanctify human beings through the love of God, for Christ assumed humanity in order that human beings may become like him, "As we shall see Him face to face" (1 John 3:2). Christ is *philanthropos,* a lover of humankind; and through this love, men and women become true lovers of God.

It is my conviction that Christianity began to lose its power of sanctification as it lost its Eastern home and character. It was in this Eastern piety and spiritual dynamism of the holy desert fathers that Islam was born and nourished. It was not dogma but holiness, victory against the demonic spirits of uncleanness, which spoke to the needs of men and women. We dismiss as a bit of Eastern superstition that Jesus cast out unclean spirits. Yet it was this piety of healing and sanctification, whose ultimate source Jesus was, that played an important role in the life of the society of the ancient Near East, and that can once again rejuvenate the materialistic society of our world today.

## God's Holiness and the Sanctification of Human Beings

Holiness is liberation, and if we seek earnestly to know the truth, the truth shall set us free (John 8:32). The Truth, or *al-ḥaqq,* is God. Thus, to know the truth is to know God. But to know God truly is to walk in His ways, the ways of peace, holiness, and righteousness. To know God is to participate in His holiness through prayer, enjoining the good and dissuading from evil, sharing God's merciful gifts with the needy and seeking the pleasure of God and His mercy.

It may be argued that the worldview of the ancients, with its demonic forces, sacred places and objects which baffled their innocent minds, is no longer tenable in a world dominated by science and technology. This may be so, but the ancients had a better sense of what was good and wholesome, and therefore holy, and what was evil and unsalutary, and therefore impure and unholy, than we now have.

The divine agency of sanctification through guidance and healing, which Christians know as the Holy Spirit and which Muslims know as God's guidance, *hudā*[11] is not affected by our science and technology. On the contrary, unless our science and technology are guided by this divine agency, and thus sanctified by being dedicated to the service of God in His world, then the dreaded conflagration of a nuclear war becomes inevitable.

The three greatest evils of the human soul are self-centeredness—

individual, national, international—arrogance, and greed. The sin of regarding man as the measure of all things is as old as humanity itself. Since the Renaissance, this sin has taken on forms of ideology—nationalism, Marxism, and humanism. This self-centeredness leaves no room for God in our lives. This is because no man can serve two masters, whether these be the nation, the flag, or material wealth, and God.

## Muslim Point of View: Holiness or Righteousness?

It is instructive that the Qur'an uses the term *holy* (*quddūs*) only of God (Q. 59:23). When it speaks of the Sacred House of Jerusalem or the Holy Land, it does so by way of reporting an alien usage. This is not to say that the Qur'an has no concept of holiness; rather, it calls it by different names. A holy life is one that is guided by God to the straight way, a balanced course between the extremes of each facet of human life (Q. 1:6 and 2:143). A holy person is one who enjoins the good and dissuades from evil. A person who purifies him- or herself by prayers, almsgiving, and other works of righteousness is a holy person. Likewise, holy things are the wholesome or good things, *al-ṭayyibāt*, and those things that are unholy are *al-ḥabāiṭ*, the filthy or unclean things.

It is also significant that Islam has no saints as such. The *walī* is not a *qiddīs*, the term used by Arabic-speaking Christians for *saint*. A *walī* is rather one who accepts God as his/her only ally or patron; such a person is a friend of God. It is more analogous to the "man of God" of the Old Testament than to the saint of the Catholic Church. This means that all human beings and things are essentially holy, and that all that is needed to recover this original state of sanctity in which God created all things is to strive to live a holy life before God. This means that life itself can be sanctified by good works, good thoughts, and relations.

Finally, Islam has no sacraments because life must altogether be sacramental in the service (*ʿibādah*) of God. The acts of worship, or *ʿibādāt*, are at the same time acts of sanctification. Those which are obligatory (*farā'iḍ*) are meant to provide the necessary discipline of holiness. Yet without good works and devotional acts of worship, *farā'iḍ* become mere mechanical acts with little meaning.

## Conclusion

I offer these contrasts between Islam and Christianity not in order to score points for either of the two faiths but to suggest that perhaps the Qur'anic vocabulary may help us all in reformulating ancient truths in a more understandable language. Muslims have much to learn from the Christian understanding of God's work through the Holy Spirit, the spirit of revivification, guidance, and sanctification. Nor is this term *holy* (*quddūs*) foreign to the Qur'an. It is rather significant that commentators have not agreed on the identity and meaning of this term.[12]

I must also stress in conclusion that I am aware that my criticisms of some Christian later views and implementations of holiness are too simplistic. I offer them, however, in the hope that they will stimulate a dialogue of love, faith, and goodwill between the people of faith of our two communities. The promise of God through Christ is for us all, a challenge and a consolation: "Blessed are the pure in heart (those who are holy), for they shall see God" (Matt 5:8).

# Notes

1. *New Catholic Encyclopedia*, s. v. "Holiness."

2. See Rudolf Otto, *The Idea of the Holy* (New York: Oxford University Press, 1970 [1950 ed.]).

3. See *Documents of Vatican II*, ed. Austin P. Flannery, document 28, "Dogmatic Constitution on the Church" (Collegeville, MN: The Liturgical Press, 1975).

4. See Mircea Eliade, *Patterns in Comparative Religion*, trans. Rosemary Sheed (Cleveland: World, 1965), chap. 5. On the introduction of baptism to Christianity through the activities of John the Baptist, see Matthew 3.

5. *Documents of Vatican II*, document 28, sections 21-22.

6. See, for example, the case of Cornelius and his family in Acts 10.

7. This practice began in the Middle Ages and was based on St. Augustine's doctrine of the sinfulness of children. For a summary of the history of this controversy as it relates to the fate of unbaptized infants, see *New Catholic Encyclopedia*, s. v. "Baptism (Theology of)," Fate of Unbaptized Infants.

8. This was an accusation first made against the Christians by Roman authorities. Its basis in the church, however, goes back to St. Ignatius, bishop of Antioch. The controversy reached its height with Berengar (d. 1088).

9. See Williston Walker, *A History of the Christian Church* (New York: Charles Scribner's Sons, 1959), 258.

10. See *Documents of Vatican II*, document 1, "The Constitution on the Sacred Liturgy," sections 47-50.

11. See Wilfred Cantwell Smith, *On Understanding Islam* (The Hague: Mouton, 1981), 242.

12. Mahmoud M. Ayoub, *The Qur'an and Its Interpreters* (Albany: State University of New York Press, 1984), 1:124-25.

# 7

# Martyrdom in Christianity and Islam

One of the most important marks of a person's faith or commitment to a religious ideology is his readiness to defend that faith with life itself if necessary. Examples of such heroic sacrifice or martyrdom abound in both ancient and contemporary society. In ancient times, the heroic indifference of such men as the Stoic philosopher Epictetus to torture and death in the affirmation of a noble ideal earned them the honor of martyrdom; their example and ideal of total indifference to passions and worldly life provided a model for early Christian martyrs. In our own time, such figures as Che Guevara and his legendary comrade, Tania, have been regarded as martyrs and even saints by some Catholic leftist priests. Martyrdom has been one of the most powerful instruments in the establishment and propagation of a faith or ideology, and hence of a new social order.

In this essay I shall examine the philosophy of martyrdom and the role of martyrs in Christianity and Islam. I shall first consider this phenomenon in each of the two traditions separately, and then briefly discuss similarities and differences of concepts and attitudes toward the martyr in the two communities. My aim is essentially to appreciate the contribution that this phenomenon has made to the religio-political situation of today's world.

The term *martyr* as used in the New Testament means "witness." A martyr is a witness not to an idea but to an event, to the faith in the crucified and risen Christ. Thus the author of 1 John writes, ". . . that which we have seen with our eyes, which we have looked upon and touched with our hands . . . we proclaim also to you . . ." (1 John 1:1).[1] The first Christian martyr, Stephen, is reported to have seen the heavens open and the Son of God seated on the right hand of God (Acts 7:55-56). Neither in the Old nor the New Testament, however, do we see any significant development of the concept beyond an almost juridical meaning of *witness*.

In biblical and postbiblical Judaism, martyrdom was considered to be an individual work of piety and resistance to evil. The cases of the woman and her seven sons in 4 Maccabees (8:3ff.) and the three young men in Daniel

---

Previously published in *Religious Resurgence: Contemporary Cases in Islam, Christianity, and Judaism,* ed. Richard T. Antoun and Mary Elaine Hegland (New York: Syracuse University Press, 1987), 67-77. Reprinted by permission.

(chap. 3) have survived as powerful symbols in the liturgy and hagiography of the church. The aim of martyrdom in Judaism was essentially to perfect the victim and edify the people. Since martyrdom, as a religious and moral concept, can best develop within an eschatological framework, it is significant that in Judaism this concept appears only in late biblical and apocryphal writings in an eschatological context. The early church fell heir to both Jewish eschatology and its moral implications.

In Acts 22:20, St. Paul acknowledges his role in the martyrdom of early Christians, "when the blood of Thy servant Stephen was shed."[2] The book of Revelation, the apocalypse of the early church, presents a vivid image of the martyrs: "I saw the woman drunk with the blood . . . of the martyrs" (Rev 17:6).[3]

During the apostolic age, the concept of martyrdom took on new meaning as the number of martyrs increased and their memory lived on. Yet the two elements of witnessing to one's faith and stoic indifference to pain continued to dominate the thinking of the early church. Thus we read in *1 Clement* 5:4-7 (written about 96 C.E.):

> Peter, who because of unrighteous jealousy suffered not one or two but many trials, and having thus given his testimony went to the glorious place which was his due. Through jealousy and strife Paul showed the way to the prize of endurance; seven times he was in bonds, he was exiled, he was stoned, he was a herald both in the East and in the West, he gained the noble fame of his faith, he taught righteousness to all the world, and when he had reached the limits of the West he gave his testimony before the rulers, and thus passed from the world and was taken up into the Holy Place—the greatest example of endurance.[4]

One of the earliest and most eager martyrs of the church was Ignatius, bishop of Antioch, who died in 108 C.E. For Ignatius, the martyr was "he who imitated Christ in His sufferings" (Rom 6:3).[5] He therefore used the term in the sense of *disciple* rather than of *witness*. His view was fully theological, and he insisted on bodily suffering as a proof that Christ, the crucified Son of God, was clothed in a real body. Ignatius wished his own body to be crushed between the teeth of wild beasts, to become a perfect loaf for Christ, whose own body is represented in the bread and wine of the eucharist, which was regarded by Ignatius as "the medicine of immortality" (Ignatius *Ephesians* 20:2).

In the account of the martyrdom of Polycarp, bishop of Smyrna, written about 155 C.E., witnessing in faith to the humanity and suffering of the Son of God was fully developed as a concept.[6] In the Leonine letters of about 170 C.E., the term *martyr* signified persecution leading to the shedding of blood for Christ. Here, the example of Stephen, who saw (witnessed) the glorified Christ before his death, was used as a proof case. The letters vehemently protest the use of the epithet *martyrs* for confessors who endured persecution but did not seal their testimony with their blood.[7] In *The Shepherd of Hermas*, this imitator of Christ through martyrdom earns the martyr's salvation and a share in the glory of Christ. "Those who suffered for the name of the Son of God are glorious. All their sins have been taken away."[8] The martyrs are also pictured as sitting on thrones with crowns on their heads, with Christ engaged in judging the world.[9] Such glory belongs only to those who have suffered stripes, imprisonment, crucifixion, and wild beasts for Christ's name, insists the author of *The Shepherd of Hermas*.

A rich and elaborate cultus evolved out of this great regard for martyrdom and the veneration accorded martyrs. We can discuss only the beginnings of this cultus, and some of its salient features. Apparently, the authorities responsible for the execution by burning of Polycarp sought to prevent the Christians from gathering his remains, which, they feared, would be venerated more than Christ. The faithful protested this accusation vehemently, arguing that the veneration accorded to martyrs for their sacrifice is not the same as worship, which belongs to God alone. The classic difference here stated and greatly elaborated in the Eastern Church is between the honor of veneration and worship. The parishioners of the bishop did gather the bones of the saint for burial, considering them "to be more valuable than precious stones and finer than refined gold . . . . [They] laid them in a suitable place. There the Lord will permit us [they said] . . . to gather together in joy and gladness and to celebrate the day of his martyrdom as a birthday, in memory of those athletes who have gone before . . . ."[10] The "birthday of the martyr" as an annual memorial was a Christian adaptation of a pagan custom that played a crucial role in the growth of the cult of martyrs.[11]

Others among the early church fathers advocated great veneration for martyrs, whom they considered to be the treasures of the church. Martyrdom was considered to be a second baptism, a baptism of blood, granting the martyr immediate remission of sin and entry into paradise. Martyrs who were imprisoned awaiting death, their families, and even the towns in which they resided were held in a high honor. Those who remained steadfast through imprisonment and torture (although escaping death) gained positions among the elite of society. This honor gave them the privilege of episcopal office.[12]

From an early period, martyrs who were imprisoned were asked to pray for the health, well-being, and salvation of the pious. It was a natural development that such requests for prayers came to be renewed after the martyr's death. This controversial point no doubt led to an even greater tension between worship of the dead—a common practice in pre-Christian pagan society—and the veneration of martyrs. The cult of martyrs with its relics and shrines became an object of scorn in the Protestant Reformation; as a result the Catholic Church was forced to define its theology of martyrdom again and again. In the words of the Council of Trent, which met in part to answer the criticisms of the Reformation: "The holy bodies of holy martyrs, and of others now living with Christ—which bodies were the living members of Christ and the temple of the Holy Ghost (1 Cor 3:16), and which are by Him to be raised unto eternal life, and to be glorified—are to be venerated by the faithful through which bodies many benefits are bestowed by God on men."[13]

While in Christianity a rich cultus arose around the shrines and relics of the martyrs, in Islam this phenomenon remained limited to Shi'i Islam, and even there took a different form and meaning. This "friend of God" or saint in Islam, whose shrine became a place of pilgrimage for the pious, was not required to be a martyr. In fact, the Prophet recommended that, whenever possible, martyrs should be buried at the spot where they fell in battle.[14] To my knowledge, there are no shrines in the Muslim world specifically erected as memorials for martyrs except those of the Shi'a imams in Iraq and Iran. Yet even here the imam's role is far greater than simply that of martyr.

The word *shahīd* (witness), with its derivatives, occurs over fifty times in the Qur'an. In most of these references, the emphasis is on its linguistic meaning and usage as witness here on earth to the Oneness of God, the apostleship of Muhammad, and the truth of the faith. Witnesses are not in a category by themselves but are classed with the prophets, the righteous, and the truthful—that is, with those who have found favor with God (Q. 4:69 and 57:19).

The first question of concern to us is, Who is a martyr? The answer, as we shall see, is in the end legally determined. A man, we are told, said to the Prophet, "A man may fight in quest of booty. Another may fight for fame and still another for a show of status. Who among these would be fighting in the way of God?" The Prophet answered, "Whoever fights in order that the word of God be uppermost, would be fighting in the way of God."[15]

The famous traditionist, Ibn Hajar al-Asqalani, comments on this hadith:

> One may fight for one of five reasons: booty; a show of bravery; or a show before others; in defense of wealth, family, or land: and out of anger. Any one of these could in itself be praiseworthy or the opposite. So long as the main purpose remains that the "word of God be uppermost" [which is here defined as defending the cause of Islam], it matters not what other reasons may exist as secondary causes.[16]

In yet another tradition, the Prophet was asked whether a man fighting for material rewards would also have a reward with God on the Day of Resurrection. The Prophet answered, "Nothing." He continued, "God would not accept a deed unless it is done sincerely for Him and that the doer seek by this only His [God's] face."[17]

At least in early Islam, the application of the term *martyr* was not limited to the person who is killed in the way of God on the battlefield. Martyrdom is an act of jihad (striving) in the way of God. Jihad, however, contrary to the common view held in the West, is not simply militancy; more basic is the jihad against the evil in one's own soul and in society. It is this inner purity resulting from the jihad of the soul that creates the right intention of serving the cause of truth in whatever way possible. In addition to dying in defense of one's faith, property, or life, therefore, the act of falling off one's mount, dying of snakebite, or drowning is also regarded as martyrdom. Likewise, he who dies from a stray arrow or bullet, or from his house collapsing down upon him, is considered a martyr. Even those who die of the plague or a stomach ailment, or a woman who dies in childbirth, are considered martyrs. The famous traditionist Ibn 'Abbas is said to have declared: "A man dies in his bed in the way of God, yet he is a martyr."[18] Nevertheless, in spite of all this, the true martyr is he who is slain in the way of God.

Early traditionists may have used the term *martyr* very broadly and with caution because they feared the rise of a special cult of martyrs. Thus, in relationship to the authority of Abu Hurayrah, the Prophet is said to have declared: "Whoever has faith in God and in His apostle, observes regular prayers and fasts the month of Ramadan, it shall be incumbent upon God to make him enter Paradise, whether he fights in the way of God or remains in the land of his birth." Yet when the people asked if they should convey this glad tiding to others, the Prophet did not answer directly. Instead, he described the high station of the martyrs in Paradise.[19] Perhaps for this reason it was the jurist rather than the orator or theologian who determined the principle according to which a man or woman may be considered to be a martyr.

I cannot enter in detail into this technical topic of the qualifications of a martyr; a few general remarks must suffice. Three categories of martyrs may be distinguished: martyr of this world, martyr of this world and the world to come, and martyr only of the world to come. The first is s/he who dies for a worldly cause other than of faith. The second is s/he who is slain for no other reason but that "the word of God be uppermost." Such a martyr is to be buried in his/her clothes, without washing or shrouding—ordinarily, necessary rites for the dead. The martyr of this world is likewise buried in his/her clothes, since in the end this person's motives are known only to God, who will reward each person according to his/her acts and intentions. 'Umar ibn al-Khattab and 'Ali ibn Abi Talib, the second and fourth of the four rightly guided caliphs, who were stabbed and died later of their wounds, were given regular burial. While both were considered martyrs in the way of God, such burial indicates that they were not, technically speaking, martyrs. The third caliph, 'Uthman, who was slain in his house, was also given a regular burial.[20]

Finally, the Qur'an counsels Muslims to make peace among themselves. Yet if one group transgresses against another, that group must be fought until it returns to the right path (Q. 49:9). Thus, we are told, after the battle of

Nahrawan against the Kharijites (659 C.E.), Ali had the dead on his side buried as martyrs. This principle has continued to be observed (and often abused) to the present day.

As in Christianity, the blood of the martyr in Islam washes away his or her sins. It is important to observe that even though women are exempted from actual fighting for religious and juristic reasons, the first martyr in Islam was a woman named Sumayya, the mother of 'Ammar ibn Yasir, who was tortured to death with her husband and son by the Makkan Arabs before the conquest of the city. The injunction to let the blood of the martyrs be their purification is said to have been given by the Prophet regarding those slain in the battle of Uhud.[21] He said: "Shroud them in their blood and do not wash them. For no man who is injured in the way of God but that he shall come on the Day of Resurrection with his blood gushing out of his veins. The color shall be that of blood and the odor that of musk."[22]

The martyrs—"those who are slain in the way of God"—the Qur'an tells us "are not to be reckoned as dead; rather, they are alive with their Lord sustained" (Q. 3:169). Islamic eschatology has always been expressed in the language and the social framework of this life. Hence, tradition very early displayed great imagination in depicting the great pleasures of the martyrs in Paradise.[23] Yet the true martyr for God retains his desire for martyrdom even in Paradise. Malik ibn Anas related that the Prophet said: "No one who enters Paradise would wish to return to this world, even if he were to possess all that is in it, except the martyr. He would desire to return to the world to be killed ten times because of the great honor [with God] which he sees in this act."[24] "The door of Paradise," we are told in another tradition, "is under the glittering swords."[25]

Tradition records numerous examples of martyrs who sensed the odor of Paradise on the battlefield and thus gladly met their death. One such example is that of a man called 'Abdallah ibn Jahsh, who prayed on the morning of the battle of Uhud, saying: "O God, let me today meet a strong and brave knight who will kill me and cut off my nose and two ears. Thus when I shall meet you tomorrow, you will say, 'My servant, for what were your nose and ears cut off?' I will then answer, 'It was in You [for your sake], my Lord, and in your apostle.'"[26]

Shi'a Muslims have made the ethos of martyrdom and suffering a basic principle of their faith and piety. Every year during the first ten days of Muharram (the first month of the Muslim calendar), they relive the experience of Husayn ibn 'Ali, the third imam, who through his death at Karbala provided for all Muslims the supreme example of self-sacrifice in the way of God. In the tragedy of Karbala in 680 C.E., the ideal of martyrdom took on new theological and pietistic significance. Thus Husayn, "the Prince of Martyrs" and "Master of the Youths of the People of Paradise," was said to have been destined for this sacrifice from the beginning of creation. History was read backward from him to Adam, and beyond and forward to the end of the world. Before him, history was a long prelude to the drama of suffering and death of which he, his friends, and immediate relatives were the central characters. After him, history is a period of intense hope in the anticipation of the return of the Mahdi (his ninth descendant and twelfth imam of the Shi'i community) to avenge the death of Husayn and vindicate the faithful for their actual and vicarious sharing in the sufferings of the holy family of the Prophet Muhammad. Yet Husayn himself was said to have been told by the Prophet in a dream that "he has an exalted station with God which he cannot attain except through martyrdom."[27]

The death of Husayn, moreover, became for Shi'a Muslims a source of redemption and healing. According to a well-known tradition, just before his death the Prophet said: "I am leaving with you [the Muslim community] the two weights onto which if you hold fast, you shall never go astray: the Book of God and my family, the people of my household. They shall never be separated until they come to me at the spring."[28] This paradisiacal spring shall be given to the Prophet on the Day of Judgment to quench the thirst of the pious "on the day of the great thirst."[29] Both the Qur'an and the family of Muhammad will judge and intercede before God and his Prophet for those of the Muslims who honored the two weights or neglected and mistreated them. Husayn will also stand before God on the Day of Resurrection as a headless body to contend with his murderers and intercede for his follow-ers.[30] For Shi'i piety it is Fatimah, the daughter of Muhammad and mother of Husayn, who has in this world embodied the suffering of her descendants and who continues to shed tears of anguish even in Paradise.[31]

This ethos of suffering stands in sharp contrast to the quick and spec-tacular success of the early generations of Muslims. Yet it is itself the prod-uct of that military and economic success, coming as it does out of the conviction that political justice must, in the end, reflect divine justice. God Himself, in Shi'i theology, is bound only by His own justice. Hence, Shi'a repeat daily in their worship the prayer "O God, we desire of You an hon-orable state in which You honor Islam and its people, and humiliate hypocrisy and its people. [We pray] that in it you render us among those who call [others] to obedience to you, and that you make us leaders to your way." This ideal order will come only when human justice will approximate divine justice most closely, which can only be achieved under the leadership of an imam protected by God from error. In this hope—or rather, humanly unrealized goal—political idealism and theology meet.

It is noteworthy that Shi'a, more than the Sunni majority of Muslims, have risked life and Muslim unity in this quest. They have, moreover, main-tained a long and recognizable list of martyrs. The list begins with Abel (Qabil) and includes the Prophet Muhammad and all the imams but one. The twelfth imam, the Hidden Imam, will return to close this long chapter of wrongdoing and martyrdom, and establish justice in the earth. Thus, the Prophet is said to have declared: "Even if there remains [only] one day of the life of the world, God will prolong that day until a man of my progeny shall appear, whose name is my name and whose agnomen is my agnomen. He shall fill the earth with equity and justice as it has been filled with inequity and injustice."[32] This tradition, with minor variations, is accepted by both Shi'i and Sunni traditionists. Thus, the ideal it expresses has gained official acceptance among Muslims of both groups.

This ideal of great justice was realized for a brief time only by the Prophet, Muhammad, in Madinah. The Qur'an refers to the realization of the ideal of a good society in a statement coming shortly before the Prophet's death and after all the obligations of Islam had been instituted: "Today have I perfected your religion for you; I have completed my favor towards you and have accepted Islam as a religion for you" (Q. 5:3). Martyrs throughout Islamic history have been an affirmation of this hope and a recognition that this hope remains an ideal unfulfilled because of human folly. Hence, the challenge remains as powerful today in Iran, Afghanistan, the Arabian peninsula, and even here in the New World as it was when it was first uttered.

"Surely God has exchanged with the people of faith their lives and wealth so that they shall have Paradise: they fight in the way of God, they kill and are killed . . ." (Q. 9:111). This verse continues, "It is a promise incumbent upon Him in truth, in the Torah and the Gospel." Thus Islam has from the beginning recognized the place and value of martyrdom in the major scriptures revealed before it. In an earlier surah of the Qur'an, revealed before the principle of jihad was established for the Muslim community, the Qur'an alludes to the famous Christian martyrs of Najran (Q. 85:4-8), who became the subject of much exegetical and hadith scholarship. It is therefore important to ask, in conclusion, about the similarities and differences in the view of and attitude toward martyrs in the two religious traditions.

Perhaps the most obvious and important historical difference is that while in Christianity martyrdom was a glorious struggle before Christendom became a world power under Constantine, in Islam the jihad, or struggle of the martyrs, was instituted *after* Islam became a religious, social, and political order. Thus, when the symbol of supreme martyrdom, the cross, became the banner under which political wars were waged, the significance of the principle altogether became subject to question and doubt. The most intense protest against this "distortion" may be seen in the radical Reformation and the rich and moving martyrologies that Mennonites and Anabaptists have left as their legacy for posterity. The ideal martyr in Christianity was, therefore, he "who suffered stripes, imprisonment, crucifixion and wild beasts. . . ." Today, one may wonder if it is because of the loss of the original meaning of this ideal that even among committed fundamentalist Christians martyrdom is no longer the impetus it was for the early church.

In Islam, the ideal martyr is someone who strives in the way of God "with his hand, with his tongue, and with his heart." Yet striving only with the heart is considered to be "the weakest of faith."[33] This emphasis on outward struggle does not imply wild and uncontrolled warfare, however; rather, it advocates a regulated struggle for the good and against evil. This struggle has definite priorities of concern: "if affliction befalls you," advised

'Abdallah ibn Jundub, the son of a well-known companion, "ransom your souls by your wealth. But if affliction increases, put your souls before your faith. For a truly deprived man is he whose religion is taken away from him. This is because there is no poverty after Paradise, nor is there any wealth after the Fire."[34]

In spite of this important difference, however, both Islam and Christianity agree on the basic concept of martyrdom as witness to the truth. The true martyr, the two religions also agree, is a person who is free from any motive but that witness. While the ideal martyr in Islam is the one who falls on the battlefield, actual fighting is not an absolute requirement for martyrdom. Islam, moreover, has its martyrs who silently and bravely endure torture and death. Finally, both traditions are in agreement regarding the exalted station of the martyr with God and the belief that the martyr will carry the marks of one's sacrifice with him or her to be displayed even in heaven.[35]

In more recent Christian developments, the two ideals may yet have more in common than ever before. Liberation theology—the product of poverty, piety, and political awareness—may yet prove to be the most important phenomenon in modern Christian history. As a Muslim, I believe that piety without political involvement is at best all theory and no practice. It shall be those who feed the hungry, clothe the naked, care for the sick, and defend the wronged in prison who will inherit the kingdom of God.

# Notes

1. All biblical quotations are taken from the Revised Standard Version.

2. See also Acts 1:8; Luke 21:13; John 15:27; and Matt. 10:28, where the term *martyr* is used in the sense of witness.

3. See also Rev 6:9-11; 20:4.

4. Cyril C. Richardson et al., eds., *Early Christian Fathers*, The Library of Christian Classics (Philadelphia: Westminster, 1953), 1:46.

5. See the entire epistle that revolves around this concept.

6. See Richardson, *Early Christian Fathers*, 149ff.

7. *New Catholic Encyclopedia* (1967; Palatine, Ill.: J. Heraty, 1981), 11:312.

8. Ibid.

9. Ibid.

10. Richardson, *Early Christian Fathers*, 156.

11. On the development of the cult of the martyrs and its relationships to Graeco-Roman antecedents, see James Hastings, ed., *Encyclopaedia of Religion and Ethics* (New York: Charles Scribner's Sons, n.d.), 9:52ff.

12. Ibid., 53.

13. Ibid., 51.

14. Hasan Khalid, *al-Shahid fi al-Islam* (Beirut: Dar al-'ilm al-Malayin, 1971), 75.

15. Ahmad ibn 'Ali ibn Hajar al-Asqalani, *Fath al-bari bi sharh Sahih al-Bukhari*, (Beirut: Dar al-Ma'rifah, n.d.), 6:28.

16. Ibid., 28.

17. Ibid.

18. Khalid, *al-Shahid fi al-Islam*, 57. See also 55-57.

19. Ibn Hajar al-Asqalani, *Fath al-bari bi sharh Sahih al-Bukhari*, 11.

20. See Khalid, *al-Shahid fi al-Islam*, 69-72.

21. Ibid., 70.

22. Ibid.

23. See Imad al-Din Abi al-Fida Isma'il ibn Kathir, *Tafsir al-Qur'an al-Azim*, 2d ed. (Beirut: Dar al-Fikr, 1389/1970), 2:153-60.

24. Ibn Hajar al-Asqalani, *Fath al-bari bi sharh Sahih al-Bukhari*, 31.

25. Ibid.

26. Khalid, *al-Shahid fi al-Islam*, 138.

27. Akhtab al-Muwaffaq al-Khawarizmi, *Maqtal al-Husayn* (Najaf: Muhammad al-Samawi, 1367/1947), 1:187.

28. Abu Ja'far al-Suduq Ibn Babawayh al-Qummi, *Ikmal al-din* (Najaf: al-Matb'ah al-Haydariyyah, 1389/1970), 62.

29. Mahmoud M. Ayoub, *Redemptive Suffering In Islam* (The Hague: Mouton, 1978), 205ff.

30. Ibid., 214.

31. Ibid., 144-45.

32. Ibid., 217.

33. Abu 'Isa Muhammad bin 'Isa bin Sawrah al-Tirmidhi, *Sunan al-Tirmidhi*, ed. 'Abdul Rahman Muhammad 'Uthman, 3rd ed. (Beirut: Dar al-Fikr, 1398/1978), 3:318.

34. Khalid, *al-Shahid fi al-Islam*, 138.

35. I have already cited Muslim tradition in support of this idea. For the Christian tradition, see Ayoub, *Redemptive Suffering in Islam*, 199, 282 n. 7.

# 8

# The Idea of Redemption
# in Christianity and Islam

Among historians of religion, the approach has largely been to categorize a religion according to its concept of God. This approach, fruitful as it may be, has problems; and it may well be a more enlightening exercise if we begin not with the concept of God alone but with the way a religious tradition views human society or, in other words, human beings' relationship to the Divine.

From that starting point, it can be said that from the earliest beginnings of human civilization, it has been a matter of human awareness of the mysteries of suffering and death. From the earliest times, in China, in Egypt, and notably in Mesopotamia with the cults of Tammuz, we find that the main concern is to understand the purposes of life and of death. (I will resist a great temptation to retell the tale of Gilgamesh as a commentary on the human predicament on life and on death.)

Muslims believe that revelation is an ongoing process. For Islam, revelation began with Adam when he received words from his Lord, and God turned toward him. And while we believe that revelation reached its technical culmination in the Prophet Muhammad through a long period of what we call progressive revelation, nonetheless, it may be said that revelation continues, not in the form of *waḥy* (revelation technically considered) but in the form of *ilhām*, or inspiration that is open to the friends and worshipful servants of God. This mode of revelation will not end. It did not begin only after prophetic revelation had ended, but rather, in my view, it always coexisted with it. In other words, the beginnings of what I may call collective revelation are our rich heritage of mythology.

Unfortunately, we call anything that is not true, that cannot be taken seriously, mythical. But if we consider seriously that mythology has been the language of faith, that religious tradition has done far better in poetry than in prose, and that poetry is usually the language of myth, then we can see the crucial importance of myth in the development of human religious con-

Previously published in *Mormons and Muslims: Spiritual Foundations and Modern Manifestations,* ed. Spencer J. Palmer (Provo, Ut.: Brigham Young University, 1983), 105-16. Reprinted by permission.

sciousness. It is in mythology also that the idea of redemption was born. As the prophet Ezekiel put it, "And there sat women weeping for Tammuz" (Ezek 8:14). On the banks of the Tigris and the Euphrates sat women and men expressing their emotions of fear and hope, as they sang dirges for the God who died in order to bring him back to life. This really meant to bring the sap back into the date palm tree, the milk to the cow and hence to the milkskin, and the grain to the surface of the earth.[1]

If we look carefully, the ideas expressed in the myths are universal—they are Greek, they are Indian. Everywhere we go there is the idea of life coming out of death, so to say, healing the world, healing nature after a period of sickness or cessation. What is *redemption* or the word *salvation*? It comes from the Latin root meaning "to be whole." Yet again, it is in the myth which from Tammuz moved a vast step forward to the suffering servant of the Lord of Deutero-Isaiah. It is important to observe that whether it be in Tammuz, or in the suffering servant of the Lord, or later in Christ, or in the prophet Muhammad and his intercessory role, or later on in the martyrdom of his grandson Husayn, redemption is not achieved by or through ideas or doctrines but through the lives and the sacrifices of human individuals. In my view, our problem has been, to a large extent, that we have taken far too seriously doctrines and theological wranglings, and not seriously enough the lives and the models, the examples, of the friends of God. The suffering servant of Deutero-Isaiah remained unidentified. Some said it was a prototypical character; others, that it referred to the entire Jewish people. Finally in the church, beginning in the book of Acts and developing more clearly through the thought of Justin Martyr, the suffering servant was identified with Christ. The Gospels also refer to this somewhat briefly. The suffering servant must be all of these and none of them. In a way, he is every one of us, both needing redemption and participating in a redemptive role for its achievement. I will return to this at greater length later.

As we come to postbiblical Judaism and especially early Christianity, there are essentially two types or ideas of redemption. It may be observed here that the Swedish writer, Gustaf Aulén, is very right when he says there is no doctrine of redemption in Christianity but only theories about it.[2] There was a redemptive act, but what was it? How can we express it in doctrinal form? It is good, perhaps, that there has not been agreement.

As I see it, there are two basic types of redemption in Christianity. The first is a death on the cross, where the cross becomes a prototype of the biblical or, more specifically, the Jewish Temple altar. That sacrifice was the final sacrifice, all others before it being only a prelude to it. Hence, the Gospel of St. Matthew tells us that when Jesus died on the cross, the veil of the Temple that separated the true place of sacrifice—the holy of holies—and the people was rent and the barrier, therefore, was removed. The idea of this type, that is, redemption through death and the shedding of blood, is worked out in the New Testament most interestingly and clearly in the Epistle to the Hebrews.

The other type is one that characterizes the Eastern Church most notably. It is redemption not by death and suffering so much as by victory. Hence, the Easter hymn for the Greek Orthodox Church goes something like this: "Christ rose from the dead, trampling death and by death giving life to those who are in the graves."

The two basic ideas developed by medieval thinkers of Christ dying in order to appease either God or Satan or to set a trap for Satan have not been, in my view, as fruitful and creative or as poetic as the other idea, which is also expressed in the thought of St. Paul that Christ really conquered death by death. More interestingly, this idea was developed in the mystical theology of the Eastern Church, which had its beginnings in the Johannine corpus—both the Gospel and the Epistles. Christ, the second Adam, came not to abolish an original sin by dying for Adam, but rather he came in order to make us divine. He came in order to achieve victory over the *demonia,* the powers of evil. It was God visiting humanity in human disguise. Hence, that Christianity which lived on strongly and converted numerous people in the Syro-Aramaic area, or what we now call mainly the Arab world, was that Christianity which has been characterized by Christian writers as the faith of the merciful, that is, *addīn arrahamānī*. It is that faith which Islam breeds, and I think we cannot understand Islam fully unless we see it in that Christian ritualistic context. It may be argued that even though the prophet of Islam lived in closer proximity to the Jewish community in Madinah and interacted with it far more extensively on a daily basis, the overall influence of the spirituality of Eastern Christianity and its idea of redemption played a greater role in the formative period of Muslim piety.

To the two types of redemption discussed in Christianity, Islam added a third and a fourth. But before I talk about the Islamic idea of redemption, it must be observed that the basic mystery which preoccupied humanity from its earliest beginning was that of suffering and death. Hence the idea or hope of redemption was born in suffering. In the West, the suffering of Christ developed into an idea of a Christ contorted with pain. For example, the gory images that we see in much of Western medieval literature characterizing the suffering Christ were the products of the first type of redemption, that is, redemption as death. In Eastern Christian piety, on the other hand, the cross is not really an altar of suffering and death but a throne of glory. In many poems, notably that of Fortunatus,[3] and echoed even in Ireland in the "Dream of the Rood," we find the same notion of the universal cross as the throne of glory. Yet suffering was not forgotten, and the Christian church, inasmuch as it itself participated in that redemptive role, did it through its witness. The greatest witness was that of martyrdom. The word *martyr* actually means witness. The point was vividly argued even in the early church when Stephen, the first martyr, at the point of death declared that he saw the heavens opened and the "Son of God" seated on the right hand of God (Acts 7:55-56). That suffering, however, had to be transferred from earth to heaven in order for it to be universal and eternal. Thus, St. John Chrysostom (in a sermon sometimes wrongly attributed to St. Augustine) declares that Christ sits in heaven still bearing the marks of the nails and the wound of the lance in his side.[4] Therefore the emblems of suffering were not only to be embodied by the church here on earth in its participatory role in the achievement of redemption, but they were also transferred to heaven, where they will be displayed before the angels until the final victory—the return of the Messiah, the Second Coming.

To understand the Islamic idea of redemption, in contrast, and the two types which I said Islam added to the Christian notion, one must look briefly at the Muslim view of human being. For a long time, Christian and Jewish orientalists in the West read the Qur'anic account of Adam as a gross distortion of the biblical account that, had he known better, Muhammad would have copied. It is only now, I think, that scholars are beginning to see the Qur'an on its own terms. However different it may be from that of Genesis, the Qur'anic account of Adam must be seen on its own terms. What does it tell us? In some ways, the Adam of the Qur'an closely resembles that of Genesis. Like the Adam of Genesis, Adam in the Qur'an is declared to be made of clay and obtains the breath of life through the divine spirit that was breathed into him. Like the biblical Adam, the Adam of the Qur'an sinned by disobeying the divine command. But here the comparison ends. The Qur'an does not tell us that Adam ate of the fruit of the tree of knowledge, because knowledge was given to him even before his sin (Q. 2:31-33). Knowledge was not the cause of his condemnation and damnation but of his salvation. Adam was saved because he received words from his Lord. He was declared higher than the angels because he knew language that they did not know. So it is not knowledge that made Adam sin, but disobedience. While the biblical Adam becomes the first sinner for Christians, for Muslims Adam is not the first sinner but the first prophet, because with him the history of revelation begins.

In nine verses in the Qur'an (Q. 2:30-39) we have a commentary on the story of Adam which was told several times in other Qur'anic verses. It is a commentary that goes beyond the creation of Adam. There God says to the angels, "Behold, I am about to place a vicegerent in the earth." The angels, knowing what we would do, said, "Would you place therein one who will spread corruption and shed blood, while we proclaim your praise and sanctify you?" He said, "I know what you do not know." Then Adam was taught the names of all creatures and the challenge was placed between knowing and choosing man and knowing and choosing the angels, who could only do that which was good. Satan, or Iblis, in the Adam story plays a role not in spite of but by the permission of God. His sin, in essence, was like that of Adam. Both rebelled. But while Adam repented and turned to God, Iblis persisted in his pride and would not accept that a creature of clay might be better than a creature of fire.

Redemption, then, in Islam begins with Adam, who was made for the earth. He descends to earth, and the battle between good and evil begins on its true stage, the earth. Redemption is when this battle is finally concluded with the divine victory, with the victory of the good.

The Qur'an speaks not of ransom by sacrifice, even though Muslims do a commemorative sacrifice at the time of the *hajj* to commemorate the sacrifice of Abraham, but the Qur'an insists that then neither the fat nor the blood of the animals reaches God. What reaches him is our piety or righteousness. So expiation, or *takfīr*, of sin must be done by the individual himself, and here, then, redemption is what men and women do with their own sin through repentance and through expiation through prayers, fasts, sharing their wealth with the poor, and so on. This is one type of redemption.

The other, and in a sense more important in that it has permeated Islamic life more deeply and is a type that may be considered as really the only legitimate type of Islamic redemption, is that of intercession—*shafā'ah*. Contrary to what many Muslims say, intercession is not denied in the Qur'an; rather, what is denied is that intercession will benefit those who are deep in sin. Any intercession must be a divine gift. The Qur'an tells us, "Who shall intercede with him, save by his leave" (Q. 2:255). Furthermore, if we examine the large number of hadiths known as *ahādīth al-shafā'ah*, or the traditions of intercession, we find so clearly the idea that it will be Muhammad who will intercede on behalf not only of the Muslims but the entire world. In a long and dramatic tradition related on the authority of Abu Hurayrah we are told that on the Day of Resurrection, people will be made to stand for seventy years. They will weep tears, and when their tears run out they will weep blood until the blood shall stop their mouths, and still they will not be judged. Then Muhammad will go and prostrate himself before God and intercede for people, not that they may be given paradise but at least that they must be heard—they must be judged—and hence the judgment begins.

While Muhammad, in popular Islam and in much of not-so-popular Islam, plays a very important intercessory role, intercession is not limited to him. Rather, in explanation of a very interesting verse in *Surat al-Baqarah*, which comes after telling the story of David and Goliath and Saul, the text adds that had not God restrained or stopped some people by means of others, the earth would have been corrupted (Q. 2:251). Most people take that to mean that there must always exist in the earth people who pray, otherwise the earth will disappear. In a comment on that verse by the sixth Shi'i imam, Ja'far al-Sadiq, we are told that God protects those who do not pray among the Muslims through those who do pray; those who do not fast through those who do fast; and those who do not go on pilgrimage through those who do go. Were they all to concur in neglecting the prayers, fasting, and pilgrimage, then they would all perish.

In another hadith we are told that God blesses, that is, gives *barakah*, through the prayerful servant of God. He gives *barakah* not only to the person's own family but to his neighbors and neighbors' neighbors to the seventh neighbor. This notion of the earth being preserved, made whole, redeemed from evil through piety and prayers is most eloquently expressed in Islamic mysticism in Sufism, and systematically in the notion of the *quṭb* or the perfect man. The *quṭb* is the person around whom the universe revolves, and every age must have a *quṭb*, otherwise the earth could not stay in its place. Through the grace of the *quṭb*, the universe goes on running. This is put rather poetically by one Sufi writer, who says, *inna lillāhi 'ibādan idha arādū arād* ("there are those servants of God who, when they will something, God wills it as well"). So, then, wholeness or redemption, salvation, restoration can be achieved through personal expiation and through intercession widely considered.

Here again in Islam, as in Christianity and Judaism and even in Buddhism, there is the notion that the world is continuously evolving toward a state of perfection. In Buddhism this is expressed in the role of the future Buddha, Maitreya. It is an interesting notion which presents a reverse of Darwinian evolution. Darwin thinks that evolution is upward from the unicellular animal to the monkey to man and whatever. It appears that the religious concept is that the world evolves downward from a golden age to a silver age to an iron age to a clay age, and then the whole thing will be dark until someone comes to restore things to their natural and earlier purity. This, in Islam, is the Mahdi.

In the idea of the Mahdi, Islam and Christianity again meet. I would like to argue here that the original notion of the Mahdi was not that a person of the family of the prophet would be born, according to the Sunni Muslim view, or that he would appear at the end of time, according to the Shi'i Muslim view. Rather, it would be Jesus who will return. If we are to find any Qur'anic basis for this eschatological event, it will not be for a future, so to say, Islamic Mahdi, but for Jesus, who is declared to be a sign for the hour (Q. 43:61). Muslim piety, in order to preserve itself and its own integrity, did not deny that Jesus will come to restore the world to its purity but affirmed that Jesus and the Mahdi will work together. Most of the hard work will be done by Jesus, who will kill *ad-Dajjāl,* the anti-Christ.

Here again, ad-Dajjal is pictured as a human individual whose appearance is deformed, who is not human as he should be. The best description of him is one that was made by the thirteenth-century Farid ud-Din Attar, a Persian mystic who said that at the end of time there will come two Dajjals, not one. (The Arabic word *dajjāl* means "one who lies.") There will be one who has only his right eye and sees the world as all spirit. He will be a liar. There will be one who has only his left eye and will see the world as simply matter and material things. He will be a liar. The true vision of reality, then, is one that sees reality as a whole—both material and spiritual. The role of Jesus is that he will kill that liar, the anti-Christ, and restore the reality of the universe to its pristine purity. Symbolically it is said that Christ, when He comes, will break the cross and kill the swine (these two being the symbols that divide Muslims from Christians), and Islam in its essential aspects will prevail. This is redemption.

I return to my earlier reference of that ethos of redemptive suffering which the Shi'i community developed. In that ethos we see a continuity of history. It was on the spot where the women sat weeping for Tammuz that Husayn, the son of Ali and grandson of the prophet, was killed on the tenth day of Muharram in the year A.H. 61 (680 C.E.). Very soon those who betrayed him formed an association, a group called *al-tawwābūn*, "the repenters." It was in that group that the seeds of a rich cult of Muharram were first sown and sprouted.

To be sure, the event was used and abused by many upstarts and pseudo-movements, but these failed, as they were doomed to failure. What remains is the following: The world, according to the Shi'i view and its history, must be read forward from creation to the imams and backward from the Day of Resurrection to the imams. In time, the notion developed that the world was created for the sake of the pious, the Prophet and his progeny. They were the lights of the world which, through a process of concretization, took on human form. All were doomed to be martyred. The idea again gradually arose, even though there is no full documentary evidence that every one of the eleven Shi'i imams were martyred. The Shi'a community, nonetheless, insisted that that was the case. Those who were supposedly the noblest, supposedly the richest, had to undergo suffering in order to redeem humanity.

But how does humanity become redeemed? It is through the suffering of Husayn's mother, who is still weeping in paradise for his death, and that of his children after him. How is the world to be redeemed? It is by participation of the community every year in that suffering that the community redeems itself. So we are told in many traditions attributed to one or another of the imams that whoever weeps even one drop of tears for the sufferings of the imams will have the reward of paradise. But in the final analysis, redemption will be through intercession because the headless Husayn will stand before God to intercede for his people.

There is, finally, another important aspect of redemption, whether it be Christian or Islamic. Redemption is only one side of the divine judgment. Redemption must also imply judgment and condemnation. Christ will return on the clouds of heaven, as the book of Revelation declares (Rev 1:7); and those who have stabbed him will mourn him. He will come not as the meek lamb of God but as the man who has a sword of fire coming out of his mouth with every word he utters. Before the new earth and the new heaven appear, replacing the old earth and heaven, judgment must be executed on the wicked. Similarly, with Islam, the Mahdi when he comes will avenge the blood of Husayn before he fulfills his main mission; on this, both Shi'i and Sunni traditionists agree. He must purify the earth of iniquity. Before he does that, he must avenge the blood of the martyrs.

The Mahdi will do his work and eventually die, but it will be Husayn who will return to rule the earth or the Muslim community for so long that his eyebrows shall fall upon his eyes from old age.[5] But the hope for a future restoration, for an eschatology of renewal, is best expressed in a Qur'anic verse and a comment by the sixth imam on that verse. The Qur'an declares that on the last day, when the trumpets shall sound and when judgment has been executed, the earth shall shine forth with the light of its Lord (Q. 39:69). The sixth imam said, "When our *qā'im* [that is, the one raised by God to renew human society and restore truth] shall come, the earth shall shine forth with the light of its Lord."[6]

Much of what has been discussed above may be regarded as poetic myth, for it is so many centuries removed from the events of Christ and Husayn and Tammuz. What does it say to us today? I have already noted that redemption in its widest sense is a corporate, not an individual, process. Whether it be the church widely viewed or the Muslim community, for redemption to be meaningful and real for us today, we all have to take part in it as an ongoing process.

On the principles of the ideas that we can learn from the mythology of the past, we see that redemption means harmony between material and spiritual things. Redemption means sharing. The people who will be put on the right hand of Christ will be those who visit the sick, clothe the naked, visit the prisoner, and feed the hungry (Matt 25:31-46). But, most of all, it remains for us to redeem the world from our own human folly—the folly that says that we will vie not with God but with the devil to make ourselves, as one Greek philosopher described us, the measure of all things. Hence, we make atom bombs and nuclear bombs; we make big skyscrapers; but with all of this we forget the purpose of life, which is to be a life of righteousness—a bridge to eternity.

In conclusion, I would like to say that Christ redeemed and continues to redeem us, not simply and only by his divine act but by his humanity, a humanity that cared. Muhammad redeemed and continues to redeem us as we follow his life, his *sunnah*, as a model for our lives. But in the end we must heed the words, "Work out your own salvation with fear and trembling." I pray that we will all be successful in that process and that we will strengthen one another as we traverse the weary way of this life into the life to come.

# Notes

1. See T. Jacobsen, *Towards an Image of Tammuz and Other Essays on Mesopotamian Religion and Culture*, ed. W. L. Moren (Cambridge, Mass.: Harvard University Press, 1970), 73ff.

2. Gustaf Aulén, *Christus Victor*, trans. A. G. Herbert (London: SPCK, 1965).

3. See the "Hymn of Fortunatus" quoted in Rev. Joseph Connelly, M.A., *Hymns of the Roman Liturgy* (Westminster, Md.: Newman Press, 1954).

4. St. John Chrysostom, "The Lord's Passion" or "The Cross and the Good Thief," *Patrologia Latina,* ed. J.-P. Migne (Paris: J.-P. Migne, 1850), 39:2047ff.

5. Mahmoud M. Ayoub, *Redemptive Suffering in Islam* (New York: Mouton, 1978), 228.

6. Ibid., 227.

# 9

# *Dhimmah* in the Qur'an and Hadith

Concepts often undergo a process of reification which reduces them from the status of broad and dynamic principles to that of mere names or designations of things and ideas. I shall study this process in one of the most important concepts in Muslim society. The lexical meanings of the term *dhimmah* as defined by some of the classical Arabic lexicographers will be examined. The study then turns to some of the general applications of this term in the Qur'an and hadith, where it is used to characterize the relationship of humanity to God and man's responsibility in this relationship. Instances in which the term *dhimmah* was used to characterize general human interrelations, and more particularly those based on the principles of Islamic faith and prophetic tradition or *sunnah,* will also be examined.

Finally, the designation of Jews and Christians by the term *ahl al-dhimmah* (people of *dhimmah)* will be analyzed. The study shows that *dhimmah* as a concept was used first to designate moral and spiritual relations among communities of faith, but was later reduced to a mere name or designation of subordinate communities. I shall limit the analysis to hadith traditions that reveal the general attitude of Muslims toward *ahl al-dhimmah* (Jews and Christians) and leave out the practical legal implications of this attitude. Both Sunni and Shi'i traditions will be considered with the aim of presenting a broad and coherent picture rather than a comprehensive one.

## Lexical Meanings of *Dhimmah*

Al-Jawhari, the author of one of the earliest Arabic lexicons,[1] defines *dhimmah* and *dhimam*, its alternate form, as "sanctity" (*ḥurmah*). *Dhimmah* also signifies "surety," or "assurance of safety" or "protection" (*aman*). In its verbal form, *dhamma,* the term has a negative meaning, "to decry a person or thing," "to find it unworthy" (*madhmūm*). It can also mean "to fall behind" because of fatigue or inability, as when a camel is unable to advance

Previously published in *Arab Studies Quarterly* 5, no.2 (Spring 1983): 172-82. Reprinted by permission.

because of fatigue. In another noun form, *madhammah*, or *madhimmah*, it means "shame" brought on by revoking the sanctity of a covenant or pact. The same form also signifies "obligation" or "indebtedness" from which a person must seek to free himself. Negative qualities such as miserliness or lying bring *madhammah* or "blame" to the person possessing them.

Both *Lisan al-'Arab*[2] and *Taj al-'Arus*[3] generally agree with Jawhari, whom they freely quote. They lay special stress, however, on the covenantal aspects of the term. Thus, *dhimmah* means both the agreement (*'ahd*) and the sanctity (*ḥurmah*) of the agreement. The author of *Lisan al-'Arab* states: "The people of *dhimmah* are also called *dhimmah* because they enter into a covenant of protection with Muslims."[4] Based on a hadith of Ali, *dhimmah* implies a binding obligation to fulfill a promise.[5] Relying on other examples of hadith usage, *Taj al-'Arus* adds: " . . . everyone has a covenant of safety and protection with God . . . ," which a human being can revoke through sets of disobedience to divine injunctions.[6] A final signification, which admirably denotes its dynamic and multifaceted application, is the use of the term to mean a banquet or wedding feast. Here a term generally denoting the depth and variety of human and divine relationships also denotes the well-known Arab ideal of hospitality.[7]

## The Application of *Dhimmah* in the Qur'an and Hadith

In contrast with this broad use of the term, the Qur'an employs the word *dhimmah* only twice and in a very narrow and limited sense, both times in one single passage revealed shortly before the Prophet's death and intended to purify the *ḥajj* ritual of any pre-Islamic characteristics and prohibit the non-Muslim Makkan Arabs from performing it (Q. 9:1-3). The passage begins by dissociating God and His Apostle from the *mushrikūn* (associators), or idol worshipers of Makkah. The word *barā'ah* (dissociation or freedom from something) means the exact opposite of *dhimmah* in its primary sense. *Barā'ah* in this context signifies the end of a pact or agreement (*'ahd*) obligation.[8] This declaration of the end of the pact was to be made at the time of the *ḥajj* (Q. 9:1ff).[9] Two kinds of people are then distinguished: those who have kept their agreement, and those who have either revoked it outright or acted hypocritically. The term of the pact with the former must be honored for the duration of the sacred months (Q. 9:5).[10]

Because the *mushrikūn* were nonbelievers, and hence because their lives were not morally regulated by worship (*ṣalāh*) and almsgiving (*zakāh*), their word cannot be trusted: "were they to prevail over you, they would regard in you neither consanguinity (*illan*) nor *dhimmah* . . ."(Q. 9:8).[11] Here *dhimmah* signifies a covenant that should be honored, as the word *illan* is coupled with it for greater emphasis. Two verses later, the same charge is repeated with even greater emphasis: "They would not observe in a believer either *illan* or *dhimmah*; those are treacherous people" (Q. 9:10).[12] In this verse the relation of *dhimmah* is narrowed to the personal level, and another of its opposite qualities—transgression (*i'tida'*)—is stressed. Throughout the passage, however, the possibility of repenting is recognized and pleaded for.[13]

These verses were explained in later hadith tradition. After the last pilgrimage before the Prophet's death, Abu Bakr and then 'Ali were sent to Makkah to deliver the following declaration: "The *dhimmah* of God and His Apostle is free (*barī'atun*) from every associator (*mushrik*). Journey on the earth for four months (i.e., the sacred months); let no *mushrik* perform the *ḥajj* after this year; nor let any naked man henceforth circumambulate the House (i.e., the Ka'bah)."[14] This hadith introduces an important element to the general scope of the term *dhimmah*, the *dhimmah* of God and His Apostle. Let us first consider the nature and implications of God's *dhimmah*, or covenant with human beings.

Two general aspects of this divine-human relationship may be distinguished. The first manifests the divine providential succor which is granted to human beings through prayers of supplication (*du'ā'*) and thanksgiving. In this context *dhimmah* generally denotes divine protection which extends beyond the short span of human life on earth. It is related on the authority of Ibn al-Asqa' that the Prophet Muhammad uttered the following prayer at a funeral:

> Oh God, behold this man (*fulān*), son of so-and-so, he is now in your *dhimmah* (protection) and within the rope (*ḥabl*) of your domain (*jiwār*). Protect him, therefore, from the trial of the grave and the torment of the fire, for you are worthy of fulfilling your covenant and worthy of all justice and truth (*ḥaqq*). Forgive him and have mercy upon him, for you are all-forgiving, all-merciful.[15]

Here man is called upon not simply to ask for divine favor and protection but to be thankful when these are granted. Ibn Hanbal related on the authority of Abu Umamah, who related on the authority of Umar, that the Prophet said: "whoever acquires a new garment should say (as it reaches his neck), 'Praise be to God who clothed me with that, which covers my nakedness and gives me comeliness in my life' then give his old garment in alms; such a person will be in the protection (*dhimmah*) of God, in His domain (*jiwār*) and His safe-keeping (*kanaf*), be he alive or dead, be he alive or dead."[16]

The second aspect of the *dhimmah* of God with man is one of reciprocity and mutual faithfulness. With regard to human beings, this means responsibility to God and for fellow human beings. It is therefore related in a number of hadiths, with varying degrees of emphasis, that any person who regularly offers the dawn prayers, or keeps prayers in general, would be in God's protection (*dhimmah*). Most hadiths add the warning, "let not God demand of you anything in violation of His *dhimmah* and thus throw you face down into the fire of hell."[17] As for a human being's responsibility toward others, the Prophet said, on the authority of 'Abdullah ibn 'Umar,

"Whoever hoards food for forty nights would be totally dissociated (*barī'*) from God the Exalted and God would likewise be dissociated from him. The people of any land, moreover among whom a man wakes up hungry, would be dissociated from God's covenant (*dhimmah*)."[18]

In both examples *dhimmah* is a covenant of protection between God and human beings. As humans have no power over God, they must satisfy God's terms of the covenant by protecting others. Indeed, on our keeping of God's *dhimmah* depends the order and well-being of the world. Thus we are told:

> When four (things) spread in the world, four (other things) appear. When adultery spreads, earthquakes occur. When tyranny spreads among rulers, rain is withheld from heaven. When *dhimmah* is revoked, the people of association are allowed to prevail over the people of Islam. When almsgiving (*zakāh*) is withheld, poverty prevails.[19]

## *Dhimmah* as a Code of Governing Human Relations

God's *dhimmah,* or covenant relationship with human beings, is given a human dimension by being identified with the *dhimmah* of the Prophet of God, Muhammad. In the Qur'an the Prophet spoke on God's behalf. Thus, his *dhimmah* was, in fact, God's *dhimmah*. Through the Prophetic tradition (*sunnah*) human beings can interiorize the *dhimmah* of God and His Prophet and make it their own. It is then their responsibility to honor the covenant of God and God's Apostle, but without having the prerogative of claiming to understand or implement fully this divine prophetic covenant. It rather must remain an ideal to be sought after but never fully attained. It is related that whenever the Prophet appointed a person to head an army in war he instructed the person to fear God and deal kindly with fellow Muslims. Then, addressing the rest of the army, the Prophet continued: "fight in the flame of God and in the way of God. Fight those who disbelieve in God, but do not overindulge, commit acts of treachery, mutilate people, or kill a child." The hadith continues: "if you besiege a fortified settlement and its inhabitants request that you give them the *dhimmah* of God and His Prophet, do not give them either the *dhimmah* of God or that of His Prophet. Rather, make with them the covenant (*dhimmah*) of yourself, your father, and your fellows. For it is better for you to violate your own *dhimmah* than to violate the *dhimmah* of God and His Prophet."[20]

The concept of *dhimmah* as a principle of honor governing human relations was not introduced by Islam. Rather, Islam gave it a divine moral basis which elevated it beyond any consideration of human power and prestige. Yet even before Islam, Arab society regarded bonds of *dhimmah* as sacred. This ancient attitude is well illustrated by an anecdote related on the authority of A'isha, daughter of Abu Bakr and wife of the Prophet. Her father decided to leave Makkah before the *hijrah* under pressure from the people of Quraysh, who protested that his piety was drawing their youths to the new religion. On his way out of the city he met a person of status who established a bond (*'aqd*) of protection with him. It was agreed that Abu Bakr would remain in his house, provided that he practice his new faith in the privacy of his home. Since Abu Bakr was unable to restrain himself, the man requested that he be released from their pact because "I do not wish the Arabs to hear that I have failed a man with whom I have established a bond." The man asked literally that his *dhimmah* be returned to him.[21]

The Islamic character of *dhimmah* may be further illustrated by two important sayings attributed, respectively, to Ali and his great-grandson Muhammad al-Baqir, the fifth Shi'i imam. After the battle of Siffin and the revolt of the Kharajites against Ali, he sent them the following warning: "beware that you shed no innocent blood, waylay travelers, or wrong a *dhimmah*.[22] If you do, we shall wage war against you; for God loves not those who transgress."[23] Al-Baqir declared: "Any man who grants another protection (*aman*) in a pact (*dhimmah*) and then kills him shall come on the Day of Resurrection bearing the banner of transgression."[24] In both traditions, the reason for keeping the covenant is not to preserve one's honor and prestige in society but to fulfill God's command. Thus, *dhimmah* becomes an obligation primarily to God; it becomes a religious rather than a social principle.

In contrast with pre-Islamic Arab society, where *dhimmah* was the privilege of the rich and powerful, Islam made it a universal obligation, binding all Muslim males and females. In a very important hadith, related on the authority of a number of the prophet's companion and by both Sunni and Shi'i traditionists, the Prophet declared: "the *dhimmah* of all Muslims is one by which even the lowliest of them can live."[25] This statement was prompted by the fact that Umm Hani, sister of 'Ali, gave a pact of protection to two men whom the Prophet honored; he went even further by stipulating that the *dhimmah* of a Muslim slave is binding on other Muslims. No doubt this attitude contributed to the designation of Jews and Christians as *ahl al-dhimmah*, people of the *dhimmah* of God and His Apostle, and, by extension, of all the Muslims.

## Dhimmah and the People of the Book

The Qur'an refers to Jews and Christians as *ahl al-kitāb* (people of the Book). The designation of *ahl al-dhimmah* is nowhere employed, nor is the term *dhimmah* used in any way to characterize the relationship of Muslims to Jews and Christians. The Qur'an uses the term in its strictly Arabian pre-Islamic context. Its absence with regard to Jews and Christians may suggest a certain level of equality of faith between the people of the Book and Muslims, who are also people of the Book in the strictest sense. The term *ahl al-dhimmah* underwent a gradual process of development both in definition and in usage. In this process it lost most of its dynamic aspects and was finally reduced to a legal term designating peoples with whom Muslims had a special relationship.

The attitude of Muslims toward *ahl al-dhimmah* likewise underwent a process of change from that of a sacred responsibility or divine charge to one of a legal relationship. Thus, a man who slapped a Jewish merchant for declaring the superiority of Moses over the rest of humankind in an oath was brought to answer before the Prophet by his opponent. The Jew protested confidently, "I have a *dhimmah* and covenant (*'ahd*); why then did this man slap my face?" The Prophet reproached the offender for his excessive zeal, and forbade the making of any claims of superiority for any prophet of God over another.[26] This early attitude and the change that was taking place is further illustrated by the following anecdote: A well-known companion saw a group of *ahl al-dhimmah* standing in the hot Damascus sun as punishment for not paying fully their land tax. He went to the governor and protested. "I bear witness that I heard the Apostle of God say, 'God the Exalted will torment on the Day of Resurrection those who torment men in this world.'"[27]

It is easy for a people in authority to abuse their power and violate their sacred trust. Thus, in order to safeguard the sanctity of this divine trust, its violation was declared to be a heinous sin. It is related on the authority of the famous companion Abu Hurayrah that the Prophet declared, "Whoever kills a man who has the *dhimmah* of God and the *dhimma* of His Apostle shall not smell the fragrance of paradise, though it may be sensed from the distance of a seventy-year journey."[28]

This attitude continued to prevail at least during the period of 'Umar, the second caliph. In his final counsel to his people he charged his successor "with the *dhimmah* of God and the *dhimmah* of His Apostle (i.e., Jews and Christians), that he fulfill their covenant, that he fight behind them (i.e., in their defense) and that they be not burdened beyond their capacity."[29] It is significant to observe that Jews and Christians in this tradition are referred to as "the *dhimmah* of God" and not as *ahl al-dhimmah*. In what appears to be a later version related by Ibn Hanbal, this injunction is put in more practical terms: "I charge you to do well toward the people of your *dhimmah*, for they are the source of sustenance for your children and the covenant of your Prophet."[30] This may be compared with a later designation of Jews and Christians in a tradition that shows both the older and more positive attitude as well as the change it underwent: Two of the companions were sitting in Qadisiyyah when a funeral passed by. They rose in reverence for the dead but were told: "it is one of the people of the earth. . . ." There was hence no need to show such deference. One of the two men replied that a funeral of a Jew once passed by the Prophet and he rose. When told that it was only the funeral of a Jew, he answered: "Is it not a soul?"[31]

It is clear that the attitude toward *ahl al-dhimmah* had to be reevaluated from time to time by the standard of the *sunnah* of the Prophet and his first companions. People had to be reminded of their original pledge under Islam to protect others and show kindness toward them. We are told that the pious caliph 'Umar II, Ibn 'Abd al-'Aziz, wished to follow the example of his namesake in the treatment of people of other faiths. Thus, he "established a bond of *dhimmah* with peoples of other religions. . . ."[32] Here we see that the covenant (*dhimmah*) of Muslims with those of other faiths had to be renewed in accordance with the norms established by the Prophet and his immediate successors.

In the Qur'an a distinction is made between the *mushrikūn* of Makkah and the people of the Book (*ahl al-kitāb*). This distinction was retained in early hadith tradition as well. Thus, in a section in Bukhari (the authoritative collection of hadith) dealing with marriage regulations between Muslims or new converts to Islam and non-Muslims a distinction is made between a *mushrik* (man or woman) and a *nasrānī* (Christian man or woman). It is interesting to observe that the former is referred to as *ḥarbī*, one with whom a state of war exists.[33] As pre-Islamic religion soon disappeared from Arabia, the term *mushrikūn* was applied to Christians. It gradually became synonymous with the word *Christian* and has largely replaced the more positive designation of *ahl al-kitāb*.

The Shi'i attitude toward *ahl al-dhimmah* is ambivalent at best. It deserves special attention for several reasons. First, Shi'i hadith collections are relatively late; hence, they may reflect the general attitude that prevailed at the time. Second, the Shi'i attitude changed from a more or less positive one in traditions attributed to the early imams to an extreme attitude in later traditions. It must also be added that the Shi'i attitude was that of an oppressed and embittered community and therefore reflected a particular psychology.

This ambivalence is well expressed in a curious and puzzling bit of double advice that Ali is said to have given to a man whom he appointed as an officer in Qadisiyyah. In public he counseled the man as follows: "Guard well your *kharaj* (land tax), that you do not overlook one *dirham* (a coin of little value) of it." He then asked the man to see him privately before he left. In private he told him: "that which you have heard from me before was only a ruse. Do not ever beat a Muslim, Jew, or Christian on account of one *dirham* of land tax, or sell a beast of burden because of a *dirham* in arrears. This is because we are commanded to take what they voluntarily give."[34]

A tradition attributed to the fourth imam, Zayn al-'Abidin, enjoins that a Muslim consider the elders of the Muslim community as his father, their old women as his mother, their youth as his brothers, and their children as his/her own. It continues: "as for the *dhimmah* (i.e., *ahl al-dhimmah*) you should accept from them only that which God has accepted from them. Do not wrong them so long as they are faithful to God's covenant."[35] This irenic and wise counsel may be contrasted with a tradition attributed to the sixth imam, al-Sadiq, in explanation of the Prophetic hadith "There is no child but that he is born with the *fiṭrah* (i.e., in a state of pure faith); thereafter his parents turn him into a Jew, a Christian, or a Magian." The sixth imam comments, "the Apostle of God gave (protection) and accepted the poll tax (*jizyah*) from those people on the condition that they would not turn their children into Jews or Christians. As for the descendants of *ahl al-dhimmah*, today they have no *dhimmah* (covenant)."[36] This being the case, a Muslim should not have any dealings with a man of *ahl al-dhimmah* nor should he show any amity toward him.[37] The Qur'anic verses allowing intermarriage between Muslims and the people of the Book, or in any way encouraging social intercourse between members of the two communities, were either declared abrogated by other verses or interpreted in ways that would give the exact opposite sense from that intended by the text.[38]

A complicating factor in assessing the Shi'i attitude toward other communities, including other Muslims, is the principle of *taqiyyah* (dissimulation). The great scholar al-Tusi, the *shaykh* of the Shi'i community, uses the principle of *taqiyyah* to harmonize contradictory traditions. Those hadiths that agree with the actual text of the Qur'an and general Muslim views he dismisses as being only concessions to prevailing sentiment, "the view of al-'*āmmah* (the general community)."[39]

It must be added that in other ways Shi'ism has shown an unusual catholicity toward Judaism and Christianity, dictated by the universal principle of the imamate. The mother of the twelfth imam was herself a Byzantine Christian; through her an important spiritual link is established between Christianity and Islam. It must be concluded that the harsh attitude of the Shi'i community in its formative period probably does not represent the imam's thought on the matter but the frustration of an oppressed minority. It may also reflect the general situation in the fourth century of the *hijrah* (tenth-eleventh century C.E.), during which Shi'i hadith tradition was largely codified.

In modern everyday speech, the word *dhimmah* has become synonymous with honor, decency, and truthfulness. One who is without *dhimmah* is not a true human being; s/he is one who refuses to live within the *dhimmah* that God decreed for humankind. Such a person refuses the divine covenant of servanthood. As we have seen, the human *dhimmah* stands beneath the divine *dhimmah,* which must not be violated. This is the meaning of the injunction of the Prophet to the armies of the Muslim community who were told not to presume themselves able to fulfill the *dhimmah* of God, and hence not to invoke it in applying the imperfect standards of human justice. That the human *dhimmah* must always be judged by the divine, primordial *dhimmah* and challenged by its demand of justice and decency is beyond doubt. In a sense, therefore, the people of *dhimmah* embodied this challenge, as may be inferred from the statement attributed to 'Umar, the second caliph. Yet as the term became reified into a technical legal concept, it lost its dimension of transcendence. Consequently, the people of *dhimmah* lost their challenge as it became a legal and not a divine charge. The question of how well or badly the Muslims treated their Jewish and Christian subjects as *ahl al-dhimmah* is, to say the least, a complex one, which, in any case, must be answered from within the historical realities of all three communities.

# Notes

1. Abu Nasr Isma'il bin Hammad al-Jawhari, *Taj al-lughah wa-sihah al-'arabiyyah*, transmitted by Shaykh Abu Muhammad Isma'il bin Muhammad bin 'Abdus al-Nisaburi; ed. Nasr al-Hurini (Cairo: Bulaq Press, A.H. 1365), 2:287.

2. Abu al-Fadl Jamal al-Din Muhammad ibn Markram ibn Manzur al-Ifriqi al-Misri, *Lisan al-'arab* (Beirut: Dar Sadir, 1375/1965), 12:221.

3. Muhibb al-Din Abu al-Fayd al-Sayyid Muhammad Murtada al-Husayni al-Wasiti al-Zabidi al-Hanafi, *Taj al-'arus min Jawahir al-qamus*, 1st ed. (Cairo: al-Matba'ah al-Khayriyyah, A.H. 1306), 8:301.

4. Ibn Manzur al-Ifriqi al-Misri, *Lisan al-'arab*, 12:221.

5. Ibid.

6. Al-Zabidi al-Hanafi, *Taj al-'arus min Jawahir al-qamus*, 8:301.

7. Ibid.

8. For the general context of these verses, see Abu 'Isa bin Muhammad bin 'Isa bin Sawrah al-Tirmidhi, *Sunan al-Tirmidhi*, 1st ed., ed. 'Izzat 'Ubayd al-Da"as (Hums: Matabi' al-Fajr al-Hadithah, 1387/1967), 8:245.

9. Ibid.

10. These are the four sacred months, during which war is prohibited.

11. Ibid.

12. Ibid.

13. Ibid. See also Q. 9:3, 5, and esp. 11.

14. Tirmidhi, *Sunan al-Tirmidhi*, 8:245.

15. Abu 'Abdullah Muhammad bin Yazid ibn Majah, *al-Sunan* (Cairo: Ihya al-Kutub al-'Arabiyyah, 1372/ 1952), 6:480. See also the Prophet's prayer for travel in Tirmidhi, *Sunan al-Tirmidhi*, 9:134; and Ahmad Ibn Hanbal, *al-Musnad*, 1st ed. (Beirut: Dar Sadir, 1389/ 1969), 2:401.

16. Ibn Hanbal, *al-Musnad*, 1:44.

17. Abu al-Husayn Muslim Ibn al-Hajjaj b. Muslim al-Qushayri al-Nisaburi, *al-Sahih*, ed. Shaykh Muhammad al-Zihani et al. (Cairo: Mustafa al-Babi al-Halabi and Sons, A.H 1377), 1:250. For other hadiths on the same theme, see also Muhammad bin Isma'il al-Bukhari, *al-Sahih*, 1st ed. (Cairo: al-Matba'ah al-Bahiyya al-Misriyyah, 1343 A.H), 1:54-55; Tirmidhi, *Sunan al-Tirmidhi*, 6:332; and Muhammad bin 'Ali bin al-Husayn bin Musa ibn Babawayh al-Qummi, *Man la yahduruh-u al-faqih* (Najaf: Dar al-Kutub al-Islamiyyah, 1376/1957), 2:367.

18. Ibn Hanbal, *al-Musnad*, 2:33.

19. Abu Ja'far bin Muhammad bin Ya'qub bin Ishaq al-Kulayni al-Razi, *al-Usul min al-Kafi*, ed. 'Ali Akbar al-Ghifari (Teheran: Maktabat al-Saduq, A.H. 1381), 2:448. See also Ibn Babawayh al-Qummi, *Man la yahduruh-u al-faqih*, 1:332.

20. Tirmidhi, *Sunan al-Tirmidhi*, 5:338.

21. al-Bukhari, *al-Sahih*, 2:25.

22. Referring to the people of the Book, who were sometimes called simply *dhimmat Allah*. See below; and Ibn Manzur al-Ifriqi al-Misri, *Lisan al-'arab*, 12:221.

23. Ibn Hanbal, *al-Musnad*, 1:86.

24. al-Kulayni al-Razi, *al-Usul min al-Kafi*, 5:31.

25. Tirmidhi, *Sunan al-Tirmidhi*, 5:306; al-Bukhari, *al-Sahih*, 1:210; and 2:127-28. See also Abu 'Abd al-Rahman bin Shu'ayb al-Nasa'i, *al-Sunan*, 1st ed. (Cairo: Mustafa al-Babi al-Halabi and Sons, 1383/1964), 8:18-22. Al-Nasa'i significantly substitutes the term *mu'minūn* (believers) for *muslimūn*. See also al-Kulayni al-Razi, *al-Usul min al-Kafi*, 1:403-4 and 542 for a different reading and interpretation.

26. al-Bukhari, *al-Sahih*, 2:154.

27. Ibn Hanbal, *al-Musnad*, 3:403.

28. Ibn Majah, *al-Sunan*, 2:896. This tradition appears in all six canonical collections as well as in most others.

29. al-Bukhari, *al-Sahih*, 1:160.

30. Ibn Hanbal, *al-Musnad*, 1:51.

31. al-Bukhari, *al-Sahih*, 1:151.

32. Abu Dawud Sulayman bin al-Ash'ath al-Sijistani al-Azdi, *al-Sunan,* 1st ed., ed. 'Izzat 'Ubayd al-Da"as and Adil al-Sayyid (Hums, Syria: Muhammad 'Ali al-Sayyid, 1392/1972), 3:364.

33. Al-Bukhari, *al-Sahih*, 3:170.

34. Ibn Babawayh al-Qummi, *Man la yahduruh-u al-faqih*, 2:13.

35. Ibid., 2:381.

36. Ibid., 2:27. See the following hadith, also related on the authority of Zirarah, an important disciple of the fifth and sixth imams.

37. See al-Kulayni al-Razi, *al-Usul min al-Kafi*, 5:286; and Ibn Babawayh al-Qummi, *Man la yahduruh-u al-faqih*, 3:145.

38. See al-Kulayni al-Razi, *al-Usul min al-Kafi*, 5:11 and 351; and 6:240.

39. See Abu Ja'far Muhammad Ibn al-Hasan al-Tusi, *al-Istibsar fi ma ukhtulifa fih min al-akhbar,* 2nd ed., ed. al-Sayyid Hasan al-Musawi al-Khurasani (Najaf: Dar al-Kutub al-Islamiyyah, 1375/1956), 1:179ff., for good examples.

# PART III

## Christological Issues

### Muslim Perspectives

# 10

# The Miracle of Jesus

## Muslim Reflections on the Divine Word

The human spirit in all its richness, its faith and hope, its love and creativity, is mirrored and indeed celebrated in the life of Jesus, who is "high honored in this and the next world" (Q. 3:45).[1] He was born in a lowly and lonely spot of God's earth, far from the power centers of this world and its empires.[2] Yet his miraculous birth was celebrated in heaven, announced by angels, and made the focus of human history. As we, Muslims and Christians, reflect on the life of Jesus and its meaning for our faith and history, we can now more than ever before strive together to hear the voice of God challenging us through our scriptures to a greater understanding of God's will for human creation.

Some of what I say in these reflections will be controversial, at least to Muslim readers. I am motivated, however, not by controversy for its own sake but by two Qur'anic challenges. The first calls us all, the people of the Book, to come together to a common resolve that we worship God alone. The challenge is for us to achieve a consensus of faith and to remind ourselves, our nations, and our societies that our loyalty must be to God alone and not to any human-made institutions: "Say, 'O people of the Book, come to common terms as between us and you: that we worship none but God; that we associate no partners with him; that we erect not for ourselves Lords and patrons other than God'" (Q. 3:64).[3]

The second Qur'anic challenge is that of the infinity and openness of God's Word, which transcends human comprehension and yet demands that it be interiorized and understood anew by the people of faith in every age. The Qur'an declares: "Were all the trees of the earth pens and the ocean [were ink] supplemented by yet seven oceans like it, the words of God would not be exhausted" (Q. 31:27).

Before reflecting on the miracle of Jesus in our two faith traditions, clarification of the meaning of the word for "miracle" in the Qur'an and the

Previously published in *Christology in Dialogue,* ed. Robert Berkey and Sarah A. Edwards (Cleveland: Pilgrim Press, 1993), 221-28. Copyright © 1993 by The Pilgrim Press. All rights reserved. Reprinted by permission.

111

Qur'anic view of miracles may be helpful. "Miracle" in the Qur'an is *āyah*, that is, a divine sign. A miracle may therefore be a universal divine sign in creation, such as the day and night and the creation of heaven and earth, the winds that carry rain clouds by means of which God revives the earth, after its death, and the seas that carry ships laden with goods for the benefit of humankind (Q. 2:164).[4] Another more inclusive meaning of the word *āyah*, or sign, is the Word of God itself. It is either the Word revealed to humankind with a challenge that it be accepted and lived by, or the creative word of command (*amr*). This is the great miracle of creation and revelation.

Early in Muslim history, the concept of miracle took on important theological and political significance. Then the burden of proof of God's election of some faithful servants to be favored with the gift of prophethood or nearness to God fell not only on God, where it ought to be, but on human logic and rationality. Thus, Muslims took it upon themselves to explain God's purposes. A miracle came to mean not a sign of God's infinite mercy and power but an act or occurrence that violates the norms of the natural order and of which none but God and God's prophets are capable.

I argue that the Qur'anic concept of miracle is far closer to the spirit of Islam as an attitude of absolute surrender to God, than that which was evolved later by Muslim theologians. The Qur'an makes frequent reference to miracles. But a miracle must have a purpose. Never in the Qur'an do we see a miracle simply as a show of power, even spiritual power; rather a miracle must speak to the situation of the people. When, for example, Abraham confronted a tyrannical king who thought of himself as God, Abraham manifested God's will and power by being thrown into a fire that God made "coolness and peace" for him (Q. 21:69). The purpose of the miracle was to show that God has power over nature as well as over human folly and arrogance.

The miracles ascribed to Moses in the Qur'an have a similar purpose and message. There again, a ruler of an admittedly great nation and of an equally great civilization saw himself as God. The miracles of Moses were designed to show that God is Lord. Thus, neither the magic nor the great civilization of Egypt would count for much before God. Indeed, the Qur'an states clearly that Moses was not sent expressly to free the children of Israel from Egypt, but primarily to call an arrogant king, pharaoh, and his people to God.[5] This, moreover, was the mission of all the prophets of God according to the Qur'an.

Jesus lived at a time when science began to grow into a systematized discipline. He lived after the rise of Greek medicine and the development of scientific thinking through Greek philosophy, culminating in Plato, Aristotle, and their successors. He, furthermore, lived among a people who were struggling to formulate a universal eschatological worldview. Some, taking the early books of their scriptures literally, denied the hereafter and the resurrection. Hence, the miracles of Jesus were miracles having to do with life—its fullness, meaning, and purpose.

Jesus is himself a divine sign, one to be celebrated with joy, marvel, and faith. In the Qur'an as in the Gospel, the angels bring to Mary the glad tidings of a great miracle—the unique birth of a unique child, the "Word of God," the "Son of the Most High" (Q. 3:45; Luke 1:32-33).

Both the Gospel of Luke and the Qur'an begin their account of Jesus' nativity with a genealogical narrative followed by a glorious annunciation to Mary of a miraculous child with a unique mission. In the Gospel of Luke, the angel says to her: "The Holy Spirit will come upon you, and the power of the Most High will overshadow you; therefore the child to be born will be called holy, the Son of God" (1:35). I will return to the significance of the epithet "Son of God" later.

In the Qur'anic narrative, the angel who appeared to Mary was sent to her by God. He was the angel of revelation. The same angel who brought the Word of God, the Qur'an, to Muhammad brought the Word of God, Jesus Christ, to Mary: "I am the messenger of your Lord," he said, "come to bestow upon you a pure child" (Q. 19:19).

We cannot fully appreciate the meaning of Jesus' birth without studying it in the context of the sanctified life of his mother. Mary was, according to the Qur'an, purified and chosen by God for God's special favor: "Remember when the angels said, 'O Mary, God has surely chosen you and purified you; He has chosen you above the women of humankind'" (Q. 3:42).[6] Only as an unblemished virgin could she serve as a receptacle of the divine Word. The parallel of Mary's sanctity and election with Muhammad's status as the recipient of the Word of God in Muslim piety deserves further study.

The Qur'an first came to Muhammad not in the humdrum of Makkah and Madinah but in the cave of Mount Hira, where the prophet was in seclusion, preparing his mind and soul for the awesome task of receiving and transmitting the Word of God to the world.[7] It was in the same solitude, in the "easterly place," where Mary secluded herself from her people, that the angel encountered her in a good, one might say handsome, human form (Q. 19:16-17). According to tradition, the angel Gabriel often appeared to Muhammad as a handsome man.[8] As the Prophet in the cave of Hira was bewildered, so was Mary. She was afraid. But the angel reassured her. The language in both the Gospel and Qur'an is one not of pure narrative but of celebration. Surah 19, which recounts the birth of Jesus, has been one of the most popular and beloved surahs of the Qur'an.

The miracle of life that is Jesus unfolds further as a life-giving and sanctifying divine force. When Mary conceived him, the Qur'an relates, she withdrew from her people. Was it only from a sense of embarrassment, bewilderment, or shame that she shunned human society? Might it also have been from a sense of gratitude for God's special favor that she wished for solitude to try to fathom the great mystery that enveloped her? The beautiful hymn of divine magnification (Luke 1:46-55) that Mary proclaimed in answer to the angel's annunciation expresses exultation and gratitude to God.

There in the place of her seclusion, according to commentators, the labors of childbirth brought her to a dried-up stump of a palm tree, which God revived to bear fruit; commentators tell us that fruit was the best food for women suffering the pangs of childbirth.[9] As Mary struggled alone with her emotions and the travails of childbirth, a voice from beneath her called out, consoling and encouraging her. This voice is said by commentators to have been that of Jesus. He comforted his mother, saying, "Do not grieve, for your Lord has made a brook pleasantly to run beneath you. Shake the palm tree, and it will drop ripe fruit down to you. Eat and drink and be consoled."[10]

The miracles that the Qur'an attributes to Jesus during his ministry are miracles of life and healing. Some are paralleled in nonbiblical traditions contemporary with the Gospel records of Jesus' birth and infancy. Among these is the miracle of fashioning birds of clay and breathing life into them by God's permission. In the infancy Gospels this miracle is given as one of the child Jesus trying to impress his playmates.[11] In the Qur'an it is intended to show God's power as the creator through the agency of the divine Word, Jesus. The Qur'an credits Jesus alone among the prophets with raising the dead, giving sight to those born blind (as the Arabic word *akmah* indicates), and healing the lepers and the sick (Q. 3:49; 5:113).

I do not advocate that we accept the theology of one tradition and reject that of the other. Rather, I wish to understand the meaning for our life of faith of the Qur'an's insistence that it confirms the scriptures that came before it, the Torah and the Gospel. This claim is based on the transcendent and timeless unity of the Word of God, as all scriptures come from one source: God.

"God brings you glad tidings of a word from Him whose name is Jesus Christ," the angels said to Mary (Q. 3:45). It is worth noting that the word *kalimah* is a feminine noun. The Qur'an is here speaking not of a name but of an actual being, of the Word of God manifested in human life and history. Is all this merely metaphorical or even metaphysical? Or is there not a mystery far greater than we have been able to fathom for the last fourteen hundred years?

The verses describing Jesus in the Qur'an are not without mystery. They continue to challenge both Muslims and Christians to understand, however imperfectly, God's will for us as people of faith. They challenge us to affirm, or at least not to lose sight of, the humanity of Christ. "I am the worshipful servant of God. He gave me the Book, and made me a prophet." In fact, was not Christ's humanity and his servantship one of the greatest challenges to the church? The humanity of Christ was one of the original doctrines of the christology of the church. It was frequently invoked against Gnostic, docetic, and other heresies that threatened the integrity of the Christian faith. This doctrine, moreover, has continued to be the focus of the christological debate, not only within the church but also between the church and the Muslim community. Muslims often remind Christians of the words of Jesus in the Fourth

Gospel: "Go to my brethren and say to them, I am ascending to my Father and your Father, to my God and your God" (John 20:17).

Who, then, is Jesus, the miracle of life, of love, and of healing? He is the Word of God and the servant of God and the messenger of God. He is the savior of us all, for what is salvation but healing? A savior is not simply one who dies for the sins of others but also one who heals the sickness of the human soul; one who infuses life into dead spirits by his own life and spirit. The original meaning of salvation is "to be healed," "to be made wholesome," "to be truly restored to life." This, according to the Qur'an, was the mission of Jesus.

Jesus' close proximity or nearness (*qurb*) to God is affirmed in the Qur'anic insistence that Jesus did not die but was taken up to God and remains with God (Q. 3:54; 4:157).[12] Hence, Jesus, who came to humanity as the Word of God to heal and to save, to carry the process of divine revelation in human history further—to make things easy, to make things that were unlawful lawful (Q. 3:50), subsists with God, awaiting a cosmic mission of healing and salvation. According to Islamic tradition, Jesus will come again and exercise his power of healing. He will forever destroy falsehood, as embodied in the Dajjal, the great falsifier, the anti-Christ. Then will God reign forever.

To return to the Qur'anic objection to calling Jesus the "Son of God": the Qur'an criticizes Christians who attribute an offspring (*walad*) to God. Only once, to my knowledge, does the Qur'an use the word *ibn* (son), and there it uses it to chastise both the Jews and Christians—the Jews for saying "'Uzayr is the Son of God," and the Christians for saying "Jesus is the Son of God."[13] *Ibn* has several meanings and connotations. A youth whom the Prophet brought up, Zayd bin Harithah, was called "the son, *ibn*, of the Messenger of God." The word *son* is generally used to express a relationship of love or care and not necessarily a physical or blood relationship.

Christians would certainly agree with Muslims that Jesus is not an offspring by generation, *walad*, of God, but that he is our brother and the older son in the family of God of which we are all members. In this human family are individuals and progenies chosen by God for a special mission.

The Qur'an presents us with the great challenge of seeing Jesus in this wider context of humanity's relationship with God. It states: "God chose Adam, Noah, the House of Abraham, and the House of Imran above all beings. They are of one progeny, following one another" (Q. 3:33-34). Jesus and his mother, as special members of this blessed progeny, symbolize the unity of the human family around the prophetic model. If all prophets are one family, then are we, their followers, not members of this family that God has favored and blessed?

If we celebrate with joy God's miracle in Jesus Christ, the Word of God, the words of the angels, "Peace on earth, and goodwill toward humankind," have a special meaning and relevance to our troubled world today. The miracle of Jesus, like the miracle of the Qur'an, is not a once-only event but an everlasting source of blessing, guidance, and salvation.

# Notes

1. In this verse Jesus is described as *wajīh*, meaning "high-honored," "notable," and, in this context, "being in the forefront among the peoples of this world and the denizens of the world to come." He is also one of the *muqarrabīn,* meaning "brought near both in intimacy and proximity to God."

2. While the Gospels stress the poor and humble circumstances of Jesus' birth, the Qur'an emphasizes Mary's loneliness and total dependence on God's succor. The nativity story in both scriptures, however, is one of celebration of a unique event of God's intervention in human history. If read carefully, the Qur'anic and Gospel accounts may be seen to complete and complement, rather than oppose or contradict, each other. See Matt 1:18-2:11; Luke 1:26-2:20; and Q. 19:16-34.

3. This is one of several verses in the Qur'an where God directly enjoins the Prophet as well as the Muslim community to deal with the people of the Book on the basis of unity of faith in the One God and in the revealed books; see Q. 3:113-15 and esp. Q. 29:46.

4. God's omnipotence and wisdom are frequently recurring themes in the Qur'an.

5. See, for example, Q. 79:15-26.

6. For the significance of Mary's election, see my commentary on this verse in *The Qur'an and Its Interpreters* (Albany: State University of New York Press, 1992), 2:122ff.

7. In two of the earliest surahs of the Qur'an, the Prophet is commanded to "recite," that is, publicly proclaim, and "warn" (see Q. 96:1-5; 74:1-2). For the intensity of the experience of the encounter with the angel Gabriel, see Muhammad ibn 'Abdallah Khatib al-Tibrizi, *Mishkat al-Masabih,* translation with explanatory notes by James Robson (Lahore: Shaikh Muhammad Ashraf, 1975), 1252-53.

8. The angel Gabriel is said to have appeared at times to the Prophet in the guise of Dahya al-Kalbi, the most handsome young man of Makkah.

9. For example, see Ismai'il ibn 'Umar ibn Kathir's comments in *Tafsir al-Qur'an* (Beirut: Dar al-Andalus, 1977), 4:449-51.

10. Ibid; see also Q. 19:24-26.

11. See the *Gospel of the Infancy of Jesus Christ* 15:1-6, in *The Lost Books of the Bible and the Forgotten Books of Eden* (New York: Meridian Books, 1974), 52-53.

12. For a detailed discussion of Muslim views of the death and ascension of Jesus to heaven, see "Towards an Islamic Christology II: The Death of Jesus, Reality or Delusion," chap. 13 in the present volume.

13. For a study of the terms *ibn* and *walad,* see the essay "Jesus the Son of God: A Study of the Terms *Ibn* and *Walad* in the Qur'an and *Tafsīr* Tradition," chap. 11 in the present volume.

# 11

# Jesus the Son of God

## A Study of the Terms *Ibn* and *Walad* in the Qur'an and *Tafsīr* Tradition

Jesus Christ, Son of Mary, the Spirit of God and His Word, has provided both a bridge between Christian and Muslim faith and piety and a great theological barrier between the Christian church and the Muslim *ummah*. For Islamic faith, Jesus, like Adam, is a special creation of God, but unlike Adam, he is free from sin. He is a "blessed" and righteous servant of God, "high-honored in this and the next world, and one of those who are nearest to God" (Q. 3:45).

For Muslim piety, Jesus is a model of true Islam, or total submission to God. He lived in God's presence, free from all attachments to this world and its vain pleasures. He is a source of hope and solace for the poor and oppressed, and a stern reproach for the rich and greedy oppressors. For the Sufis, the "friends of God," he is an example of true piety and trust in God, and through his gracious miracles he embodies for all faithful Muslims God's gift of life and healing.

This Jesus of faith and piety, the man who "went about doing good" (Acts 10:38), feeding the hungry, healing the sick in heart and body, and restoring dead brothers and sons to their bereft mothers and sisters (Luke 7:12-17; John 11:1-44), is the bridge linking the two communities in their quest for faith and holiness. Jesus the "Christ," the "eternal logos," the "Word made flesh," the "only-begotten Son of God" and second person of the Trinity, has been the barrier separating the two communities and long obscuring the meaning and significance of Jesus, the "Word of God," to Muslim faith and theology. Doctrines such as the divinity of Jesus and the Trinity have been the subject of sharp debate between Muslims and Christians, a debate that transcends the plane of human history and that will finally be decided between God and Jesus on the Day of Resurrection (Q. 5:116-19).[1]

Previously published in *Christian-Muslim Encounters*, ed. Yvonne Y. Haddad and Wadi Z. Haddad (Gainesville: University Press of Florida, 1995), 65-81. Reprinted with permission of the University Press of Florida.

I am convinced that this theological barrier is not an impenetrable wall dividing our two communities. Rather, in the spirit of the divine challenge for Muslims to seek harmony and concord with the people of the Book through dialogue and "fair exhortation,"[2] this wall could be transformed into a beacon of light guiding us all to God and the good. This essay is a humble attempt to make a small breach in this wall.

The present essay will examine the theological significance of two important Qur'anic terms: *ibn* and *walad,* both signifying a filial relationship. *Ibn* ("son"), which is used only once in the Qur'an in relation to Jesus, may be understood metaphorically to mean "son" through a relationship of love or adoption. The term *walad,* on the other hand, means "offspring," and thus primarily signifies physical generation and sonship. It is this latter term that is often used by Qur'an commentators to argue against the Christian concept of Christ's divine sonship. The Qur'an, however, as we shall see when we study these two terms closely, does not use the term *walad* specifically to refer to Jesus. That is to say, the Qur'an nowhere accuses Christians of calling Jesus the *walad* offspring of God.

The purpose of this endeavor is twofold. It is first to stress the need to take our scriptures seriously in what they say and not to use one as a criterion to judge the truth and authenticity of the other. This does not mean that we should treat our scriptures as isolated sacred texts completely divorced from their own time and history. God speaks to us in our historical and existential human condition, and to attempt to hear His voice in isolation from human history is to miss the essential message of His Word.

The second purpose is to reflect on the situation to which the Qur'an seems to have addressed its critique of the Christian doctrine of the divine sonship of Christ. If, as we may well discover, the historical situation that the Qur'an presupposed in its primary address no longer obtains, then the challenge for us all is to go beyond that situation and seek other and deeper meanings of God's Word to our own existential situation.

To do full justice to this subject is far beyond the scope of this study. I shall therefore limit myself to the Qur'an and some of its representative commentators. Before turning to these, however, a few remarks on God's role in the conception of Christ as presented in the Gospel and the Qur'an are necessary. Before examining more closely the language that grew out of the Qur'anic account for Muslims, we shall as well take a brief look at a classical Arab-Christian theologian for a concrete example of the language Arab Christians used to translate the Gospel account. It is hardly necessary to argue that neither the Qur'an nor early Muslim traditionists were aware of the theological doctrines of the church fathers and church councils in their debate with Christians, but they were aware of Christian piety, liturgy, and worship.

The language of the two scriptures is highly symbolic and allegorical. The Gospel of Luke, which is our primary source on the nativity of Christ, analogous to the Qur'an, describes the conception of Jesus thus: "'The spirit of the Lord shall come upon you,' the angel said to Mary, 'and the power of the Highest shall overshadow you: therefore also that holy thing (*hagion*)³ which shall be born of you shall be called the Son of God'" (Luke 1:35).⁴

The language of this verse is clearly circumspect. It implies no sexual union or divine generation of any kind. Furthermore, while Luke's description agrees both in form and spirit with the Qur'anic idea of the conception of Christ, the language of the Qur'an is far more graphic and open to interpretation.

The Qur'an makes two references to God's direct intervention in the conception of Jesus. The first is put in the context of the miraculous birth of John (Yahya) to Zechariah and his wife, who was long past the age of childbearing. God says, "We answered his prayers and granted him Yahya and restored for him his spouse. They were surely diligent in the performance of good deeds and called upon Us in fervent hope and fear. They truly lived in awe of Us." Then of Mary He continues, "And she who guarded well [lit., fortified] her chastity [lit., generative organ], and thus We breathed into her of our spirit, and We made her and her son a sign [or miracle, *āyah*] for all beings" (Q. 21:90-91). Here God includes Mary among the prophets and the righteous, those who call upon Him in fervent devotion and righteous fear.

In the second instance the Qur'an speaks of Mary as a righteous woman who lived in strict chastity and obedience to God: "And Mary daughter of 'Imran who guarded well her generative organ (*farjahā*), and thus We breathed into it of our spirit" (Q. 66:12). This bold and graphic statement appears to have shocked traditionists and commentators, so that most of them either tried to cover it up with different and farfetched significations or glossed over it without comment.

Al-Tabari, and following him a number of other commentators, interprets the verse as follows: "God means to say that she guarded her bosom with her garment from Gabriel, peace be upon him." Al-Tabari then explains: "Any opening or hole in a chemise is called *farj*. Likewise, any crack or opening in a wall is a *farj*." Thus al-Tabari interprets the verse to read: "'and thus We breathed' into the opening of her chemise which is her *farj* 'of our spirit' of Gabriel who is the 'spirit.'"⁵

Ibn Kathir interprets the phrase "guarded well her generative organ" to mean "safeguarded and protected it. Guarding well *iḥsān* signifies chastity and high birth." He comments on the phrase "and thus We breathed into it of our spirit" thus: "that is, through the angel Gabriel. This is because God sent him to her, and he took for her the form of a man of good stature (Q. 19:17). God commanded him to breathe into the breast of her chemise. His breath went down and penetrated her generative organ, and thus caused her to conceive Jesus."⁶ Ibn Kathir, like al-Tabari and all other commentators and traditionists, insists on God's transcendence; hence, it is inconceivable that He would directly intervene in such intimate human affairs. Ibn Kathir also tries to harmonize later Muslim tradition with the Qur'an without resorting to a radical interpretation of the sacred text.

The Malikite jurist al-Qurtubi observes that early *tafsīr* authorities held that by *farj* God here meant "bosom," *jayb*. This, he argues, is because "God said, 'and thus We breathed,' for Gabriel breathed into her bosom not into her generative organ." Al-Qurtubi further reports that the reading (*qirā'ah*) of Ubayy is, "and thus We breathed into her bosom of our spirit." Al-Qurtubi concludes: "It is possible that the verse means that Mary safe-guarded her generative organ, and that God breathed the spirit into her bosom." He interprets the phrase "and We breathed" to mean: "We sent Gabriel and he breathed into her bosom of our spirit, that is one of our spirit, which is the spirit of Jesus."[7]

Abu Ja'far al-Tusi, the jurist doctor of the Shi'i community, as well as his well-known disciple al-Tabarsi, read the words "We breathed into it" literally. Al-Tusi says, "It has also been held that Gabriel breathed into Mary's generative organ, then God created Christ in it." Al-Tabarsi reports yet another interpretation which he obviously does not accept: "It is said that the verse means, 'We created Jesus in her womb and breathed into him the spirit, and thus he became a living person.'" This reading rests on the fact that both *farj* and *masīḥ* (Christ) are masculine. Hence, the word *fīhi* (into him/it) could refer to either. This interpretation is perhaps meant to dissociate both God and Gabriel from the impurities of human generation.[8]

It is noteworthy that contemporary commentators have nothing significant to say about this verse. The late Iranian religious scholar Muhammad Husayn Tabataba'i simply observes that Mary is the only woman mentioned by name in the Qur'an, and that she is mentioned in over thirty surahs. The assertion, moreover, that Mary "guarded well her chastity" is meant to exalt her above the calumnies of the Jews. This is also the view of Sayyid Qutb.[9]

The language of both the Gospel and the Qur'an is poetic and celebrative, not scholastic, or even, strictly speaking, theological. In both, this marvelous event is announced as glad tidings to Mary and linked to prophetic history as a miracle of special significance. In both scriptures, it is God and not an angel who manifests His power directly in the conception and birth of Christ.[10] God breathed His spirit into Adam directly,[11] and this gave him priority over the rest of His creation. God also declares, using the "We" of majesty, that He directly breathed of His spirit into Mary, thus making her and her child a divine sign for humankind, and making the miraculous child a manifestation of divine mercy.

From the foregoing it must be concluded that the Gospel and the Qur'an are speaking about the same Christ, the "son of Mary," child of God, His Word and spirit. Furthermore, neither the Qur'an nor the Gospel nativity story implies that God had a female consort in Mary, or a physically engendered son in Christ. But have the two theological and scholastic traditions been speaking about the same Jesus?

The question posed here has concerned Muslim and Christian thinkers from the beginning and has thus produced a vast and fascinating body of literature on both sides. We shall choose one Christian savant, theologian, and cleric as representative of the classical Syro-Arabic Christian tradition. In his interesting work *Maymar fi wujud al-khaliq wa al-din al-qawim*,[12] Theodore Abu Qurrah attempts, in the spirit of reasonable and "fair dialogue," to prove God's attributes of engendering (*wilādah*) and procession or emanation (*inbithāq*). His argument rests on an analogy not between Adam and Christ but rather between Adam and God. It is an unusual argument.

Abu Qurrah begins by asserting that God's existence can be known, or inferred, from Adam's existence. He then contrasts the nature of the two: Adam is finite but God is infinite in life, power, knowledge, and all the other attributes that He shares with Adam. Adam, moreover, was a creature of God; hence all his attributes or excellences over other earthly creatures were bestowed upon him by the creator.

The most excellent attributes that Adam possessed are *wilādah*, engendering; *inbithāq*, emanation or procession; and *ri'āsah*, headship. He thus argues: "We saw that Adam did engender [another being] who was like him in nature, and proceeded, or issued forth, *inbathaqa* from him [another being]. We also saw that he was head over the one [Eve] who was like him. Since, therefore, Adam was a progenitor, and was head of her who issued forth from him, it follows that He who made him progenitor and head must necessarily Himself be father and head over him who is like Him." Abu Qurrah again contrasts the essential differences between Adam and God. Adam engendered his son through a female by means of sexual union and brought him up. Eve came out of Adam's body, and thus diminished him. Moreover, Adam preceded both his spouse and sons, and his headship over them is not one of like nature and desires between him and them.

Abu Qurrah continues:

> On the other hand, God's engendering of His son was from Him, and in like manner was the procession of His Holy Spirit. There was no female, sexual union, conception, or rearing; nor was any priority in time among them. Rather, from eternity they all were together. God's headship, moreover, over those who are of Him presupposes no difference among them. Rather they are like Him in nature, will, eternity and desire (*hawā'*). There is no difference whatsoever among them except one is father and the other begotten, and the third issued forth. The father among them is also the Godhead.

Abu Qurrah further argues that it is by means of the attributes of engendering and headship that Adam was distinguished from the dumb beasts and other lowly creatures. If therefore God does not possess these two excellences, then Adam is more excellent than God. Nor is it rational to suppose that Adam was head over those who were like him, but God is head of all creatures. If neither Adam nor any other human being would accept to be head of swine, beasts, and bedbugs, then how can we describe God as head of such creatures? Nor can it be said that God is only head of angels and humankind because His nature is more different from human nature than is that of the lowliest creatures.

Abu Qurrah concludes: "God, blessed and exalted be He, is without doubt head or chief. He is not, moreover, the head of all creatures, but the head of those who are like Him. He thus begot a son, and a spirit proceeded out of Him. He is therefore like Adam and Adam is like Him in engendering and headship." This mystery, Abu Qurrah asserts, fulfills God's word: "So God created man in His own image, in the image of God he created him" (Gen 1:27 RSV).[13]

It can be clearly seen from the foregoing that Christian theology, and this may be asserted of creed and liturgy as well, has used human language to describe divine activity. It went far beyond the third evangelist in speaking of Jesus as the actual Son of God. Abu Qurrah's language in particular would leave no doubt in the mind of a Muslim reader that Jesus is the Son of God, engendered by Him from eternity. For, while Abu Qurrah uses *ibn* for son, he always uses the verb *walada*, "to engender," or "give birth to," when speaking of God the father and Jesus His Son. In fact, this direct language remains the language of Syro-Arabic liturgy and worship to this day.

As we shall see presently, on the basis of the Gospel and the Qur'an the disagreement between Christians and Muslims is not over the divine sonship of Christ, figuratively speaking, but over his divinity. This is understandable, for christology remains the foundation stone of the church and the greatest challenge to her unity and faith.

As has already been observed, the term *ibn* with reference to Jesus as Son of God occurs only once in the Qur'an. We have also noted that this term has both an actual and metaphorical or figurative connotation. This fact has been recognized by most commentators. Two issues will concern us in this discussion. The first is the source or origin of this concept, in the view of Qur'an commentators, and the second, its significance to Christian faith and history.

The term in question occurs in verse 30 of Surah 9, which is one of the latest surahs of the Qur'an. The verse, furthermore, is part of a crucial passage that regulates the socio-political and religious relations of an already well established Muslim state with the communities of the Book, particularly Jews and Christians. The tone of the entire passage is highly polemical; this is reflected especially in later commentaries, which in turn reflect the political and military tensions between Christendom and the world of Islam. There is as well a broader religious and moral dimension to this debate which is clearly discernible in the verse under discussion as well as the one following it. The two verses read: "The Jews say 'Uzayr [Ezra?] is the Son of God, and the Christians say Christ is the Son of God. That is their saying with their own mouths; they resemble the saying of those who rejected faith before them. God curse them, how they perpetrate falsehood! They took their rabbis and monks as lords instead of God, as well as Christ the son of Mary. Yet they were commanded to worship the One God, there is no god but Him; glorified is He over all that they associate with Him."

With regard to this alleged error, commentators relate the following tale: When Jesus was taken up to heaven[14] his "true followers" lived by the true religion. They fasted during the month of Ramadan and prayed facing the Kaʻbah. In other words, they were Muslims. Then arose many wars between them and the Jews.

Among the Jews lived a brave man called Bulus (Paul) who persecuted the Christians and killed many of them. Paul one day said to his fellow Jews: "If Jesus had the truth, then we have been rejecters of faith, and our abode shall be the Fire. We shall surely be losers if they enter Paradise and we be consigned to Hell. I will therefore deceive them and lead them astray."

To this end he hamstrung his horse and threw dust on his head, pretending remorse. He claimed that a voice addressed him from heaven, saying, "No repentance will be accepted from you unless you become a Christian."

Christians believed him and took him to their church where he remained for a whole year, never leaving the sanctuary. There he learned the Gospel, and all Christians believed him. He then went to Jerusalem and left a man called Nastur (Nestorius) as his representative over his followers.

Paul then began to teach his followers that Jesus, God, and Mary were three gods. He sent emissaries to Byzantine territories to teach the people that Jesus had a divine and a human nature.[15] He also taught that Jesus was not a man or a body; rather, he was God. He propagated this doctrine through another of his emissaries, called Jacob. He chose a third representative, a man called Malka, and taught him that Jesus was, is, and will forever be God.

Paul told each of the three men, "You are my representative; go forth, therefore, and call others to your belief." Having thus completed his scheme, Paul then told his followers, "I saw Jesus in a dream, and he was pleased with me. I shall therefore sacrifice myself for his pleasure." He thus went to the altar and slew himself.[16]

The purpose of this tale is to explain the origin of the three major Eastern Christian sects: the Jacobites, Nestorians, and Melkites, as the names of the three men indicate. The assertion that early Christians were actually *muslims* reflects, first, the high place that Christ occupies in Muslim faith and piety and, second, the persistent belief that Christianity is essentially a true religion. For this reason many commentators, even recent ones, insist that not all Christians say that "Jesus is the Son of God."[17] It must also be remarked that a number of commentators seriously doubted the truth of this tale. Thus al-Alusi, for instance, remarks that this is "a strange [tale] which can hardly be true."[18]

It was earlier observed that this debate has a political dimension which is clearly reflected, according to changing circumstances, in different commentaries. Ibn Kathir, who lived in Syria in the aftermath of the Crusades, puts the verse squarely in its polemical framework. He says, "This is an incitement by God of the people of faith to fight with the rejecters of faith of the Jews and Christians for uttering such evil words and for their calumny against God."[19]

Fakhr al-Din al-Razi, a noted theologian/philosopher and Qur'an commentator who lived closer in time if not in place to the Crusades, goes even further in his invective against this concept and those who subscribe to it:

> There is no meaning to association (*shirk*) except if a person takes another object of worship beside God. If we were to ponder well this point, we would surely see that the rejection of faith of idol-worshippers is less serious than that of the Christians. This is because an idol-worshipper does not say that his idol is the creator or god of the universe. Rather he regards it as an object which would bring him nearer to God. Christians, on the other hand, profess divine incarnation (*ḥulūl*) and union (*ittiḥād*), and this is the worst kind of rejection of faith.

Thus, Razi continues:

> God favored the Christians with the acceptance of the *jizyah* or poll tax from them because they allied themselves outwardly to Moses and Jesus and claimed to live by the Torah and the Gospel. Hence, because of these two great apostles and their two great scriptures, and because the forefathers of these Jews and Christians followed the true religion, God decreed acceptance of the *jizyah* from them. Otherwise, there is in reality no difference between them and the associators.[20]

In spite of his harsh denunciations, Razi was a rationalist theologian who did not accept easy answers and thus generally gave his opponents a fair hearing. He asks rhetorically how all Christians could come to believe in this concept when neither Jesus nor his disciples could have uttered such a falsehood? Razi was not convinced by the Paul story. He rather says, "I believe it to be nearer to the truth to say that perhaps the word *son* (*ibn*) occurs in the Gospel to denote high honor, as the word *khalīl* (intimate friend of God) denotes high honor.[21] Then, because of the enmity between Jews and Christians, the latter wishing to exalt Jesus by claiming a similar falsehood to that of the Jews, they exaggerated their claim and interpreted the word *son* literally to signify actual sonship. This idea was accepted by the foolish among them, and thus did this false belief spread among the followers of Jesus; but God knows best the truth of the matter."[22]

The view that the word *ibn* is used metaphorically in the Gospel to express a relationship of love and intimacy is shared by most commentators. Some have even concluded that Christians misunderstood their own scriptures. Al-Alusi, who was a well-known Sufi and thus more prone to look for mystical inner meanings in all scriptures, says, "It seems to me that Christians found the term *ibn* used for Jesus and the word *father* for God in their Gospel, and erred in their understanding of what is actually intended by these terms, hence they said what they said."[23]

Muhammad Mahmud Hijazi, a more recent commentator, blames this grave misunderstanding on foreign ideas and philosophies. "Ancient Christians used this term to express love and high honor. But when pagan philosophy spread among them, they began to apply it literally claiming that Christ was the Son of God, or that he was God. They are, moreover, all agreed that a unitarian *muwaḥḥid* is not a Christian."[24]

The well-known reformer Muhammad Rashid Rida in his *Tafsir al-Manar* devotes much space to this verse. He uses as one of his primary sources the Arabic encyclopedia of the famous Christian thinker Butrus al-Bustani. Rida agrees that ancient Christians used the word *ibn* to denote one who is beloved or especially favored by God. They were, however, influenced in their error by Indian beliefs concerning Krishna, and other such heathen ideas. Under the influence of Greek philosophy, church councils, three hundred years after Christ, and his disciples formulated the doctrine of the Trinity. Rida insists, however, that there are many Christian thinkers who have rationally rejected the Trinity, and thus are true unitarians. He may have heard of the Unitarians or perhaps other nineteenth-century Western critics of the Trinity.[25] Sayyid Qutb, who was one of the sharpest critics of the West and of Western civilization, also argued that the idea of divine sonship has no basis in either original Judaism or Christianity.[26]

Whereas the term *ibn* occurs only once in the Qur'an and clearly refers to Jesus, the term *walad* occurs fifteen times, although only two refer to Jesus directly. Moreover, the majority of these verses are referred by most commentators to the Makkan Arabs who claimed that their goddesses Allat, al-'Uzza, and Manat were daughters of God and that angels were also His daughters.[27] Thus Jews and Christians are often added by implication.

It must be further observed that in most cases the Qur'an uses the verb *ittakhadha* (took unto Himself) rather than *begot*, or any other verb suggesting actual generation. The verb *ittakhadha*, if anything, implies a relationship of adoption. Yet most commentators argue strenuously against attributing an offspring to God, this being allegedly an erroneous Jewish and Christian belief.

As we review some of these verses it will become clear that both the Qur'an and its exegetes are actually arguing for God's absolute Oneness and transcendence. Moreover, since the three most immediately known communities—the Jews, Christians, and non-Muslim Arabs—were accused of this form of associationism, then by analogy the concepts of God's transcendence, *tanzīh*, and Oneness, *tawḥīd*, came to distinguish Muslims from all other communities. While this conclusion is nowhere stated, it seems to be behind the arguments of both the Qur'an and its interpreters.

Finally, before we turn to the verses themselves, it must be observed that the language in most of them is the same. They contrast God's transcendence, omnipotence, origination of all things, and sovereignty over all His creation with human non–self-sufficiency, and hence the need for offspring.[28]

The Qur'an declares, "They say that God took unto Himself an offspring; glorified be He! Rather to Him belongs whatever is in the heavens and the earth; all are subservient to Him. The originator of the heavens and the earth, when He decrees a thing He says to it 'be,' and it is" (Q. 2:116-17). These two verses are typical of the Qur'anic arguments against the error of ascribing offspring to God. It may be that the emphasis on God's power to create *ex nihilo* through His word of command, *kun*, led commentators to include the Christians in their critique. Otherwise, the two verses just cited constitute an independent statement following a reference to the direction of prayer. Some commentators relate the two verses to verse 114, which reproaches those who bar people from entering God's places of worship and seek to destroy such places. This surely cannot at that time have referred to the Christians.

Al-Tabari nevertheless simply states, "These are the Christians who claim that Jesus is the Son of God." He then advances the following argument against this claim: "How could Jesus be an offspring (*walad*) of God when he must be in one of these places, either in the heavens or in the earth. Yet to God belongs all that is in them." Then addressing the Christians directly, al-Tabari continues, "If Christ was a son as you claim, he would not have been like all the other subservient creatures of God which are in the heavens and the earth in manifesting God's handiwork in him."[29]

Ibn Kathir regards the two verses under discussion as a refutation of the claims of Christians, Jews, and the "associators" among the Arabs. Ibn Kathir generally repeats al-Tabari's argument but in somewhat stronger language. He argues, "An offspring is engendered by two compatible beings. But God, exalted and blessed be He, has no equal or partner in His greatness and majesty. Since, moreover, He has no consort, how could He have an offspring?"

Ibn Kathir concludes his critique with two hadith traditions stressing the gravity of such an error. The first is a *hadīth qudsī* (prophetic hadith or report of divine utterances) in which God says, "The children of Adam have uttered lies about me, yet they had no reason. They have insulted me and they had no right to do so. As for their lies, it is their saying that I cannot bring them back to life as they were before. Their insult is their saying that I have an offspring. Far glorified am I above having a consort or offspring." The second is a prophetic hadith in which the Prophet is reported to have said, "No one is more patient with the hurt He hears from human beings than God. They ascribe to Him offspring, and yet He provides for them and grants them sound health."[30]

A good example of the argument from transcendence is stated by the Andalusian jurist and Qur'an commentator al-Qurtubi. He first argues that the verse applies to all Jews, Christians, and Makkans. He continues, "Far exalted is God above their claim that He took unto Himself an offspring. He is God the Exalted, one in His essence and attributes. He did not engender, so that He would need a female consort, and how could He have an offspring when He has no consort? He created all things, nor was He begotten so that other things preceded Him, high exalted is His majesty above what the wrongdoers and deniers say."

Al-Qurtubi then advances the usual argument, namely, that "God is the creator of all that exists in His creation, and if all is His creation, then none of His creatures can be His offspring: *waladiyyah* (engendering), implies sameness of species and temporality; while *qidam* (eternality), implies unicity (*wiḥdāniyyah*) and permanence. God, glorified be He, is eternal (*azalī*), the One and 'Unique (*aḥad*), eternal refuge (*ṣamad*), who does not beget, nor was he begotten. Nor is there anyone equal unto Him' (Q. 112). Furthermore, sonship clearly contradicts slavehood (*riqq*) and subservience. How can an offspring be a slave? This is impossible, and anything which implies an impossibility is itself impossible."[31]

Few among the commentators here studied see a difference between *ittikhādh*, "taking something unto oneself," and actual engendering. The Turko-Persian Sufi Isma'il Haqqi discusses this important difference thus: "Taking something unto oneself can mean either making or creating such a thing, in which case [the maker is one and unique], or it means making, that is to say, God made one of His creatures a child and claimed that he is His child, not that He engendered him in reality. As it is impossible for God to engender in reality, it is likewise impossible for Him to adopt or take unto Himself a child. Thus God elevated Himself above what they say about Him in His saying, 'glorified is He.'"[32]

Abu Ja'far al-Tusi argues in a scholastic fashion that this verse indicates the impossibility of God having a child in any way. This, he argues, is because "if all that is in the heavens and the earth is His possession, then both Jesus and the angels who are brought near to Him are slaves under His dominion. A child must by necessity be of the same genus as his father, but the object of an act is never of the same genus as the subject. Every corporeal being is an object of God's act. There is therefore no one like Him in any way. Exalted be He above the attributes of His creatures."[33]

The great theologian-philosopher Fakhr al-Din al-Razi advances several scholastic arguments against the possibility of God engendering or in any way having offspring. The first is the argument from necessity and contingency. God alone necessarily exists in Himself, and the existence of all else is contingent on Him. Moreover, God alone is eternal and all else is created in time. "It therefore follows that everything other than God is created in time, and hence preceded by nonbeing. This also means that all things came into being through God's creative act and His power of bringing things from nonbeing into being. From this it follows that everything other than God is His slave and possession. It is therefore impossible that anything other than He be His offspring."

Al-Razi's second argument is that of eternity and temporality. "This being which is ascribed to God as His offspring must be eternal. If he is eternal, then it matters not which of the two we regard as father and which as son. If, on the other hand, the child is temporal, then he was created by him who is eternal, and is therefore his slave, and thus cannot be his child."[34]

Al-Alusi sums up most of the arguments so far discussed and others as well in the following brief commentary on the statement "To Him belongs whatever is in the heavens and the earth":

This is a refutation of their claim and an explanation of the things which follow from that erroneous claim, namely: likening [God the eternal] to temporal phenomena of human generation and begetting, and the need of the father for a child who would fulfill his need, as well as the inevitable passing away of all composite beings which are dependent on one another. For the wisdom in human generation is to preserve the human species through the continuous succession of its examples. This is because no one individual can last forever. All this is impossible for God, for He is eternal and everlasting, absolutely self-sufficient, most exalted above resembling His creatures.[35]

Sayyid Qutb always sought to relate early Muslim history to present realities. He thus argues that this erroneous belief was held by all three communities, Jews, Christians, and Makkan Arabs, all of which are represented today by international crusadism, Zionism, and communism. The original source of such ideas was Greek philosophy, the Muslim champions of which introduced into Islam ideas alien to it. Islam draws an absolute distinction between the creator and all created things. Yet ideas such as Ibn al-'Arabi's *wahdat al-wujud*, "unity of being," can easily accommodate notions of divine sonship.[36]

We have discussed these two verses at some length because, although they do not refer to Jesus, commentators have used them to advance most of their arguments against the view that God may beget or in any way have a child. There is no need for us in the limited scope of this essay to study each of the remaining occurrences of the term *walad*. Two, however, do call for some attention because they refer directly to the Christian belief in Christ's divine sonship. In the first, God reproaches the Christians for holding such an extreme position in their faith. In the second, Jesus counsels his people not to hold such a view:

O people of the Book, do not exceed the proper bounds in your faith, and speak only the truth about God. Christ Jesus, the son of Mary, was only a messenger of God and His Word which He sent forth to Mary, and a spirit from Him. Accept faith, therefore, in God and His messengers, and do not say three. Desist, and it will be better for you. God is only one God, glory be to Him that He should have an offspring. To Him belongs all that is in the heavens and the earth, and God is a sufficient guardian. (Q. 4:171)

It must be noted that the Qur'an declares the Christian belief in the Trinity to be an extremist religious position. The matter of God having a child is mentioned only in passing as part of this extremism in faith. The verse further asserts that Jesus, Mary's child, is God's Word which He "sent forth," or cast, into Mary, as the word *alqāhā* seems to suggest. Here again, what is God's role in the conception and birth of Christ? Commentators unfortunately have not pondered this question.

Al-Tabari comments briefly on the verse as follows: "God is not as you say, you who claim that God is the third of three. This is because he who has an offspring is not God. Likewise, it is not possible that he who has a consort can be a god worthy of worship. Rather, God to whom belongs true Divinity and worship is one God alone worthy of worship. He has no offspring, progenitor, consort, or partner."[37]

Al-Zamakhshari presents the following brief but interesting exegesis: "Jesus is called 'Word of God' and 'word from Him' because he came into being only through God's word and His command without the intervention of a father or sperm. He is also called 'the spirit of God' and 'a spirit from Him' because he is possessed of a spirit and a body, and because he came into being not through a part of one possessed of a spirit, such as a sperm which proceeds from a living father. Rather, Jesus was a special original creation, originated (*ukhturi'a ikhtirā'an*) by God in His power."

Al-Zamakhshari interprets the word *alqāhā*, "sent it forth," to mean "He caused it to reach Mary and be in her." Following a brief analysis of the doctrine of the Trinity, al-Zamakhshari concludes, "God called Jesus son of Mary to affirm that he is her child, and not the Son of God."[38]

After repeating the usual argument that Jesus cannot be God's offspring because he is part of His creation, al-Qurtubi adds with rhetorical sarcasm, "If it is possible for God to have one offspring, then why not many? Thus anyone in whom is wrought a divine miracle would be a child of God."[39]

For al-Tabarsi, God's Oneness is the word of truth which Christians are enjoined to "speak about God." He says, "Say that He, exalted be his majesty, is One without associate, consort or offspring. Say not of Jesus that he is the Son of God, or that he is like Him because this is not 'speaking the truth.'"[40]

While earlier commentators saw a special creation in Jesus as "the Word of God," more recent ones have consistently attempted to play down any distinction between Jesus and the rest of humankind. For example, al-Tabarsi reports that some say the meaning of the phrase "and His Word which He sent forth to Mary" is "He created it in her womb."[41] The contemporary Egyptian thinker Muhammad Mahmud Hijazi, as a good representative of this modern trend, says, "Every birth of a child has one manifest cause which is the coming together of two people of the opposite sex, and a real cause which is the will of God expressed in His word 'be.' Since in the case of Jesus the first cause does not apply, there is no doubt that he was created through the second cause which is the word 'be' which God conveyed to Mary through the angel Gabriel."

Hijazi further argues that Jesus is not the spirit of God but he was strengthened by a spirit from God. "It is a spirit which God brought into being, and not a part of Him, as Christians have understood it. Otherwise everything would be part of God." The author then blames the church for deviating from original Christianity which was founded on faith in the One and only God.[42]

Muhammad Rashid Rida addresses more directly than any other commentator the question why the term *walad* is used in the Qur'an to critique the Christian belief in the divine sonship of Christ rather than the term *ibn*, which is more commonly used by Christians to express their belief. "The reason for this choice," he argues, "is to show that if they intend actual son, then this son must be a child born through the insemination of his mother by his father, and this cannot be said of God. But if they mean son in the metaphorical rather than the true sense, as the term is used in the books of the Old and New Testaments to refer to Israel, David, the peacemakers and others of the righteous, then it has nothing to do with divinity, nor would Jesus have any special status." Rida then compares Jesus with Adam, Eve, and the angels, all of whom came into being without the process of human generation, and concludes, "They are all God's servants and His creatures."[43]

The last instance I wish to consider in this study is not without difficulty. The relevant passage reads, "This is Jesus, the word of truth concerning whom they are in doubt. It is not for God to take a child unto Himself; glory be to Him, when He decrees a matter He says to it 'be,' and it is. God is surely my Lord and your Lord, so worship Him. This is a straight way" (Q. 19:34-36).

These three verses raise many crucial questions. How are we to understand the statement "This is Jesus, the word of truth"? Is Jesus himself "the word of truth," or is what the Qur'an says about him the word of truth? Does the doubt—and hence conflict and arid debate—that has characterized Muslim and Christian relationship with Christ concern him or the "word of truth"? Finally, is the Prophet Muhammad or Jesus the Christ counseling us all to worship God our Lord?

These and many other questions have not concerned Qur'an commentators. To repeat what they have said in interpretation of this passage is to repeat the same arid and by now all-too-familiar debate.

The Qur'an and the Gospel are both agreed that God is God, the Lord of all His creation. They both affirm that "His will is done" in His universe. Jesus himself insisted that not his will but the will of Him who sent him must be done. What then is the message of the Qur'an in its insistence that God alone is God?

The words with which I began this essay, and with which I will conclude it, enjoin that God alone should be worshipped: "They took their rabbis and monks as lords instead of God," and yet, "they were enjoined to serve God alone" (Q. 9:31). Were the Qur'an to speak to today's Muslims directly, it might add, their *'ulamā'*; their *imāms* ; their politicians; their ideologies; and even "their religion." The message of these verses is not meant for Christians only but for Muslims as well. For Christians, it is to remind them that God alone is God. As for Muslims, it is to remind them that the Truth is God.

# Notes

1. This is a colloquy between Christ and God, and which, according to Qur'an commentators and traditionists, is yet to take place on the Day of Judgment. See Michel Haik, *al-Masih fi al-Islam*, 2d ed. (Beirut: Catholic Press, 1961), 278.

2. Striving for a unity of faith and purpose between the Muslims and the people of the Book is an oft-repeated injunction in the Qur'an. See, for example, Q. 3:64; 29:46; 16:125.

3. I am grateful for the help of my friend and colleague Gerald Sloyan, who gave me a literal translation of this verse.

4. I have followed the punctuation of the King James Version.

5. This interpretation is reported by commentators on the authority of the well-known early traditionist/jurist of Basra Qatada ibn Di'ama al-Sadusi (Muhammad bin Jarir al-Tabari, *Jami' al-bayan 'an ta'wil ay al-Qur'an*, 30 vols. [Beirut Dar al-Fikr, 1398/1978], 28:110).

6. 'Imad al-Din Abi al-Fida' Ibn Kathir, *Tafsir al-Qur'an al-'azim*, 2nd ed., 7 vols. (Beirut: Dar al-Fikr, 1389/1970), 7:65.

7. Abu 'Abd Allah Muhammad bin Ahmad al-Ansari al-Qurtubi, *al-Jami' li-ahkam al-Qur'an*, ed. Ahmad 'Abd al-'Alim al-Burduni, 2nd ed., 20 vols. (Cairo: Dar al-Katib al-Arabi, 1387/1967), 18:203-4.

8. Abu Ja'far Muhammad ibn al-Hasan bin 'Ali ibn al-Hasan al-Tusi, *al-Tibyan fi tafsir al-Qur'an*, ed. Ahmad Qasir al-'Amili, 10 vols. (Beirut: al-A'lami, n.d.), 10:54-55; and Abu 'Ali al-Fadl ibn al-Hasan al-Tabarsi, *Majma' al-bayan fi tafsir al-Qur'an*, 30 vols. (Beirut: Dar Maktabat al-Hayat, 1380/1961), 28:129.

9. See Muhammad Husayn al-Tabataba'i, *al-Mizan fi tafsir al-Qur'an*, 2nd ed., 20 vols. (Beirut: al-A'lami, 1394/1974), 19:345; and Sayyid Qutb, *Fi zilal al-Qur'an*, 7th ed., 8 vols. (Beirut: Dar Ihya' al-Turath al-'Arabi, 1391/1971), 8:174-75.

10. The phrases in Q. 19:21, "it is a thing easy for me. . . . It is a matter already decided" and in the Gospel of Luke 1:35, "The spirit of the Lord shall come upon you and the power of the Highest shall overshadow you," suggest God's direct involvement in and control of the conception, birth, and life of Jesus.

11. See Q. 15:29 and Q. 38:72 where God declares (addressing the angels concerning Adam, his earthly creature) in exactly the same words: "When I shall have shaped him and breathed into him of my spirit, then fall prostrate before him."

12. Theodore Abu Qurrah (d. ca. 825) was a noted Jacobite theologian and bishop of Harran. The work under consideration is vol. 3 of the series *al-Turath al-*

'Arabi al-Masihi (Christian Arab heritage). The work is a pietistic theological argument for the existence and nature of God and the truth of the Christian faith edited by Fr. Ignatius Dik (Vatican City: Institute of Islamic and Arabic Studies, 1982).

13. Ibid., 221-22.

14. For a discussion of Muslim views of Jesus' ascension to heaven, see the article "Towards an Islamic Christology II: The Death of Jesus, Reality or Delusion?," chap. 13 in the present volume.

15. I have thus rendered the vague phrase *wa-wajjaha ilā al-Rūm wa-'allamahum al-lāhūt wa al-nāsūt*.

16. Nizam al-Din al-Hasan ibn Muhammad ibn al-Husayn al-Qummi al-Nisaburi, *Ghara'ib al-Qur'an wa-ragha'ib al-furqan*, ed. Ibrahim 'Atwa 'Awad, 1st ed., 30 vols. (Cairo: al-Babi al-Halabi, 1384/1964), 10:72; and 'Ala' al-Din 'Ali Ibn Muhammad Ibn Ibrahim al-Baghdadi al-Khazin, *Lubab al-ta'wil fi ma'ani al-tanzil*, 4 vols. (Beirut: Dar al-Ma'rifah, n.d.), 2:319.

17. See, for example, Isma'il Haqqi, *Ruh al-bayan*, 10 vols. (Beirut: Dar al-Fikr, n.d.), 3:415; and Muhammad ibn 'Ali ibn Muhammad al-Shawkani, *Fath al-Qadir: al-Jami' bayna fannay al-riwaya wa al-dirayah min 'ilm al-tafsir*, 3rd ed., 5 vols. (Beirut: Dar al-Fikr, 1393/1973), 2:352.

18. Abu al-Fadl Shihab al-Din Mahmud al-Alusi, *Ruh al-ma'ani fi tafsir al-Qur'an al-'azim wa al-sab' al-mathani*, 30 vols. (Beirut: Dar al-Fikr, 1398/1979), 10:82.

19. Ibn Kathir, *Tafsir al-Qur'an al-'azim*, 3:385.

20. Fakhr al-Din al-Razi, *al-Tafsir al-kabir*, 1st ed., 30 vols. (Cairo: al-Matba'at al-Bahiyya al-Misriyya, 1357/1938), 16:33-34.

21. This is applied to Abraham in the Qur'an: "God took Abraham for an intimate friend" (Q. 4:125), which has come to be used by Muslims as part of his name: Ibrahim al-Khalil.

22. al-Razi, *al-Tafsir al-kabir*, 34.

23. al-Alusi, *Ruh al-ma'ani*, 10:82.

24. Muhammad Mahmud Hijazi, *al-Tafsir al-wadih*, 6th ed., 30 vols. (Cairo: Matba'at al-Istiqlal al-Kubra, 1389/1969), 10:45.

25. Muhammad Rashid Rida, *Tafsir al-Manar*, 2d ed., 12 vols. (Beirut: Dar al-Ma'rifah, n.d.), 10:328-29.

26. Qutb, *Fi zilal al-Qur'an*, 8:171

27. See Q. 53:22 and below in this discussion.

28. See in this regard Q. 10:68 where God is called *al-ghanī* (the rich, self-sufficient, or one who has no need of any kind). This verse is referred by most commentators, however, primarily to the Makkan Arabs.

29. al-Tabari, *Jami' al-bayan*, 1:403.

30. Ibn Kathir, *Tafsir*, 1:280-81.

31. al-Qurtubi, *al-Jami' li-ahkam al-Qur'an*, 2:85.

32. Haqqi, *Ruh al-bayan*, 1:213.

33. al-Tusi, *al-Tibyan*, 1:426-27.

34. al-Razi, *al-Tafsir al-kabir*, 4:25-27.

35. al-Alusi, *Ruh al-ma'ani*, 1:136.

36. Qutb, *Fi zilal al-Qur'an*, 1:142-44.

37. al-Tabari, *Jami' al-bayan*, 6:26; see also 24-26.

38. Abu al-Qasim Mahmud ibn 'Umar al-Zamakhshari, *al-Kashshaf 'an haqa'iq*

*al-tanzil wa-'uyun al-aqawil fi wujuh al-ta'wil*, 4 vols. (Beirut: Dar al-Kitab al-'Arabi, n.d.), 1:584.

39. al-Qurtubi, *al-Jami' li-ahkam al-Qur'an*, 6:25.
40. al-Tabarsi, *Majma' al-bayan*, 5:300.
41. Ibid.
42. Hijazi, *al-Tafsir al-wadih*, 6:18-20.
43. Rida, *Tafsir al-Manar*, 6:87.

# 12

# Toward an Islamic Christology I

## An Image of Jesus in Early
## Shi'i Muslim Literature

### Introduction

It is hoped that this essay will be the first of a series of studies presenting the rich and varied images of Christ in Islamic piety. Such an undertaking would, we trust, present a definite view of Christ in Islam that may be considered as yet another, and legitimate, christology, albeit a christology that is outside the Christian tradition.

By christology is meant not a theological formulation analogous to the christologies of the early church, but, rather, an understanding of the role of Christ within the divine plan of human history, of Christ the man, one of the servants of God, but also of Christ, the Word of God, His spirit and exalted friend. These ideas are clearly stated in the Qur'an and thus provide the basic framework of the image of the Christ of Muslim piety. I wish to argue, however, that the Qur'an alone is not a sufficient source for the understanding of Christ in Islam. Hence, it may be more profitable to study the Christ of Islamic piety with the Qur'anic background in mind, but without taking the Qur'anic view as the one and only static view of Christ. Indeed, the Christ of Muslim piety has continued to be a living personality, humble and pious, forever thundering against the wrongs of society, and full of wisdom and the Holy Spirit.

I shall, in the following pages, first present my own approach and indicate the results we hope it will yield. Then I shall discuss briefly the unique case of Shi'i Islam, which presents its own interesting kind of christology. Finally, a brief discussion of the sources will introduce the two texts translated below which constitute the central concern of this study.

Previously published in *The Muslim World* 66, no. 3 (July 1976): 163-88. Reprinted by permission.

## Scope, Method, and Sources

"What think ye of Christ?"[1] This question which the Christian church has addressed to itself more than once, and even to the world, has been put to Muslims in a great variety of formulations throughout Islamic history. To the church it has remained a challenge to the faith and basic social and ethical values operating in the lives of its members. To Muslims, on the other hand, this question has been presented with its Christian answer as the truth against which Islam altogether has been judged and found wanting. That Muslims have thought much about Christ, and that the Qur'an presents at least the basis of an Islamic christology is a fact that has not so far concerned Christians in any profound way.

There is, to be sure, a positive change of attitude among Christians toward other religious traditions, including Islam. This is due, first, to an increased knowledge of the fundamental principles of other religious traditions and the cultures and lives of the men and women living by these principles. Second, the new theological understanding of Christ and of the Christian message has made its impact on Christian society at large. More significant, however, in my view, has been the change in the socio-economic and political structure of the world from colonized peoples and colonizing powers to that of free and independent states and nations. The fruits of these changes may already be discerned in the laudable efforts of such organizations as the World Council of Churches to promote a greater tolerance, if not understanding and appreciation, of the faith and spiritual heritage of other people. This has been achieved through direct dialogue and other means of communication.[2] Moreover, there is a clearly discernible change in the approach of many Western scholars, notably of the younger generation, to the study of Islam. It is a change from the polemical approach which, by "explaining" Islam in Christian terms, remained devoid of any real understanding, to an approach that instead seeks to understand and to appreciate Islam on its own terms. There has not been, however, to our knowledge, a study of the image of Jesus in Islamic sacred or pietistic literature consciously based on this approach.[3]

This final stage in the long history of Muslim-Christian relations is still in its beginnings. When it is fully realized, it will, I hope, lead to true ecumenism, an ecumenism that will accommodate Islam not as a heresy of true Christianity but as an authentic expression of the divine and immutable truth. In this spirit of mutual recognition and appreciation, Islam may have something to teach Christians that would strengthen their own faith in the Truth, the Truth which is greater than the expression of any one religious tradition or the understanding of any single individual or community. In order to realize this ideal, Muslims must likewise rethink their own understanding of the true meaning of Islam as the living up to the primordial covenant between God and all human beings and the divine reaffirmation of this covenant in a variety of expressions to a religiously pluralistic world.

Earlier research on the subject of Jesus in Islam has been comparative and usually judgmental, the yardstick being the New Testament record of the life, teaching, and significance of Jesus, the Christ. Useful as this research may have been for the wealth of information it had uncovered on Christian-Muslim relations, it often harbored old prejudices and fostered new hostilities. At any rate, all the work that can be done on that aspect of Christian-Muslim interaction has been exhausted. It is time for scholars, both Christian and Muslim, to go beyond this cataloging of points of difference and similarity, and drawing of old conclusions.

What I propose as a new approach is to start with the given data and work on them as they are. No matter how different the Qur'anic and later Islamic view of Jesus may be, it is nonetheless the view that Muslims have to struggle with and understand and that Christians must take as a Muslim view and accept as such, at least as the methodological basis for their research and study. It is no longer profitable to take Qur'anic statements about Jesus simply as distortions of, or borrowings from, the Gospels. Rather, they should be accepted as authentically Islamic statements and as expressing an Islamic view.

One such statement that has occupied the attention of Western scholars is the Qur'anic verse asserting the servanthood of Jesus to God. It reads as follows: "The Messiah will never scorn to be a slave unto Allah, nor will the favored angels. Whoso scorneth His service and is proud, all such will He assemble unto Him" (Q. 4:172).[4] In itself, this short statement is precise and unequivocal. It seeks to balance the status of Jesus as the Word of God and His spirit (Q. 4:171), and one who is highly honored (*wajīh*) in this world and the next (Q. 3:40) with his humanity thus declaring him to be, in spite of this high status, a servant (*'abd*) of God without considering this in any way to be a denigration of his lofty rank. Had scholars[5] not taken this to be a distortion of the Pauline hymn addressed to the Philippians (Phil 2:7) and gone to great length first to prove this hypothesis, and then to reject the verse altogether, they would have seen the profound significance of this Qur'anic verse for Muslims, in its proper context.[6] In fact, the parallel of the Qur'anic text with the famous hymn just mentioned is at best superficial and far-fetched. This view of Christ, with all its implications for the Qur'an and later Islamic piety, has been the basis for the total image of Christ in Islamic literature throughout the centuries. It is the view that characterizes the first of the two traditions presented in this study.

Jesus in Islam, as in the Gospels, is the messenger of forgiveness and love. Thus, the injunction of turning the other cheek, which Christ preached in the Gospel, is, in the first tradition we shall discuss below, put in the form of a command to Christ by God. Similarly, the poverty, austerity, and detachment from this world of the Christ of the Gospels receives, in Islamic piety, a far greater emphasis. Hence, for the Sufis, Jesus becomes the example of piety, renunciation of worldly pleasures, and poverty, the one after whom they sought to pattern their lives and conduct.

The reason why nothing has been said in this essay about the central role of Christ as the savior is that Islam has no concept of sin and redemption analogous to the fundamental Christian view of fallen humanity and its need of redemption. Yet Christ, as were all the messengers of God before and after him, was a savior in that he, by his message, helped to save humanity from error and to guide its steps further on the path to God, to whom we all belong and to whom we all shall return (Q. 2:156).

Moreover, Shi'i Islam, from the devotional literature of which the selections below are taken, has developed its own quasi-soteriological christology in the doctrine and role of the imams, the spiritual heads of the community.[7] It is noteworthy that 'Ali, the first imam of Shi'i Muslims, is often compared to Jesus.[8] In a highly interesting statement attributed to 'Ali, he had the following to say about himself and his descendants, the remaining eleven imams. Beginning by declaring that God is One and Unique in His unity, he goes on: "He uttered a Word which became a light. From that light He . . . created me and my progeny. Then God uttered another Word which became a spirit, and that spirit He made to dwell in the light. The light, moreover, He made to dwell in our bodies. Thus, we are the Spirit of God and His Words. . . ."[9]

The imams, for the Shi'i community, are the true mediators between God and man. They were with God from the beginning as His first act of creation. With them, the primordial history of all creation began, and through them it will be finally judged and consummated. They are a source of salvation on the Day of Reckoning for those who accept their status as the friends (*awliyā'*)[10] of God, and true heirs of the prophets. Conversely, the imams will be the stern judges of those who have rejected their lofty status. The twelfth and last of the imams will return at the end of time as the awaited messiah (*Mahdī*) to establish divine rule over the earth.[11] Jesus, son of Mary, will also descend from heaven to aid him in this task, thus playing some part in the imam's final act of redemption and judgment.[12]

Shi'i Islam sees human history, and the divine role in it, as having two related, yet distinct, cycles. Outwardly, humanity is guided by the large number of prophets sent by God for this purpose. Five of these occupy a special place in the prophetic history and are known as the "Prophets of Power" (*ulū al-'azm*).[13] Jesus, the Christ, son of Mary, is one of them. Inwardly, to every prophet God appointed twelve vicegerents, or executors (*awṣiyā'*), who are interested in his esoteric knowledge. The mission of all the vicegerents of the prophets before Muhammad was a preparatory one for that of his vicegerents, the imams, who are regarded as the seal of *walāyah*, as Muhammad is the seal of prophethood. The *walī* is another term for the vicegerent (*waṣī*), and the cycle of *walāyah* is, in a sense, the esoteric, or inward, side of the cycle of prophethood. The work of salvation belongs to this inward cycle and is thus reserved for the imams who, in this and many other respects, collectively play a role similar to that of Christ.

Jesus, however, does occupy a unique place in Shi'i piety. In addition to being the recipient of the Gospel and other direct divine communication, he is the wise ascetic endowed with esoteric gnosis. He, therefore, belongs both to esoteric and exoteric cycles of history. A third important aspect of Christ's prophetic personality is that of the humble slave of God whose life hangs, so to speak, between fear and hope. He is threatened and counseled, and reprimanded and exalted by God. This, according to Islamic piety, is one of the ways God deals with His friends (*awliyā'*) who, though near to God, are, nonetheless, His creatures and humble servants.[14] All three aspects (prophet, ascetic sage, and mystic) of the personality of the Christ of piety are present in the two texts translated below. Jesus, the mystic, friend, and servant of God of our first text, is also the recipient of special divine communication, which is delivered, or in some cases echoed, in the second text. In the second text, Jesus is essentially the teacher, whose sayings are an interesting mixture of the Synoptic Gospels and sayings attributed to him by Islamic piety. Both texts were, and still are, used as homiletic materials by popular preachers in services commemorating the sufferings of the imams. Thus, they are supposed to convey a message of suffering, wisdom, piety, and divine mercy.

Our first selection is reported by al-Kulayni, the famous Shi'i hadith traditionist, on the authority of the imams, without specifying the exact authority. It is included in the eighth and last volume of his hadith collection entitled *al-Kafi* (the sufficient in hadith). The last volume is subtitled *al-Rawda min al-Kafi* (the garden of al-kafi). This volume consists of a large number of miscellaneous traditions dealing with a variety of subjects. The author died in A.H. 328 or 329/939 C.E., thus making his work one of the earliest large hadith collections in Islam.

The tradition with which I am concerned in this section is simply entitled "That with Which God Has Instructed or Counseled 'Isa." It belongs to the genre of hadith collections known as *ḥadīth qudsī*, or divine utterance.[15] Throughout this colloquy, God is the speaker, and Jesus asks one brief question toward the end. The same text is reported in a shorter version under the title "Munajat 'Isa," or "The Colloquy [of God] with Jesus," by Ibn Shu'ba al-Harrani, the traditionist, who died toward the close of the fourth or the beginning of the fifth Islamic century. His work is entitled *Tuhaf al-'uqul 'an al al-rasul* (the delight of minds in the words of the descendants of the Apostle [Muhammad]). It contains sermons and sayings of the imams chronologically arranged. Both traditions, offered below in translation, are placed at the end of the book, without any explanation or mention of the authority on which they were reported. The second tradition, containing sermons and sayings of Jesus, is not reported in Kulayni's work; thus, my translation will be based only on the text of Ibn Shu'ba. As far as the first tradition is concerned, my translation will be based on the same text, which is clearer and more concise than that of al-Kulayni. Where the latter version adds something substantial to the version I have chosen, the relevant passages will be preceded by the letter "K" in parentheses, indicating the title of the book *al-Kafi*, and inserted into the text where they most suitably fit.

I have endeavored to keep as close as possible to the language and idiom of the text. This has meant some unavoidable repetition of both phrases and ideas. In a number of cases, certain redundant phrases or short sentences have been omitted. I trust, however, that the texts will fulfill the main purpose of this essay: to present an image of Jesus in early Shi'i Muslim literature. In general, this image is typical of the traditional Islamic view of Jesus, which is largely based on the Qur'anic presentation of the life, personality, and mission of Jesus, the Christ, son of Mary. It will be seen, however, that the author or authors of the traditions here presented must have had some knowledge of the Gospel sayings and possibly even of other popular Christian sources.

## Texts in Translation

### "A Colloquy of God, Exalted Be He, with Jesus, Son of Mary, May God's Prayers Be upon Them Both."[16]

The following selection presents Jesus as the humble and penitent servant of God, listening to God's wise council and harsh reproach. He is also the exalted messenger commissioned by God to transmit His revelation to humankind, but especially to be a teacher to the children of Israel. Although the Qur'anic condemnation of the divinity of Jesus and the doctrine of the Trinity is not mentioned, the text insists on God's unity, absolute power, and justice. Jesus is warned and threatened with hell fire if he associates other things with God. Thus, by implication, the text is meant to counter the Christian claims of the divinity of Jesus and the doctrine of the Trinity.

O Jesus, I am your Lord and the Lord of your fathers. My name is One (*wāḥid*) and I am the unique One (*aḥad*). Alone have I created everything. I made all things and all things shall return to me.

O Jesus, you are the Christ by my command (*amr*)[17] and you create out of clay by my leave [Q. 5:110],[18] and you revive the dead by your words.[19] Be, therefore, desirous of me and fear me, for you shall find no refuge from me except in me.

O Jesus, I counsel you as one who is compassionate and merciful toward you. You have truly obtained the favor of nearness (*walāyah*)[20] from me for your earnest seeking of my pleasure. Blessed, therefore, are you, as a child and a grown-up man, wherever you may be.[21] I bear witness that you are my servant (*'abd*), the son of my handmaid. Draw nigh unto me through supererogatory prayers (*nawāfil*)[22] and put your trust in me, for I suffice you. Take no one else as your master lest I abandon you.

O Jesus, be patient with affliction and accept that which is decreed. Seek my pleasure through obedience, for I wish to be obeyed and never disobeyed.

O Jesus, make constant mention of me with your tongue and keep my love in your heart. Be vigilant during the hours of sleep and be mindful of my gracious wisdom. Be diligent and fearful and mortify your heart with awe of me. Be watchful in the nights, striving after my pleasure, and mortify your body with thirst in the days for the day of your need [the Day of Judgment].

O Jesus, you shall be accountable to me, be merciful, therefore, toward the weak as I am merciful toward you, and do not oppress the orphan [Q. 93:9]. Weep for yourself in private and rise up on your feet at the appointed times of prayer.[23] Let me hear the penitent cries of your soul; for good are all my dealings with you.

(K) O Jesus, judge among my servants according to my counsels and deal with them in accordance with my justice. For to you have I sent down that in which there is healing from the disease of Satan.[24]

O Jesus, many a nation have I caused to perish in punishment for sins from which I have protected you. Show compassion toward the weak and turn your weary gaze to heaven and call upon me, for I am near [Q. 2:186; 50:16]. Remember me with a contrite heart and make me your sole concern; for as you make supplication to me, thus will I answer you.

O Jesus, do not be deceived by the sight of a stiff-necked and disobedient man who eats my sustenance and worships another. Yet, when, in times of hardship, he calls upon me, I answer him. But then he returns to his old ways in times of ease. Is it against me that he sets himself ? Or can he withstand my wrath? By myself have I sworn that I will seize him with my wrath from which he shall find neither salvation nor refuge. Where can he flee from my heaven and my earth ?

O Jesus, say to the wrongdoers of the children of Israel, "Do not call upon me while you trample the poor under your feet [that is, through usury] and keep idols in your homes. I shall surely answer them who call upon me, but I shall make my answer a curse upon them until they shall be scattered in the earth."

O Jesus, there is no good in a pleasure that does not last, or an ephemeral life that shall come to an end. O son of Mary, if your eye were to see what I have prepared for my faithful friends, your heart would melt and your soul expire in longing for it. For there is no abode like the abode of the hereafter. In it dwell the pure ones of my servants, visited by angels nearest the throne. They shall be safe from the fearful portents on the Day of Resurrection. It is an abode whose bliss shall never cease. O son of Mary, strive for it with those that strive, for it is the wish of all that desire the good, beautiful to behold. Blessed are you, O son of Mary, if you were to be counted among those that strive for it, to be with your fathers, Adam and Abraham, in gardens of bliss everlasting, wishing for nothing else instead. Thus will I favor those that fear me.

O Jesus, flee to me with those that run away from a fire of great flames, a fire of chains and torment into which neither air enters nor out of which black smoke escapes.[25] It is as though made of layers of darkness, layers that resemble the black night. Happy is he that shall be spared its torments. It is the abode of the proud, stiff-necked and wrongdoers and every haughty and arrogant man. Miserable is that abode, and miserable are those that shall dwell therein. I therefore warn you for your good, so be mindful of me.

O Jesus, wherever you may be, fix your gaze upon me. Bear witness from me that I created you, and that you are my servant. I formed you and sent you down to earth. Restrain your soul from deadly lusts and abandon any desire that may separate you from me. Know that you are before me of high station, the station of a faithful messenger . . . for I created you by my word [Q. 3:69], and Mary gave birth to you by my command. To her did I send my faithful spirit, Gabriel, one of my angels. Thus were you able to rise up and walk on the earth. All this we determined in my foreknowledge.

O Jesus, consider Zechariah as a father to you, for he was the guardian of your mother. Whenever he entered her prayer-chamber he found sustenance with her [Q. 3:37]. John the Baptist [Yahya] is like you; I granted him to his mother in her old age, when she had no strength left in her [Q. 19:8-9]. I wished to manifest my sovereign power to her, as I showed my power to you.

O Jesus, if I am wroth with you, the pleasure of no one else will avail you anything. And if I am pleased with you, no wrath will do you harm. Remember me in your heart and mention me in public that I may remember you in an assembly better than all human assemblies. Call upon me with the invocation of a man about to drown who has no one to help him. Do not swear by me falsely, lest my throne shake with wrath.

(K) O Jesus, let your speech be one in private and in public. Restrain your heart and tongue from unlawful things and your eye from evil sights. Often would a glance sow in a man's heart lust, and thus lead him into perdition.[26]

O Jesus, how would it be if I were to bring forth for you [and the children of Israel] a book speaking the truth and you would witness to the truth thereof, but keep what you know as a secret and seek to hide your own actions?[27]

O Jesus, say to the wrongdoers of the children of Israel, "You have washed your faces but kept your hearts unclean. So lightly do you take my injunctions and dare to stand against me. You anoint yourselves for the people of this world outwardly, but inwardly you are like filthy corpses and dead men in my sight."[28] Tell them, O Jesus, "Clip your fingernails from unlawful gain, and deafen your ears to words of vanity. Turn to me with your hearts for I desire not your outward appearances."

O Jesus, rejoice with a good deed, for it is pleasing to me, and weep for a bad deed, for it is evil. That which you do not wish others to do to you, do not do to others; and if someone strikes your right cheek, turn your left cheek to him.[29] Strive to draw nigh unto me through love, and give no heed to the foolish. Be humble among men of good deeds and associate yourself with them and be a witness over them. . . .

O Jesus, say to the wrongdoers of the children of Israel, "Wisdom weeps in awe of me, but you laugh and engage in vanities. Do you think that you have received my acquittal, or have you any security against my torments, or do you dare to withstand my punishment? By myself have I sworn. I shall make you an example to those that shall come after you."

At this point the subject changes, and God tells Jesus of the coming of Muhammad and describes him and his community in exalted words of praise. God, moreover, commands Jesus to announce this great Arabian apostle to the children of Israel and enjoin them to believe in his message, and follow him. The entire passage echoes the Qur'anic verse in which Jesus is said to announce the coming of Muhammad in the words, "I am the messenger of Allah unto you . . . bringing good tidings of a messenger who cometh after me, whose name is the Praised One (Ahmad)" (Q. 61:6). The colloquy then continues:

O Jesus, all that draws you near to me have I declared to you, and all that separates you from me have I warned you against. This world is sweet, and I have placed you in it as my vicegerent. Avoid that in it against which I have cautioned you, and take from it that which I have allowed you. Look upon your own deeds as would a transgressing servant (*'abd*), and do not judge the deeds of others. Renounce this world and desire it not, lest you be harmed.

O Jesus, be wise and prudent and look around you in the earth, and see how was the end of the wrongdoers [Q. 10:39 (verse 40 in Pickthall) and 16:36].

O Jesus, all my counsels to you are truthful, and I am the Truth manifest and clear. For, verily I say to you, if you would disobey me after I have informed you, you shall find neither friend nor supporter against me. Discipline your heart with fear of me, and look not up to him who is above you but to him who is below you. Know that the beginning of every sin and transgression is love of this world, so do not love it, for I love it not.

O Jesus, purify your heart before me, and make much mention of me in secluded places. Know that my pleasure is that you lift your eyes toward me. In this be vigilant and alive, not dead.

O Jesus, do not associate anything with me and beware my wrath. Do not be deceived by health or rejoice in this world for it is like a passing shadow. . . . (K) that which remains of it is no better than that which has passed away. Be diligent, therefore, in the performance of good deeds. Be with the truth wherever it may be, even if you were to be cut to pieces and cast into the fires. Do not deny, or disbelieve in me, after you have known; do not be counted among the foolish.[30]

O Jesus, pour out for me the tears of your eyes and humble your heart before me. Turn to me in times of hardship, for I alone succor those that are in deep sorrows, and hearken to those who are in difficult straits; for I am the most merciful.

### *"Sayings of Jesus, Peace Be upon Him, from the Gospel and Other Sources."*[31]

This text consists of a great variety of sayings and little sermonettes attributed to Jesus. A large number of them are either taken directly from the Gospels or written with the Gospels as the model. In this text, Jesus is clearly the stern teacher, counseling and condemning, and preaching the message of love so familiar to the Gospel readers. The Sermon on the Mount appears to

be the primary model for all the sayings. The woes of the Gospels pro-
nounced upon the Pharisees and scribes are here multiplied many times over.
To document every saying or group of sayings with Gospel references would
make for tedious reading; only where an obvious need for it exists has a footnote been added.

Of his sayings:

> Blessed are the merciful, for they shall find mercy on the Day of Res-
> urrection. Blessed are they who make peace among people, for they
> shall be brought near to God on the Day of Resurrection. Blessed are
> the pure of heart, for they shall visit God on the Day of Resurrec-
> tion. Blessed are the humble in this world, for they shall inherit the
> thrones of dominion on the Day of Resurrection. Blessed are the
> poor, for theirs shall be the kingdom of heaven. Blessed are the sor-
> rowful, for they shall rejoice. Blessed are those who hunger and
> thirst in meekness, for their thirst shall be quenched. Blessed are they
> that do good, for they shall be called the pure elect of God.[32] Blessed
> are those who are robbed of all their possessions for the sake of
> purity, for theirs shall be the kingdom of heaven. Blessed are you if
> you are envied and maligned, and is said of you every unsavory and
> false word. Rejoice, and be of good cheer, for your reward shall be
> increased in heaven.[33]

He said further:

> O you slaves of evil, you blame other men for their doubt, but do
> not reproach yourselves for certainty.[34] You slaves of this world, you
> wish to be said of you that which is not true of you, and you wish
> to be pointed at with fingers. You slaves of this world, you shave
> your heads and bow them down, and you shorten your garments,
> yet you do not remove malice from your hearts. You slaves of this
> world, you are like well-constructed graves, pleasant to behold from
> the outside, but inside are full of dead bones and transgressions. You
> slaves of this world, you are like a lamp that gives light to men, but
> burns itself.[35]

> O children of Israel, run to the assemblies of the learned, even if
> crawling on your knees. For God revives the dead hearts with the
> light of wisdom as He revives the dead earth with heavy rain. O chil-
> dren of Israel, little speech is sound judgment; observe, therefore,
> silence. Silence, indeed, is a good duality, for it leads not to grave
> sins. . . . Guard well the gate of knowledge, for its true gate is
> patience. God despises him who laughs without reason, and him
> who walks, but not to a place of good council. God loves the ruler
> who is like a good shepherd who does not neglect his flocks.[36] Be

ashamed before God in secret as you would be ashamed before men in public. Know that a word of wisdom is the desire of a man of faith. Seek it, before it disappears with the death of its transmitters.

O man of knowledge, revere the learned for their learning and oppose them not. Do not revere the foolish because of their foolishness, but do not drive them away; be kind to them and teach them. O man of knowledge, know that every bounty for which you are not thankful is like a sin for which you shall be held accountable. O man of knowledge, know that any disobedience for which you do not repent is like a punishment for which you shall suffer. . . .

Again he said, peace be upon him, to his companions:

Think you if one of you, while passing by, sees the garment of his brother fallen, exposing the nakedness of his body, should he cover his brother's nakedness, or rather, expose it even more? They said No, that he should rather cover it. Jesus answered, Not so, rather he should expose it more. Then they understood that it was a parable he made for them. They therefore asked, How can that be, O Spirit of God? He answered, Even so, you look at your brother's nakedness, but do not try to help him cover it up.[37]

Verily I say to you, I teach you so that you may know; I do not teach you in order that you may admire yourselves. You shall not obtain that which you want except if you renounce that which you desire. Nor will you achieve that for which you hope, except if you are patient with afflictions. Beware vain looks, for they sow lust in the heart. . . . Blessed is he who has his sight in his heart and not his heart in the sight of his eyes. Look not on the faults of others as though you were lords; rather, look at their faults as though you were the servants of men. In truth, men are of two kinds, one afflicted, and the other sound. Be merciful toward him who is afflicted, and thank God for sound health.

O children of Israel, do you feel ashamed before God? You clear your drink of all impurities, but would devour unlawful things, like elephants. Have you not heard what you were commanded in the Torah, "Do good to your kin, and reward them well"? But I say unto you, give to him who withholds from you and be generous toward him who refuses your wishes, and be good to him who treats you badly. Say "Peace" to him who reviles you. Show justice to him who shows enmity toward you. Forgive him who does you wrong, as you wish your wrongdoing to be forgiven. Be mindful of God's forgiveness toward you. Do you not see that His sun shines over the righteous as well as the reprobates among you? He sends his rain likewise over the pious as well as the sinners among you. If you love only them that love you, or be good only toward them who are good toward you, . . . what virtue have you over others? This, even the fools who are without virtue or compassion, do. But if you wish to be beloved of God, and be counted among His elect, do good to them that do you wrong. Forgive them who do you harm, and salute with the salutation of peace those who heed you not. Listen to my words and keep my commandments; guard well my covenant so that you may be truly men of knowledge and understanding.

Verily I say to you, your hearts are where your treasures are. For this reason, men love their wealth and their souls yearn for it. Lay your treasures in heaven where neither moth shall eat them, nor thieves reach them. Verily I say to you, no servant can serve two lords; rather, he would certainly prefer one over the other, even though he may try. Likewise, you cannot love both God and this world. Verily I say to you, the most foolish of men is a wise man who prefers the world over his knowledge, . . . for what would the brilliance of the sun's light benefit a blind man when he cannot see it? Likewise, knowledge would avail nothing a man who does not live by it. Many are the fruit of trees, but not all are good to eat, and many are the wise, but not all of them benefit by their wisdom. Large is the earth, but not all the space thereof is habitable, and many are those who speak much, but not all their words are true. Beware the false wisdom of those who don garments of coarse wool, with heads bowed down to the earth, yet they indulge in every sin.[38] They slyly glance from beneath their eyebrows like wolves, and their words do not concur with their deeds.

Can grapes be gathered from thistles, or figs from colocynths? Likewise are the words of a false man of knowledge, they are to be rejected. Verily I say to you, crops grow in leveled fields, and not on the rocky hillside. Similarly, wisdom dwells in the heart of the humble and not in that of the haughty and arrogant man. Know you not that he who lifts up his head so high that it touches the ceiling would split it, but he who keeps his head down would find refuge under the ceiling? Likewise, he who does not humble himself before God, him will God bring low, and he who humbles himself will be exalted.

It is not always possible to keep honey in a skin, nor can in all hearts wisdom dwell.[39] If the skin is not torn, or rotten, it can be used as a vessel for honey. Likewise, hearts, if they are not torn asunder by lust, made unclean with greed, and separated [from God] through pleasure, they can be a dwelling place of wisdom.

Verily I say to you, if a fire were to start in one house, and that house is not destroyed from its foundations, the fire would spread into many houses.[40] Likewise a wrongdoer, if his hands were not restrained, other wrongdoers would have a leader to emulate. . . . Verily I say to you, if one sees a serpent drawing near to his brother until it bites him and he dies, that man would be as though he had a share in his brother's blood [that is, if he does not prevent the snake from biting him]. Similarly, he who sees his brother indulging in iniquity and does not warn him of the consequences thereof, . . . he would have a share in his brother's iniquity. Thus, he who is able to dissuade a wrongdoer and does it not is himself committing a wrong. . . . It is not enough for a man to say "I do no wrong, but let him who wishes to do wrong do so"; thus he sees wrongdoing and opposes it not. If the matter were as you think, would you then be punished among the wrongdoers in whose acts you have no share? . . .

Woe to you, O slaves of iniquity, how can you hope in God's protection from the fears of the Day of Resurrection, when you fear men rather than God, and obey them, while you disobey Him? You keep their covenants which are in violation of His covenant. Verily I say to you, God would not protect from the fears of that day those who take men as their lords in His stead.

Woe to you, O slaves of iniquity, for a worthless world and an evil lust you lose the dominion of paradise and forget the fears of the Day of Resurrection.

Woe to you, O slaves of this world, for an ephemeral life and pleasures that will vanish you run away from God and despise His presence. How would God wish you to come before Him when you despise His presence? . . . How can you claim to be of all men the friends (*awliyā'*) of God when you run away from death and seek protection in this world. Of what use is the fragrance of a dead man's embalming spices to him, or the whiteness of his shroud when all this will decay in the earth. Likewise, the pleasures of this world which you so value will benefit you naught when they will all disappear. . . .

Woe to you, O slaves of this world, for you carry a lamp in bright sunlight when the light of the sun would suffice you, and claim to walk by the sun's light in the night. Thus do you walk by the light of knowledge, seeking worldly affairs, when God gave it to you for your hereafter. You consent that the hereafter is an inescapable reality, yet you cling to this world. You say death is an inescapable reality, yet you run away from it. You say that God hears and sees, but you fear not His reckoning of your deeds. How could anyone hearing you believe what you say? For it is excusable for a foolish man to lie, but a wise man has no excuse.

Verily I say to you, if a beast of burden is not ridden, and thus broken in and used to carry loads, it becomes uncontrollable, as its nature would change. Likewise, your hearts, if they are not made tender by the remembrance of death, or be engaged in acts of worship, would become hard as stones. What benefits a dark house if a lamp is placed on its roof, while inside darkness prevails?[41] Likewise, the light of knowledge will avail you nothing when it shines only through your mouths while your hearts are left in darkness. Hasten to your homes and illuminate them, and to your hearts, and illuminate them with wisdom before they are overcome with sins and made harder than stones.

How can a man, having no help, carry heavy burdens? How can a sinner be relieved of the heavy burdens of sin if he does not beg divine forgiveness? Would a man have clean garments if he does not wash them, or would a man be acquitted from his transgressions without expiating them? Nor would a man escape drowning in the sea if he tried to cross without a boat. Would a man, likewise, escape the temptations of this world without the healing of true endeavor? Would a traveler reach his destination without a guide, or a man attain paradise without due regard to the fundamentals of faith (*dīn*)? Nor would he who does not obey God obtain His pleasure with him. . . .

Verily I say to you, as the sea would suffer no decrease or harm if a boat sinks therein, likewise, you shall cause God no want or harm by your sins. Rather, it is your own souls you harm. As the sun will suffer no harm or decrease of luminosity because of the multitudes of men basking in the light thereof, so it is with God's bounty, it suffers no decrease because He bestows it on you. Rather, it is by His bounty that you live and have your being. God multiplies His bounties to those who are thankful, for He is the one deserving of all praise and He is all-knowing.

Woe to you, you unfaithful servants! You receive your wages, clothe yourselves, are well sustained and build houses, yet you perform badly the work of your Master. Soon will the Master of the work investigate the work you do, punish you severely, and order your necks cut off at the roots. He will have your hands cut off at the joints and your bodies dragged face down and left by the wayside.[42]

Thus, you shall be an example to those who fear God and a warning to the wrongdoers.

Woe to you, O evil men of knowledge! Do not tell yourselves that your lives shall last forever and that you shall not die. Indeed, you are already in the grip of death. Begin now to understand and weep for yourselves. Lament your sins. Hasten now and be ready. Repent soon and turn to your Lord. . . .

Is it not, you slave of this world, by knowledge that you were given authority over all things; yet you despise knowledge and live not by it. Instead, you cling to this world to rule over it, making it your sole desire. You live in it as though it will never end. How long will you cling to this world while God has no share in you? Verily I say to you, you shall never attain the exalted status of the hereafter unless you abandon the things you love. Do not wait until the morrow for repentance, for between now and the morrow is the night wherein God's decree comes and goes.[43]

Verily I say to you, small sins are the temptation of the devil. He makes your sins seem small and insignificant in your eyes until they multiply and overtake you. . . . Verily I say to you, there is nothing better that would secure a high status in the hereafter and is of more succor in the face of hardships in this world than continuous prayers. Prayers are the best means of bringing you nigh unto the Merciful. Pray therefore, much and always.

Verily I say to you, a wronged man who finds no supporter in this world by word or deed shall be greatly requited in the kingdom of heaven. Who among you has seen light which was named darkness, or darkness which was called light? Likewise, no man can be both a man of faith and an unbeliever, or one loving this world and striving for the hereafter. Is it possible that those who sow barley can reap wheat, or those who sow wheat reap barley? Thus shall also every servant in this world reap the fruits of what he had sown here, in the hereafter, and will be rewarded for his deeds.[44]

Verily I say to you, he who does not weed the grass from his field, it shall multiply and kill his crops. Thus also, he who does not remove the love of this world from his heart, his heart shall be captured by it, and he will never be able to taste the love of the world to come.

Woe to you, O slaves of this world, make the houses of the worship of your Lord prisons for your bodies and your hearts houses of piety, not dwelling places of every lust. . . . Woe to you, evil men of knowl-edge, were you not dead, and He [God] revived you, but when you were revived you made yourselves dead again? Were you not fool-ish and He instructed you, and you soon forgot His instructions? Were you not fools and He gave you understanding, but you chose ignorance? Woe to you! Were you not gone astray and He guided you, but you went astray after you were guided? . . . (He continues with blindness and sight, deafness and hearing, poverty and riches, and humility and exaltation.) Woe to you, therefore, on the Day of Resurrection, for God shall humiliate and upbraid you. . . .

Verily I say to you, Moses commanded you not to swear by God, truthfully or falsely, rather say "Yea" or "Nay." [45]

O children of Israel, eat the herbs of the field and barley bread, and avoid eating wheat bread, for you may not be able to be thankful enough for it. Verily I say to you, every evil word you utter in this life you shall answer for it on the Day of Resurrection.

O slaves of vanity, if one of you goes to sacrifice an animal [as a burnt offering, *qurbān*] and remembers that his brother is angry with him, let him leave his sacrifice and make peace with his brother; then let him return and offer his sacrifice [Matt 5:23].[46] O slaves of wickedness, if someone asks one of you for his shirt, let him give his garment as well. If someone strikes the cheek of one of you, let him offer his other cheek also. If one of you is forced to walk one mile for another man, let him walk two miles.

Verily I say to you, what good is a body if from the outside it appears healthy but inside it is sick . . . ? Of what benefit is it to you to wash clean your skins but leave your hearts full of impurities?

Verily I say to you, be not like a sieve that throws out the good flour and retains the chaff. Likewise, you bring out words of wisdom from your mouths, but retain hatred in your hearts. Verily I say to you, abandon evil and seek the good, for if you combine good with evil, the good will avail you nothing. . . .

Verily I say to you, blessed are those who spend their nights in prayer, for they shall have everlasting light. They stood in the dark-ness of the night in prayer in their prayer chambers supplicating their Lord to save them from the hardships of the Last Day. . . . Verily, I say to you, O slaves of this world, neither this world you truly love, nor for the next do you hope. For if, indeed, you love this world, you should have rendered good the actions through which you obtained it. If you truly hope for the hereafter, your deeds should have conformed to your hopes. . . .

Verily I say to you, evil spirits have found no better place to dwell than your hearts. Behold! God gave this world to you that you may work in it for the world to come, and not that it should make you forget the hereafter. He made the earth wide for you that you may use it as a place of worship and not that you should use it as a stage for your sins. He enjoined you to do good and to be obedient to Him in it and not to be disobedient and sinful. . . . Verily I say to you, as a tree is not perfect until it gives good fruit, so also your faith (*dīn*) will not be perfect until you avoid evil and seek the good.

Verily I say to you, as plants will not grow except through water and soil, so also faith will not be perfect except through knowledge and good deeds. Verily I say to you, as water extinguishes fire, so prudence extinguishes wrath. Verily I say to you, as water and fire cannot be in one vessel, so also blindness and understanding cannot dwell in one heart. . . .

Verily I say to you, the sun is the light of everything, and wisdom is the light of every heart, and piety is the beginning of all wisdom. Truth is the gate to all goodness, and the mercy of God is the gate to every truth. The keys to all these are invocation, supplication, and good deeds. No door can be opened without a key. . . .

Verily I say to you, the carrying of heavy stones from mountaintops is easier than speaking to a fool who comprehends not your speech. . . . Blessed is he who makes his words few and good, fearing by excessive speech the wrath of his Lord. Blessed is he who makes clear his speech and praises nothing until he discerns its consequences. Blessed is he who learns from the learned that which he did not know, and teaches the ignorant that which he learned. . . .

Verily I say to you, O my disciples,[47] you are among men as the living among the dead. Do not die with those who die.

Then Christ, peace be upon him, said, God, exalted be He, says, "My faithful servant grieves when I take away from him the pleasures of this world, but this I do because I desire to draw him nearer unto me. He rejoices when I bestow ease and comfort upon him in this world, yet this I love not, for it separates him from me."[48]

# Conclusion

The image of Jesus that emerges from the two preceding texts is a composite one. In the first we see the master as the humble servant of God, but one who is at the same time a highly favored and exalted friend of God. Jesus is commissioned to teach men the truth and thus to bring them nearer to God. Yet, he is sternly warned not to overstep his human limits of humility and servanthood before the divine majesty.

The second text breathes more the familiar air of the Synoptic Gospels, both in language and in ideas. Here, Jesus is the stern teacher and warner, instructing men and also passing harsh judgment on their folly, foolishness, and hypocrisy. Even here, however, the victims of this judgment are not specifically the Pharisees and scribes of the Gospel, but imperfect humanity in general. Here again, Jesus is to be regarded as the chosen messenger sent to warn men and to preach to them the divine revelation, even though he speaks the language of the Gospel. He remains, therefore, the Jesus of the Qur'an, one in the long series of prophets and messengers of God for humankind.

Thus we see that like the Christ of Christian faith and hope, the Jesus of the Qur'an and later Muslim piety is much more than a mere human being, or even simply the messenger of a Book. While the Jesus of Islam is not the Christ of Christianity, the Christ of the Gospel often speaks through the austere, human Jesus of Muslim piety. Indeed, the free spirits of Islamic mysticism found in the man Jesus not only the example of piety, love, and asceticism which they sought to emulate, but also the Christ who exemplifies fulfilled humanity, a humanity illumined by the light of God. This reflection of the divine light in the human heart and soul is known in the language of Islamic mysticism as *tajallī*, the manifestation of divine beauty and majesty in and through man.

In this concept of divine manifestation, the Christian and Muslim images of Jesus converge at many points. Islam says that human beings can and must draw nearer to God, and in the *mi'rāj* (the physical ascension of the Prophet to heaven) and the "lifting up" of Jesus to God (Q. 4:158), this takes on a most concrete form. Nevertheless, Islam insists on "man being man" and God being God in the absolute sense. Christianity, springing up in a different spiritual and cultural milieu, begins not with the ascent of man to the divine but rather the descent of the divine to man. Thus, the "Word was made flesh, and dwelt among us" becomes the expression of this encounter of man with the divine. In a way, therefore, the two approaches to the question of the divine–human relation here presented are widely divergent; yet this is only true in points of emphasis and in the position from which each of the two religious traditions start. In spite of these and other differences, however, we insist that Muslims and Christians can, and must, learn much from the man Jesus of Islam and from Christ the Lord of Christianity. This can only be achieved through honest and sincere efforts by us all to be existentially involved in the meaning and purpose of our existence in a world of sin and imperfection, but a world sanctified by the divine presence among and within us.

# Notes

1. This question was adopted as the theme of the ecumenical sessions by the World Council of Churches in a variety of formulations and answers in most of its conferences. See, for example, the themes of the 1964 and 1961 conferences. Cf. Matt 22:42. (All biblical references will be made to the *Oxford Annotated Bible*, Revised Standard Version [New York: Oxford University Press, 1962].)

2. Most fruitful have been the occasional consultations sponsored by the World Council of Churches where groups from many different cultures and religious traditions took part in the dialogue on the meaning of faith to the peoples of different religious traditions. Such a meeting on Muslim-Christian dialogue, in which the author participated, was held in Lebanon in 1972. The results have been published in a booklet entitled *Christian-Muslim Dialogue*, ed. S. J. Samartha and J. B. Taylor (Geneva: World Council of Churches, 1973).

3. Much has been written, of course, on Jesus in Islam by Western scholars, but for the most part the purpose has been either to compare the Jesus of Islam with the Christ of Christianity or to demonstrate the false understanding of Jesus by Muslims. A notable exception to this approach is Kenneth Cragg, who, while remaining a Christian committed to the task of explaining the Gospel to Muslims, nonetheless is ready to wrestle with Islamic concepts and thus shows a unique appreciation of the faith of Muslims. Other exceptions can also be cited.

4. All Qur'anic references in this essay are taken from *The Meaning of the Glorious Koran*, trans. Mohammed Marmaduke Pickthall (New York: New American Library, n.d.). For the Christian view, see Geoffrey Parrinder, *Jesus in the Qur'an* (London: Faber & Faber, 1965), 34. Kenneth Cragg holds a similar, albeit more complex, view, as the author has discussed it with him on many occasions.

5. See note 4 above.

6. Islam, like Christianity, lays a great emphasis on divine guidance as the basis of its faith and history. Any reference to Jesus in the Qur'an must be viewed in the light of this fundamental concept.

7. See Mahmoud Ayoub, *Redemptive Suffering in Islam: A Study of the Devotional Aspects of 'Ashura' in Twelver Shi'ism* (The Hague: Mouton, 1978), chaps. 2 and 6.

8. Muhammad Baqir, *Bihar al-anwar*, vol. 13 of the old, traditional edition, vol. 53 of the modern edition (Tehran: al-Maktaba al-Islamiyya, A.H. 1384), 46-47, where many texts are given in support of this idea. See also Abu Ja'far Muhammad bin Yaqub bin Ishaq al-Kulayni al-Razi, *al-Usul min al-kafi* (Tehran: Dar al-Kutub al-Islamiyya, A.H. 1381), vol. 1 ("Kitab al-Hujja"): 194-90, and 293-94, where the comparison of 'Ali to Jesus is described in a similar way.

9. Baqir, *Bihar al-anwar*, 53:46.

10. The Arabic word *wali*, plural *awliyā'*, means "friend," "confidant," and "master." It also signifies theologically one who has authority. All these meanings are implied when the term is applied to the imams.

11. See Ayoub, *Redemptive Suffering in Islam,* chap. 6, 442ff.

12. Ibid., for a detailed discussion of the subject.

13. See al-Kulayni al-Razi, *al-Usul min al-kafi,* 1:224-25. The prophets here mentioned are Noah, Abraham, Moses, Jesus, and Muhammad.

14. See, for a vivid example, the colloquy between God and the ancient prophet *Ilyās* (Elijah), reported on the authority of the sixth imam, in al-Kulayni al-Razi, *al-Usul min al-kafi,* 1:227-28.

15. For an excellent discussion of this genre of hadith, see William A. Graham, *Divine Word and Prophetic Word in Early Islam* (The Hague: Mouton, 1977).

16. From Abu Muhammad al-Hasan bin 'Ali bin al-Husayn bin Shu'ba al-Harrani, *Tuhaf al-'uqul 'an Al al-Rasul,* ed. and introduced by Muhammad Sadiq Bahr al-'Ulum (Najaf, Iraq: Haydariyya Press, 1383/1963), 373-78. al-Harrani was a famous traditionist of the fourth century A.H.

17. The divine creative command by which God says to a thing "Be" and it is. See Q. 3:47.

18. Cf. the *Infancy Gospel of Thomas* 2:2, in *New Testament Apocrypha,* trans. Edgar Hennecke (Philadelphia: Westminster, 1963), 1:393.

19. Ibid.

20. Meaning "friendship" or "authority." See note 10 above.

21. Cf. Q. 19:33; 3:45-46.

22. *Nawāfil* are the extracanonical prayers usually offered at night. They are regarded as especially meritorious by the Sufis. See the famous *hadīth qudsī* known as *hadīth al-nawāfil,* in Muhammad bin Isma'il al-Bukhari, *al-Jami' al-Sahih,* ed. Ludolf Krehl and T. Juynboll (Leiden: E. J. Brill, 1862-1908), 81, 38, 2.

23. That is, the five prayers, and especially the dawn prayer.

24. al-Kulayni al-Razi, *al-Usul min al-kafi,* ed. Akbar al-Ghaffari (Tehran: al-Maktaba al-Islamiyya, Haydari Press, n.d.), 8:131-32, hadith no. 103.

25. This highly metaphorical description of hell, occurring in many sources, is a favorite of early Shi'i writers. Hell is a closed well of darkness and smoke, and the passage describing that is too eloquent to be rendered into clear English.

26. Cf. Matt 18:9.

27. This refers to the Qur'an, which was sent, according to Muslims, not to deny but to confirm previous revelations, among which is the *Injīl,* revealed to Jesus. Men shall be judged by the revelations sent to them by God. Hence, the next sentence, in a way, continues the same theme, although under a different subject.

28. Cf. Matt 23:27, and possibly Luke 11:44.

29. Cf. Matt 5:39 and Luke 6:29. The same command in repeated in the next section by Jesus to his hearers. So, in a way, Jesus is commanded to do what he later preaches. Perhaps this is significant, because it shows the essential equality of Jesus with other men.

30. al-Kulayni al-Razi, *al-Usul min al-kafi,* 8:141.

31. Ibn Shu'ba al-Harrani, *Tuhaf al-'uqul 'an Al al-Rasul,* 378-89.

32. The deviation from the Sermon on the Mount in the preceding sayings can be easily explained as an Islamic way of saying more or less the same thing. Cf. Matt 5:3-10.

33. Matt 5:11-12. It is interesting to note the substitution of the word "purity" (*t)ahārah*), which implies physical ritualistic purity, for the word "righteousness."

34. It shall be clear from the following that mere certainty without action is useless, hence the seemingly vague condemnation.

35. Compare this and the Gospel sayings in Matt 5:15 and 23:27 for differences and similarities.

36. Perhaps this is an allusion to John 10:1-18.

37. The model for the saying is perhaps Matthew 7, where it appears in various verses, but the saying itself is rather strange.

38. The *'ulamā'* of both Shi'i and Sunni Islam have always been very critical of the Sufis. The saying here may be a somewhat indirect condemnation of Sufis.

39. The substitution of honey for wine is, again, an accommodation to the Islamic prohibition against wine. Cf. Matt 9:17; Mark 2:22; and Luke 5:38.

40. The reference here is to houses made of wood, or at least with a wooden roof.

41. Cf. Matt 5:15.

42. The author may have had the parable of the unfaithful tenant in mind (Luke 20:16 and Matt 21:41), or the parable of the unfaithful servant (Matt 25:15).

43. The meaning here is that perhaps they will not live until the morrow, since God's decrees are unknown to men. This passage may echo the parable of the rich fool in Luke 12:16-21.

44. Cf. Matt 7:16. This metaphor may have been suggested by Matthew. What is of special significance, however, is that it expresses clearly the Islamic emphasis on works as opposed to faith only.

45. The author confuses the commandment in Exod 20:7 with the injunction of Christ not to swear at all (Matt 5:34).

46. This and the following three statements are taken directly from the Sermon on the Mount.

47. The disciples of Christ are given a high status in the Qur'an. They are called *al-ḥawāriyyūn*. In Shi'ism they are the true heirs of Jesus' prophetic knowledge and wisdom and are his vicegerents.

48. This last saying is a typical divine utterance (*ḥadīth qudsī*). It resembles in both words and ideas the divine sayings attributed to the Prophet Muhammad.

# 13

# Toward an Islamic Christology II

The Death of Jesus, Reality or Delusion—
A Study of the Death of Jesus in *Tafsīr* Literature

## Introduction

This is the second of a series of studies of the Islamic view of Jesus the Christ. In the previous chapter I argued that Muslims have thought much and seriously about Christ and that there is an authentic Islamic understanding of Christ that deserves careful consideration as a legitimate christology. The Christ of Islam, we wish to insist further, must not be dismissed as a distorted image of the true Christ of the Gospels, but must rather be seen as a living and dynamic personality, addressing humanity in many languages and across the barriers of dogma, creed, and even scriptures.

The purpose of the present essay is to study some of the ways in which Muslim commentators (*mufassirūn*) of the Qur'an have understood the Qur'anic verses dealing with Jesus. Our main concern is with one verse, and more specifically a single clause, one that boldly denies the death of Jesus on the cross at the hands of his opponents. They plotted to kill him, but God saved him and "it (or, he) was made only to appear so to them" (Q. 4:157).[1] I shall endeavor in what follows to examine the meaning of this difficult and controversial clause. The words *wa lākin shubbiha lahum* have generated much discussion, myth, and legend throughout the long history of Islamic *tafsīr*. They have presented Muslims with a challenge, first, to understand God's ways with humanity, and, second, to answer convincingly the charge of history.

The Qur'an offers itself as a Book of guidance to humankind (Q. 2:1). For it to fulfill this purpose in human life, it must speak to the situation of the community of its receivers at every stage of its earthly existence. This the Qur'an has done in large measure through *tafsīr*, or the science of Qur'anic exegesis. As one writing from within the community, my task will not be

Previously published in *The Muslim World* 70, no. 2 (April 1980): 91-121. Reprinted by permission.

simply to present and analyze the opinions of the commentators on the subject. Rather, having done that, I wish to engage in the process of *tafsīr* myself by presenting my own understanding of this clause, which is crucial to the Qur'anic view of Christ. In this I will be accepting the challenge of the divine Word, and that of history.

Three main stages in the history of the *tafsīr* of the verse with which we shall be concerned suggest themselves. The classical tradition is epitomized in the monumental commentary of Tabari (d. 310/923), which has influenced subsequent commentators down to the present. Other works of the classical period differ little from that of Tabari which they take as their source and starting point. The second stage, which may be considered as the middle period, shows a greater interest in history as well as a greater awareness of Christian views. This stage is represented, on the one hand, by the polemical approach of the historian Ibn Kathir (d. 774/1373), and by the brilliant, analytical, and questioning mind of the theologian Fakhr al-Din al-Razi (d. 606/1209), on the other. The irenic, spiritual, and universal interpretation of the Sufis, of which examples will be considered in the essay, represents still another important trend. The third and final stage constitutes the modern period, beginning in the late nineteenth century with modernist reformers such as Muhammad 'Abduh and his successors. Both the methodology and the concern of modern commentators are radically different from those of their predecessors. The views of some of the most important modern thinkers will be considered.

Shi'i commentators, especially of the classical period, present a unique approach to the problems raised by the Qur'anic verse under consideration. It must be observed, moreover, that modern Shi'i thinkers, such as 'Allamah Tabataba'i, while employing the methodology of modern commentators, clearly continue the Shi'i philosophical and theological tradition.

We shall follow a loose chronology, aiming not so much at a strict historical survey but at a presentation of the major developments in *tafsīr* relevant to the subject at hand. Two texts of special importance will be translated in an appendix. The first presents an interesting parallel to the passion in the Fourth Gospel. The second is a selection from a Sufi *tafsīr* presenting what may be considered a "Sufi christology." Finally, the ultimate aim of this study is to promote constructive and meaningful dialogue among the men and women of faith in the two communities.

## Jesus, "The Word of Truth" (Q. 19:34)

Prophethood in Islam is the divine answer to human folly and false confidence, a source of guidance for men to God and the model of a fulfilled humanity. In every prophet, speaking on God's behalf to humankind, there is both a challenge and a judgment. The challenge is in the call to men and women of every age to return to their prophetic origins as exemplified in

Adam, the first prophet, before whom the angels were commanded to prostrate themselves (Q. 7:11). Human fulfillment must be achieved through human prophets; the Qur'an therefore insists on the humanity of God's messengers (Q. 6:8, 9, 50; 11:31; 17:94, 95; 25:7).

In the long drama of human prophets and a humanity challenged to seek prophetic fulfillment, Jesus plays a unique role. In him there is an originality of being that is akin to that of Adam (Q. 3:59). In him, as in Adam, the divine power over and within creation is manifested. He represents a special creation; he is the Word of God injected into the human plane of existence (Q. 3:45; 4:171). Yet like other prophets, Jesus remains a human being created by God, His servant and messenger (Q. 4:171-72; 5:17, 75).

Later Islamic tradition not only affirms the high status accorded to Jesus by the Qur'an; it makes still greater claims of uniqueness for him. It is reported in a very early hadith that the Prophet declared, "Every child born of the children of Adam Satan touched with his finger, except Mary and her son, peace be upon them both."[2] Jesus is therefore free from the taint of evil and impurity. That his mother shares in this great honor is only because she was accepted by God to be a pure vessel for His Word and messenger (Q. 21:91; 66:12). This purity, which Adam had till he was touched by Satan's finger and thus lost it, now remains exemplified in Jesus alone.

When the Qur'an speaks of earlier prophets, it does so by way of examples of God's dealings with faltering humanity. Jesus alone is presented as a challenge and a judgment. In the famous passage of the Qur'an ending with the verse of the *mubāhalah*, God confronts humanity with the challenge, "And whosoever disputes with you concerning him [Jesus], after the knowledge which has come unto you, say: 'Come! Let us summon our sons and your sons, our women and your women, ourselves and yourselves, then we will pray humbly and invoke the curse of God upon those who lie'" (Q. 3:61).[3] The knowledge that "came" to the Prophet concerning Jesus presents a rare instance of theology proper in the Qur'an. The Christ of the Qur'an is according to this theology fully human, in spite of his miraculous birth and special status. Like Adam, he is the creature of God not through the law of human generation; rather, he is the object of the divine *amr*, or command (Q. 3:59). Again, in spite of his humanity, and perhaps because of it, Jesus is made the agent of divine acts through his special miracles. To him alone among the prophets God gave the power to give health to the sick, life to the dead and even to crude matter. All this he did "by God's leave" (Q. 3:49).

The Qur'an presents a christology of the human Christ, empowered by God and "fortified with the Holy Spirit" (Q. 2:87, 253). It is a fully Islamic christology based not on borrowed distortions of early Christian heresies but on the Islamic view of man and God. There are, no doubt, some resemblances between the Qur'anic story of Jesus and early Christian sources;[4] these are at best, however, similarities of framework and story, not of theology or essential view. Islam differs from Christianity on two crucial points. First, it denies the divinity of Christ, but without denying his special humanity. Second, it denies the expiatory sacrifice of Christ on the cross as a ransom for sinful humanity, but again denies neither the actual death of Christ nor his general redemptive role in human history. Enough has been said about the first point. It is with the second that this essay is concerned.

## Who Died on the Cross?

In a series of verses directed against the children of Israel, to whom Jesus was sent as a messenger (Q. 3:49; 61:6), the Qur'an first accuses them of killing prophets unjustly. It then reproaches them for uttering great calumnies against Mary, perhaps accusing her of adultery. Finally, the Qur'an reproaches them for claiming to have killed Jesus the Christ:

> and for their saying: "We have surely killed the Christ, Jesus son of Mary, the messenger of God." They did not kill him, nor did they crucify him; rather it was made only to appear so to them. And those who have differed concerning him are in doubt regarding him [or it, the truth]; they have no knowledge of him [or it], except the following of conjecture. They did not kill him [or it, their doubt] with certainty. Rather, God took him up to Himself, for God is Mighty and Wise. (Q. 4:157-59)

These two verses constitute the answer to a divine challenge, "They devised and God devised, and God is the best of devisors" (Q. 3:34). The important question here is, What do the words *wa lākin shubbiha lahum* mean? In answer to this question, a number of different theories have been formulated and elaborated by Qur'anic exegetes throughout Islamic history. For the most part, their purpose has been to answer the question, Who was killed and crucified if Jesus was saved by divine intervention? In their eagerness to confirm the denial of the death and crucifixion of Christ at the hands of his enemies, commentators have generally interpreted the words *shubbiha lahum* to mean that another was made to bear his likeness (*shabah*) and die in his stead. Although later commentators questioned this reading on grammatical grounds, as will be seen below, they nonetheless continued to propound theories about who that substitute may have been.

Christian scholars, likewise, accepted this interpretation and propounded their own theories. Michel Hayek, a modern Lebanese theologian, comments as follows: "This opinion may be related to a Christian heresy which had many supporters in Najran just before the rise of Islam. This was the heresy of the docetics who denied the sufferings of Christ. Some of them claimed that Simon the Cyrene was the man who bore the likeness of Christ (and died in his stead)."[5] Docetism, in whatever form it appeared, sought to preserve the divinity of Christ from the indignities of suffering and death. Islam, however, does not admit of docetism in any form. Its very human images of the life to come, as well as its insistence on the humanity of God's messengers, argues against such a view. Furthermore, neither the Qur'an nor later Islamic tradition suggests a phantomlike appearance of Christ. He was, rather, a man, born in the usual way (Q. 19:22, 23), lived like other men, and like them must die and be resurrected for the final reckoning (Q. 19:33).

It must therefore be argued that the Qur'an only denies the death of Jesus on the cross and leaves open the question of his actual death. From the beginning, the commentators had some knowledge of the Christian insistence on the crucifixion as a historical fact. They did not, however, grasp the implication of this fact for Christianity, and therefore tried to harmonize the Qur'anic denial with the Christian affirmation. They accepted a crucifixion as a historical fact, in agreement with Christians, but denied it of Jesus, in agreement with the Qur'an. They adopted not a docetic position in interpretating the words *shubbiha lahum* but a substitutionist one. Thus, any parallels that this position may present with docetism can be only incidental.

The substitutionist solution to the problem raised two further questions. Why would God cause one person to suffer the trials of another, even if for the purpose of sparing His own messenger the ignominy of a shameful death? Second, what would the implications of this confusion of identities by God be for social norms and the credibility of historical testimony? The second of these two questions was eventually raised, and therefore deserves some attention later in this discussion. The first, however, underlies the choice of alternative solutions preferred by different commentators. To these, I shall now turn.

The traditions relating the story of Jesus are told on the authority of either Jewish converts such as Wahb bin Munabbih or of unnamed Christian converts as in the traditions of Ibn Ishaq. Tabari relates on the authority of Wahb the following story. When God revealed to Jesus that He would take him up to Him, Jesus and seventeen of his disciples went into a house (perhaps to celebrate the Passover). There, they were surprised by the Jews who were seeking Jesus. God, however, cast the likeness of Jesus on every one in the group so that he could not be distinguished from the rest. The Jews exclaimed, "You have bewitched us! Either bring forth Jesus or we shall kill you all."[6] They then took one of the group and killed him, believing him to be Jesus. Hence, "It was made only to appear so to them." After reviewing a number of traditions, Tabari himself prefers the one just discussed. He bases his preference on two major considerations. The Jews, who denied the truth of what Jesus brought them from their Lord, deserved to be frustrated and to have their plan against Jesus, the prophet of God, thwarted. The disciples, *ḥawāriyyūn,* and the Christians who followed them were not telling a lie by asserting the crucifixion, as they did not see Jesus taken up to heaven.

They thought, rather, that he was killed because he told them on the night before that his end was at hand. This interpretation, however, was not accepted by most commentators because it was related on the authority of only one traditionist, albeit the famous Wahb bin Munabbih.

Tabari presents a possible alternative which, in his view, serves the same purpose. This is the story, again related on the authority of Wahb, which declares that Jesus was deserted by all his companions at the time of his arrest.[7] He was tied with a rope and dragged through the streets to the place where he was to be crucified. At that moment, he was taken up to heaven and his likeness cast on another whom the Jews killed, thinking him to be Jesus. Thus they were frustrated and the disciples were not telling a lie since they did not see him taken up. This solution, however, creates more problems than it solves. It makes historical Christianity based on a divine deception which was not disclosed until the Qur'an was revealed centuries later. We shall return to this problem later.

Important to most of the substitutionist interpretations is the idea that whoever bore the likeness of Jesus, and consequently his suffering and death, did so voluntarily. It must have been felt by hadith transmitters and commentators that for God to cause an innocent man to die unjustly to save another would be divine wrongdoing (*zulm*), which cannot be predicated of God. Thus, the theory which eventually gained most popularity was that one of the disciples voluntarily accepted death as a ransom for his master.[8]

This theory in its simplest form was related by Tabari on the authority of Qatada (a well-known companion and hadith transmitter). He said:

> It has been related to us that Jesus son of Mary, the prophet of God, said to his companions, "Who among you would consent to have my likeness (*shabahi*) cast upon him, and be killed?" One of them answered, "I would, O prophet of God." Thus that man was killed and God protected His prophet and took him up to Himself.[9]

In what appears to be the second stage in the development of this theory, the number of the disciples is set at nineteen. One of them consents to die in his master's place; then Jesus is taken up to heaven before their eyes. When the disciples came out of the besieged house, they declared that their master was taken up. The Jews verified this claim by counting the men several times; each time one was missing. Still, they took the man and killed him, thinking him to be Jesus.[10]

The next stage in the development of the theory presents a growing interest in historical accounts. The result is an interesting story composed of diverse elements, Gospel materials, and hagiography. It was related on the authority of Ibn Ishaq (the famous biographer of the Prophet) that the king of the Jews who sought to kill Jesus was a man called David. When all the people had concurred, Jesus was greatly frightened by death. He prayed, "O God, if Thou wouldst take away this cup from any of Thine creatures, then take it away from me."[11] His skin was dripping with blood, from grief and fear (Luke 22:44). Then he and his twelve disciples entered a house where he offered a place with him in paradise to the one who would bear his likeness and die in his stead. The man who volunteered, according to this tradition, was not one of the twelve. His name was Sergus; he took the seat of Jesus and the master was taken up to heaven.[12] It is of special interest that this story is supposed to have been related to Ibn Ishaq by a Christian convert. Whether this reflects a local Christian tradition, or was an echo of docetic theology, albeit in a crude form, cannot be determined with certainty given the present state of our knowledge of Arabian Christianity of that period.

In time, however, we see a preference for what we may call punishment substitutionism. Here, God is completely absolved from the responsibility of injustice or wrongdoing. According to some versions of this theory, Jesus was sought by his enemies, who intended to kill him. God, or Gabriel, made him enter a house for refuge. His pursuers sent a man in to kill him. The man's name is variously given as Tityanus, Titabus, or Titanus. Jesus was taken up through an opening in the roof. Not finding him, the man came out to report to the people. But God had turned him into the likeness of Jesus, and he was killed in spite of his protests. God, however, cast the likeness of Jesus only on the man's face and not on his body.[13] Thus, the people were confused as to the identity of the man they killed. This is added to explain the rest of the verse, which declares that those who differed concerning him followed only their conjecture.

By the sixth Islamic century (twelfth century C.E.), we witness yet another development that seeks to interpret the entire passage in one complete story.[14] The Jews, the Qur'an tells us, uttered great calumnies against Mary. A group of them reviled Jesus and his mother, calling him "sorcerer, son of a sorceress, reprobate, son of a loose woman." Jesus prayed, saying, "O God, You are my Lord and I from Your spirit came into being and with Your Word You did create me. I did not come to them of my own accord. O God, curse those who reviled me and my mother."[15] God answered his prayer and turned the calumniators into apes and swine. The king and notables of the Jews, fearing a similar punishment, sought to kill Jesus. They besieged him and his disciples in a house, and one of them agreed to bear the likeness of his master and die in his place in order that the others may be saved. According to other versions of the same tale, the Jews sent the man Tityanus to kill Jesus who was alone hiding in a house. But he himself was killed, as we have already seen.

Judas Iscariot has had an interesting history in Christian piety and folklore. He appears in Muslim *tafsīr* very early, clearly introduced by Christian or Jewish reporters. Reporting on the authority of Wahb bin Munabbih, Tabari tells the story of Judas selling his master for thirty pieces of silver; later he regrets his evil deed and hangs himself. At that early stage, however, Judas is not yet identified. Later, when Judas is specifically mentioned, his name is confused. In a tradition related on the authority of Ibn Ishaq, who heard it from a Christian convert, Yudas Zechariah, Yutah, or Butah (Judas

Iscariot) led the Jews to Jesus and was himself made to bear the likeness of the master. Jesus was taken to heaven and Judas was seized by the mobs who crucified him, thinking him to be Jesus. All the while, he cried out, "I am not the one you want! I am the one who led you to him."[16] This tradition has since been reported by most commentators.[17] Modern thinkers have generally preferred this alternative on special historical and psychological grounds, as will be discussed below.

Many commentators questioned the entire theory and sought to go beyond the literal meaning of the text. Others tried to present the whole episode in a credible historical account without rejecting the substitutionist interpretation. The account of the historian Ibn Kathir. (d. 747/1373) is one of the most interesting examples of this historical approach. It is a narrative account showing definite dependence on Gospel materials. We present it here in some detail.

The Jews envied Jesus for what God had given him, manifest revelations (*bayyināt*) and power to perform miracles (*mu'jizāt*), and sought to kill him. Jesus did not dwell with them; rather, he roamed the earth, often with his mother. The Jews wrote to the king of Damascus, who was a worshipper of the stars, accusing Jesus of sedition and leading the people astray. The king then wrote to his governor in Jerusalem ordering him to arrest Jesus, place thorns on his head (Matt 27:29; Mark 15:17; John 19:2), and crucify him. Thus, a group of Jews went with soldiers to the house where Jesus lodged with his twelve, thirteen, or seventeen disciples. They besieged them on a Friday past the mid-afternoon hour. Jesus asked his disciples, "Who among you would consent to bear my likeness and be my companion in paradise?" A young man volunteered, but Jesus, thinking the youth too young for the task, repeated his request three times. Each time, however, only the youth indicated his readiness to ransom the master. Jesus then agreed and an opening appeared in the roof of the house through which he ascended to heaven. After this the companions of Jesus went out of the house, and the youth was seized and killed.[18]

Thus, the Jews and some Christian groups thought that it was Jesus, as did those of his companions who did not see him ascend to heaven. It is also said that his mother sat at the foot of the cross and wept and that the man spoke to her.[19] The author, however, doubts this and adds, "but God knows best." Then, commenting on the entire episode, he writes, "And all this is so that God may try His servants according to His infinite wisdom."[20]

The first to seriously question the substitutionist idea altogether was the famous commentator Abu'l Qasim al-Zamakhshari (d. 538/1143). His objections are based only on grammatical considerations. Nevertheless, he provides new arguments for many commentators after him. He begins by asking to what the verb *shubbiha* refers. If it is made to refer to Christ, then Christ is the one to whom something else is likened, not the one likened to something else. The verb, however, cannot have as its subject the one killed, since he is never mentioned in the Qur'an. Thus it must refer to the preposition "to" (them), that is, "they were made to imagine it." It is possible also to make the verb *shubbiha* refer to the one slain, as in the clause, "We have surely killed the Christ, Jesus," that is, the one who was made to appear to them like Jesus.[21] His famous disciple, Nasir al-Din al-Baydawi (d. 685/ 1286), repeats the same objections, and then adds, "or it may be that no one was killed; rather his being killed was falsely claimed and spread among men."[22] Baydawi does not, unfortunately, develop the idea further.

The thinker who really faced the theological and philosophical issue that the substitutionist interpretation implies was Fakr al-Din al-Razi (d. 606/ 1209). Razi was not satisfied with repeating the views of his predecessors; rather, he subjected every view to the careful scrutiny of his sharp analytical mind. He begins by raising two questions. The first is the one raised by Zamakhshari, already discussed. The second and more important question concerns what would happen if it is supposed that the likeness of one man could be cast on another. Two problems would result. First, it would open the gate of sophistry so that no social norm such as marriage or ownership rights could be ascertained. Further, this would lead to doubt in historical testimony, that is, the ongoing transmission of historical reports (*tawātur*). This historical transmission provides a sure source of knowledge, provided that *tawātur* is based on concrete data. If, however, we allow the possibility of the occurrence of such confusion of identity, this would necessitate in the end doubt in all sacred laws (*sharaʿī*). Nor can it be argued that such an occurrence is possible only during the ages of prophets. This is because although the age of prophetic miracles (*muʿjizāt*) has ended, nonetheless the age of *karāmāt* (miracles as divine favors) has not, for miracle as divine favors are possible in every age. "In sum, the opening of such a gate necessitates doubt in *tawātur*, and this in turn necessitates doubt in fundamentals (*uṣūl*), and this in turn necessitates doubt in the prophethood of all prophets. This is a branch (*farʿ*) necessitating doubt in fundamentals and must therefore be rejected."[23] Razi then suggests that perhaps when Christ was taken up, the Jews took a man whom they killed, claiming that he was Jesus, for Jesus was a man little given to social intercourse, and thus known only to a few chosen companions. "The Christian agreement in the transmission (of the crucifixion event) goes back to a few people whose agreement on a false report is not improbable."[24]

Having thus criticized the principle of the substitutionist theory, Razi reviews the various opinions without endorsing any of them. He saw these as only conjectures transmitted from one generation to the next; the acceptance or rejection of any of them would be in itself a matter of opinion. Razi was more concerned with the understanding of Christ, the spirit of God and His Word. But before we turn to this more important point, we should consider a few other examples of the substitutionist solution to complete our discussion.

The idea that no one actually bore the image of Christ and suffered in his stead may have had its origins in Muʿtazili circles (*Muʿtazili* was a rationalist school of thought in early Islam). To the Mu'tazili, the notion that God could commit acts of injustice, for any reason, was most repugnant. Furthermore, for God to allow such confusion of identity for whatever reason, would be too irrational and therefore inadmissible. Shi'i authors, who had much in common with Mu'tazili thought, report an interesting tradition to this effect on the authority of Abu 'Ali al-Jubba'i (d. 303/ 915), a well-known Mu'tazili theologian. Al-Shaykh al-Tusi (d. 459/1067) reports that the Jews sought to kill Jesus, but God took him up to Himself. They therefore took another whom they crucified on a high and isolated hill, allowing no one to come near him until his features had changed beyond recognition. They were thus able to conceal the fact of Jesus' ascension, which they witnessed, and to spread false reports of his death and crucifixion. This they did to prevent his ascension from becoming a reason for other Jews to believe in him. In this solution, the requirements of both justice and rationality are met. Moreover, those who later disagreed concerning Christ's end were not those who crucified him. Hence, the contention of both the Jews, who claimed to have crucified Jesus, and of the Christians, who asserted that he died on the cross and was then taken up to heaven, are—from the point of view of Jewish and Christian reporters—historically true.[25]

Shi'i popular piety presents Jesus from a definite Shi'i perspective. According to Shi'i piety, human beings are either in the wrong or in the right, depending on whether or not they follow the right authority or guidance of God's prophets and their true vicegerents, the imams. We are told on the authority of the fifth imam, Imam al-Baqir, that Jesus called his disciples together one evening to tell them of his coming ascension and asked who would consent to bear his image, be killed, and be his companion in paradise. A young man accepted and Jesus assented as well. He then told them that one of them would deny him twelve times before the morning, and one confessed his intention to be that person. Finally Jesus predicted, "You shall indeed be divided after me into three sects. Two of these will be calumnious toward God, and thus be destined for the fire; the third will follow Sham'un (Simon Peter), will be truthful toward God, and hence be destined for paradise."[26] Jesus, as a true Shi'i ascetic, then ascended to heaven wearing a woolen shirt, spun and sewed by Mary, his mother. As he reached the heavenly regions, he was addressed, "O Jesus, cast away from you the adornment of the world."[27]

Shi'i authors in general report the usual traditions on the authority of the same traditionists cited by Sunni commentators. Shi'i traditions, however, and these are few, present, as we have seen, typically Shi'i interpretations. To the element of human plotting (*makr*) and divine counterplotting, Shi'i exegesis adds an element of divine mystery. Those who imagined that Jesus was killed and crucified did so in ignorance of the truth. Their conjecture (*zann*) was based on an incomplete knowledge of the facts. Thus the famous fourth-Islamic-century theologian and traditionist Ibn Babawayh quotes the eighth imam, Imam al-Rida, as saying:

The case of no one among the prophets of God and His proofs (or witnesses, *hujaj*) has been obscured (*shubbiha*) to men except that of Jesus alone. This is due to the fact that he was taken up from this world alive, and his spirit taken away from him between heaven and earth. He was taken up to heaven and there his spirit was returned to him.[28]

The word *shubbiha* in this context means not only "it was made to appear so" but also that the matter was made obscure. This interpretation is not at all implausible if we consider the rest of the verse, as we shall now do.

## Did Jesus Die?

The Qur'an, we have argued, presents Jesus as a challenge not only to human folly and unbelief (*kufr*) but equally to human ignorance and the reliance on mere conjecture. Indeed, the Arabic word *zann is* the opposite not only of knowledge (*'ilm*) but also of absolute certainty or faith *(yaqīn)*. The Qur'an declares, "Those who differed concerning him [Jesus] are in doubt regarding it [the truth]; they have no knowledge of it [the truth] save the following of conjecture (*zann*)" (Q. 4:157). In this reading, we may differ from some commentators, yet we have not forced the text to yield any meaning or idea not in consonance with the Qur'anic view of Christ. Nor were commentators from the earliest time unaware of this interpretation.

The famous scholar Ibn Qutayba (d. 276/889) comments on the passage, "They have no knowledge concerning it save the following of conjecture, and they did not slay him [or, it] with certainty" (meaning, "they did not slay knowledge with certainty").[29] This interesting interpretation is based on a tradition attributed to the first actual commentator, Ibn Abbas, the cousin and companion of the Prophet. According to Tabari, the disagreement *(ikhtilāf)* here concerns Jesus, whether he was the one who was killed by the Jews or someone else. Their having killed him was only a conjecture, the opposite of knowledge and certainty. "And this is like one man saying to another, 'You have not killed this matter with knowledge, nor have you killed it with certainty,'" Tabari argues therefore that the *hu* ending of the word *qatalūhu,* "they slew him (or, it)," refers to *al-zann,* conjecture.[30]

If this interpretation is at all plausible, then the Qur'an is addressing not only the Jewish contemporaries of Jesus but all human beings of all times. The disagreement for which the Qur'an reproaches the contemporaries of Jesus is not absent from Muslim thinking about Christ. In their earnest search for truth, many commentators obscured the essence of the Qur'anic view of Christ behind the veil of their own conjecture. The substitutionist theory will not do, regardless of its form or purpose. First, it makes a mockery of divine justice and the primordial covenant of God with humanity to guide human history to its final fulfillment (Q. 7:172; 2:38). Would it be in consonance with God's covenant, his mercy and justice, to deceive humanity for so many centuries? Or, can it be said that the argument of the commentators would be really meaningful to Christians? Muslim commentators have generally assumed an attitude of overconfident superiority toward the Christians whom they were supposed to guide to the truth. This attitude has been generally a polemical one in that it assumes, as we have seen, that the Christian witness to the cross of Christ is based on a divine deception and is therefore false.

To be sure, there were those who sought to minimize or reject this attitude. In this they came nearer to the Qur'anic spirit of conciliation and search for meaning beyond the mere facts of history. This effort was made mainly by Sufi exegetes, although it was not limited to them. Razi, after reviewing and criticizing the various theories and notions of his predecessors, explains the Christian idea that only the human body of Christ suffered and died:

> For his [Jesus'] soul is of the substance of sanctity (*qudsiyyah*) and exaltation (*'ulwiyyah*). It is a celestial [soul] of intense luminosity, with the divine lights, and of great proximity to the angelic spirit. A soul such as this would not suffer because of the darkness of the body. For after its separation from the darkness of this body, it is liberated into the open courts of the heavenly realms and the lights of the world of majesty. There its exaltation and bliss are increased beyond measure.[31]

This statement goes a long way toward meeting the Qur'anic challenge of Jesus, the Christ. It also provides a good starting point for Muslim-Christian understanding.

Muslim commentators had some awareness, however imperfect, of the christological issues in Eastern Christian theology. They therefore attributed this disagreement and conjecture to Christian errors concerning Jesus.[32] Yet even here, we see operating the Islamic view of the truth as transcending the flow of historical events. Islam, according to this view, is as old as history itself. It is the truth which all prophets have claimed, but which was forgotten or distorted until revealed with definite force and clarity in the Qur'an. Thus Ibn Kathir relates, in his interpretation of the verse in question, that the followers of Jesus were divided after him into three sects. One of them asserted, "God was among us for as long as He willed, then went up to heaven." This was the Jacobite sect. The second said, "The Son of God dwelt among us so long as he willed, then God took him up to Himself." These were the Nestorians. The third group declared, "The servant of God and His apostle sojourned among us for as long as God willed, then God took him up to Himself." These were the Muslims. "Since that time, Islam remained obscured until God sent Muhammad."[33]

This view of the universality of the truth could be the basis of unity and dialogue within the diversity of humankind. If all human beings are seen as committed (*muslim*) to the divine will within the context of the spirit and cultural heritage of each human community, then the spirit of tolerance and understanding would prevail. If, on the other hand, the Islam of the Muslim community, with all its institutions as a reified religion, is to be used as the measure of religious truth, everywhere and in every age, then the divine wisdom in creating a world of religious and cultural plurality (Q. 49:13) has been in vain. The denial of this is possible, in our view, only on the most superficial level, where facts, not meaning, become the point of contention and polemics on both sides.

The Qur'an, as I have already argued, does not deny the death of Christ. Rather, it challenges human beings who in their folly have deluded themselves into believing that they would vanquish the divine Word, Jesus Christ, the messenger of God. The death of Jesus is asserted several times and in various contexts.[34] Two of these are of special interest to the argument of this study. In Surah 5, God questions Jesus directly, "O Jesus, son of Mary, did you say to mankind, 'Take me and my mother as two gods beside God?'" To this Jesus answers:

> I did not say to them save that which you commanded me (to say), "Worship God, my Lord and your Lord." I was a witness over them, as long as I was among them, but when You took me (or, caused me to die), You were the Watcher over them, and You are a witness over all things. (Q. 5:117)

Here the Oneness of God is contrasted with the humanity of Christ, which is stressed by the reference to the fact of his mortality.

The other verse I wish to discuss at some length is put in the context of confrontation or struggle between Jesus and his opponents, where God intervenes directly on behalf of His messenger. The struggle begins when Jesus senses the denial or unbelief of his people. He asks his disciples, "Who shall be my supporters (*anṣār*) to God?" They pledged their support in the words, "We shall be God's supporters; we believe in God, so bear witness that we are Muslims" (Q. 3:52). Then in answer to the plot of the people against Jesus, God assures him, saying, "O Jesus, I am surely taking you (or, causing you to die, *mutawaffīka*) and lifting you up to me" (Q. 3:55). The verse goes on to promise Jesus salvation from the impurities of unbelief and to his followers authority over the people of unbelief until the Day of Resurrection, when all men shall return to God, who will judge among them. The verse clearly states an end to Jesus' earthly life followed by a celestial life with God.

Commentators went to great length in their attempts to harmonize this statement with what appears at first sight as its opposite. It is the declaration that Jesus did not actually die on the cross but was taken up to heaven. The solutions offered were, first, that the word *mutawaffīka* means "receiving you."[35] The verb *tawaffa* literally means "to reclaim a debt or a charge in its entirety from another person." In general usage, however, it means in its passive form *tuwuffī*, "to die," hence the verbal noun *wafāt*, "death." Thus, the dilemma is whether Jesus died and his soul was received by God, or his soul and body were both reclaimed and he went to heaven alive. The second solution implies that Jesus is still alive in heaven, having been taken up in his sleep so that he would not be frightened by the experience.[36] Tabari cites Ka'b al-Ahbar, the Jewish chief rabbi, as saying:

> God, exalted be His Majesty, would not have caused Jesus, son of Mary, to die. . . . Thus, when Jesus saw the small number of those who accepted him and the multitude of those who rejected him, he complained to God. Then God revealed to him, 'Surely I am receiving you (*mutawaffīka*) and lifting you up to me. For the one whom I take up to Me is not dead, and I shall send you against the one-eyed liar (*al-A'war al-Dajjāl*) and you shall kill him. After this, you shall live for twenty-four years, then will I cause you to die the death of the living.[37]

It was early reported on the authority of Ibn Abbas that the word *mutawaffīka* means "causing you to die," *mumītuka*.[38] Perhaps contemporary with this tradition was the alternative equating of *tawaffī* (receiving or reclaiming) with *rafa'a* (to take up to heaven).[39] Still another tradition suggests that Jesus was taken to heaven and will die later, since the sequence of the action of receiving and taking up does not necessarily require the order given in the literal reading of the text.[40]

The traditions related on the authority of converts such as Wahb bin Munabbih retain a strong echo of Gospel accounts. Wahb declared, "God caused Jesus, son of Mary, to die for three hours during the day, then took him up to Him." It is possible that the three hours here mentioned refer to the darkness that was supposed to have covered the earth at the time of Jesus' death.[41] Ibn Ishaq reports on the authority of a Christian convert that God caused Jesus to die for seven hours, an idea that later commentators attribute to Christian reports.[42] There is no evidence of such a notion in Christian tradition. There were even suggestions that Jesus died for three days, then was resuscitated and taken up to heaven.[43]

Again, as usual, we find in Razi a genuine attempt to go beyond the literal reading of the text. He first interprets the word *mutawaffīka* as possibly meaning "completing the term (*ajal*) of your life," and "protecting you from the evil schemes of your enemies." This also means that Jesus was taken up to heaven both in body and spirit, that is, as a complete person. Razi then argues that the word is to be understood metaphorically: "I [God] shall render you [Jesus] as though you are dead," because when Jesus was taken up to heaven and no news or trace was left of him on earth, he became as one dead.[44] The author takes the term *tawwafī* to include death, without being synonymous with it. It is rather a general term requiring specification of the kind intended; hence, "and 'taking you up to Me' is . . . a specification of the kind."[45] It could also mean that God accepted the deeds (*a'māl*) of Jesus, which He caused to be brought before Him.[46] Razi concludes:

> What is meant by this verse is that the Exalted One gave Jesus the glad tidings that his acts of obedience and good deeds were accepted. He informed him also that what troubles and hardships he had suf-fered at the hands of his enemies in the cause of manifesting his faith (*dīn*) and sacred law (*sharī'ah*) would not be lost, nor would his reward be destroyed.[47]

In this interpretation, Razi may have been influenced by the Sufi view of Christ. He quotes the statement of the famous Sufi Abu Bakr al-Wasiti that God said, "I am causing you to die to your desires and the limitations of your cardinal soul (*nafs*)."[48] Razi does not, however, carry this interpretation far enough for him to be a good representative of the Sufi view.

The Sufis, while not rejecting the traditional interpretation completely, have attempted to see Christ as the universal perfect man through whom all religions will be unified and humanity brought nearer to God. The signifi-cance of the death of Jesus is not in the how and when of history but rather in its meaning to a humanity bound to this material plane of existence by lust, greed, and anxiety. Nor is the significance of his heavenly subsistence with God dependent on whether his body, his spirit, or both were assumed to heaven. Rather, the significance of Christ's life in heaven is his example as a specially favored human being who has risen beyond this world of mate-rial existence to the divine presence. He was taken to the heaven, which, according to al-Hasan al-Basri, "is the locus of the grace (*karāmah*) of God and the dwelling place of His angels."[49] God wished him to be with the angels in order that "they may attain his grace (*barakah*), because he is the Word of God and His Spirit." Jesus may be taken as a concrete example of the spiritual journey of the man of faith from the plane of material existence to the celestial plane where God alone is; there to Him alone belongs judg-ment and to no one of His creatures.

Jesus will return to share in our human life, and more fully than he did during his first sojourn on earth. He shall then purify the earth from all false-hood and dissension. He shall kill the one-eyed liar, the symbol of all evil in the world. He shall remove the barriers that divide humanity spiritually. He shall marry and beget children. He shall die and be buried with Muhammad in his grave, and the two will be resurrected together.[50] In this final com-mingling of the bodies of the founders of two of the world's largest religious communities, we have perhaps the myth expressing hopes often drowned by the clamor of our empty words.

## The Search for Meaning: Some Modern Attitudes

The Sufi approach had been unique in the long history of Muslim-Christian relations. It has not, unfortunately, received the attention it deserves as a possible basis for constructive dialogue. In fact, modern thinkers have generally ignored Sufi ideas along with much traditional literature dealing with the interpretation of the life, death, and mission of Jesus.

The Shi'i view of Christ resembles that of the Sufis in some important respects. First, it does not always insist on a literal understanding of the text. Second, it presents an ascetic image of Jesus, and finally, it does not generally favor a bodily ascension of Christ to heaven.

Modern Shi'i thinkers have allowed the possibility that Jesus died and only his spirit was taken up to heaven. One modern commentator has argued that the Jews crucified not Jesus but another whom they mistook for him. Jesus, however, escaped and with his mother spent the rest of his life in hermetic seclusion. The author finds support for this view in the verse, "And we have made the son of Mary and his mother a sign, and led them for refuge to a hill of comfort and flowing water" (Q. 23:50).[51] Jesus then died a natural death, and his body was buried in that hill, while his spirit went up to heaven.

The well-known contemporary Shi'i scholar Sayyid Muhammad Husayn Tabataba'i takes the same view, but on different grounds. He first argues that *wafāt* does not necessarily mean death, unless specified.[52] He argues further that although a literal reading of the words "rather, God took him up to Himself" may suggest a bodily ascension, "God actually meant a spiritual (*ma'nawī*) and not a formal (*ṣuwarī*) assumption, because the Exalted One has no place of the kind occupied by bodies."[53] In this, the author follows a time-honored tradition in Mu'tazili and Shi'i thought that sought to explain metaphorically all anthropomorphic references to God in the Qur'an. Even, he concludes, "if the text indicates literally bodily assumption, heaven means only the locus of proximity to Him and His blessings."[54]

Again, in agreement with the Mu'tazili insistence on divine justice and the rationality of all things, Sayyid Tabataba'i interprets the words *shubbiha lahum* as "seizing someone else unknowingly."[55] For the Roman soldiers who arrested Jesus and crucified him did not know him. He bases this argument on the role of Judas, who identified Jesus for them. Thus, *tashbīh*, seeming or appearing, could also mean "mistake" (*shubha*), and not the casting of the image (*ṣurāh*) of one man on another. The author offers a final curious suggestion:

> Perhaps some historians have mentioned that the stories relating to Jesus, his mission, and the historical events of the rulers and other preachers of his time refer to two men called Christ. The two may have lived five hundred years or more apart. The earlier was the true Messiah, neither killed nor crucified, and the later, the false Mes-

siah, was crucified. Thus, what the Qur'an mentions concerning *tashbīh* is that of Jesus, son of Mary, with the crucified Christ.

Perhaps aware of the historical problems that this suggestion raises, the author adds, "and God knows best."[56]

In contrast with the Sufi and Shi'i views of the death and assumption of Christ, contemporary Sunni thinkers have shifted the emphasis of their arguments to a discussion of the meaning of the cross in the Christian faith and to the question of the authenticity of the Gospel accounts regarding the death of Christ. In this, they have taken an important step toward facing the crucial issues involved in the Christian assertion of the cross as a historical fact of cosmic dimensions, transforming and transcending history. Commentators of the classical and postclassical periods sought through an earnest and painstaking study of the Qur'an to question the historicity of the cross, without, however, grappling with the problems of its significance for Christianity. Modern thinkers, on the other hand, have turned to history, including the Gospel story, for support of their interpretations. They exhibit a fairly accurate knowledge of primary Christian sources, which they discuss not from a Christian but from a strictly Islamic perspective. This approach can hardly serve as the basis for a fruitful encounter of the two faiths.

The modern approach is dialectic and personal, and while it takes traditional ideas into account, it is generally not bound by them. Hence, it is not to tradition that modern thinkers turn for their criticism of Christianity but to the nineteenth-century humanist attacks on religion. In this we see a kind of crystallization of a modern tradition. Early modernists in the Arab world, such as Muhammad 'Abduh and his immediate successors, all belong to the nineteenth century. Their views have been adopted and in large measure repeated by later thinkers interested in Christianity in general.

Another important characteristic of the modern approach is a tendency to demythologize the Christ of the classical tradition, whether by rejecting tradition altogether or by interpreting it metaphorically. Sayyid Qutb, the famous leader of the Muslim Brothers, relies on the Gospel accounts only for the background of his interpretation of the verses under consideration. His purpose was to "remain in the shadow of the Qur'an."[57] He accepts only what the sacred text states concerning the death and assumption of Jesus Christ, commenting that "as for the manner of his death and assumption, these are matters belonging to the unseen (*ghaybiyyah*), and they fall in the category of obscure (*mutashabbihāt*) verses, whose exegetical meaning (*ta'wīl*) is known to God alone."[58]

Another modern thinker, Ahmad Mustafa al-Maraghi, offers a rationalistic view of Christ by interpreting tradition metaphorically. He argues from historical examples of identity confusion that it was possible for the Jews and the Roman soldiers to mistake another for Jesus.[59] Like Moses, who disappeared under the eyes of thousands of his people, Jesus disappeared and died a natural death. As for his ascension, it must be understood as the raising of status or degree with God; as we read of Idris (Enoch), "and We raised him into a high station" (Q. 19:57). Similarly, what is meant by Christ's return to the earth and his rule over it is "the domination of his spirit and the mystery of his message over humanity in order that men may live by the inner meaning of the law (*sharī'ah*) without being bound by its outer shell."[60] For Jesus did not bring a new law to the Jews. He was rather a reformer who sought to manifest the truth. Likewise, the liar (*al-Dajjāl*) whom Jesus is to kill at the end of time is only a symbol of empty legends, falsehood, and all the evils which would disappear were men and women to live by the spirit of the sacred law and fulfill its injunctions.[61]

It must be emphasized that Muslim thinkers do not reject the Gospels out of hand as complete distortions of the truth. They are regarded, on the contrary, as containing clear evidence of the essential truth of God's Oneness and the humanity of Jesus. It is interesting to observe further that throughout Islamic history, the Fourth Gospel, with its Logos christology, has been the one most often cited by Muslim thinkers in support of their arguments. Another document that provided the answer to many christological questions for modern commentators is the *Gospel of Barnabas*. This is most probably a late work, written under Islamic influence and agreeing with Islam on many crucial points.[62] It was translated into Arabic in the early decades of this century by Antun Saadi, a Lebanese Christian. Since then, it has been regarded by Muslim scholars as coming nearest to the lost *Gospel of Jesus* (*Injīl 'Īsa*), and has therefore been the source of many of their arguments against Christianity.[63] The *Gospel of Barnabas* tells us that Judas Iscariot led the Jews and Roman soldiers to arrest Jesus at night in a house where Jesus and the disciples were sleeping. As he entered the house, Jesus was taken away by the angels, who carried him up to heaven. His likeness and his voice were cast upon Judas, who woke up the other disciples to ask where the master had gone. They, however, hailed him as the master and thought him distraught by the fear of death. This Judas was taken and crucified. He lost his mind, so that his incoherent protests were considered as those of a madman. Jesus, however, appeared after three days to his mother and the rest of the disciples to comfort and reassure them, announcing the coming of the Prophet Muhammad, who would fulfill all the things he had taught.[64]

The *Gospel of Barnabas* has provided modern commentators not only with a supposed firsthand report in support of the substitutionist theory but also with what appears as a plausible justification. Thus, we have come full circle back to the earliest interpretation of the words *shubbiha lahum* as meaning "another took his likeness and was substituted for him." Modern Muslim thinkers have been aware of the claim that *Barnabas* is a late document. Some have therefore used it only as partial evidence,[65] while others have argued that it is the true Gospel in full or in part, which Christians had hidden for many centuries until it was found in their most sacred institution, the Vatican library. The question of the historicity of the event of the cross remains open, nonetheless, and a more up-to-date study of the *Gospel of*

*Barnabas* would help greatly in moving Christian-Muslim dialogue from scriptural polemics to the more important task of understanding and appreciating the significance of Christ for the two religious traditions. The critique of the cross as the instrument of redemption by Sayyid Muhammad Rashid Rida in *Tafsir al-Manar* typifies both the problem as well as the effort for greater Christian-Muslim understanding. We shall conclude our discussion of Muslim views of the death of Jesus with a brief analysis of this critique.

Rashid Rida agrees with other contemporary commentators in taking the traditions regarding the ascension of Jesus and his return at the end of time metaphorically and with caution. He sees in the Qur'anic reference to Jesus as the apostle of God whom the Jews wrongly claimed to have killed an assertion of Christ's apostleship, not divinity. He argues further that the Gospels indicate that Jesus himself proclaimed the Oneness of God in the words, "and this is eternal life, that they know Thee, the only true God, and Jesus Christ whom Thou hast sent."[66] He likewise finds support in the same Gospel for the idea of doubt and conjecture concerning Jesus' identity even by the disciples: "You shall doubt me tonight."[67] These works are quoted by most modern commentators, all of whom miss their real significance, both for the evangelist and for Christian tradition in general. The author concludes from this that if the disciples, who know him most intimately, doubted him, then a mistake in identity would not be impossible. Therefore, this story is based on a historical account with an incomplete chain of transmission. Here again, the author of *al-Manar* echoes the usual demand that the only measure of true report is the model of hadith transmission.

Having thus established his position regarding the problems of interpreting the Qur'anic text, the author adds: "The actual fact of the crucifixion is not itself a matter which the Book of God seeks to affirm or deny, except for the purpose of asserting the killing of prophets by the Jews unjustly, and reproaching them for that act."[68] The author then proceeds to the more important matter, namely, the Christian belief concerning Christ and the crucifixion. He begins with a detailed discussion of original sin, then the incarnation, and finally the work of redemption.

The author insists throughout on the necessity of reason in judging and accepting the truth of divine revelation. Thus he argues that the story of the crucifixion and redemption is unacceptable to anyone who believes in rational proof. The story implies that when Adam fell, God was for thousands of years seeking a way to reconcile His justice with His mercy. This imputes ignorance to God, and thus it is an act of unbelief (*kufr*). No one in possession of an independent reason could accept the idea:

> that the creator of the universe could be incarnated in the womb of a woman in this earth which, in comparison to the rest of His creation, is like an atom, and then be a human being eating and drinking, experiencing fatigue and suffering other hardships like the rest of mankind. Then His enemies would level at Him insults and pain, and finally crucify Him with thieves and declare Him cursed accord-

ing to the Book He revealed to one of His apostles, exalted be He over all this![69]

No one could believe in such a story on which, Christians claim, depends the salvation of humanity. "We say rather no one believes it because belief (*īmān*) is the affirmation (*taṣdīq*) by reason of something that it can apprehend."[70]

The author goes on to ask how can we say that God had reconciled His justice with His mercy through the crucifixion of Christ when in reality this had nullified them both. For God allowed Jesus to suffer as a man without having committed any sin that merited this great punishment. God, therefore, cannot be both just and merciful if in attempting to reconcile the two, He loses them both. Perhaps referring to the doctrine of salvation by faith, the author protests that if the crucifixion would save the person believing in it, no matter how grave his sins and evil his deeds, where would the justice of God and His mercy be? "The claim of the people of the cross, therefore, that clemency and forgiveness are opposed to justice, is unacceptable."[71] Sayyid Rashid Rida then continues by contrasting this with the idea of salvation in Islam.

Obviously, these criticisms are not new, nor are they limited to Muslims. This study is not the place for us to argue for or against them. It must be observed, however, that reason has not been considered, even by Islam, as the final arbiter of faith. Indeed, the Qur'an is replete with instances extolling the divine mystery in creation. Nor does the Qur'an reject the nonrational conception of Jesus, outside the biological law of procreation. Christians have insisted from the start that the cross is an obstacle to human wisdom and rationality. Faith is not logic but the divine gift to man transcending and transforming human wisdom and rationality.

Rashid Rida and Muhammad 'Abduh were subject to missionary and secularist pressures. Thus, their polemical arguments against Christianity must be seen in the context of Christian polemic against Islamic tradition, both in its religion and its culture. Times have changed, and with the change of time there is a change of attitude. In his *Qaryah zalima*,[72] Kamil Husayn presents perhaps the first Muslim attempt to see the cross in its true meaning. It is a judgment not against any group of people but against humanity, a repeatable act in any city, large or small, whose inhabitants choose to turn it into a "City of Wrong." In deciding to crucify Christ, the zealously religious men of Jerusalem agreed to crucify their conscience. Christianity would perhaps agree with this, but it would assert (and here the difference is vast and instructive) that in choosing to crucify their conscience, men and women everywhere and in every age crucify Christ anew.

# Conclusion

It has been often argued by Christian scholars of Islam that because Islam was not forged in the face of persecution and martyrdom, it has no place for the mystery of suffering, which in Christianity becomes the foundation for faith, hope, and love. This view, I believe, is at best a simplistic one. The distraught Jacob, the patient Job, the persecuted Abraham, and the martyred Zechariah and his son, John the Baptist, are but a few of the many examples of suffering in the way of God. Their stories, told and retold to the pious throughout Islamic history, have played an important, although little recognized, role in Muslim piety. The Shiʻi ethos, which sees suffering as a dominant force in human history, has also played its important role in sensitizing Muslims to the power and profundity of human suffering. Finally, the Prophet, in his moments of agony and depression, under the burden of the divine commission and in his moments of fear and loneliness, had to be reassured by God with the words, "Have we not relieved your breast for you?" (Q. 93:1). Why then, it must be asked, does the Qurʼan deny the crucifixion of Christ in the face of apparently overwhelming evidence? Muslim commentators have not been able convincingly to disprove the crucifixion. Rather, they have compounded the problem by adding the conclusion of their substitutionist theories. The problem has been, we believe, one of understanding. Commentators have generally taken the verse to be a historical statement. This statement, like all the other statements concerning Jesus in the Qurʼan, belongs not to history but to theology in the broadest sense. It is similar to the Qurʼanic assertion that Mary, the mother of Christ, was the sister of Aaron. In answer to the historian's protest, the Qurʼan declares that all the prophets are a continuous progeny (Q. 19:28; 3:34), not, of course, in the strict physical sense. Let us, then, look at the verse again, this time from the point of view of theology, not of history.

The reproach of the Jews, "for their saying: 'We have surely killed Jesus the Christ, son of Mary, the apostle of God,'" with which the verse starts, is not directed at the telling of a historical lie or at the making of a false report. It is, rather, as is clear from the context, directed at human arrogance and folly, at an attitude toward God and His messenger. The words identifying Jesus are especially significant. They wished to kill Jesus, the innocent man, who is also the Christ, the Word, and God's representative among them. By identifying Christ in this context, the Qurʼan is not only addressing the people who could have killed yet another prophet but is telling all of humanity who Jesus is.

The Qurʼan is not speaking here about a man, righteous and wronged though he may be, but about the Word of God who was sent to earth and who returned to God. Thus, the denial of the killing of Jesus is a denial of the power of human beings to vanquish and destroy the divine Word, which is forever victorious. Hence the words "they did not kill him, nor did they crucify him" go far deeper than the events of ephemeral human history; they penetrate the heart and conscience of human beings. The claim of humanity (here exemplified in the Jewish society of Christ's earthly existence) to have this power against God can only be an illusion. "They did not slay him . . . but it seemed so to them." They only imagined doing so.

The words *wa lākin shubbiha lahum* do not disclose, therefore, a long-hidden secret of divine deception; rather, they constitute an accusation or judgment against the human sin of pride and ignorance. They are explained further in what follows: those who have disagreed about Christ are surely in doubt concerning the truth. They have no knowledge; they follow only conjecture, the foolish imaginings of their minds. What is this truth? It is, I think, the affirmation, once again, that God is greater than human powers and empty schemes: "They did not kill him [that is, Jesus the Christ and God's apostle] with certainty; rather, God took him up to Himself, and God is mighty, and wise." Again, human ignorance, delusion, and conjecture are all identified as a lack of certainty or firm faith. In the statement "and God is Mighty and Wise," these human limitations are contrasted with divine power and infinite wisdom.

The same verse presents Christ the Word as a challenge to human wisdom and power, and a judgment against human folly and pride. Men may "wish to extinguish the light of God with their mouths," that is, with their words of foolish wisdom, but God will perfect His light in spite of our foolishness and obstinacy (Q. 9:32).

In their earnest striving for a true understanding of the scared text, Muslim commentators did more than indulge in an exercise of textual analysis. The Qur'an insists on "letting God be God," and this the Muslim community has taken with uncompromising seriousness. The commentators expressed this insistence with eloquence and power, even at the risk of denying man the privilege of being man. On this privilege, with all its implications, the Qur'an also insists, and with equal emphasis. Man, the crown of creation, "made in the best of forms" (Q. 95:4), is also a "wrongdoing, foolish" creature (Q. 33:72). Yet, in the end, the righteous men and women among God's servants will inherit the earth (Q. 21:105). Humanity must be fulfilled, and that is possible only through its exemplars, God's prophets and friends (*awliyā'*).

Christianity has insisted, and with equally uncompromising seriousness, on "letting God be man" in order for "man to be divine." The gap between an extreme Islamic and an extreme Christian position on this point is admittedly vast. The difference is, I believe, one of theological terminology rather than intent. The final purpose for the two communities of faith is one: let God be God, not only in His vast creation but in our little lives as well. Then and only then could man be truly man, and the light of God would shine with perfect splendor in our mouths and hearts.

## Appendix I: An Early Muslim Account of the Passion[73]

When God informed Jesus, son of Mary, that he would soon be departing this world, he was disheartened by death, and sorely grieved. He therefore called the disciples (*ḥawāriyyūn*) together for a meal which he had prepared for them. He said, "Come to me all of you tonight for I have a favor to ask of you." When they had all come together in the night, he served them himself, and when they had finished eating, he washed their hands and helped them to perform their ablutions with his own hands and wiped their hands and garments.[74]

The disciples regarded this as an act below the master's dignity and expressed their disapproval. But Jesus said, "Anyone who opposes me in what I do tonight is not of me (that is, of my faith) nor I of him." Thus they concurred. When he had finished, he said, "As for what I have done for you tonight, serving you at table and washing your hands with my own hands, let that be an example for you. You regard me as the best of you, so let no one among you regard himself as better than the others, and let each one of you offer his life for the others as I have laid down my life for you.[75] As for the favor for which I have called you, it is that you pray God fervently that He may extend my term (*ajal*)."

But when they stood up in prayer, wishing to prolong their earnest supplications, they were overcome by sleep, so that they were unable to pray. He began to rouse them, saying, "To God be praise, could you not bear with me one night and render me help!" They answered, "We know not what had befallen us. We used to stay up the night in long fellowship (*samar*), but tonight we cannot keep ourselves from sleep, and whatever supplication we wish to make, we are being prevented from making." Then Jesus said, "The shepherd will be taken away and the sheep will be scattered."[76] With similar words he went on foretelling and lamenting his end. He continued, "in truth, I say to you, one of you will deny me three times before the cock crows. And another will sell me for a few pieces of silver and consume my price."[77]

After this, they went out, each his own way, and left him. The Jews then came seeking him, and they seized Sham'un [Simon Peter], exclaiming, "He is one of his companions," but he denied, saying, "I am not his companion." Others also seized him and he likewise denied. Then he heard the crowing of a cock; he wept bitterly (Matt 26:75).

The next morning one of the disciples went to the Jews and said, "What will you give me if I lead you to Christ?" They gave him thirty pieces, which he took and led them to him. Prior to that, however, he [or: it] so appeared to them. [The clause *wa kāna shubbiha 'alayhim qabla dhālik* is inserted here without further explanation. It could mean that the disciple Judas bore his likeness or that they imagined something; no doubt the phrase is inserted to harmonize a Gospel account with Islamic exegesis. From here on, it is not clear who the actual object of the story is.] Thus they took him, after ascertaining that it was he, and tied him with a rope. They dragged him, saying, "You raised the dead and cast out Satan, and healed those who were possessed, can you not save yourself from this rope?" They also spat on him and placed thorns upon his head. Thus they brought him to the wood on which they wished to crucify him.[78] God, however, took him up to Himself and they crucified what seemed [like Christ] to them. [It is interesting to observe that the clause *faṣalabū mā shubbiḥa lahum* does not necessarily imply a person but a thing; otherwise, *man shubbiḥa lahum* would have been more appropriate.]

Then Jesus remained seven [days?] [we are not told where, but perhaps in heaven.]. Then his mother and the woman whom Jesus cured from madness [Mary Magdalene?] came to weep in the place where the crucified one was. Jesus came to them and said, "For whom do you weep?" They answered, "for you." He said, "God has taken me up to Himself and no harm befell me. For this is a thing which only appeared to them. Go now and tell the disciples to meet me at such and such a place." So they met him, eleven, but the one who sold him and led the Jews to him was missing. Jesus asked his companions about him and they said, "He regretted what he did, so he hanged and killed himself." Jesus said, "Had he repented, God surely would have turned toward him." [It is clear from this that Judas was not the one substituted for Jesus. At this early stage, the identity of the substitute was left unspecified.]

Jesus then inquired from them concerning a youth who followed them called John (Yuhannah). [The use of the Syriac "Yuhannah" rather than "Yahya," as well as the fact that John has no special place in this story, indicates that the source of the tradition was clearly the Fourth Gospel.] He answered, "He is with you. Go now for everyone of you will speak the language of a different people. [This is perhaps a vague allusion to the descent of the Holy Spirit.[79]] Let him therefore warn them and leave them."

## Appendix II: The Christ of Sufism[80]

Jesus was taken to heaven because his entrance into worldly existence was not through the gate of lust; therefore his departure from it was not through the gate of death. He rather entered through the gate of power (*qudrah*) and departed through the gate of majesty (*'izzah*). [In heaven] God gave him wings and clothed him with light and removed from him the desires for food and drink, Thus he flies with the angles, and is with them around the throne. For he is human and angelic, heavenly and earthly.

If, then, it is asked, why did God not return Jesus to the world after He had taken him up to heaven, the answer is that he shall return in the end to be a sign for the hour (*'ilm li sā'a*), that is, the Day of Resurrection and the seal of general *walāyah* [saintship]. For after him, there is no *walī* (saint or friend of God) with whom God would close the Muhammadan cycle (*al-dawrah al-Muhammadiyyah*). [For in this] is its great ennoblement, in that it will be closed by a prophet-messenger who will be subject to the *sharī'ah*. Both Jews and Christians will believe in it [that is, Islam]. Through him [Jesus] God will renew the age of prophethood for the community (*ummah*). He shall be served by the Mahdi and the men of the cave. He shall marry and beget children. He shall be one of the community for Muhammad as the seal of his *awliyā'* and heirs with regard to *walāyah*. [Sufi theology posits two concentric cycles of prophethood and *walāyah*, beginning with Adam and ending with Muhammad, the seal of the prophetic cycle. That of *walāyah* will continue until the end of time. Jesus, however, will have the great privilege of culminating both cycles, being the perfect *walī* and perfect prophet.] For the spirit of Jesus is the manifestation of the greatest name, and an effulgence of divine power . . . ; he is the manifestation of the universal divine name, a primordial inheritance.

# Notes

1. The numbering is of the Egyptian edition and all Qur'anic translations are my own.

2. Ahmad ibn Hanbal, *Musnad,* ed. Ahmad Muhammad Shakir (Cairo: Dar al-Ma'arif, 1375/1955), vol. 15, hadith 7902ff. See also Muslim bin al-Hajjaj al-Qushayri al-Nisaburi, *Sahih Muslim,* ed. Muhammad Fu'ad Abd al-Baqi, 1st ed. (Cairo: Dar Ihya' al-Kutub al-'Arabiyya, 1375/1955), vol. 4, hadith 141-49.

3. See also Abu Ja'far Muhammad bin Jarir al-Tabari, *Jami' al-bayan 'an ta'wil ay al-Qur'an,* ed. Mahmud Muhammad Shakir and Ahmad Muhammad Shakir (Cairo: Dar al-Ma'arif, n.d.), 6:461.

4. See, for example, the *Infancy Gospel of Thomas* and the *Protevangelium of James* in Edgar Hennecke, *New Testament Apocrypha,* vol. 1, trans. and ed. R. McL. Wilson (Philadelphia: Westminster, 1963).

5. Michel Hayek, *al-Masih fi al-Islam* (Beirut: Catholic Press, 1961), 21.

6. al-Tabari, *Jami' al-bayan 'an ta'wil ay al-Qur'an,* 9:367, hadith 10779.

7. See appendix I for the complete text of this tradition.

8. See, for example, Abu'l-Faraj Jamal al-Din 'Abd al-Rahman bin 'Ali bin Muhammad al-Jawzi al-Qarashi al-Baghdadi, *Zad al-masir fi 'ilm al-tafsir,* 1st ed. (Beirut: al-Maktab al-Islami, 1384/1964), 2:224; Abu 'Abdallah Muhammad bin Yusuf bin 'Ali bin Yusuf al-Hayyani, commonly known as Abu Hayyan, *al-Bahr al-muhit* (Riyadh: Maktabah al-Nasr, n.d.), 2:373 and 3:389; and for a good review of the various ideas up to his time, see 'Imad al-Din Abu'l-Fida' Isma'il ibn Kathir, *Tafsir al-Qur'an al-'azim* (Cairo: Dar Ihya' al-Kutub al-'Arabiyya, n.d.), 1:573ff.

9. al-Tabari, *Jami' al-bayan 'an ta'wil ay al-Qur'an,* 9:370, hadith 10781.

10. Ibid., 370.

11. Ibid., 370-71; cf. Matt 26:39; Mark 14:36; Luke 22:42.

12. See Baghdadi, *Zad al-masir fi 'ilm al-tafsir,* 2:244ff.; Abu Tahir bin Muhammad al-Fayruzabadi al-Shirazi, *Tanwir al-miqbas min tafsir ibn 'Abbas,* 2nd ed. (Cairo: Mustafa al-Babi al-Halabi, 1370/1951), 68; for Shi'i examples, see Abu 'Ali al-Fadl bin Hasan al-Tabarsi, *Majma' al-bayan fi tafsir al-Qur'an* (Tehran: Sharikat al-Ma'arif al-Islamiyya, A.H. 1373), 3:135.

13. See the previous footnote. See also Abu'l-Barakat 'Abdallah bin Ahmad bin Mahmud al-Nasafi, *Madarik al-tanzil wa haqa'iq al-ta'wil* (Cairo: Dar Ihya' al-Kutub al 'Arabiyya, n.d.), 1:203; and Muhiy al-Sunna bin Muhammad bin al-Husayn bin Mas'ud al-Baghawi, *Ma'alim al-tanzil* (n.p.: Matba'at al-Salihi, A.H. 1249). See the commentary on Surah 4:157-58, no pagination.

14. See the two previous footnotes, and Ibn Kathir, *Tafsir al-Qur'an al-'azim,* 1:366ff. and 573ff.

15. Isma'il Haqqi, *Tafsir ruh al-bayan* (Istanbul: al-Matba'a al-'Uthmaniyyah, A.H. 1130), 2:317. See also al-Qadi Sana'allah al-'Uthmani al-Mazhari, *Tafsir al-mazhari* (Hyderabad: n.p., n.d.), 2:280.

16. al-Tabari, *Jami' al-bayan 'an ta'wil ay al-Qur'an*, 9:370-71.

17. See, for example, Abu Ja'far Muhammad bin al-Hasan al-Tusi, *al-Tibyan*, ed. Ahmad Shawqi al-Amin and Muhammad Habib Qusayr (Najaf: Maktabat al-Amini, n.d.), 3:383; and Ibn Kathir, *Tafsir al-Qur'an al-'azim*, 1:575, for his discussion of the various traditions.

18. Ibn Kathir, *Tafsir al-Qur'an al-'azim*, 1:574.

19. Ibid., 574; cf. John 20:26-27.

20. Ibn Kathir, *Tafsir al-Qur'an al-'azim*, 1:574.

21. Abu'l-Qasim 'Abdallah Mahmud bin 'Umar al-Zamakhshari, *al-Kashshaf 'an haqa'iq ghawamid al-tanzil wa 'uyun al-aqawil fi wujuh al-ta'wil* (Beirut: Dar al-Kitab al-'Arabi, n.d.), 1:587.

22. al-Qadi Nasir al-Din al-Baydawi, *Tafsir al-Baydawi* (Cairo: Muhammad 'Ali Sabih, 1951), 135.

23. Fakhr al-Din al-Razi, *al-Tafsir al-kabir,* 1st ed. (Cairo: al-Matba'a al-Bahiyya, 1357/1938), 11:100.

24. Ibid.

25. Ibid., 11:101.

26. al-Sayyid Hashim bin Sulayman bin Isma'il bin Sayyid 'Abd al-Jawwad al-Husayni al-Bahrani, *al-Burhan fi tafsir al-Qur'an* (Tehran: Chapkhaneh Aftab, n.d.), 285.

27. Ibid., 285. See also 'Abd 'Ali Janqalarusi al-Huwayzi, *Tafsir nur al-thaqalayn* (Qom: Matba'at al-Hikma, A.H. 1382), 1:287.

28. al-Bahrani, *al-Burhan fi tafsir al-Qur'an*, 285.

29. Abu Muhammad 'Abdallah bin Muslim bin Qutayba, *Tafsir gharib al-Qur'an*, ed. Ahmad Saqr (Cairo: Dar Ihya' al-Kutub al-'Arabiyya, 1348/1958), 136.

30. al-Tabari, *Jami' al-bayan 'an ta'wil ay al-Qur'an*, 9:376.

31. al-Razi, *al-Tafsir al-kabir*, 11:101. See also Haqqi, *Tafsir ruh al-bayan*, 2:318.

32. See, for example, al-Razi, *al-Tafsir al-kabir*, 11:101; Ibn Kathir, *Tafsir al-Qur'an al-'azim*, 1:573. For a different view, see Baghawi commentary on Surah 4:158.

33. Ibn Kathir, *Tafsir al-Qur'an al-'azim*, 1:574-75.

34. See, for example, Q. 3:55; 5:117; 19:33.

35. See al-Tabari, *Jami' al-bayan 'an ta'wil ay al-Qur'an*, 6:455, for his detailed discussion. See esp. Zamakhshari, *al-Kashshaf 'an haqa'iq*, 1:366.

36. Zamakhshari, *al-Kashshaf 'an haqa'iq*, 1:366.

37. al-Tabari, *Jami' al-bayan 'an ta'wil ay al-Qur'an*, 6:456-57.

38. Most commentators mention this as an alternative. Modern thinkers generally insist on it.

39. al-Tabari, *Jami' al-bayan 'an ta'wil ay al-Qur'an*, 6:457.

40. See al-Shirazi, *Tanwir al-miqbas min tafsir ibn 'Abbas*, 39.

41. See Michel Hayek, *al-Masih fi al-Islam*, 225; cf. Matt 27:45; Mark 15:33; Luke 23:44.

42. See al-Tabari, *Jami' al-bayan 'an ta'wil ay al-Qur'an*, 6:458; and Ibn Kathir, *Tafsir al-Qur'an al-'azim*, 1:366.

43. Muhammad bin 'Ali bin Muhammad al-Shawkani, *Fath al-Qadir: al-Jami'*

*bayna fannay al-riwaya wa al-diraya min 'ilm al-tafsir* (Cairo: Mustafa al-Babi al-Halabi, n.d.), 1:346, citing Ibn Asakir, who reports on the authority of Ibn Munabbih.

44. al-Razi, *al-Tafsir al-kabir*, 7:72.

45. Ibid.

46. Ibid.

47. Ibid.

48. Ibid. See also al-Shirazi, *Tanwir al-miqbas min tafsir ibn 'Abbas,* 39: "I shall cause your heart to die to the love of this world."

49. Haqqi, *Tafsir ruh al-bayan,* 2:318.

50. Mazhari, *Tafsir al-mazhari,* 2:57.

51. Muhammad 'Ali Hasan al-Hilli, *al-Mutashabah min al-Qur'an,* 1st ed. (Beirut: Dar al-Fikr, 1965), 1:204.

52. Muhammad Husayn Tabataba'i, *al-Mizan fi tafsir al-Qur'an* (Beirut: Mu'assasat al-A'lami, 1970), 3:207.

53. Ibid., 3:208; see also al-Tusi, *al-Tibyan,* 2:478.

54. Tabataba'i, *al-Mizan fi tafsir al-Qur'an,* 5:132.

55. Ibid., 5:133.

56. Ibid.

57. Sayyid Qutb, *Fi zilal al-Qur'an,* 5th ed. (Beirut: Dar Ihya' al-Turath al-'Arabi, 1386/1967), 4:587.

58. Ibid., 1:595-96.

59. Ahmad Mustafa al-Maraghi, *Tafsir al-Maraghi,* 2nd ed. (Cairo: Mustafa al-Babi al-Halabi, 1373/1953), 6:12-13.

60. al-Maraghi, *Tafsir al-Maraghi,* 3:169.

61. Ibid., 3:170.

62. *Gospel of Barnabas,* ed. and trans. by Lonsdale and Laura Ragg (Oxford: Clarendon, 1907).

63. See, for example, Shaykh Muhammad Abu Zahra, *Muhadarat fi al-nasraniyyah,* 3rd ed. (Cairo: Matba'at Yusuf, 1385/1966), 57ff.

64. *Gospel of Barnabas,* 481ff.

65. See, for instance, al-Maraghi, *Tafsir al-Maraghi,* 3:13; and Sayyid Qutb, *Fi zilal al-Qur'an,* 6:587.

66. Sayyid Muhammad Rashid Rida, *Tafsir al-Manar,* 2nd ed. (Cairo: Dar al-Manar, A.H. 1367), 6:18; *Oxford Annotated Bible,* Revised Standard Version, ed. H. G. May and B. M. Metzger (New York: Oxford University Press, 1973), John 17:3; see also John 20:17.

67. Rida, *Tafsir al-Manar,* 6:19. This does not appear to be a direct quotation from the Gospels. Cf. Matt 28:17 for a possible parallel.

68. Rida, *Tafsir al-Manar,* 6:23.

69. Ibid., 6:26.

70. Ibid., 6:26-27.

71. Ibid., 6:27.

72. Muhammad Kamil Husayn, *Qaryah zalima* (Cairo: Matba'at Misr, 1958), 1-3; trans. Kenneth Cragg under the title *City of Wrong* (Amsterdam: Djambatan, 1959).

73. al-Tabari, *Jami' al-bayan 'an ta'wil ay al-Qur'an,* 9:367ff.

74. The author changes the washing of feet to that of the hands; cf. John 13.

75. I translate this word *nafs* as "life" in this context. This clearly theological

statement has never been investigated by Muslims thinkers. Cf. John 15:12-14, for parallels.

76. Cf. Matt 26:31.

77. Cf. John 13:38 and 13:21.

78. This is no doubt a telescoped account of the trial of Jesus, based essentially on John but echoing the passion story of Matthew and Luke as well.

79. Cf. Acts 2:1-11.

80. Haqqi, *Tafsir ruh al-bayan*, 2:318ff.

# PART IV

## Muslim-Christian Dialogue in the Modern World

*Comparative Studies*

# 14

# Nearest in Amity

Christians in the Qur'an and
Contemporary Exegetical Tradition

## Introduction

The Qur'an frequently urges Muslims to reflect on its revelations. Yet the Qur'an is not meant to be simply an object of contemplation but a divinely revealed scripture whose precepts and worldview are meant to be pondered, comprehended, and implemented in the life of human society: "Will they not ponder the Qur'an, for had it been from other than God they would have found in it much discrepancy?" (Q. 4:82).[1]

The Qur'an presents itself as an ultimate source of moral guidance and social harmony among its devotees and between them and other scripture-based faith communities. Muslims took the challenge to comprehend the Qur'an and ponder its verses so seriously that they have dedicated their best minds to the interpretation of their sacred Book and elucidation of its meanings. Consequently, Qur'an exegesis (*tafsīr*) is one of the earliest and most important religious sciences, whose beginnings go back to the Prophet and his immediate companions. By the fifth/eleventh century, *tafsīr* had become a highly developed literary genre with a number of ancillary linguistic, legal, theological, mystical, and sectarian disciplines.

Throughout Muslim history, and particularly in the twentieth century, Qur'an commentaries have served as an effective platform for the propagation of diverse beliefs and ideologies. Furthermore, producing a popular commentary on the Qur'an is still regarded as a supreme pious act, a sign of superior religious knowledge, and a source of prestige and even political power for its author. It may, in fact, be argued that the Qur'an shaped Muslim society through its interpreters.

Since the rise of Islamic reform movements in the late nineteenth and first decades of the twentieth centuries, Qur'an commentaries have conferred on both their authors and the movements they championed legitimacy and

Previously published in *Islam and Christian Muslim Relations* 8, no. 2 (July 1997): 145-64. Reprinted by permission.

authority. Hence, practically every Muslim thinker of note must produce a complete, or at least partial, commentary on the Qur'an. Nor has Qur'an exegesis been limited to the Arabic language. Rather Qur'an commentaries have been, and still are being, produced in or translated into most Islamic vernacular as well as Western languages.

It is no exaggeration to say that Qur'an exegesis provides one of the best indicators of the ideological and religious moods of Muslim societies today. While the Qur'an speaks to the hearts of pious Muslims through its reciters, it speaks to the socio-political and religious situation of the Muslim community through its interpreters. In view of all this, the present study will investigate the attitudes of a few well-known contemporary thinkers and Qur'an commentators to Christianity and Christians, and, by implication, their openness to interreligious dialogue. These thinkers have been carefully chosen on the basis of their prominence as religious leaders and scholars and their lasting influence on Muslim thought and piety. Some are still alive, and others have died within the last few decades.

Although the majority of the sources examined in this study are in Arabic, to demonstrate the universality of Qur'an interpretation, two partial commentaries in Persian and English have been included. Important *tafsīr* literature emanating from places such as south and southeast Asia, Turkish speaking areas, and non-Arabic speaking African countries is left out only because of my lack of knowledge of the relevant languages. It is, nonetheless, hoped that this essay will make some contribution to the promotion of better Muslim-Christian understanding in a religiously and culturally pluralistic world.

## The Religious Worldview of the Qur'an

It must be observed at the outset that the attitudes of Qur'an commentators toward the people of the Book have always been colored by the fluctuating political, social, and economic relations between the Muslim world and the Jewish community and Western Christendom. It is necessary, therefore, to begin with a brief analysis of a few Qur'anic verses that seem to present a clear and coherent religious worldview. The verses selected for investigation may be read as categorical statements that need not be limited to specific occasions of revelation, as many classical and contemporary commentators have done, but only for the purpose of limiting the perspective of such verses.

Religiously speaking, the Qur'an divides humankind into two categories: the people of faith (*mu'minūn*) in the One God—creator and sovereign Lord of the universe—and the rejecters of faith (*kāfirūn*) who associate other gods with God. It is noteworthy that the Qur'an has no conception of atheism, either in theory or in practice. Faith in God and the last day, rather than religious affiliation, is the sole criterion of right and wrong, truth and falsehood, and salvation or damnation on the Day of Judgment.[2] The diversity of races and languages, and by implication of religions and cultures, is a sign of divine wisdom in the ordering of human society.[3] The Qur'an asserts that to every people a messenger was sent to call them in their own tongue to God and to elucidate God's holy law for them.[4] Moreover, every human being is created with the innate disposition or capacity (*fiṭrah*) to know God and have faith in Him.[5]

Both the Qur'an and early Prophetic tradition clearly indicate that Muhammad was convinced that the biblical personages of the Old and New Testaments were prophets like him and that the scriptures they brought were divinely revealed Books. In spite of their diversity of form and contents and historical and cultural frame of reference, all sacred scriptures emanate from a single archetypal heavenly source of revelation called in the Qur'an *umm al-kitāb* (essence of the Book).[6]

On this unity of revelation is based the Qur'anic imperative to believe in all of God's messages and prophets, for in essence God's religion is one and prophethood is one. This means having faith not only in well-known prophets and their scriptures, such as Moses and the Torah, Jesus and the Gospel, and Muhammad and the Qur'an, but in "whatever Book God may have revealed" (Q. 42:15).[7]

In this Qur'anic dialectic of revelation in human history, the archetypal heavenly Book, which is manifested in an indeterminate number of scriptures and revealed to an indeterminate number of prophets, is the source of both the unity and the diversity of religion. "Humankind," the Qur'an asserts, "was all one community." Then God sent prophets with the Book to judge among peoples concerning that in which they differed. Disagreement arose, however, only after scriptures had come to human communities. The cause of disagreement, the verse just cited asserts, is religious jealousy. Yet had God not so willed, religious communities would not have quarreled with one another (Q. 2:213).[8]

This important verse describes not religious diversity but discord. Diversity is a divinely instituted law of human society, which no one can alter: "Had your Lord so willed," the Qur'an categorically states, "He would have made humankind one single community" (Q. 11:118, 119; 16:93, and 42:8). Yet they continue to be in discord. It must, therefore, be concluded that while religious diversity is a necessary consequence of human racial and linguistic differences, religious discord is the result of human folly, envy, and arrogance.

It is significant that the Qur'an never discusses religions as ideologies, philosophies, or theological systems. Rather, it is primarily concerned with concrete human attitudes, such as *islām* (total surrender or obedience to God), *īmān* (sincere faith in God), and *iḥsān* (righteous living, or the performance of good deeds). The Qur'an further asserts that true faith in God and righteous works are not the prerogative of any one religion or religious community. Moreover, it is for God alone to decide the ultimate destiny of the followers of every religion on the Day of Resurrection.

## Qur'anic Pluralism and Muslim Exclusivism

It was observed above that the Qur'an speaks not about religions but about religious people. It must be again stressed that the Qur'an recognizes the plurality of religious communities and the essential validity of their faiths. The sharp reproaches which the Qur'an frequently levels at Jews and Christians are for the most part directed at particular beliefs, attitudes, or actions of particular persons or groups with whom the Prophet had direct dealings, and not at their faith or religious affiliation. This seemingly hostile attitude, however, is as often balanced with approbation and calls for unity of faith in the One God.[9]

A careful look at the chronology of Qur'anic revelation seems to indicate a broad development in its approach to other faith communities. While Jews and Christians are mentioned often either separately or together as "people of the Book," they are mentioned along with other faith communities only four times. The first is in Surah 22, *al-Hajj*, which is a Madinan or perhaps late Makkan surah.[10] Verse 17 reads,

> Surely those who have accepted faith, those who are Jews, the Sabeans, the Christians, the Magians and those who have associated other gods with God, God will judge among them on the Day of Resurrection. God is Witness over all things.

It must be noted that this verse simply observes the obvious fact of religious difference and leaves the ultimate judgment as to the validity of faith to God alone. It is also significant that it does not impute association (*shirk*) to any of the recognized religious communities it mentions, but places those who associate other gods with God in a separate category.

The three other instances are undoubtedly Madinan revelations. The first is in Surah 2, *al-Baqarah* (the Cow), and the other two are in Surah 5, *al-Ma'idah* (the Table Spread). It is noteworthy that these two surahs occur near the beginning and end of the Prophet's Madinan career. This is important in view of the fact that verses 62 of Surah 2 and 69 of Surah 5 are a verbatim repetition of the following categorical statement:

> Surely those who have faith, those who are Jews, Christians, and Sabaeans—whosoever has faith in God and the last day and performs good deeds—these will have their reward with their Lord. No fear shall come upon them, nor will they grieve.

This important statement, which occurs at the beginning and end of the Prophet's political career, indicates that the principle of religious pluralism it espouses is not subject to any political or theological considerations. It is rather a fact of divine wisdom operating in human history. Nevertheless, this Qur'anic view of religious diversity has constituted a serious legal and political problem for Muslim rulers, jurists, and political ideologues throughout Muslim history. Thus, most Qur'an interpreters have gone out of their way to negate this central Qur'anic teaching.

Since a comprehensive historical study of representative interpretations of the Qur'anic view of Christians has recently been undertaken,[11] I shall limit my investigation to the two verses just mentioned and verses 82-85 of Surah 5. I shall likewise consider the view of contemporary Qur'an commentators not discussed in that study. The commentators selected for the present essay represent traditional as well as ideologically motivated approaches to the Qur'an. They also illustrate both Sunni and Shi'i juridical and ideological standpoints.

One of the most influential religious and political thinkers of post–Second World War Muslim society has been the Egyptian Islamic activist Sayyid Qutb, who was executed by President Nasser of Egypt in 1966. Sayyid Qutb interprets verse 62 of Surah 2 as asserting decisively that any one of these four communities who accepts faith in God and performs good deeds will have its reward with their Lord. He continues:

> The important issue is the truth of faith rather than any ethnic or nationalistic loyalty. But this, of course, was the case before the Muhammadan dispensation; thereafter, however, the final form of faith has been forever fixed.[12]

Sayyid Qutb is more explicit in his commentary on verse 69 of Surah 5. He first identifies the four religious communities mentioned in the verse. As for the conditions of having faith and performing good deeds, he says,

> This means that if they do so in accordance with that which the last Messenger has brought, they would be saved. They need not worry about what faith they had previously professed, nor about the name or identity of the religion they held. The important thing is the final identity [i.e., Islam].[13]

This is because, Qutb argues, Muhammad was sent as a messenger to all of humankind,[14] and they are all invited to believe in what he brought from God, regardless of their religious affiliations. Therefore,

> anyone who does not believe in what Muhammad has brought, and that he is the last Messenger, will be unacceptable before God on the last day, nor would he enter into the company of those "upon whom there is no fear, nor will they grieve."

Sayyid Qutb then draws the logical socio-political conclusion from his interpretation of the verses under discussion. It is that social and political realities should not force Muslims to compromise this truth by conceding that the followers of any other religion would be acceptable before God. Nor should they have any serious dealings with them.[15] This, of course, implies that all Qur'anic injunctions to live in amity with the people of the Book are to be ignored. It also implies that the sole aim of any relations of Muslims with other faith communities or individuals should be to bring them into Islam, voluntarily, or by force if necessary. In other words, Qutb's position means the return to old confrontations and conflicts.

It must be observed that this attitude, with minor variations, is as old as Muslim–Christian relations.[16] Thus, 'Abd al-Qadir bin Shaybat al-Hamd, a traditional scholar living in Saudi Arabia, begins his discussion of Q. 2:62 with what he calls "a fundamental principle which is valid for all times and binding on all rational human beings." This principle is the demand to have faith in all the prophets and messengers of God, "the first of whom is their chief (*shaykh*), leader (*imam*), and master (*sayyid*), Muhammad son of Abd Allah." This is because, bin Shaybat al-Hamd argues, God decreed that after Muhammad's dispensation, "no one would enter paradise except by following Muhammad's way and his life-example (*sunnah*) and abiding by his sacred law (*sharī'ah*)." The author then quotes a sacred tradition (*ḥadīth qudsī*) in which God declares, "By my might and majesty, were human beings to come from every way and knock at every door, I would not open for them unless they come through your way."[17]

Bin Shaybat al-Hamd identifies the *naṣārā* as "those who claim to follow the religion of Christ, which implies that in reality they do not. For, were they truly to follow Christ's religion, they would be Muslims." He then asserts that the verse means that no true happiness in the world to come can be attained by any religious community or individual except through faith and good works, including belief in the resurrection and last judgment. God, he further argues, presents two basic conditions in this verse for the attainment of felicity in the hereafter. The first is that good deeds should be performed solely for God's good pleasure. Second, "good deeds should be performed in accordance with the way of God's Messenger Muhammed."[18] The author repeats the same ideas and even phrases in his interpretation of Q. 5:69.[19]

While Sayyid Qutb, as we have seen, bases his argument for the invalidity of all religions after the coming of Islam on the principle of Islamic supersessionism, bin Shaybat al-Hamd makes the same argument on the basis of the superiority of Muhammad over all prophets. Yet both principles are diametrically opposed to the Qur'anic theology of the universality of faith and plurality of religions and the equality of all God's messengers. These two principles are in fact stated as a single truth in the assertion that both the Prophet and all faithful Muslims "have faith in God, His angels, His Books and His messengers—we make no distinction between anyone of His messengers . . ." (Q. 2:285).[20]

Muhammad Sayyid Tantawi, the grand mufti of Egypt and Shaykh al-Azhar, first affirms the Qur'anic view of the priority of faith over religious affiliation, but then negates it by asserting Islam's supersessionism. He argues that God begins with "those who have faith," that is, the Muslims, to indicate that the religion of Islam is based on the principle that "God's good pleasure cannot be attained except through sincere faith and good deeds." Consequently, no community can claim greater favor with God over another community except through sincere faith manifested in righteous works.[21]

After asserting that faith and righteous acts can elevate a person to the highest stations, even if he had fallen into the lowest pits of wickedness, Tantawi asserts that true faith for non-Muslims can only be in accordance with Islam, "the religion of truth." He who has not received the call to Islam and lived by a religion which is originally true, such as Judaism and Christianity, he will have his good reward with God. As for those who had received the call to Islam but do not accept it, they will not be saved from God's chastisement on the Day of Judgment. This is because, his Eminence argues, "the Islamic sacred law (*sharī'ah*) has abrogated all the religions that came before it."[22]

Tantawi presents with approval another interpretation of the verse under consideration. According to this view, "those who have faith" are those who believe in the Prophet Muhammad and all that he brought from God, regardless of their religious affiliation. According to this interpretation, the verse is simply meant to attract the followers of the other faiths mentioned to Islam by presenting an alternative universal model of faith. The intent of the verse would then be the following:

> Those who have faith in God with sincerity and total obedience, and in addition perform righteous deeds in this life, deeds which will benefit them on the day they meet Him, they will have their reward with their Lord. They will not fear the terrors of the Day of Resurrection as the rejecters of faith will, nor will they grieve for eternal bliss, as will they who fall short [in fulfilling God's commandments].[23]

The author simply summarizes these ideas with minor elaborations in his commentary on Q. 5:69.[24]

In contrast with the two previous commentators, Tantawi bases his arguments for Islamic supersessionism on the principle of *naskh* (abrogation).[25] He does not, however, hold the view that Q. 2:62 was itself abrogated, as many classical as well as contemporary commentators have done, but that the Muhammadan sacred law has abrogated all previous religious dispensations. This is essentially the view of Sayyid Qutb as well. It must be noted that this more inclusive view of abrogation has no clear Qur'anic basis, nor has it been universally accepted.

Our next example is the well-known Syrian jurist Wahba al-Zuhayli. His voluminous commentary *al-Tafsir al-munir* covers the legislative, theological, and linguistic aspects of the Qur'an. Zuhayli begins his commentary on Q. 2:62 with a brief and general linguistic and exegetical discussion. He derives the word *naṣārā* from the name of the city *al-nāṣirah* (Nazareth), without mentioning other possible derivations. He interprets the words "whosoever accepts faith in God and the last day" to mean anyone who did so "in the time of our Prophet." By "and performs good deeds" is intended "those who abide by Muhammad's law." Zuhayli continues, "Such people will be well rewarded for their good deeds." He then relates the well-known story of Salman the Persian's long quest for true faith and his ultimate discovery of Islam as the occasion of revelation of the verse.[26]

Following this general elucidation of the verse, Zuhayli presents what he takes to be its general juridical purport:

> Anyone who believes in God, holds fast to the strong rope of faith, and performs righteous deeds will be among those who will attain salvation. It matters not whether he lived as a Muslim, Jew, or Christian, or was one of those who had irrevocably abandoned their religion and accepted Islam.[27]

Zuhayli seems to vacillate between accepting the verse in its obvious sense and negating it through the usual juristic strictures. After clearly affirming that faith and good deeds rather than religious identity are the ultimate cause of salvation, he counters this by asserting that only those Jews and Christians who change their faith and profess faith in the One God and the truth of all that Muhammad brought from God will be saved. Yet when the author deals with the legislative aspects of the verse he says, "The sole cause of felicity and salvation is true faith in God coupled with righteous deeds." While he rejects the view that the verse was abrogated, he still argues that it refers only to those who stand firm in their faith in the Prophet Muhammad.

Zuhayli acknowledges the intimate social relations that the Qur'an legislates for Muslims with the people of the Book. He observes that on account of the scriptures of the Jews and Christians, "it is lawful to marry their women, eat their food, and levy the poll tax (*jizyah*) on them."[28] Zuhayli seems to want to take an open and liberal attitude toward Christians, yet he appears to be constrained by his juristic training.

Christians and Muslims have since the rise of Islam lived in the Levant as neighbors and friends. They have, furthermore, shared a common ethnic and cultural heritage, as well as a historical destiny. Zuhayli is a child of this common heritage. It may therefore be that he had the Christian West in mind when he wrote as follows:

> The previous verse alludes to the fact that the people of the Book did not establish God's religion. They neither kept the texts of revealed scriptures, nor did they preserve intact the sacred Books they possessed; rather they misinterpreted them. Thus they neither accepted faith in God and the last day, nor did they perform good deeds.[29]

The previous verse (Q. 5:68) reads in part: "Say, O people of the Book, you have nothing on which to stand until you abide by the Torah and the Gospel, and that which has been sent down to you from your Lord." It then observes that the revelation vouchsafed to the Prophet Muhammad only increases some of them in rejection of faith. Although this verse alludes to the natural resistance and even hostility of some of the people of the Book to the new faith, it in no way alludes to or supports all that the author reads into it. Furthermore, the challenge to abide by God's revelations could as well be addressed to Muslims.

One of the most popular religious orators in Egypt in recent times has been the Azharite shaykh Muhammad Mutwalli Sha'rawi. His "Reflections in Qur'anic Exegesis," which he has regularly presented on Egyptian radio and television, have also appeared in small pamphlets. While the shaykh's reflections are neither scholarly significant nor ideologically sophisticated, they are important because of his social standing and religious authority.

In his brief commentary on Q. 2:62 Sha'rawi advises anyone who follows a religion that came before Islam, and who thinks that such a religion will benefit him on the last day, to abandon that religion and accept Islam. To such a person, Sha'rawi unequivocally says:

> God, glorified and exalted be He, has definitively decided this issue in His saying, "Anyone who seeks a religion other than *islām*, it will not be accepted from him," and His saying, "Surely, the true religion with God is *islām*." (Q. 3: 85 and 19)[30]

Sha'rawi presents an unusual and ultimately uncompromising supersessionist interpretation of Q. 5:69. By "those who have accepted faith" is meant not sincere Muslims or believers in God in general, he argues, but "the hypocrites *(munāfiqūn)* who accepted faith with their tongues, and not with their hearts." He concludes,

> God wishes to bring about a final and conclusive delimitation of faith in the world. Thus he who hastened to enter into this divine delimitation would be saved from the evil of whatever he did before the coming of Islam.[31]

Thus the shaykh negates the verse completely by placing all four groups outside the purview of Islam. This interpretation is meant to stress that even sincere faith in God outside the Islamic *ummah* is unacceptable. Moreover, it goes not only against the letter of the verse but also against its spirit.

I began this discussion of contemporary Sunni commentators with Sayyid Qutb who was a prominent leader of the Society of Muslim Brothers. I shall end with another prominent member of the society, the late Syrian ideologue Said Hawwa. Hawwa was a modernist *salafī* ideologue. He held an elitist view of faith, the truth of which can be judged only by the standard

set by the Prophet and the pious forebears *al-salaf al-ṣāliḥ* of the first generations of Islam. Hawwa argues that there should always be people in every
religious community who have faith in God and do righteous deeds. Therefore, "those who have accepted faith," mentioned in the two verses under
discussion, should not be limited to Muslims. This is because, of course, not
all Muslims can be regarded as having true faith. It is concerning such people of faith that the verse was revealed. They would be saved from divine ret-
ribution in both this world and the next. Yet such people must by necessity
be Muslims, because Islam is the only true religion.

Hawwa identifies *naṣārā* as "those who supported Christ (*nāṣarū*)." As
for the Sabaeans, they are either the followers of a particular religion, whose
remnants can still be found in Iraq, or "all those who abandon falsehood
and turn to God, but do not yet know the true religion." These would be
people with an innate disposition (*fiṭrah*) to know God and have simple faith
in Him. They would be people who either lived before Islam or are living
now but have not received the call to Islam.[32]

After this general introduction, Hawwa categorically states,

> In order that no confusion may occur, we say that there is no salva-
> tion now for any Jew or Christian, nor for any Sabaean, Magian, or
> any other except through faith in Muhammad, that is, unless they
> had not received the call to Islam.[33]

In support of this extreme position the author quotes the following well-
known Prophetic hadith from the *Sahih* of Muslim: "By Him in whose hand
is my soul, no one of this community—Jew or Christian—who hears of me
but does not accept that with which I was sent by God, but that he would
be of the inmates of the fire." Thus the Jews intended in the two verses are
the Jews who lived before Jesus. As for those who came after him and
rejected faith in him, they will perish. Likewise, the Christians here intended
are those who lived before Muhammad. But those who have come after him
and would not accept Islam, they will not be saved.[34]

This supersessionistic view is clearly reiterated in Hawwa's commentary
on Q. 5:69. It is, of course, based on the principle that the Muhammadan dispensation has completely annulled and superseded all other previous religions. Hawwa's position is rendered even more narrow through his own
peculiar ideological view of Islam. He thus argues that those Jews, Christians, Sabaeans, and even nominal Muslims who lived at the time of the
Prophet, if they had accepted faith in God and the last day and performed
good deeds, would be rewarded by God to the extent that their faith and
actions had been in accord with the Muhammadan dispensation. Before
Muhammad's apostleship, however, such righteous believers in God would
have been saved if they had fulfilled the righteous deeds their own religions
had enjoined upon them.[35] But after the death of the Prophet and the final
institutionalization of Islam, no other faith would be accepted.

The commentators so far discussed differ not in substance, as we have seen, but only in approach. While, moreover, the approaches of Sayyid Qutb and Said Hawwa are dictated by their ideological standpoints, other commentators are, generally speaking, traditional scholars with differing shades of conservatism. Yet in the end they all deny all other faith communities the right to live by their faith in friendly relations with Muslims. They do not even recognize the legitimacy of their faith.

The four Shiʻi examples that will be next considered present a greater diversity of views and approaches. Muhammad Jawad al-Balaghi was a modernist/traditional scholar who wrote a comprehensive polemical work against Christianity.[36] Thus, his interpretation of the verses under discussion was no doubt colored by his anti-Christian polemical attitude.

In his brief commentary, Balaghi treats Q. 2:62 and 5:69 together. After a brief and traditional comment on the term *naṣārā*, Balaghi categorically states, "It is clear that belief in the Messenger of God Muhammad and in what he brought from God is necessary for the reality of faith and good deeds intended in this verse."[37] The author further argues that none of the groups mentioned in the two verses have true faith in the final return (*miʻād*) of all beings to God and the last day, as specified in the Qurʼan. Nor do they, in the view of the author, have true faith in God, His majesty, holiness, and unity.[38]

It is not true, of course, that Christians do not believe in the return of all creatures to God for judgment on the last day. Nor is the biblical view of the resurrection and final judgment essentially different from that of the Qurʼan. Nor do Christians deny the majesty, holiness, and unity of God. Balaghi should have known all this through his extensive research into the Christian faith and scriptures. Still, Christians cannot be included among the felicitous people of faith mentioned in the two verses simply because they are not Muslims.

Balaghi wrote his commentary in the narrow framework of the religious schools of Najaf in the post–Second World War era of political turbulence throughout the Arab world, and particularly in Iraq. In contrast, the late Lebanese scholar Muhammad Jawad Mughniyya produced his commentary in a multireligious society in which religious leaders are expected to respect the faiths of their fellow citizens and promote interreligious harmony. In fact Mughniyya was financially helped to travel to Najaf, where he obtained his formal religious education, by an Armenian Christian.

Mughniyya's straightforward and brief commentary was written in a contemporary idiom and intended for young educated people. He too does not treat Q. 2:62 and 5: 69 separately. Mughniyya explains the adjectival ending *i* (*ya*) of the word *naṣrānī* (Christian) not as indicating relation to either the town Nasira or to the helpers (*anṣār*) of Jesus; rather, it is an emphatic ending. Thus, the true *naṣārā* are those who completely follow Christ.

Mughniyya then succinctly comments on Q. 2:62 as follows:

> Anyone of these four groups who follows a just or middle course and thus has sincere faith in God, His messengers and the last day and performs good deeds, "they shall have their reward with their Lord. . . ."[39]

It should be noted that reason (*'aql*) and justice (*'adl*) are two fundamental and interdependant principles of Shi'i theology and worldview. Since, therefore, reason and justice are the basis of true faith, and hence of reward and punishment on the last day, Mughniyya leaves the final judgment as to the rationality and justice of the faith of any people to God.

In contrast with Mughniyya's Shi'i theological interpretation, Nasir Makarim al-Shirazi, a contemporary Iranian scholar, presents an essentially juristic interpretation of the two verses under consideration. He argues that Q. 2:62 presents a general criterion according to which both individuals and communities must be judged. This divine criterion is that only true faith in God and good deeds can be used in deriding the status of any person before God. In support of this broad and pluralistic view, Shirazi cites the following occasion of revelation of Q. 4:123-24 as the basis for the interpretation of 2:62.

> A group of Jews, Christians, and Muslims met and each boasted of his own religion. The Jews claimed: "Our religion is better than your religion, for our scriptures were before your scriptures and our prophet was before your prophet. We follow the religion of Abraham, and no one shall enter paradise except those who are Jews." The Christians made the same claim. Then the Muslims said: "Our Book came after your Book, our prophet came after your prophet and our religion came after your religion. You have been enjoined to abandon your religion and follow us, for we are better than you. We follow the religion of Abraham, Ishmael, and Isaac, and no one will enter paradise except those who follow our religion." Thus God revealed: "It is not in accordance with your desires nor the desires of the people of the Book. Whosoever does evil, he will be recompensed for it, nor would he find against God friend or supporter. And, whosoever does good deeds, be it male or female, and is a person of faith—these will enter paradise, and they will not be wronged in the least."

Shirazi comments, "in this, Muslims are the same as the followers of all other religions."[40]

Having made this assertion, the author hastens to clarify his own position on this important matter. "There remains," he argues, "an important issue." The issue in question is that some misguided people have used these verses as an argument in favor of religious pluralism. This erroneous view holds that:

Abiding by any of the divine religions would be well rewarded by God. It is not therefore necessary for a faithful Jew or Christian to embrace Islam. Rather, it is sufficient that such a person have true faith in God and the last day and perform good deeds.

This is, of course, what all the verses under discussion affirm. Shirazi, however, blatantly denies this clear Qur'anic teaching and cites in support of his denial the verse "Anyone who seeks a religion other than *islām* it will not be accepted from him" (Q. 3:85). This and Q. 3:19 have been used by most other commentators to counter the Qur'an itself. They ignore the fact that the term *islām* has been used in many senses in the Qur'an and that in neither verse does it necessarily signify the legal Islamic identity of the *ummah* but the primordial way or *sunnah* of God for all His creation, including His human creatures. The author appears to take all Qur'anic uses of this term to refer to Islam as simply a legal identity. This is because he insists that "the Qur'an is full of verses that call the people of the Book to Islam."

Perhaps aware of the inconsistency of his position, Shirazi offers two possible significations of Q. 2:62. The first is that were Jews and Christians truly to abide by their own religions, they would necessarily believe in Muhammad and his message. This is because Muhammad's prophethood is foretold in the scriptures of both communities. Hence, "abiding by the Torah and the Gospel," as called for in Q. 5:68, includes faith in Muhammad and his religion. It must, however, be observed that the Qur'an asks no more of Jews and Christians than to acknowledge Muhammad as a prophet of God and that the Qur'an is a divine revelation, confirming their own scriptures. The Qur'an, moreover, addresses the people of the Book as Jews and Christians, and not as potential or errant Muslims.

The second possible interpretation of the verse is that it refers to faithful Jews and Christians who lived before Islam. It was therefore meant only to answer Salman's anxious enquiry about the fate of his fellow seekers for the truth who died before they met the Prophet Muhammad. It seems that the author accepts this interpretation because he concludes, "Those Jews who had faith in God and performed good deeds before Christ are saved; likewise, are the faithful Christians who performed good deeds before the coming of the Prophet of Islam."[41]

Sayyid Mahmud Taliqani, the revolutionary Iranian cleric (d. 1979), presents a unique and philosophical discussion of Q. 2:62. His voluminous socio-political and philosophical commentary covers only the first two surahs of the Qur'an. Taliqani's discussion is rooted in the Shi'i philosophical tradition and would thus be equally applicable to other verses dealing with the people of the Book.

Taliqani discusses Q. 2:62 in the general context of the human potential for faith. The four religions mentioned in the verse represent all the religions or spiritual paths in the Middle East, the cradle of prophethood and revelation.

Taliqani's view implies that human civilization is rooted in religion. He argues that human beings are by nature inclined toward rationality and right guidance. But as civilization develops, such moral and spiritual potentials become obscured, and social immorality and lawlessness ensue. This in turn leads to the institutionalization of harsh and unjust laws. Then prophets and reformers appear to counter these laws and preach instead spiritual faith and moral commitment. They are thus opposed and persecuted as lawbreakers and destroyers of the social order. The same process also takes place in societies dominated by established religions, where ancient customs, vain desires, and self-interest predominate. It is for this reason that the verse under discussion insists on the general principle of sincere faith and good works.

It is in this philosophical framework of universal faith and morality, which are introduced into human civilization by God, that Taliqani interprets this verse. He asserts that in every age, God manifests His true religion as an act of mercy for humankind. In this call to God by God's own prophets there is no place for tribal or ethnic solidarity or religious exclusivism. Thus, the verse "admits of no interpretation or limitation in its meaning; it insists on sincere faith and good deeds."

Taliqani was a Shi'i *mujtahid* (one who practices independent analysis/ interpretation of Islamic law); therefore he could not completely ignore the traditional jurisprudential interpretation of this verse. He thus interprets the "Jews" and "Christians" mentioned in the verse to mean those who had entered into Islam. But he interprets "whosoever has faith in God" to mean "whosoever has true faith in the heart." By this he means "faith which is confirmed by native reason (*'aql fiṭrī*) and illumination of the soul." It is spiritual faith that elevates the soul above any form of associationism and worldly desires.

Taliqani also cites Q. 4:123-24 in support of his mystical and philosophical interpretation of the verse in question. Unlike Shirazi, however, he insists that the four religions referred to in this verse are to be accepted without conditions or qualifications, since none are mentioned.[42]

It was argued above that the Qur'an deals with the people of the Book not as misguided Muslims but as followers of divinely revealed religions. It calls upon them to worship God alone in accordance with their own scriptures and in harmony with Muslims who worship the same God. It does not demand that they abandon their religions and embrace Islam but that they should have sincere faith in God and perform righteous deeds, which is the essence and goal of all true religions. Yet, as the late Fazlur Rahman rightly says concerning the two verses under discussion,

> . . . the vast majority of Muslim commentators exercised themselves fruitlessly to avoid having to admit the obvious meaning: that those—from any section of humankind—who believe in God and the last day and do good deeds, are saved.[43]

The Qur'an not only affirms the validity of the faith of the people of the Book, especially the Christians, but sets them up as an example of fervent worship, sincere faith, and humility before God for Muslims to emulate. It commends their amity towards Muslims, and calls upon both communities to engage in a dialogue of faith and love. It is to the answers to this call of some of the commentators represented in this study that I shall now turn.

## The Qur'anic Call for Dialogue and Muslim-Christian Rivalry

I have shown in the foregoing discussion that the Qur'an bases interfaith relations not on any religious or ethnic identity but on a life of faith manifested in works of righteousness. The Qur'an also maintains that this universal faith in God encompasses, but at the same time transcends, all religions. In this framework of the universality of faith within a great diversity of religions, the Qur'an calls upon faithful Christians and Muslims to live in amity and engage in a genuine dialogue of faith.

This call, however, has for fourteen centuries been drowned out by the clamor of religious, political, economic, and military rivalry. I shall briefly examine the answers to this call of some of the commentators discussed above. But I must first discuss the concrete and vivid picture that the Qur'an presents of Christians, the Christians with whom Muslims are called upon to engage in fair and fruitful dialogue.

The Qur'anic term for dialogue is *jidāl*, which means to be intimately engaged with someone in discussion or debate. This intimate and purposeful dialogue is called in the Qur'an "the best" or "fairest debate" (*al-jidāl al-ahsan*). It requires wisdom and fair exhortation; as the Qur'an enjoins Muhammad, "Call to the way of your Lord with wisdom and fair exhortation; and debate with them in the fairest manner" (Q. 16:125). This fair dialogue, moreover, must be based on common and sincere faith in God and His revelations:

> Do not [you Muslims] debate with the people of the Book save in the fairest manner—except those among them who have committed wrong—and say, "We believe in that which was sent down to us and sent down to you. Your God and our God is one, and to Him we are submitters (*muslims*)." (Q. 29:46)[44]

The reality of faith, according to the Qur'an and Prophetic tradition, is ultimately known to God alone. Therefore, Muslims must judge the faith of any person or community by its manifestation in worship and good deeds. In accordance with this principle, the Qur'an presents a graphic description of the faith and righteous works of the Christians with whom Muslims must live in harmony and fellowship of faith.

The Christians whom the Qur'an describes appear to be desert monks and other pious men and women who lived as hermits and in small communities in the Arabian desert and whom the Prophet and early Muslims must have observed firsthand. The verses describing them, moreover, belong to both the Makkan and Madinan periods of revelation. The Qur'an states,

> Those to whom We had given the Book before it [i.e., the Qur'an], they believe in it. When it is recited to them, they say, "we believe in it; it is the truth from our Lord. For, before it, we were submitters (*muslims*)." (Q. 28:52-53)

The passage under discussion then describes these people of the Book as steadfast and magnanimous people who avoid vain and contentious talk. Hence, "These shall receive their reward twofold for their steadfastness. They counter evil with good, and they spend in alms of what we have bestowed upon them." Their peaceful temperament and deep piety are depicted thus: "When they hear vain talk they turn away from it and say, 'To us belong our actions and to you belong your actions. Peace be upon you; we seek not the foolish'" (Q. 28:54-55).

Although the verses here cited do not specifically mention the Christians, they no doubt refer to them. This is because they clearly echo other verses which extol the piety and humility of Christians, as we shall presently see. It should also be noted that these verses closely resemble verses describing the piety and humility of "God's faithful servants" among the Muslims (Q. 25:63-67). By depicting such common piety, the Qur'an aims at establishing a fellowship of faith among the faithful of the two communities.

The verses just cited were revealed in Makkah, and thus explicitly indicate the permanence of this Qur'anic view of Muslim-Christian relations.[45] The verse we shall now discuss belongs to a crucial period of the Prophet's Madinah political career. It confirms and completes the picture that these verses present. The verse in question is one of the concluding verses of Surah 3, *Al 'Imran*, which deals at length with the relations of the nascent Muslim commonwealth with the people of the Book after the painful experience of the defeat of Uhud in the third year of the *hijrah*, 625 C.E. It reads,

> There are among the people of the Book those who have faith in God and in what God revealed to you and in what He revealed to them. They are humble before God and do not exchange God's revelations for a trifling price. They shall have their reward with their lord, and God is swift in reckoning. (Q. 3:199)[46]

It is clear from our discussion thus far that verses 82-85 of Surah 5, which we shall now consider, cannot be regarded as an isolated statement. Rather, they describe in concrete terms an ideal relationship of amity and harmony between Muslims and Christians. Nor are they limited to a particular time or place, but apply to Christians of all times whose life of faith complies with the conditions these and other verses present. An important verse that supports this general thesis is the following:

> We then made our messengers to succeed in their footsteps. Then we followed with Jesus, son of Mary, and gave him the Gospel. We placed in the hearts of those who follow him compassion and mercy. . . . (Q. 57:27)

Furthermore, like the verses just considered, these verses confirm the people of the Book in their own religious identities and expect from them no more than the recognition of Muhammad as a Messenger of God and of the Qur'an as a genuine divine revelation confirming their own scriptures. Verses 82 and 83 of Surah 5, with which we are primarily concerned, read,

> You [Muhammad] will surely find strongest in hostility among men toward those who have faith the Jews and those who have associated other gods with God; and you will find nearest in amity to those who have faith those who say we are Christians. This is because there are among them learned pastors (*qiṣṣiṣīn*) and monks, yet they are not arrogant. And when they listen to what was sent down to the Messenger, you see their eyes well up with tears because of what they recognize of the truth. They proclaim, "Our Lord, we have faith, inscribe us therefore with the witnesses [to the truth]."

The three remaining verses affirm the faith of these humble Christians and their hope of being included among the righteous. They also promise them eternal bliss in paradise for their faith and humble submission to God.

Like verses 62 of Surah 2 and 69 of Surah 5, the verses under discussion are not a legislative but a narrative statement. Because of their clear and positive tone, moreover, they could not be explained away through the principle of abrogation. They have nonetheless been negated by being assigned to a specific occasion of revelation, and thus applied to a limited group of Christian converts to Islam.

According to most classical and contemporary commentators, these verses were revealed concerning the Abyssinian ruler al-Najashi (the Negus), who with a group of his bishops and monks accepted Islam. In Makkah, the Prophet advised a number of Muslims who had no tribal or clan protection against increasing Makkan persecution to seek refuge in Christian Abyssinia. They were, according to tradition, well received, as al-Najashi refused to turn them over to a Makkan delegation that was expressly sent by the hostile men of the Quraysh to bring them back to Makkah.

Najashi instead brought the two contending groups together and asked Ja'far bin Abi Talib, the spokesman of the Muslims, to explain their new faith in the presence of his learned bishops and monks. In the course of his explication of the basic principles of Islam, Ja'far recited the beginning of Surah 19, *Maryam* (Mary), which recounts the story of Mary and the miraculous birth of Jesus. As they listened, al-Najashi and his fellow Christians are said to have wept till their beards were soaked with their tears. He then exclaimed, "By God, this and what Jesus brought from God issue from one niche [of divine light]."[47]

In order to bring into accord even more closely the occasion of revelation of these verses with their actual text, more elaborate versions of this and similar hagiographical tales have been related. These tales have generally been uncritically accepted by contemporary commentators. An obvious problem with the Najashi tradition with all its variants, for example, is the fact that the Abyssinian migration happened in Makkah, many years before the revelation of these late Madinan verses.[48]

Sayyid Qutb, for instance, repeats the fanciful tale that seventy Christian men, clad in ascetic woolen garments, accompanied Ja'far bin Abi Talib on his return from Abyssinia. Among them were eight Syrian Christians, including the famous monk Bahira. The Prophet recited the Qur'an to them; their eyes were filled with tears, and they accepted Islam. In the same breath, Qutb also reports another variant of the same tale, namely, that after hearing Ja'far's Qur'anic recitation, al-Najashi sent a delegation of thirty of the most learned Christians to the Prophet in Makkah to learn more about the new faith. They wept when they heard Surah 36, *Yāsīn*, acknowledged it as the same truth that was revealed to Jesus, and became Muslims. Qutb relates still another tradition about a group of men of the Christian community of Najran who voluntarily came to the Prophet in Madinah, again to learn about Islam. The Prophet recited to them the same surah, and they likewise wept as they heard the truth and accepted Islam.[49]

Sayyid Anwar Ali, a Pakistani scholar who was perhaps the first to attempt to produce a comprehensive commentary on the Qur'an in English, offers an unusual interpretation of these verses. It should first be observed that he adopts a generally traditional view of the two verses discussed in the previous section and those under consideration here. This he does in spite of the fact that in his commentary he relies on the Bible, as well as on general works on Christianity and other religions in English.

Ali asserts that the followers of Christ were originally all known as *naṣārā*. They then split into two factions, the followers of Christ's true vicegerent, Simon Peter, and the followers of Paul. The former were called *naṣārā,* and the latter came to be known as Christians. The *naṣārā,* or true followers of Christ, eventually believed in the Prophet Muhammad and became Muslims. It was concerning them that the verse "and you will find nearest in amity to those who have faith those who say we are *naṣārā* " (Q. 5:82) was revealed.[50]

In spite of his familiarity with Christian sources, Ali's remarks on the formative period of Christianity bear no relation to historical facts. He pres-

ents an essentially traditional Shi'i view of Jesus as a prophet and his true successor, or imam after him, who was Simon Peter. He also repeats the usual
Islamic polemic against Paul as the one who distorted Christ's origin and salvation through Christ's death. This means that since those who were true
followers of Christ became Muslims fourteen centuries ago, all Qur'anic
verses dealing with Christians have since that time been irrelevant.

It was observed above that commentators have rendered the generally
positive Qur'anic approach to Muslim-Christian relations irrelevant to the
historical realities of the two communities. This they did by denying outright
the continued applicability of Qur'anic verses enjoining such an approach.
Otherwise, they limited them to a small number of Christians with whom the
Prophet had direct contact and who consequently accepted Islam.

The primary motivation behind this approach, we believe, has been the
continued religious, political, social, and economic rivalry between Western
Christendom and the world of Islam. To demonstrate this point, we shall
briefly look at three of the Sunni and one of the Shi'i commentators discussed
in this essay. It should, however, be noted that the others on the whole share
the same motivation and come to similar conclusions.

Sayyid Qutb argues that Q. 5:82-85 conclude a long narrative about the
corrupt beliefs of the Jews and Christians. They should, therefore, not be
read in isolation from other verses that call upon Muslims not to trust either
of the two communities.[51] As we have already seen, the author limits the
verses to a specific group, "those who said we are Christians." Thus their
saying "inscribe us therefore with the witnesses" means "their entry into the
*ummah* of Islam in word and deed." Their witnessing would then be their
sacrifice of life and possessions in the cause of Islam. Qutb reads these verses
not as a call to an amicable dialogue but as a warning to Muslims to beware
the historic enmity of all other Christians. They are, in fact, intended by
those "who reject faith and deny God's revelations," who are mentioned in
the concluding verse of this passage.[52]

Qutb appears to favor the view of the well-known early traditionalist
Qatada, who did not refer these verses to any particular group. Rather, the
faithful Christians here intended "were people who followed the way of truth
which Jesus brought from God. But when Muhammad came, they believed
in him; thus God praised them." Otherwise, Qutb asserts that the enmity of
the Christians to Islam and the Muslims goes back to the battle of al-Yarmuk
in which Khalid defeated the Byzantine army in 636 C.E. He, however,
excepts those "whose hearts answered the call of Islam" as well as those
"who sought refuge in the justice of Islam against the oppression of other
Christians." Qutb concludes,

> The overall historical perspective of most Christians has been [deter-
> mined by] the Crusades, whose spark has never really been extin-
> guished since Islam and the Romans met on the banks of the
> Yarmuk river.[53]

Sayyid Qutb was an eloquent but also an uncompromising anti-establishment, anti-Western Muslim activist. In his view, any economic, political, or social cooperation between any Muslim country and Western Christendom was a foolish capitulation on the part of these Muslims to Christian world hegemony. In contrast, Sha'rawi—while taking Muslim-Christian rivalry to be the cause of antagonism between the two communities—is far less harsh and more didactic in his approach. This no doubt is due to the fact that he speaks for the Egyptian religious and government establishment, and through its media he addresses Egyptian citizens directly, both Muslims and Christians. He also appears to have in mind Egyptian militant Islamists, as he counsels dialogue rather than violent confrontation as a way to solve religious and social problems.

The Christians whom Sha'rawi imagines are not those of modern rival nation-states, but small traditional and peaceful *dhimmī* communities living under Muslim protection. He thus argues that the rivalry between the Jews and Muslims has always been over temporal authority. As for the Christians, so long as they remained occupied with worship and devotions in their churches and monasteries, there were no grounds for conflict between them and their Muslim overlords. This is because, Sha'rawi further argues,

> He who holds no temporal power would not show hostility to someone who attempts to seize it from oppressive rulers in order to establish justice among men, as the Muslims did towards Eastern Christians and Jews when they conquered Egypt, Syria, and the Iberian peninsulas.[54]

So long, therefore, as Christian authority is limited to learned pastors and monks who seek to maintain moral and religious leadership among their followers, Christians would remain nearest in amity to Muslims.

It is clear that Sha'rawi approaches these verses as a traditional Islamic jurist. He thus interprets the words "yet they are not arrogant" to mean, "they do not aspire for any leadership, but remain humble and morally upright." All this stems from the nature of their religion, which gives them great spiritual capacities, manifested in the principle of "turning the other cheek." He concludes,

> They shall remain nearest in amity to us so long as they possess the qualities of moral uprightness, humility, and disinterestedness in aspiring for temporal authority. But if they abandon any of these characteristics and seek temporal authority, then this would mean that they had abandoned the characteristic on account of which God declared them to be nearest in amity.[55]

Unlike Sha'rawi, Zuhayli adopts a traditional and historical approach to these verses. He comes closer to accepting the apparent sense of the text than any of the Sunni commentators here discussed. Although he relates the usual stories as possible occasions of the revelation of the verses, he still attempts to understand them in their religious and historical context. He writes,

> Learned pastors and monks undertake to call others to faith, virtue, meekness, and ascetic non-attachment to the world. They are not haughty in regard to hearing the truth and justly following it. God thus characterized them by learning, devotion, and humility.[56]

Zuhayli then interprets the weeping of the Christians as an emotional appreciation of the word of God. They also admit that Muhammad is the prophet foretold in their scriptures. Still, Zuhayli could not accept that Christians could do all this and remain Christians. Rather, "they then hasten to accept the call of Islam, saying, 'Our Lord, we have faith; inscribe us therefore with the witnesses.'" He then interprets the rest of the passage in this vein.[57]

Zuhayli asserts that the *naṣārā* are those whom God mentioned in Q. 3:199 and 28:52-55, which we have already discussed. He does not identify "those who reject faith and deny God's revelations" as all other Christians, as Sayyid Qutb does, but as "those who reject faith in God's Oneness and the prophethood of Muhammad."[58] This may be interpreted to mean those who do so but without necessarily becoming Muslims. It is nonetheless significant that Zuhayli leaves some room for dialogue by leaving the question open.[59]

Among the Shi'i commentators examined in this essay, Mughniyya offers the most interesting and original commentary on the passage under discussion. He clearly refers the verses to the time of the Prophet and the Makkan-Jewish alleged alliances against the Muslim state of Madinah. He cites the account of al-Najashi and his people as the occasion of the revelation of the verses. Yet he argues that there is nothing in these verses concerning whether Christians prefer Muslims, or that they hate the Jews more than those of them who accept Islam. Rather, he says: "These verses indicate that Christian thought—with its humanism—is closer to Islam and its humanism than it is to Jewish thought." This is clear, Mughniyya further asserts, to anyone who reads the Hebrew Bible and the Gospel. He continues,

> The God of the Gospel is the God of love and mercy toward all of humanity, and this is exactly what the Qur'an teaches. As for the God of the Hebrew Bible, he is inextricably bound to the Jews, and they are His chosen people.

The author then wonders how Christians could believe at one and the same time in the fanatical God of the Hebrew Bible and the God of the Gospel "whose mercy encompasses all things."

In keeping with this view of Christians, Mughniyya asserts that good Christians "are not arrogant toward any of God's servants and His children." He still wishes to limit the verses to a special event, so that they do not refer to all pastors and monks. "This is why," he argues, "God uses here no definite articles for the 'learned pastors and monks.'" Mughniyya concludes with the following brief commentary on Q. 5:86 in support of his ideas: "Thus the doer of good is not equal before God's justice with the doer of evil. For, an evildoer may escape the punishment of men, but he shall have no escape from God's punishment."[60]

## Conclusion

I have endeavored to show in this study that the Qur'an accepts religious diversity but censures religious discord and conflict. Religious diversity should, however, exist within a universality of faith in the One God and acceptance of all His prophets and revelations. I have also maintained that this universal faith in God and His revelations and prophets does not mean religious uniformity. This means that Muslims, Christians, Jews, and indeed all other faith communities who share this universal faith are called upon to accept the authenticity of all God's revelations and the veracity of all His prophets. Yet each community can and should worship God in its own way and in accordance with the scripture revealed to it. This diversity of religion and unity of faith should foster a spirit of amity and dialogue of faith among all the people of faith.

Against my thesis, it may be argued that the Qur'an also contains verses that foster disunity and discord. Such statements as, "O you who have faith, do not take the Jews and Christians as friends or allies (Q. 5:51)," and "Neither the Jews nor the Christians would be pleased with you [Muhammad] unless you follow their religion" (Q. 2:120), can hardly be said to encourage amicable relations among the three Abrahamic communities.[61] I have argued elsewhere[62] that the Qur'an is generally ambivalent in its attitude toward Jews and Christians. This ambivalence is largely due to particular circumstances and problems between Muslims and the people of the Book. Therefore, verses like those I have just cited often referred to specific political problems between the Prophet and the Jews of Madinah or neighboring Christians. They should not, therefore, be used to negate the positive verses which are, in any case, more numerous and more emphatic in their insistence on mutual recognition and fair dialogue between Muslims and the people of the Book.

I admit that ultimately my interest in interreligious dialogue is not simply an academic one. Without denying the need for academic integrity, it must be recognized that we live in a religiously, culturally, and ideologically pluralistic world which we can either share or destroy. We must therefore be selective in our choices of sacred texts and concepts, and should give preference to those which encourage greater understanding and cooperation among the people of different faiths and ideologies. This need is specially pressing for the followers of such world religions as Christianity and Islam. I therefore fully accept the charge of being highly selective in my use of Islamic sources to this end.[63]

The Qur'an presents to the three peoples of the Book a challenge and a promise. The challenge is for all of them to live by the moral and spiritual dictates of the Torah, the Gospel, and the Qur'an. The promise is that if they do so, both the sky and earth would freely bestow on them their blessings: "were they to abide by the Torah, the Gospel, and that which was sent down to them from their Lord, they would have provisions from above them and from beneath their feet" (Q. 5:66). Can Jews, Christians, and Muslims hear the voice of God speaking to each in their own language through all three scriptures? This is the challenge for the twenty-first century.

# Notes

1. All Qur'anic translations are mine. Pondering the Qur'an is a frequently repeated injunction; see, for example, Q. 47:24 and 83:29.

2. This principle is frequently stated in the Qur'an; see, for example, 2:62 and 5:69, which will be discussed below.

3. See Q. 30:22 and 2:213, to which I shall return later in this discussion.

4. The Qur'an states: "There is not a community but that a warner came to it" (34:24). And, "No messenger have we sent except in the tongue of his people" (14:4).

5. See Q. 30:30 and 6:76-79, which recount Abraham's quest for the knowledge of the creator through his own unaided reason.

6. See, among many Qur'anic verses asserting this concept of revelation, Q. 43:4; 13:39; and 86:21-22.

7. For a good discussion of this point, see Fazlur Rahman, *Major Themes of the Qur'an* (Minneapolis: Bibliotheca Islamica, 1980), 162ff.

8. The idea of religious differences being willed by God is suggested in a number of other verses. See 2:253.

9. See esp. Q. 3:64, 191.

10. Early traditionists and commentators have differed as to the place and time of its revelation. It seems that some of its verses were revealed in Makkah and some in Madinah. The first thirty verses, which include the one just cited, are reported to be Madinan revelations. For a good discussion of this issue, see Abu al-Faraj 'Abd al-Rahman ibn al-Jawzi, *Zad al-masir fi 'ilm al-tafsir*, 9 vols. (Beirut: al-Maktab al-Islami lil-Tiba a wa'l-Nashr, 1384/1964), 5:401-2.

11. Jane McAuliffe, *Qur'anic Christians* (Cambridge: Cambridge University Press, 1991).

12. Sayyid Qutb, *Fi zilal al-Qur'an,* 7th ed., 8 vols. (Beirut: Dar Ihya' al-Turath al-'Arabi, 1391/1971), 1:95-96.

13. Ibid., 4:811.

14. Q. 7:158 states, "O humankind, I am God's Messenger to you all." See also Q. 34:28.

15. Sayyid Qutb, *Fi zilal al-Qur'an*, 4:811-12.

16. For classical *tafsīr* examples, see Mahmoud Ayoub, *The Qur'an and Its Interpreters*, 2 vols. (Albany: State University of New York Press, 1984, 1992), 1:109-12.

17. 'Abd al-Qadir bin Shaybat al-Hamd, *Tahdhib al-tafsir wa-tajrid al-ta'wil mimma uliq bihi min al-abatil wa-radi' al-aqawil*, 5 vols. (Riyadh: Maktabat al-Ma'arif li'l-Tawzi wa al-Nashr, 1993), 1:157. Note the polemical title: "Rectifying the Science of *tafsīr* and Freeing Interpretation (*ta'wīl*) from All Accretions of Falsehoods and Bad Imputations." Note also the author's unusually traditional and pompous-sounding name.

18. Ibid.

19. Ibid., 4:221.

20. This doctrine is also expressed in Q. 29:46, which will be discussed below.

21. Muhammad Sayyid Tantawi, *al-Tafsir al-wasit*, 15 vols. (Cairo: Dar al-Ma'arif, 1412/1992), 1:156.

22. Ibid.

23. Ibid., 158; see also 157.

24. Ibid., 4:228-30.

25. For a brief discussion of this principle, see Ayoub, *The Qur'an and Its Interpreters*, vol. 1, commentary on Q. 2:106, 138-40.

26. Wahbah al-Zuhayli, *al-Tafsir al-munir fi al-'aqidah wa al-shari'ah wa al-manhaj*, 16 vols. (Beirut: Dar al-Fikr al-Mu'asir, 1411/1991), 1:177. On the story of Salman's faith, see Ayoub, *The Qur'an and Its Interpreters*, 1:110-12.

27. Ibid., 178. The author here interprets the word *saba* from which the word *ṣābi'īn* (Sabaeans) is derived in its pre-Islamic connotation to mean "abandoning one's tribal religious affiliation in favor of a new and unfamiliar religion," as Muhammad was accused of doing by his Makkan compatriots.

28. Ibid., 177-78; see also Q. 5:5 and 9:29.

29. Ibid., 165; see also 164.

30. Muhammad Mutwalli Sha'rawi, *Tafsir al-Sha'rawi khawatir hawl al-Qur'an*, 53 vols. (Cairo: Akhbar al-Yawm, 1411/1991), 5:378-82.

31. Ibid., 41:3300. See also 3298-3302.

32. Said Hawwa, *Asas al-tafsir*, 11 vols. (Cairo: Dar al-Salam, 1405/1985), 1:153.

33. Ibid., 1:154.

34. Ibid.

35. Ibid., 3:1453.

36. *al-Huda ila din al-mustafa*, 2 vols. (Qum: Dar al-Kutub al-Islamiyya, 1966) is a systematic and detailed refutation of Christianity.

37. Muhammad Jawad al-Balaghi, *Ala' al-Rahman fi tafsir al-Qur'an*, 2 vols. (Beirut: Dar Ihya' al-Turath al-'Arabi, n.d.), 1:97.

38. Ibid., 98.

39. Muhammad Jawad Mughniyya, *al-Tafsir al-mubin* (Beirut: Dar al-Ta'aruf, 1398/1978), 15.

40. Nasir Makarim al-Shirazi, *al-Amthal fi tafsir kitab allah al-munzal*, 20 vols. (Beirut: Mu'assasat al-Bi'tha, 1413/1992), 1:217-18. See also the commentary on this verse in Muhammad Rashid Rida, *Tafsir al-Manar* (Beirut: Dar al-Manar, n.d.), on which Shirazi relied in his commentary on this verse.

41. Ibid., 219.

42. Sayyid Mahmud Taliqani, *Partawi az Qur'an*, 6 vols. (Tehran: Shirkat-i Sehami-i Intishar, 1362 [Hijri-Solar, Iranian calendar]), 1:180-82.

43. Fazlur Rahman, *Major Themes of the Qur'an*, 166.

44. See also 3:64, where this faith commitment is called "a word of common purpose between us and you."

45. Ibn al-Jawzi says that the entire surah was revealed in Makkah. He, however, reports that Muqatil alone held that only the verses just cited were revealed in Madinah. See Ibn al-Jawzi, *Zad al-masir*, 6:200.

46. It should be noted that many commentators have attempted to negate this verse by assigning it to a specific group of Christians, or questioning whether it can even be applied to non-Muslims. See Ayoub, *The Qur'an and Its Interpreters*, 2:414-15.

47. Bin Shaybat al-Hamd, *Tahdhib al-tafsir*, 4:240-41.

48. Because of this time discrepancy, Ibn Kathir questions the veracity of traditions that relate these verses to the Najashi story. See Abu al-Fida Isma'il ibn Kathir, *Tafsir al-Qur'an al-'azim*, 4 vols. (Beirut: Dar al-Ma'rifah, 1402/1982), 2:85. See also McAuliffe, *Qur'anic Christians*, chap. 7, where these traditions are critically examined.

49. Sayyid Qutb, *Fi zilal al-Qur'an*, 7:16-18.

50. Sayyid Anwar Ali, *Qur'an: The Fundamental Law of Human Life* (Karachi, Pakistan: Hamdard Foundation Press, 1982-84), 2:270. For his commentary on Q. 5:82-85, see 5:393.

51. See, for example, Q. 2:120; 5:151; and 5:68, which the author cites among other verses.

52. That is Q. 5:86, which Qutb sees as completing the contrast between the few Christians who accepted Islam and the rest who constitute Christendom today. See Qutb, *Fi zilal al-Qur'an*, 7:8-16.

53. Ibid., 19. See also Said Hawwa, *Asas al-tafsir*, 3:1453-84. Hawwa generally agrees with Sayyid Qutb, whom he quotes extensively.

54. Sha'rawi, *Tafsir al-Sha'rawi*, 42:3336.

55. Ibid., 3341-42; see also 3336-42.

56. Zuhayli, *al-Tafsir al-munir*, 7:9; see also 7:5-9.

57. Ibid., 9.

58. Ibid., 10.

59. See ibid., 10-12.

60. Mughniyya, *al-Tafsir al-mubin*, 129.

61. In fact Sayyid Qutb uses these verses in his argument against such amicable relations; see note 51 above.

62. See, for example, the essays "The Islamic Context of Muslim-Christian Relations," "Islam and Christianity: Between Tolerance and Acceptance," and "Roots of Muslim-Christian Conflict," chap. 2, 3, and 4 in the present volume.

63. Kate Zebiri, "Relations Between Muslims and Non-Muslims in the Thought of Western-Educated Muslim Intellectuals," *Islam and Christian-Muslim Relations*, 6, no. 2 (December 1995): 267; see also 264-67.

# 15

# Muslim Views of Christianity

## Some Modern Examples

### Introduction

Islam as a religious and cultural tradition grew in a milieu permeated with Judaeo-Christian ideas. It was further nourished by the rich legacy of Greek wisdom and science, a legacy which had previously shaped Christian civilization. Ancient Greek philosophy and science, revitalized and remolded by Islam, combined with the Qur'an and Arab tradition to give Islam its *Weltanschauung* and framework for its cultural heritage. Islam, in turn, gave back to the West this Graeco-Islamic legacy which provided medieval Christendom with its *Weltanschauung* and the impetus for its Renaissance, Enlightenment, and even its modern technology. Thus, the relationship between Islam and Christianity is not that of superficial acquaintance; it is rather one of interaction touching the very roots of the two traditions.

This fruitful interaction in philosophy, the arts, and sciences has been, with a few notable exceptions, all but absent in the sphere of religious thought and piety. Very early, each of the two communities formed its conceptions and misconceptions of the faith of the other and refused to have its image challenged either by direct dialogue or the contradiction of actual facts when these were known. Islam has always venerated some of the most important personages of the Christian tradition: Jesus and his disciples, his mother Mary, "The Mistress of the Women of the World" (Q. 3:42),[1] and Zechariah and his son, John the Baptist. Yet whereas the Qur'an sought to go beyond mere historical facts in its characterizations of these and other biblical personalities, Muslims have, in the main, taken such characterizations as actual facts of history. When, therefore, their reading of these facts differed from that of Christians, they dismissed the latter as willful distortions of the truth. Christians, on the other hand, from that position despised Islam, its Holy Book and Prophet and considered the entire venture as the work of Satan or more compassionately, perhaps, as a Christian heresy too

Previously published in *Islamochristiana* 10 (1984): 49-70. Reprinted by permission.

stubbornly tenacious to be eradicated. The result on both sides has been irreligious and often inhuman polemics which bred hatred, fear, and distrust.

The religious isolation of Muslims and Christians from each other may be contrasted with a long history of political and military relations which took the form of conquest and re-conquest, religious warfare, and finally colonial domination and its aftermath. In each period of this long history, religious interrelations reflected not only deeply entrenched misconceptions and negative feelings but also the political and military situation. Muslim-Christian dialogue, for the most part and until very recently, took place either on the battlefield or between colonizing and colonized.

The four Muslim thinkers with whom this study is concerned represent the last two stages of this long history. Shaykh Muhammad 'Abduh (d. 1905) and his disciple, Sayyid Muhammad Rashid Rida (d. 1935), witnessed the collapse of the Ottoman Empire and its breakup into different regions dominated by one or another colonizing Western power. They addressed themselves to the problems resulting from the defeat of Muslims, and hence their feeling of inferiority in the face of Western technology and liberalism and their growing doubt in their own faith and tradition. 'Abduh concerned himself with the defense of Islam against the secular threats of Western humanism, science, and philosophy. He appropriately entitled his book *Islam and Christianity: Between Science and Civilization*.[2] Rashid Rida, on the other hand, addressed himself to the attack of Christian missionaries on Islam. His work bears the title *Shubuhat al-nasara wa hujaj al-Islam* (criticisms by the Christians and the proof of Islam).[3]

The two other thinkers who will be considered in this essay, Shaykh Muhammad Abu Zahrah and Ahmad Shalabi, lived and wrote after the Second World War.[4] They witnessed the end of the colonial era. Both claim to be writing an objective, scholarly study of Christianity intended for Muslim students in Egyptian colleges and universities. In actual fact, however, they continue the usual polemics using the same old charges and countercharges, albeit in a different style.

All four thinkers sought to answer actual or hypothetical Christian arguments against Islam. The works of 'Abduh and Rida are generally an apologetic defense of Islam, while those of Abu Zahrah and Shalabi are a polemical refutation of Christianity. All four lived and worked in Egypt. Rashid Rida, although originally Syrian, spent many years in Egypt, where he carried on the work of his teacher, 'Abduh. All except Shalabi were recognized religious teachers not only in Egypt but throughout the Muslim world.

## Apologetics: In Defense of Islam

Imam Muhammad 'Abduh may be regarded as one of the most important architects of the modernist movement in Islam. He was the child both of traditional Islamic piety and learning and of nineteenth-century Western humanism. As one firmly rooted in the traditional Islamic worldview, he advocated a return to the golden age of Islam, the age of the "Pious Forebears" (*al-salaf al-ṣāliḥ*), in which he saw both the norm and inspiration for reform and progress. As a humanist, he regarded the normative age as not only the model for great piety and pure faith, but also that of cultural creativity, freedom of thought and expression, and the confidence enabling both the civil and religious authorities to seek knowledge, whatever its source and manner of acquisition. This vibrant civilization in all its cosmopolitan diversity, built by Muslim, Christian, Jewish, and other scholars, was for Shaykh Muhammad 'Abduh the model of true Islam, which he sought to defend against the attacks of Western secular humanism.

This defense was contained in a series of articles that first appeared in the periodical *al-Manar al-Islami*, of which 'Abduh was the founder and chief editor. The defense was prompted by a long study of the great Muslim philosopher Ibn Rushd (Averroes), made by a Syrian Christian scholar, Farah Antun, and published in *al-Jami'ah*, a humanistic philosophic journal. The author was in reality critical of religion as such, which he regarded as an obstacle to progress and free inquiry. He considered Islam only as an example of this charge, which he would have as readily laid against Christianity. Antun, again influenced by nineteenth-century critiques of Islam, compared the nature and function of authority in the two religions. He argued that Christian Europe had finally achieved the separation of religious and secular powers, thus allowing for greater freedom of thought and expression. In Islam, on the other hand, the position of the caliph as both the religious and political leader led to the restriction and opposition of this freedom.

The following brief discussion of 'Abduh's defense of Islam will be concerned with his views of Christianity as the religious framework of a civilization.[5] 'Abduh begins his critique of Christianity with a detailed discussion of what he calls "the nature of the Christian religion."[6] He sees Christianity as essentially based on nonrational elements of faith and doctrine which in the end determined both the growth and character of Western religion and culture. He constructs his argument around six principles which he considers as the fundamental bases of Christianity.

The first of these is the principle of miracles, or supernatural phenomena. Jesus, our author argues, based his message on the power to perform miracles and gave that power to his disciples. Still more, he taught that if a person had faith and commanded a mountain to move and be cast into the sea, his prayers would be answered (Matt 21:21; 22:24).[7] If, then, 'Abduh concludes, everyone had the power of contravening the natural order, there would no longer be laws of nature guaranteeing this order. 'Abduh's argument is clearly based on a strictly literal reading of the text, which misses its real purpose. The problem arises, perhaps, from the fact that Muslims have judged the question of miracles (*mu'jizāt*) which God allows His prophets to perform only as proof of their claim to prophethood or apostleship. The tendency of both Muslims and Christians to judge the tradition and the faith of each other by their own standards has been a major obstacle in the way of meaningful dialogue.

The absolute authority of the clergy constitutes the second fundamental principle of Christianity in the view of Muhammad 'Abduh. Again, this is based on the words of Jesus, who gave his disciples the authority to "bind and loose" both on earth and in heaven (Matt 16:19; 18:18). This principle places the faith of the individual and his salvation in the hands of church leaders. Even if some Christians have managed to abandon this principle, 'Abduh argues, nonetheless "Christianity upheld it for fifteen long centuries."[8]

The third fundamental principle of Christian faith and worldview is that of world renunciation. Jesus himself taught, "do not be anxious about tomorrow" (Matt 7:34) and declared that it is easier for a camel to go through the eye of a needle than for a rich man to enter the kingdom of heaven (Matt 19:24). If his principle were to be applied fully, human society would altogether disintegrate. As proof of this argument, 'Abduh quotes the words of Christ, "For there are eunuchs who have been so from birth, there are eunuchs who have been made eunuchs by men, and there are eunuchs who have made themselves eunuchs for the sake of the kingdom of heaven. He who is able to receive this, let him receive it" (Matt 19:12).

Not only are such principles unsuited to serve as bases of human order, they are also irrational. 'Abduh thus gives the fourth principle as "faith in the irrational." St. Anselm, for example, advised Christians, to believe first, then to seek understanding, because in reality there is no need for understanding in the certainty of faith. 'Abduh then comments with an obvious tone of irony, "But woe to him who seeks understanding, if his search leads him to anything opposing the requirements of his faith."[9]

The notion that the sacred scriptures of the community of faith contain all the knowledge necessary for man's happiness and salvation is common to Islam and Christianity. Muhammad 'Abduh, however, presents this as his fifth principle of Christianity. He cites Tertullian as asserting that all branches of learning which humankind could ever seek are contained in the Bible. Hence, there is no need for resorting to any other source of knowledge. It must be observed, however, that Tertullian himself was an intellectual firmly rooted in Greek wisdom. As a Christian he sought to demonstrate the equality of biblical wisdom with that of Greece. This apologetic approach was common to many intellectual circles, particularly that of Alexandria. In this as in his other principles, 'Abduh pushes his argument too far, reaching conclusions not justified by the original ideas he seeks to emphasize.

What 'Abduh considers as the sixth and last fundamental principle is a case in point. Christianity, he asserts, calls for divisiveness and discord between Christians and others and even among Christians themselves. In support of this claim he cites the words of Christ, "Do not think that I have come to bring peace on earth; I have not come to bring peace, but a sword"

(Matt 10:34). The influence of this saying, 'Abduh claims, has remained in the hearts of Christians even though there were other sayings of Jesus free from this spirit of violence.[10] 'Abduh then goes on to consider the consequences of these principles for the development of Western science and civilization. These were, first, limiting the reading and understanding of the sacred scriptures to the ecclesiastical authorities alone, who even forbade the laity to read the Bible. Second, the principle of divisiveness inspired by the supposed teachings of Jesus and his refusal even to recognize his own mother, brothers, and sisters (Luke 8:19-21) was applied in its cruelest forms during the Inquisition.[11] The suppression of the quest for knowledge in any form by the church in the belief that the Bible is sufficient was expressed in the dictum, "Ignorance is the mother of piety."[12] Thus the West after the fall of the Roman Empire and the adoption of Christianity as the only religion fell into the torpor of the Dark Ages. The reawakening and renaissance of Europe was possible only when the light of knowledge shone from the world of Islam, dispelling the darkness of many centuries. 'Abduh therefore concludes that Christian Europe was able to reach the high level of progress and wealth it had obtained only when it abandoned religion or relegated it to the periphery of social and intellectual life. The Muslim community, on the other hand, lost its place of prominence in world society inasmuch as it abandoned Islam. In this view, 'Abduh was followed by most apologists for Islam against Western religion, science, and culture. One of the most eloquent spokesmen for this view was Sayyid Muhammad Rashid Rida, to whom we shall now turn.

Muhammad 'Abduh aimed his defense of Islam, as we have seen, against secular attacks. Although his small book first appeared in a series of articles, it presents a sustained and well-developed argument. Rashid Rida, in contrast, wrote his defense against virulent attacks and invectives which Christian missionaries waged against the Islamic faith, the Qur'an, and the Prophet. Thus, Rida had to answer such attacks as they were made in Christian books, tracts, and journals. In addition, he had to answer questions which these attacks raised in the minds of Muslims. His book, *Shubuhat al-nasara wa hujaj al-Islam,* is made up of a number of articles that treat a variety of subjects in a variety of ways, as the occasion demanded. We shall choose for discussion a few salient themes of the book, imposing on them a certain measure of coherence for the sake of a clearer presentation.

Rida begins his discussion with the Qur'anic injunctions, "Call to the way of your Lord, with wisdom and good counsel . . . ." and, "Do not debate with the people of the Book, except in the best manner, save those among them who have committed acts of wrongdoing. Say, 'We believe in that which was sent to us, and that which was sent to you; our God and your God is One, and to Him we are submitters [Muslims]'" (Q. 16:125 and 29:46). He then goes on to bemoan the sad state of Muslims which made it possible for the opponents of Islam to deprecate it in its own home. "Muslims have become powerless because they have weakened Islam, so that Europeans lorded over them everywhere. Christian missionaries have, moreover, established themselves throughout Muslim lands, denigrating the Qur'an and spreading doubt concerning the Prophet."[13] The author was not worried about Muslims converting to Christianity, since a Muslim would not accept the divinity of anyone other than God in spite of any influence on his thinking. Rather, he feared that Muslim youths might begin to doubt the validity of religion as such and thus succumb to libertinism.

Rida saw it as his duty as a religious thinker and teacher to answer the doubts and queries raised in the minds of Muslim readers by Christian missionary writings. He also felt an obligation to society to counter the hostilities and distrust fostered by such missionary activities. He therefore distinguishes throughout between what he calls "paid preachers," whose zeal for the faith always depended on their salaries, and the "wise and virtuous Christians," who, like him, wished that each community would respect the faith of the other and together work for the good of all. Religion is in essence one, which is the worship of the one and only God. It is for this reason that Rida entitled his series of articles "Criticisms or Suspicions by Christians, and the Arguments (or proofs: *ḥujaj*) of Islam." This is because "the Christian religion itself does not contradict the Islamic faith; it is rather the Christians themselves who seek to contradict it. The incontrovertible proofs or contentions against them are not what the Muslims say, [in fact Muslims] themselves have become an argument against their own religion. Rather, these proofs are found in the Islamic religion itself."[14] This universalistic view of religion as the submission (*islām*) to God dominates the author's approach.

The most important subject of contention between Rida and his opponents was the scriptures of the two religious traditions. Thus, articles one, six, eight, and nine seek to answer Christian arguments for the truth of the Bible and the falsity of the Qur'an. The remaining articles, while dealing with other matters, touch indirectly on the same issues.

Rida begins by presenting the Muslim view of the Old and New Testaments. He goes far beyond the usual offhand Muslim rejection of these scriptures. He argues that the Qur'an bears witness to the Torah (*Tawrāt*) as a book of sacred law (*sharī'ah*) which God instituted through the prophet Moses. It is not a book of Babylonian and Assyrian mythology, as much of the Old Testament appears to be. Where its contents go against reason or science, such portions must be considered simply as myths or calumnies against God (as, e.g., the assertion that God felt regret in His heart, Gen 6:6). The Torah, therefore, is "true, it is the sacred laws and decrees which Moses and subsequent prophets of the children of Israel and their rabbis (*aḥbār*) followed."[15] The Qur'an does not, however, bear witness to the books of prophets such as Isaiah, Ezekiel, and Daniel. As for the Gospel (*Injīl*), "it is, in the views of Muslims, the sermons, maxims, and precepts that God revealed to Christ and with which he imparted guidance and good counsel to his people. What is contained beyond that in the books which Christians call [the] Gospel belongs, in the view of Muslims, either to history if it is a report or to its authors if is a matter of belief or sanction."[16] There are, Rida argues further, no authorities of transmission (*asānid*) for either of the two testaments.

The Qur'an contends further against Christians, saying, "And among those who say, 'We are Christians,' we took their covenant but they forgot a portion of that which they were given for remembrance [i.e., the scriptures]" (Q. 5:14). The Qur'an reproaches Jews and Christians who neglect their own scriptures by not abiding by their laws and judgments. It refers to the scriptures which the two communities possess, even though the sacred books were intermingled with history and legend. This conclusion led the Prophet to say, "Do not believe or disbelieve the people of the Book when they relate to you what is in their Book."[17] This is because, Rida argues, we have no criterion (*furqān*) by which we can distinguish between original revelation and what was interpolated in the process of writing. It is possible, however, to accept as reasonably probable that the laws, sanctions, and prohibitions attributed to Moses in Exodus, Leviticus, Numbers, and Deuteronomy "are most if not all parts of the Torah, for if they are not Torah, then where is the Torah? We similarly accept the Sermon on the Mount and other such teachings as reported in Matthew."[18]

As has already been observed, Rida did not wish to engage in anti-Christian polemics; rather, he felt compelled to answer the charges that Arab Christian thinkers and missionaries advanced against Islam in their various writings. He realized the futility of such polemical endeavors and repeatedly called instead for mutual respect and cooperation between the two communities. Both Rida and his opponents judged the faith and the scriptures of the others by the standards of their own tradition. Nonetheless, it must be said that Rida was more convincing, calm, and rational. Like Muslims, fundamentalist Christians—and especially those of the Middle East—have considered their sacred scriptures as the actual Word of God. Yet while Muslims in accordance with the Qur'anic view must regard previous revelations as coming from God, the Christian view of revelation excluded any revelations after the New Testament, which also superseded the Hebrew scriptures or Old Testament, the only true revelation before the Gospel. Against this view, Rida asks first, "How is it possible for Paul to annul the law of Moses and Jesus and yet not possible for God to send another Prophet with a law more perfect and nearer to reason than both; a Prophet, moreover, who came to confirm the truth brought by other apostles, and to contend with Jews and Christians as did Jesus with the scribes and Pharisees?"[19] Second, the Qur'an urges the people of the Book to accept all the scriptures revealed by God, including the Qur'an, and to live by them. Finally, the Gospels themselves assert that Jesus came with the evangel to the children of Israel; hence the Qur'an challenges them and those who accepted the Gospel to fulfill its injunctions.[20]

Modern Muslim thinkers have laid much stress on reason as the final arbiter of truth, again in accordance with the Qur'anic emphasis on the necessity of understanding and reason.[21] Their argument is that, at least in matters fundamental to the truth of any religious faith, revelation must accord with reason. Otherwise, how can we accept as actual facts things which science and reason would regard as impossible? Evidently the argument is appealing, and Christian thinkers have used it often in support of the view that the Bible was sent by God as a guide for the daily life of society and that God sent prophets to guide humanity to Him. Starting from this assumption, Rida asks why God left humanity for so many thousands of years without the Bible. Moreover, why should God have favored the Jews with His guidance when all men are His creatures and servants? Rida then asserts that if we were to consider the Bible as the only guide for humankind, then we would have no way of explaining the fact that China and India, both before and after the coming of Christianity, possessed civilizations higher than those of both Jews and Christians. This does not constitute a problem for Muslims because, Rida goes on, "in accordance with the guidance of the Qur'an they admit the possibility that God has sent prophets to the ancient Chinese and Indians to lead them to the level of felicity they had enjoyed. Then, with the passing of time, they contaminated their pure faith with polytheistic tendencies so that it was completely altered, as we believe."[22] Similarly, the author argues, "Christianity was originally a heavenly religion of divine unity but Christians later turned it into the worship of human beings such as Jesus and his mother."[23]

This comprehensive view of religion is unique. It asserts that God indeed "did not leave Himself without a witness" (Acts 14:17) and thus, "There is no people but that a warner [i.e., a prophet] was sent to them" (Q. 35:24). It further asserts that a civilization with a sound religious tradition based on faith in the One God produces a strong and prosperous society. Christianity, therefore, inasmuch as it is in essence a unitarian religion, has in itself the potential of an advanced religious tradition. The Dark Ages, which followed the corruption of the faith of Christ, ended only with the introduction to the West of Islamic science and philosophy. Europeans, Rida asserts, "are the nearest people to the religion of Islam in their good character, their self-dignity, industriousness, seriousness of action, veracity, and trustworthiness. They are guided by the laws (*sunan*) of the universe. They follow the laws of the original state (*fiṭrah*) [of things] and seek knowledge through experimentation and empirical verification." The author expresses the hope that "as they have been led to all this by free investigation and broadening of knowledge, they will likewise be guided to the rest of what Islam brought: sound beliefs, moral principles, spiritual virtues and good deeds."[24]

True Islam, which is the religion of God, is one: "Had this Islam not been veiled from the eyes of men by Muslims themselves, all the wise among the Europeans would have followed it."[25] Rida therefore suggests that the best service that can be rendered to religion as such is to make Islam known truly, for that would help people to know Judaism and Christianity as well. This can be achieved not by arguing from the Qur'an for the truth of the Torah and the Gospel, then arguing from them to prove the falsehood of the

Qur'an, as Christian missionaries have done, but rather by finding common ground of harmony and concord among the three sacred scriptures. As we have seen, however, Rida considers the books of the Old and New Testaments to be a mixture of myth, legend, and history along with the true biblical message as revealed by God. Thus, the Qur'an alone remains as the source concerning which there is no doubt, whether of authorship and compilation or in transmission. It is, moreover, the only book containing a message that human reason can readily accept. Rida illustrates this by briefly examining basic Christian concepts such as the Trinity and redemption. He decides that these concepts are based on pagan and philosophical ideas and not divine revelation.[26] Salvation, he argues, depends on faith in the One God and the performance of good deeds.

Rashid Rida presents what he considers three fundamental aims of religion in light of which he compares Islam and Christianity. He begins by asserting that the probability of the truth of any idea must in the end be determined by reason. If, on the one hand, a Holy Book proclaims things that reason must judge impossible, then what other criterion can we apply? If, on the other hand, all scriptures are in agreement, then religion is one. The three aims of religion are, first, to lead humanity to sound beliefs which, second, lead to the perfection of reason and the moral discipline of character. This will lead further to good deeds and the perfection of the soul. On this depends, third, the social welfare (*maṣlaḥah*) and benefits on which also depend the perfection of the individual. As for the first principle, the Qur'an demands the acceptance of matters of faith through reason and demonstration and condemns conjecture (*ẓann*). With regard to moral discipline, the Qur'an enjoins justice and moderation in contrast to the Gospels, which advocate excess and immoderation as, for example, in the injunctions of turning the other cheek and renouncing the world. Again in contrast to the Gospels, the Qur'anic teachings aim at the greatest benefit of society and protection against its own evils.[27]

It is clear from our discussion so far of both Muhammad 'Abduh and Rashid Rida that Muslim thinkers have generally missed the real challenge of the Sermon on the Mount. This they did by regarding it as law in the strict Islamic sense rather than as an ideal to be striven for but never fully attained. Christians have, similarly, sought to compare Muhammad with Christ, only to conclude that the Prophet of Islam was a sinner unable to save other sinners like him. On the basis of this assumption, Christian missionary scholars have regarded Islamic piety, which is based on fear of God and hope in His mercy, as an admission of despair in the face of sin, without a savior. Many have therefore issued passionate calls to Muslims to come to Christ and be saved. The entire debate, especially when it concerns itself with the faith of believers of both communities, can only breed insensitivity and misunderstanding. In all fairness, it must be said that Rida was generally guilty of exaggeration and misunderstanding, while his Christian opponents were guilty of both misunderstanding and insensitivity. Rida, for example, argues that salvation by faith alone and the practice of confession in the non-Protestant churches can lead to license for lewdness and cruelty. He based this statement at least in part, no doubt, on colonial policies in North Africa and Egypt.

Nevertheless, he continues to distinguish between what he calls "wise and virtuous Christians" and "paid preachers" seeking discord, criticizing Islam, and ignorantly misrepresenting what they wished to criticize. In fact, they did not seek to call Muslims to Christ but rather to their own sects. Here again, Rida is generally correct in his assessment of many local Protestant missionary activities. Rida concludes by calling again on the Christians of Egypt to work together with Muslims for the good and prosperity of the country. "The wise Qur'an teaches us that the religion of God, the Exalted, is one in its essence. It teaches us further that all the prophets and the righteous among those who believe in their message lived by it. It is the proclamation of the Oneness of God and His disassociation (*tanzīh*) from all attributes of change, and that He alone should be worshipped. It is also the fear which can deter human beings from acts of disobedience and evil deeds, and the hope which leads to goodness and piety."[28] The author then observes that prudent Christians all agree with him on this principle. Like him, they wish that "the missionaries and leaders of every religion be guided to it. In this way religion would be what God had decreed: a source of happiness for human beings, not of misery and suffering or an impetus to spread discord and hatred among them."[29]

## Polemics: Refutation of Christianity

The attitudes of both Muhammad 'Abduh and Rashid Rida were not intransigent; they could be regarded as conciliatory. 'Abduh was certainly correct in his basic assumption that Islam is neither the source of social, political, and economic problems affecting Muslim society nor the cause of the society's lagging behind the West in science and technology. Such a charge indeed flies in the face of the actual facts of Muslim history. Likewise, while Rida asserted the superiority of Islam as a comprehensive guide for human living and a rational faith, he wished that the men of faith in both communities would live in harmony and amity. Such misunderstandings and exaggerations evident in the works of both thinkers could be cleared up through direct dialogue and interaction in an atmosphere of mutual respect and appreciation. This challenge remains for us today.

One would have hoped that the two authors who will concern us in the remaining pages of this study represent a step toward better Muslim-Christian understanding. In fact, they represent an unfortunate regression to the classical patterns of polemics and counterpolemics. Although they display greater acquaintance with primary Christian sources as well as the early development of modern biblical scholarship, the purpose of their research was not to understand but to refute Christianity. Of the two, Shaykh Muhammad Abu Zahrah, a traditional scholar, is more serious, objective, and original. Doctor Ahmad Shalabi was trained at Cambridge University as a historian. He displays in his book *Muqaranat al-adyan, II: al-Masihiyyah* (Comparative Religions II: Christianity)[30] neither a high level of political thinking nor rigorous scholarship. Therefore it may be more useful to follow the argument of Abu Zahrah and refer to Shalabi only where he presents important points setting forth his own view.

Abu Zahrah begins with what he considers as true Christianity, or the Christianity that Jesus taught. He admits that this true Christianity cannot be learned from the scriptures and history books of the Christians because these have been tampered with, so that they can no longer be considered trustworthy. The religion of Jesus must therefore be sought in the Qur'an.

According to the Qur'an, Jesus believed and taught the religion of absolute divine Oneness (*tawḥīd*). This is of two kinds, the Oneness of God as the sole creator of all things, and His Oneness in Himself, in that His essence (*dhāt*) is free from anthropomorphism, composition, and change.[31] Furthermore, Jesus received from God a Book which is the Gospel (*Injīl*), confirming the Torah, revitalizing its laws, and supporting its true sanctions. It is a book of light and guidance to the God-fearers. It announced the coming of an apostle after Jesus, whose name was to be Ahmad (Q. 61:6). It is the Gospel by which the Qur'an challenges both Jews and Christians to abide (Q. 5:47).

In his presentation of the actual message of Jesus, Abu Zahrah tries to synthesize Gospel material with the Qur'anic view. Thus, Jesus taught first that there are no mediators between God and human beings except the piety and good deeds of an individual believer. Second, Jesus called men and women to asceticism and renunciation of worldly wealth. He finally warned them against divine wrath on the Day of Judgment. This emphasis on asceticism was necessary because the Jews of his time were dominated by a materialistic view that denied the life to come—both its rewards and its punishments.[32]

Shalabi wrote after Abu Zahrah and thus he uses the latter's work as one of his main sources. In his discussion of Jesus and his significance within the divine plan of guidance, Shalabi begins with the story of Mary and Zechariah, relying on the Qur'an as well as the Gospel accounts. The Qur'an tells us that God breathed into Mary a spirit from Him (Q. 29:91; 66:12). The author first discusses the various meanings of the word *spirit* (*rūḥ*), one of which is the vital force that instills new life into living beings or, in other words, it is the divine creative word (*amr*).[33] Thus, God "breathed into Mary a spirit which He created without the mediation of a human father. The meaning of breathing here is the act of instilling life in the body."[34] Shalabi then asserts that the creation of Jesus in this way does not give him priority over other prophets.

There is a new tendency among modern Muslim thinkers to demythologize Jesus and play down the miraculous aspect of his life. This tendency is no doubt a reaction to classical Islamic hagiography, on the one hand, and to the christological theology in Christianity, on the other. Both authors therefore present rational explanations of the life and miracles of Jesus. Thus, Abu Zahrah comments on the manner of the creation of Jesus as follows: "This bringing into being [of Jesus] was an act whose agent was an angel, one of the pure spirits who breathed into the garment of Mary, and thus was brought into being a man without human seed."[35] Abu Zahrah similarly asserts that although Mary conceived Jesus in a miraculous way, nevertheless the duration of that conception and the manner of the birth of the child were normal. Likewise, although the Qur'an states that Jesus talked to men in the cradle (Q. 19:29-33), he thereafter ceased speaking until God gave him the power of speech in the normal way of children. Here we see an interesting view of Jesus; he was not himself a miracle, but God wrought miracles through him and for a special purpose.

The wisdom in the birth of Jesus without human father, in the view of both thinkers, is first to manifest the power of God and His will in creation, which He created out of nothing. It is, second, in order for God to manifest the spiritual aspect of humankind to a people who denied the soul, thinking man to be the body only. Similarly, as with Christ's miracles, every prophet wrought miracles to suit his time and counter the errors of his people. Therefore, the miracles of Moses were designed to counter the magic of the ancient Egyptians and those of Jesus, Greek medicine, and the materialism of his own society.

As has already been observed, miracles in Islam are granted by God to his prophets and righteous friends (*awliyā'*) only as proof of their status. Shalabi therefore rejects the Gospel account of Christ's miracles because, first, they were too many and, second, because they are like theatrical acting without a purpose. He protests, "God causes to die and Jesus revives."[36] He further criticizes the Gospel assertion that the master gave this power to his disciples and the church after them. He objects, "Were the pope able to raise the dead and heal the deaf and the leper, as Jesus did . . . all disagreement among religions would cease and all men would follow him."[37] Yet if Jesus did come with such great miracles, a fact on which both Muslims and Christians agree, why did people not only disbelieve him but even seek to kill him? But from the Islamic point of view, of course, Shalabi's objections would apply to all the prophets whose people rejected them in spite of their miracles.

With regard to the end of Christ's earthly existence, both writers accept the general modern Muslim view which is based on traditional Qur'anic exegesis (*tafsīr*) and the *Gospel of Barnabas*. In agreement with traditional ideas, they have denied the crucifixion of Christ, claiming instead that another bore his likeness and was killed in his place. Relying on the *Gospel of Barnabas,* they argued that Judas Iscariot bore the likeness of Jesus' face and voice and was deservedly killed. Shalabi, however, realized that the Gospels speak of Judas as having lived after his master's death and therefore offered the possibility that Jesus escaped and lived in hiding until he died a natural death. He writes, "Because the message of Jesus was meant especially for the children of Israel (Q. 3:49), and because he abandoned them, then his apostleship was ended. He therefore lived his appointed term and died."[38]

Both Shalabi and Abu Zahrah argue, as did Muslims before them, that Christianity which grew after the death of Jesus, its supposed founder, bears at best a vague resemblance to his original message. They present three main causes for this distortion. The first is the persecutions which Christians suffered during the formative period of their religion. The Gospels, as well as all the other books of the New Testament, were written during this period. Abu Zahrah argues that all historical sources agree that these not only made martyrs of Christians but forced many of them to renounce their faith and deliver its sacred scriptures to the fire. They had no protection until the reign of Constantine, which "was an age of ease and blessing for Christians, but not for Christianity."[39] The age of persecution left its indelible mark on Christianity. It destroyed for subsequent generations of Christians all links between the master and those who wrote his teachings in their Gospels. Thus, he argues, we have no trustworthy record of the historical transmission of these books, and therefore they cannot serve as the basis of a religious tradition.

The second cause was Neoplatonic philosophy, which dominated the intellectual scene during the early period of Christian history. The third and equally important cause was the syncretistic character of Roman religion. The poverty and social instability which Roman society endured at the time led many to seek consolation and hope in religion. This tendency, of course, needed a metaphysical framework within which a synthesis of religion and philosophy may be found. The religions that were to be included in this schema were Roman paganism, Judaism, and Neoplatonism.

The author argues that Christianity became the actual result of this synthesis. From Neoplatonic philosophy Christianity adopted the doctrine of the Trinity. If, he concludes, "we were to consider the first cause or the One as the father, the *nous* [reason or logos], emanating from the One as the son, and the universal soul or spirit as the Holy Spirit . . . we would not have gone wrong in our analogy."[40] The main difference between the two is that Christianity finally asserted the divinity of the Son and the Holy Spirit, while Neoplatonism did not regard the *nous* and the universal soul as divine. Abu Zahrah bases this theory on the fact that the Trinity, as a worked-out doctrine, appeared after the establishment of the Alexandrian philosophical school. He therefore asserts, "The one who comes first must be the teacher of the one who follows."[41]

Both Abu Zahrah and Shalabi cite a large number of sources. Abu Zahrah depended mainly on traditional Eastern Christian works, while Shalabi used, in addition, modern studies by Western scholars as well as polemical works by Muslims and Christian converts to Islam. In his discussion of what he considers as the "real source of Christianity," Shalabi argues that

Christianity is a mixture of Paul's teachings and pagan ideas and rituals. He presents a comprehensive table, demonstrating that the birth, trial, and resurrection of Christ were modeled after the legends of the Buddha and pagan deities of India and the Near East.[42]

It must again be observed that no religious tradition was born in a vacuum. Therefore, no religious tradition is free from the rites, myths, and ideas of its so-called pagan environment. It may be further argued that this fact is proof not of the falsehood of a religious tradition but rather of the universality of truth. Can Muslims deny, for example, the pre-Islamic Arabian roots of the pilgrimage ritual? Conversely, can anyone deny the Islamic character and significance of this rite? Such charges and arguments in the end defeat their own purpose and would not convince anyone.

Abu Zahrah remains to a large extent within the framework of Christian history. He thus regards "the real sources of Christianity" as, first, the New and Old Testaments and, second, the ecclesiastical tradition. He devotes a great deal of space to the consideration of each of the four Gospels and the rest of the books of the New Testament. As a Muslim, however, he puts far too much stress on the Gospels, which he examines by the standards of the Qur'an and hadith tradition. He therefore sees the large number of Gospels from which the four canonical ones were chosen as indisputable proof of their inauthenticity. He repeats the usual Islamic charge that "the four Gospels were not dictated by Jesus, nor were they sent down to him as a direct divine revelation. They were rather written after him."[43] Abu Zahrah uses the traditional Christian disagreements concerning the exact date and authorship of each Gospel, as well as the findings of modern biblical scholarship, not as tools for understanding Christianity but as weapons for its refutation. There is, of course, nothing to be gained from trying to reproduce all the minutiae of his tedious but impressive endeavors.

Abu Zahrah takes the term *Injīl* to refer always to an actual book although he realizes that it actually means "good news" (*bishārah*). Thus, referring to the statements in Matthew and Mark that Jesus preached the good news of the kingdom and that Saint Paul also spoke of the "Gospel of the Son" (Matt 24:14 and Mark 1:15)[44] he asks whether or not there was a true Gospel of Jesus. He admits that none of the four Gospels has been so designated. Therefore, he concludes, "Should we then understand that there actually was a true Gospel that was revealed to Jesus and which he preached as they [the Christians] claim? . . . and that this Gospel must be considered as the foundation of this religion?"[45] He sees a possibility for this in the "Q" document which he renders into Arabic as *al-qalb* (the heart). It is interesting to observe what he would expect from such a Gospel, had it been preserved. "Can we then say that this was the Gospel that was sent down to Jesus and that it is his Gospel and the Gospel of God? . . . Would that the church had preserved this Gospel and endeavored to protect it, so that it would be as a sharp sword against dissension and the final arbiter among men of controversy and contention. . . . It also would have been the scientific source for all those wishing to write about early Christianity and follow its stages of development across the ages and the controversies of history."[46]

Modern Muslim thinkers have sought to reconstruct in part the Gospel of Jesus from the four Gospels where these agree with the Qur'an and the *Gospel of Barnabas*. Shalabi states unequivocally, "the disappearance of the Gospel of Jesus was an intentional act because it had a close relationship to the Qur'an . . . the disappearance of this Gospel, moreover, smoothed the way for interpolations, deletions, and alterations in the teachings of the Christian religion so that its foundations collapsed and its features as a revealed religion were lost."[47] As an example of Gospel distortions, Shalabi summarizes a study by an Egyptian Christian convert proving that the angelic hymn announcing the birth of Jesus to the shepherds was in fact an announcement of the coming of Muhammad and Islam. The angels must have spoken to the shepherds in Aramaic and thus must have said, "Praise be to God in the Highest; Islam is about to come to the earth, it will be brought to humankind by Muhammad."[48]

The *Gospel of Barnabas* appears to be a late apologetic work, perhaps written by a Christian convert to Islam. In it Christ denies in no uncertain terms all claims to divinity and sees himself as the precursor of Muhammad. It puts in his mouth the words of John the Baptist, "even he who comes after me, the thong of whose sandal I am not worthy to untie . . ." and thus declares Muhammad to be the true Messiah.[49] In this, the *Gospel of Barnabas* departs sharply from Islamic belief, according to which Muhammad is only a prophet and not a Messiah. The *Gospel of Barnabas* was discovered in 1709 in the Vatican library and was translated into Arabic in the early decades of the twentieth century. Since its appearance in Arabic, Muslim scholars have relied heavily on it in their disputes with Christians. Abu Zahrah alleges, therefore, that the *Gospel* is ancient and may have figured among the books which the church, under Pope Gelasius I in 492, forbade the laity to read. The church rejected this *Gospel* for many reasons, among which are, first, its denial of the divinity of Jesus;[50] second, for declaring the victim of the Abrahamic sacrifice to have been Ishmael and not Isaac; and third, for asserting that the coming Messiah was Muhammad and not Jesus.[51] Finally, the *Gospel of Barnabas* denies the crucifixion of Christ and asserts instead that Judas bore his likeness and was killed.[52] Abu Zahrah discusses in great detail the life and status of Barnabas in the early church and his disagreement with Paul. He further asserts on the authority of early Christian historians that Peter and Mark both denied the divinity of Christ.[53]

The "insidious error" began with Paul, who had no authority to transmit from Jesus, being neither one of his disciples nor even a disciple of his disciples. Paul, according to our author, was a scheming genius who constructed a Christianity foreign to the teachings of Christ and his disciples, a Christianity concocted from diverse elements of Graeco-Roman philosophy and religion. Abu Zahrah argues further that because ancient Christian sources do not tell us where Paul received his instruction in Christianity, we have no reason to suppose that he was inspired by God. Thus Paul, the actual founder of Christianity according to our authors, was himself neither a trustworthy source nor a man of righteous character.[54]

Abu Zahrah attempts to show that neither the Gospels nor the Epistles of St. Paul are beyond suspicion. He endeavors further to prove, on the basis of Christian sources, that doubts were raised from the beginning with regard both to the date and the authorship of the Gospels. Although he admits the Pauline Epistles to be genuine, he denies the veracity of their author and his claim to revelation or inspiration. This he does on the basis of certain conditions which, he asserts, any sacred scriptures must meet if they are to be considered as divinely revealed or inspired. First, the veracity of the recipient must be beyond any doubt and must be proved by miracles as a challenge to those who deny it. It must be accepted across the centuries and supported by an unbroken chain of trustworthy transmitters. Second, the sacred book must not contradict itself nor any part deny or invalidate any other part. It must further be characterized by wisdom and high moral principles. Third, the apostle to whom the book is revealed must himself claim revelation (*wahy*) and prove his claim by miracles and unbroken testimony. Finally, the chain of authority guaranteeing the historicity of the apostle and his revelation must consist at each link of a large number of men whose truthfulness must be beyond doubt, and their agreement complete.

Abu Zahrah then concludes that neither the apostles nor the books attributed to them meet these essential conditions; hence, Christianity altogether rests on a shaky foundation. He does not accept the role of the Holy Spirit on Christian terms since Luke, neither in his Gospel nor in Acts, gives a list of the names of the seventy or the hundred and the seventy apostles on whom the Spirit descended in the Upper Room. The author also cites modern Christian writers who have asserted that not everything in the New Testament is inspired. Furthermore, Luke, who is our main source on the apostles, was himself neither a disciple of Christ nor a disciple of his disciples. Therefore his claim for the apostleship of Paul or any of the other apostles cannot be accepted. Or did any of the disciples make such a claim? Paul only called himself the apostle of Christ and not the apostle of God.

Likewise, Abu Zahrah sees in the contradictions and disagreements among the books of the New Testament still another proof of the fact that they were neither revealed nor inspired by God. He argues that Matthew and Luke differ markedly in their report of the genealogy of Jesus. He also sees basic disagreements among all four Gospels regarding the trial and crucifixion of Jesus and also concerning his resurrection, subsequent appearances, and ascension. The Gospels, Abu Zahrah contends, report several natural portents accompanying the death of Jesus, such as darkness and earthquakes, which are not mentioned by any of the historians of the time. He thus concludes, "If these books appeared to be full of contradictions, disagreements, and fallacies . . . then they cannot be considered as revealed scriptures."[55]

After proving to his own satisfaction that the very bases of the Christian faith are in doubt, Abu Zahrah goes on to refute the creed, or substance of the Christian faith. He analyzes the various components of the Nicene Creed and argues that it is not based on the faith and teaching of Jesus but that it is rather the eclectic innovation of the church in its various councils. He takes issue not with the religious significance of Christ's divinity but with the theological formation of the doctrine of the Trinity. He admits that Christians do not consider the sonship of Christ as a physical relationship with God; still he objects to the irrational attempts of Christians to harmonize between tritheism and unitarianism. Like Muhammad 'Abduh and Rashid Rida, and indeed Muslims in general, Abu Zahrah asserts that what cannot be comprehended by human reason cannot be believed by the heart either. On similar grounds, he rejects the concept of redemption.

Abu Zahrah then analyzes the major councils and their major theological conclusions. He attempts to demonstrate the gradual development of Christian theology which, he argues, contradicts the teachings of Christ even as preserved in the Gospel.[56] Early Christianity, until the time of Constantine, represented a struggle between belief in the One God and pagan tritheism. The first to sow the seeds of such erroneous ideas was St. Paul, who was opposed even by the disciples.[57] The role of the Alexandrian theological movement was, Abu Zahrah argues, "the key" to the actual history of Christian theology. He therefore counsels those who are interested in knowing "how Christianity was changed from a unitarian faith to one deifying Jesus" to study carefully this movement.[58] The second step, that is, the deifying of the Holy Spirit, followed naturally in the process of modeling Christianity on Neoplatonic philosophy. Abu Zahrah identifies the Holy Spirit as a spirit from God "which He created and made a messenger between Him and those to whom He wished to make a direct revelation (*waḥy*) or communicate a matter of universal significance. It is not the spirit of God [in the sense that] it is related to His essence."[59]

The struggle between unitarianism and trinitarian innovation may be seen in the assertion of Paul of Samosata, "I do not know what the Word (*Logos*) is nor what is the Holy Spirit," as well as in his denial of the eternity of the Son.[60] Abu Zahrah therefore divides Christian history into two main periods, the period of unitarianism, which went to the Council of Nicaea, and that of trinitarianism, which continued from then to the present. Similarly, he categorized Christian sects into the old ones, most of which were unitarian in belief, and the later sects, which were based on trinitarian ideas. He sees, furthermore, direct Islamic influence on the iconoclastic movement in Byzantium in the eighth century as well as in the Reformation, seven centuries later.

Islam, in spite of all disturbances in its early history and the attempts of new converts to bring into it foreign notions, remained pure because its foundation, the Qur'an, was preserved without any change or alteration. Thus our author presents the Qur'an, "the luminous star illuminating the deep darkness" to be the decisive criterion of distinguishing Christianity and truth from the legends and fables that corrupted it.[61]

Both Abu Zahrah and Shalabi call on the Christians of today to carry the Reformation, which began in the sixteenth century, to its natural conclusion. This, of course, means the rejection of the Trinity and return to the worship of the One God. People such as Leo Tolstoy did in fact repudiate the old beliefs, according to Abu Zahrah; in that sense, such people were essentially Muslims. The challenge presented by Muslims is thus not for Christians to become Muslims but to return to original Christianity, which is Islam in its essence.

## Conclusion

The picture presented by the four thinkers considered in this study is a typical one. Moreover, were we to make a similar presentation from the Christian side, the results would have been similar. Neither Muslims nor Christians in the Middle East try to study each others' traditions on their own terms. If Abu Zahrah compares Christian sacred writings with those of Islam, only to find the former wanting, he finds a Christian-Egyptian minister doing exactly the same thing only to prove the opposite. Ibrahim Saʻid, a well-known Protestant minister, used the same method of polemical presupposition and arguments to prove the truth and authenticity of Luke's reports against those of the hadith. Thus, in his attempt to refute the minister, Abu Zahrah changes his approach from a calm and even tedious examination of Christian sources to a lively diatribe against his opponent.[62] In fact, the Muslim view of revelation with its emphasis on a book is essentially shared by Eastern Christians. This may be due not so much to the interaction of the two communities but rather to an ancient common heritage to which the Jewish, Christian, and Islamic traditions are heir. Only recently has liberal Christian scholarship begun to take a broad view of revelation as the divine involvement in history, of which the Bible is only a human record or interpretation. Muslims have so far dealt mainly with Middle Eastern and fundamentalist Christianity. In a sense, therefore, Muslim-Christian dialogue is behind the times both in its assumptions and conclusions.

True dialogue is conversation among persons and not a confrontation between ideas. If Muslim-Christian dialogue is to be at all meaningful, it must go beyond the letter of scriptures, creed, and tradition. Men and women of faith in both communities must learn to listen to the divine voice speaking through revelation and history, and together seek to understand what God is saying to Muslims through Christianity and to Christians through Islam. In more practical terms, this means that Christians and Muslims must go beyond the history of a reified religion and try instead to share in the commonality of faith. Then it will, we hope, be realized that although Christians and Muslims have followed different roads toward the goal of human fulfillment in God, the goal is one and the roads meet at many points.

# Notes

1. All Qur'anic translations are my own.

2. Imam Muhammad 'Abduh, *al-Islam wa al-Nasraniyyah ma'a l-'ilm wa al-madaniyyah*, 8th ed. (Cairo: Dar al-Manar, A.H. 1373), a collection of articles originally published in the periodical *al-Manar*.

3. Sayyid Rashid Rida, *Shubuhat al-Nasara wa hujaj al-Islam* (Cairo: Nahdat Misr, 1375/1956).

4. Shaykh Muhammad Abu Zahrah was professor at al-Azhar and was on the faculty of law of Cairo University. Ahmad Shalabi, Ph.D. from Cambridge, had been head of the Cultural Centre of the then United Arab Republic in Jakarta, Indonesia.

5. For a fuller analysis of 'Abduh's work, see my article "Islam and Christianity, a Study of Muhammad 'Abduh's View of the Two Religions," *Humaniora Islamica* 2 (1974): 121-36.

6. 'Abduh, *al-Islam wa al-Nasraniyyah ma'a l-'ilm wa al-madaniyyah*, 21ff.

7. All citations from the Bible are from the Revised Standard Version.

8. Abduh, *al-Islam wa al-Nasraniyyah ma'a l-'ilm wa al-madaniyyah*, 22.

9. Ibid., 24.

10. Ibid., 26.

11. See ibid., 31ff., where the author argues that often confessions were extracted from members of a family against one another.

12. Abduh, *al-Islam wa al-Nasraniyyah ma'a l-'ilm wa al-madaniyyah*, 28.

13. Rida, *Shubuhat al-Nasara wa hujaj al-Islam*, 9.

14. Ibid.

15. Ibid., 2.

16. Ibid., 3.

17. Ibid.

18. Ibid.

19. Ibid.

20. Ibid., 18.

21. See, for example, Q. 2:164; 5:153 and 8:22.

22. Rida, *Shubuhat al-Nasara wa hujaj al-Islam*, 29.

23. Ibid.

24. Ibid., 30.

25. Ibid., 5.

26. Ibid., 47ff. (article 10); see also *Tafsir al-Manar* by the author and his teacher, Muhammad 'Abduh, 2nd ed. (Beirut: Dar al-Manar, n.d.), vol. 5, commentary on Surah 4:122, 431.

27. Rida, *Shubuhat al-Nasara wa hujaj al-Islam*, 12.

28. Ibid., 41.

29. Ibid.

30. This is the second in his series of books on comparative religion: Ahmad Shalabi, *Muqaranat al-adyan, II: al-Masihiyyah*, 3rd ed. (Cairo: Matba'at Yusuf, 1835/1966), 11.

31. Shaykh Muhammad Abu Zahrah, *Muhadarat fi al-Nasraniyyah*, 2nd ed. (Cairo: Maktabat al-Nahda al-Misriyah, 1965).

32. Ibid., 12-13. He refers specifically to Ernest Renan, *Vie de Jésus* (Paris: Michel Levy Frères, 1863). See esp. chap. 2, "Enfance et Jeunesse. . . ."

33. He cites the verse, "They will ask you [Muhammad] concerning the Spirit (*rūḥ*); say, "The Spirit is of the command (*amr*) of my Lord" (Q. 17:85).

34. Shalabi, *Muqaranat al-adyan, II: al-Masihiyyah*, 26.

35. Abu Zahrah, *Muhadarat fi al-Nasraniyyah*, 17.

36. Shalabi, *Muqaranat al-adyan, II: al-Masihiyyah*, 30.

37. Ibid., 31.

38. Ibid., 34.

39. Abu Zahrah, *Muhadarat fi al-Nasraniyyah*, 31.

40. Ibid., 35.

41. Ibid., 38; see also Shalabi, *Muqaranat al-adyan, II: al-Masihiyyah*, 47, 130ff.

42. See Shalabi, *Muqaranat al-adyan, II: al-Masihiyyah*, 132.

43. Abu Zahrah, *Muhadarat fi al-Nasraniyyah*, 41.

44. See also Rom 1:9 and Corinthians, *passim*.

45. Abu Zahrah, *Muhadarat fi al-Nasraniyyah*, 56.

46. Ibid., 57.

47. Shalabi, *Muqaranat al-adyan, II: al-Masihiyyah*, 43.

48. Ibid., 46; see Luke 2:14.

49. John 1:17; see also Laura and Lansdale Ragg, eds., *The Gospel of Barnabas* (Oxford: Clarendon, 1907), chap. 42 (p. 99).

50. *Barnabas,* chap. 70 (p. 163); and chap. 93 (pp. 214-17).

51. Ibid., chaps. 43-44 (pp. 101-6).

52. Ibid., chaps. 216-17 (pp. 471-81).

53. Abu Zahrah, *Muhadarat fi al-Nasraniyyah*, 71.

54. Both Abu Zahrah and Shalabi are aware that Paul wrote before the Gospels and thus argue that the Gospels were deeply influenced by him. See Abu Zahrah, *Muhadarat fi al-Nasraniyyah*, 71ff; and Shalabi, *Muqaranat al-adyan, II: al-Masihiyyah*, 48ff.

55. Abu Zahrah, *Muhadarat fi al-Nasraniyyah*, 92.

56. Ibid., 134ff.

57. See Acts 14 and 15, esp. 15:36. Abu Zahrah seems to have in mind Paul's opposition to the law being observed by Gentile converts and his final break with Barnabas.

58. Abu Zahrah, *Muhadarat fi al-Nasraniyyah*, 183

59. Ibid., 141-42.

60. Johannes Quasten, *Patrology* (Utrecht: Spectrum Publishers, 1953), 2:140-42.

61. Abu Zahrah, *Muhadarat fi al-Nasraniyyah*, 173.

62. Ibid., 93-97.

# 16

# Pope John Paul II on Islam

Muslim-Christian relations are as old as the Islamic tradition itself. Before his Prophetic mission, while still a youth, Muhammad's prophethood is believed to have been recognized and foretold by the Christian monk Bahirah.[1] The truth of Muhammad's mission and authenticity of the scripture revealed to him were confirmed by the aged Christian savant Waraqah bin Nawfal. Waraqah's testimony to the truth of Muhammad's apostolic mission confirmed him in his resolve to preach his new message of faith in the One God to an idolatrous and stubborn people.[2] When some of the Prophet's followers could no longer endure the persecution of the hostile men of Makkah, he advised them to seek protection with the Christian king of Abyssinia.[3]

## Historical Overview

Christians are described in the Qur'an as "the nearest in amity" to the Muslims (Q. 5:82). Twice they are numbered among the religious communities whose faith and good works will be richly rewarded by God, "and no fear shall come upon them nor will they grieve."[4] Yet the Christians are sternly reproached for their extremist claims concerning Jesus and even accused of rejection of faiths.[5]

Thus, the Islamic position towards Christians has from the beginning been an ambivalent one. This ambivalence is characteristic not only of the Islamic view of Christians but of Christian-Muslim relations generally. One fundamental reason for this ambivalence is that both faiths are intensely missionary oriented. Each claims to have exclusively a universal message of truth and salvation for all of humankind. Each community, moreover, considers the other to be in grave error in its basic understanding of God, his nature, and relationship to humanity and its history.

While it may be argued that Muslim-Christian relations are now better than they have ever been,[6] in fact little has changed in the basic attitudes of the church and the *ummah* toward each other. There has been on both sides

Previously published in *John Paul II and Interreligious Dialogue*, ed. Byron L. Sherwin and Harold Kasimov (Maryknoll, N.Y.: Orbis Books, 1999), 169-84. Reprinted by permission.

a grudging recognition of their common faith in the One God but also a deep mistrust of the aims and intentions of each community toward the other. This mistrust stems from long-held distortions and misrepresentations of the faith and culture by both communities. These distorted images have often been used to justify long and bloody conflicts between Western Christendom and the world of Islam.

On the basis of this common faith in God and commitment to do his will, in 1077, Pope Gregory VII wrote to the sultan, al-Nasir, ruler of Bejaya, in present-day Algeria, reminding him of this common faith and commitment. The pope admonished the Muslim ruler, "God approves nothing in us so much as that after loving Him, one should love his fellow." He continued, "You and we owe this charity to ourselves, specially because we believe and confess one God. . . ."[7] Less than two decades later, in 1095, Pope Urban II sounded an entirely different note at the Council of Clairmont, which he used to launch the First Crusade against the Muslims. In his famous address the pontiff contrasted the Franks, "the beloved of God," with the Muslims, whom he called, "an accursed race, a race utterly alienated from God. . . ."[8]

## New Hopes and Old Prejudices

The millennium following these harsh words has seen many positive changes in Muslim-Christian relations. A new era of meaningful and constructive dialogue began with Vatican II (1962-1965). In this essay we are concerned with the position of the Catholic Church toward Islam and Muslims, and more specifically, with the pronouncements of Pope John Paul II on Islam. It must be noted at the outset that the following analysis of His Holiness's pronouncements will mirror the same ambivalence that has characterized the relations between the two communities throughout their long history.

In many ways the pronouncements of Pope John Paul II on Islam echo the spirit and letter of the Vatican II. In particular, *Nostra Aetate,* one of the council's major documents expressing the church's new spirit of openness to dialogue with "non-Christians," has been the primary inspiration for the pope's approach to Islam. Nevertheless, His Holiness often returns to old and conservative attitudes of the church toward Islam and Muslims. This is particularly the case, as we shall see, when he addresses Catholic clerics living in Muslim lands. The issue that will concern us in this study is, therefore, the apparent inconsistencies in the Holy Father's pronouncements on Islam and what this means to the commitment of both the church and the *ummah* to interfaith dialogue.

Pope John Paul II has been more prolific on Islam than any pontiff before him. This is undoubtedly due in large part to his numerous pastoral visits to Christian minorities living in Muslim lands.[9] No less important in this regard is the participation of the Pontifical Council for Interreligious Dialogue in international interfaith activities. On such occasions the pope addressed

Muslim participants on behalf of the Catholic Church. Other reasons for the pope's concern with Muslims and Islam have been international conflicts such as the Lebanese civil strife, the Gulf War, and the tragic interreligious conflict in the former Yugoslavia. Still another reason is the diplomatic relations of the Vatican with many Muslim nations.

I shall selectively examine the statements of Pope John Paul II on Islam chronologically over a fifteen-year period (1979-1994). These statements will be considered under three categories, those addressed to Muslims directly and those addressed to Christians about Islam. The third and equally important category is the pope's writings, especially his encyclical *Redemptoris Missio* (*Mission of the Redeemer,* 1991) and the book *Crossing the Threshold of Hope* (1994). These two recent documents provide the theological framework for the pope's personal position toward other religions in general and Islam in particular.

The first journey of the pope to a predominantly Muslim country was to Turkey in November 1979, slightly over a year after his accession to the pontifical office. In a homily delivered at the chapel of the Italian embassy in Ankara, the pope exhorted the Catholic community to live in peace and amity with fellow Muslim citizens. He praised Turkey's secular system, which allows all citizens to practice their own religion without any discrimination. "Although they do not acknowledge Jesus as God," the pope observed, Muslims "revere him as a prophet, honor the Virgin Mary and await the Day of Resurrection." He extolled Islamic moral, spiritual, and social values, which Christians also hold. The pope finally called on both Muslims and Christians to collaborate on the basis of their common faith in God in promoting peace and brotherhood "in the free profession of faith proper to each."[10]

It is important to note here that honoring Jesus and his mother is not an Islamic gesture of goodwill toward Christians. It is rather an essential part of their faith. But to "acknowledge Jesus as God" is for Muslims to associate other gods with God, which is the only unforgivable sin.[11] While we believe such theological issues should not be ignored by Christians and Muslims in their efforts to promote better understanding through honest dialogue, they should be recognized and dealt with patiently and with great sensitivity.

In May 1980, first in Kenya and then in Ghana, the pope echoed the same sentiments in his addresses to Muslim leaders of the two African countries. He found in the worship of the One God, the creator of heaven and earth, a bond uniting Christians and Muslims. He affirmed the church's commitment to dialogue with Islam, but also asked that "her own heritage be fully known specially to those who are spiritually attached to Abraham and who profess monotheism."[12] This somewhat veiled reference to missionary work among the Muslims of Africa is more openly expressed in later speeches, particularly to African bishops and missionaries engaged in medical, educational, and other humanitarian services.

The dual mission of the church as a good Samaritan to the poor and suffering peoples of the world, and also as the maker of disciples for Christ "of all nations" (Luke 10:25-37; Matt 28:19), was emphasized by the pope during a two-day stop in Pakistan on his way to the Far East. His holiness exchanged expressions of goodwill with the late Pakistani President Zia-ul Haq. He observed that, while the primary mission of the church is a spiritual one, she nonetheless always seeks to promote the dignity of all human beings through schools and other educational, charitable, and social institutions. Then reflecting the spirit of Vatican II, the Holy Father concluded his address with the prayer that mutual understanding between Christians and Muslims grow deeper and that ways of greater cooperation be found "for the good of all."[13]

The attitude of mutual mistrust and hostility which have on the whole characterized relations between the Christian West and the Muslim world had its roots not only in fundamental theological differences but also in political, economic, and military rivalries. Within less than a century of the Prophet's death, Christendom lost to Muslim domination some of its most central provinces. Asia Minor, Egypt, and North Africa were very early irrevocably lost, and for centuries the Iberian peninsula and other important parts of Christian Europe were centers of Islamic learning and power.

While, moreover, significant Christian minorities survived in Egypt and other Middle Eastern lands, in North Africa, or the lands of the Arab West (*al-Maghrib*), the home of Cyprian, Ambrose, and Augustine, Christianity disappeared forever. Yet North Africa's pre-Islamic religious heritage left an indelible mark on its popular Sufi piety. This piety, in turn, provided the basis of spiritual fellowship with mystically inclined Christians such as the well-known Christian marabout Charles de Foucauld. De Foucauld tried and succeeded in sharing his Christ-like life with Muslims in Algeria, who saw in him a Sufi saint as well as a saintly Christian hermit. He thus broke the religious barriers that had long separated Muslims and Christians without compromising his own religious convictions.[14]

Another equally significant point of contact with the West has been the deep penetration of French education and culture of most North African societies. Therefore, in spite of the disappearance of indigenous Christianity in North Africa, the church has enjoyed long and spiritually fruitful relations with the region.

In his address to North African bishops on November 23, 1981, the pope spoke of the need to strengthen the small Catholic communities in that region in order that they may "bear a genuinely Christian witness among those who receive them." He also observed that this witness may be enriched by Muslim culture and piety. The pope, however, cautioned that empathy for Islamic spirituality should not obscure the primary responsibility of the Christian, which is to "witness to the faith in Christ and to Christian values." He finally counseled that Catholic women married to Muslim men should always be an object of solicitude by the church. For, he asserted, their presence in Muslim families allows them to witness directly to their faith.[15]

The approach of Pope John Paul II to Muslims centers on two essential concepts, interfaith dialogue and Christian witness. These appear to be in the Holy Father's mind two closely interrelated terms. Thus, the purpose of dialogue is to facilitate Christian witness. But the aim of both is ultimately the conversion of Muslims to Christianity.

This goal was enjoined upon the bishops of Mali during their *ad limina* visit to Rome on November 26, 1981. The Holy Father encouraged the bishops to engage in dialogue with Muslims as well as with people of other faiths. "But dialogue itself," he asserted, "would lack an important dimension if it did not foresee the possibility of one freely asking for baptism."[16]

Were this goal to be directed at the followers of African and other non-monotheistic traditions, an argument could be made that the aim is to lead them to faith in God. But with Muslims, dialogue ought to be a dialogue of faith among the worshipers of the God of Abraham and all the prophets, including Muhammad. Otherwise dialogue, whatever form it may take, would be simply a cover for some form of postcolonial proselytization. This is particularly the case when dialogue is conducted in the context of Western church-related medical, social, and educational missions.

The pope is, according to Catholic tradition, not only the successor of St. Peter as the head of the universal church; he is also an international political figure. Understandably, therefore, the pope would have many and at times conflicting agendas, depending on the time, place, and audience that he addresses. This may account, at least in part, for the apparent inconsistencies in his statements.

Speaking to Muslims in Nigeria on February 14, 1982, the pope called for better understanding and cooperation between Christians and Muslims on the basis of common spiritual and moral values: faith in God and submission to God's holy will, and the commitment to defend human life and dignity. The context of this address was the family and its sanctity as "a precious nucleus of society." On the basis of a common spiritual and moral patrimony, he insisted, we can "in a true sense call one another brothers and sisters in the faith of the One God."[17]

The Holy Father called for safeguarding religious freedom, particularly in the education of children, which is usually taken to mean the freedom to teach the Christian faith. Yet there was no allusion to missionary activities of any kind. Rather, he counseled that religious education be used as a means to "counter the efforts of those who wish to destroy the spiritual aspects of man."[18]

In a highly significant speech addressed to the leaders of the Muslim and Jewish communities in Lisbon on May 14, 1982, the pope presented a genuinely pluralistic theology of dialogue among the peoples of the Abrahamic traditions. Behind this religious pluralism, he averred, there must exist a unity of faith confirmed by personal conduct. The spiritual life of the faithful of all three communities would, the pope further argued, help those who are searching for the Transcendent. It may help such sensitive souls to enjoy an inner glimmer of the reality of God in their lives. He continued, "Since, convinced as we are of the good which belief in God constitutes for us, the desire to share this good with others is spontaneous."[19]

The pope went on to assert that for many people in today's world, God is either unknown or erroneously symbolized by ephemeral human powers. Therefore, interfaith dialogue could foster greater appreciation of the spirituality of every religious tradition. In this way interreligious dialogue could expose the myth of building a new and harmonious world order without God, one that is based solely on anthropocentric humanism. In doing this, the pope concluded, we would contribute to the common good of humanity.[20]

This theology of reconciliation and the freedom of faith, spiritual reform, mutual tolerance, and dialogue among peoples of different faith traditions constituted an essential component of the pope's message to the world, at least in the early years of his papacy. Concrete expression of this theology of universal faith in the One God was given in the apostolic letter of John Paul II, in celebration of the jubilee year of redemption.[21] One of the themes of this letter is the role of Jerusalem as a symbol of peace and harmony for the followers of the three Abrahamic faiths.

After speaking of the place of the Holy City in the devotional life of the three faith communities, the pope declared:

> I think of and long for the day on which we shall be so taught by God, that we shall listen to His message of peace and reconciliation. I think of the day on which Jews, Christians and Muslims will greet each other in the city of Jerusalem with the same greeting of peace with which Christ greeted the disciples after the resurrection, "peace be with you" (John 20:19).

The diversity of expressions of faith and culture in the Holy City should, His Holiness counseled, be "an effective aid to concord and peace."[22]

The theology of the unity of faith among all the believers in God, which the pope so eloquently presented to the leaders of the three monotheistic religions in Lisbon in May 1982, was again expounded at the Vatican three years later. The occasion was a colloquium on the theme of holiness in the two traditions.[23] The Holy Father began his address to that interfaith, international gathering with the Qur'anic affirmation, "Your God and ours is one and the same, and we are brothers and sisters in the faith of Abraham."[24] He then compared and contrasted the concept of holiness in the three monotheistic traditions and its manifestation as a quality of life in the Christian and Muslim communities. He contrasted the holy life of such virtues as uprightness, righteous living, and goodness, which the two religions enjoin, with such "self-centered tendencies as greed, the lust for power and prestige, competition, revenge, lack of forgiveness and the quest for earthly pleasures." These and similar vices, the pope observed, turn humankind away from the path to goodness, "which God has intended for all of us." He concluded by observing that there are countless men and women—Muslims, Christians, and others around the world—who "quietly live authentic lives of obedience to God and selfless service to others." Such holy lives "offer humanity a genuine alternative—God's way to a world which otherwise would be destroyed in self-seeking hatred and struggle.[25]

To Muslims and Jews, as we saw, the pope's message of goodwill and cooperation in promoting peace and social justice is usually based on a common faith and religious kinship. But when he spoke to Muslim and Hindu representatives in Nairobi, Kenya, on August 18, 1985, he emphasized social action based on general moral and spiritual values common to all the major religions. He thus argued that the communities of these world religions should not remain passive in the face of spiritual and social needs, violations of human rights, wars, and other disasters.

In that gathering the pope acknowledged religious diversity but also unity in the worship of God. He asserted, "God's will is that those who worship him, even if not united in the same worship, would nevertheless be united in brotherhood and in common service for the good of all." This common quest for spiritual and moral fulfillment, the pope asserted, should motivate us all to work together in facing the challenge of helping the world to "live in peace and harmony with respect for the human dignity of all."[26]

In a notable address to Moroccan youths delivered on the following day in Casablanca, the pope added a humanistic dimension to this universal message of goodwill. Since the pope referred often to this address in later encounters with Muslims, it must be regarded as an especially significant statement of his position toward Islam and Muslims. The irenic tone of this speech was perhaps determined by its audience. Among other world issues, the pope addressed the need for more justice in world affairs, the lack of North-South solidarity, and the plight of refugees. The earth, the pope asserted, is God's gift to all of humankind. All are equally entitled to its resources, and all have the right to live on it in peace and security. Furthermore, since every human being is in a certain sense the image and representative of God, we must love and respect every human being. He added, "Man is the road that leads to God. . . ."[27]

For the purpose of this study, however, it must be noted that in this address the pope spoke unequivocally of the common religious heritage of Muslims and Christians. He said, "I believe that we Christians and Muslims must recognize with joy the religious values that we have in common and give thanks to God for them."

In keeping with his role as a pastor, the pope presented to Moroccan youths a long list of common beliefs and practices that bind Muslims and Christians. These include prayers, fasting, and almsgiving, as well as hope in God's mercy both in this world and the next. He concluded, "We hope that after the resurrection God will be satisfied with us, and we know that we will be satisfied with him."[28]

His Holiness repeated many of the same ideas in a homily that he preached in the same city and on the same day. But since he was speaking then to Christians, he repeated his call for witness to Christ to Muslims. Again, he couched this call to witness in the pastoral language of Christian love and charity. In their dialogue with Muslims—which the pope admitted was not always easy—Christians should be ever conscious of the mystery of salvation, which they must communicate to others with love. As the theme of the homily was love, the Holy Father concluded, "If we have no love, our presence here will do nothing. Our witness will remain empty."[29]

On February 26, 1986, in Vatican City, the pope received in audience Jewish, Christian, and Muslim participants in a colloquium organized under the auspices of the Jerusalem Hope Center for Interfaith Understanding and Reconciliation. The theme of the colloquium was "One God and Three Religions." The pope appropriately highlighted the two divine attributes of mercy and justice, which both the Bible and the Qur'an teach. He also expressed the oft-repeated hope of peace and reconciliation among the three faith communities through the city of peace, Jerusalem, which is a living symbol of God's will for all to live in peace and mutual respect. He continued, "In today's world it is more important than ever that people of faith place at the service of humanity their religious convictions, founded on daily practice of listening to God's message and encountering Him in prayerful worship."[30]

It is noteworthy that when the Holy Father speaks to representatives of the three religions, he places the three faiths on an equal footing as legitimate paths to God. Furthermore, his call for placing religious convictions at the service of humanity gives dialogue its true meaning and purpose. Still another noteworthy point is the absence in such addresses of any missionary motives.

This conciliatory attitude, however, raises an important question. Why does the Holy Father insist on missionary work among Muslims when he talks to Christians, and even to Muslims, but avoids any reference to it when he addresses Jews? One reason, I believe, is that Jewish-Christian dialogue has made far better progress toward achieving a common language among equal participants than has Muslim-Christian dialogue. Another reason is that most of world Jewry has for centuries shared with the West a common history and culture. Islam, on the other hand, has for long been "the mysterious other," and the Muslim world has been an archrival to Western Christendom. Be that as it may, at a time when Christians and Muslims live as neighbors in every Western metropolis, the old ambivalence which remains characteristic of some of the pope's pronouncements on Islam is hardly conducive to constructive dialogue.

Despite the fact that the Holy Father has enthusiastically participated in interfaith gatherings, he nonetheless appears to be uncomfortable with such undertakings. This may be because interfaith activities mean de facto recognition of the equal validity of all religions as paths to the divine or ultimate reality. This admission would, of course, question the pope's view of the church's missionary mandate. The pope's cautionary attitude may conversely be due to the recognition of the uniqueness and integrity of every religion, which must not be compromised through interfaith activities, particularly those involving interfaith common prayers.

Both the enthusiasm and ambivalence of the pope toward interreligious common devotions were clearly evinced in his opening address to the World Day of Prayer for Peace, held in Assisi on October 27, 1986. His Holiness began by observing the great value of so many religious leaders coming together for such a noble cause. This shows, he said, "that there exists another dimension of peace and another way of promoting it, which is not the result of negations, political compromise or economic bargaining."[31] Through religious diversity, the pope further asserted, prayers for peace express a common spiritual bond and a relationship with the power that surpasses all our human capabilities.

As for His Holiness's ambivalence, it may be discerned in the following qualifications that he placed on the aims of the meeting under discussion. He argued that the purpose of the gathering was not to seek religious consensus among the participants or negotiate their faith convictions. Nor does it mean, the pope said, that "religions could be reconciled at the level of common commitment in an earthly project which would surpass them all." Nor should such a gathering be regarded as a concession to relativism in religious beliefs, "because every human being must sincerely follow his or her upright conscience with the intention of seeking and obeying the truth."[32] But is not the ultimate goal of dialogue to achieve a fellowship of faith, a sort of "religious consensus" that would see in the diversity of expressions of this common faith a divine blessing?

## Dialogue or Evangelization?

It was observed above that Vatican II ushered in a new era of Muslim-Catholic relations. The council, however, did not declare acceptance of Islam as a theological belief system but only an end to hostility toward Muslims and an appreciation of Muslim piety. All that the council did, therefore, was open the door for Muslim-Catholic dialogue in an atmosphere of mutual respect and tolerance. This new approach, however, still calls for the evangelization of Muslims, as the pope's attitude toward Islam indicates. But the question remains, Is this openness true dialogue, or could it be simply condescending tolerance aimed at facilitating evangelization?

Since the beginning of his pontificate, Pope John Paul II has been consciously urging African and Asian bishops to engage in friendly dialogue with Muslims, but at the same time to intensify their efforts in "spreading the Good News."[33] Yet in an address to a Christian-Muslim colloquium on religious education in modern society, he went a long way toward espousing a completely free and open approach in dialogue with Muslims and others on the basis of their common humanity. The pope first admitted that there are basic differences between the two faiths, but he continued, "Christians and Muslims both hold that the true path toward human fulfillment lies in carrying out the divine will in our personal and social lives."[34] A precondition for dialogue is sound religious education, which should inculcate respect for others and openness to them as children of God, regardless of race, religion, economic status, gender, or ethnic identity.[35]

From this limited survey of his pronouncements, it appears that the Holy Father's attitude toward Islam and religious pluralism in general grew more conservative through the years of his papacy. This may perhaps be a reaction to the epochal world events of the last two decades, as well as the increasing secular and liberal challenges within the church itself. The pope's attitude toward religious pluralism is expressed in a growing emphasis on evangelization.

In a papal letter addressed to the fifth plenary assembly of the Federation of Asian Bishops, held in Bandung, Indonesia, in July 1990, His Holiness advocated an ever-greater commitment to evangelization for the Asian local churches. The praise that he lavished on these churches for their dynamic "witness to the Gospel" is significant in view of the fact that among the most "dynamic local churches" is the Indonesian church. Thus, Muslims around the world believe that Indonesia's large Muslim population is a prime target of this evangelization. Whether true or not, this belief helps perpetuate old Muslim suspicions of Christian motives.

The pope grounded his strong call to evangelization in the document of Vatican II *Nostra Aetate*, which declares,

> Although the Church gladly acknowledges whatever is true and holy in the religious traditions of Buddhism, Hinduism and Islam as a reflection of the truth which enlightens all men, this does not lessen her duty and resolve to proclaim without fail Jesus Christ who is "the way, the truth and the life" (John 14:6).[36]

Moreover, he acknowledged the validity of the theological idea—based on the classical notion of the seminal divine word (*logos spermatikos*)—that the righteous followers of other religions may be saved by Christ without the ordinary means which God had established for salvation. Yet he still insisted that this "does not cancel the call to faith and baptism which God wills for all people."[37]

Carrying the logic of this argument to its ultimate conclusion, His Holiness repudiated the principle of religious pluralism, which is crucial to any meaningful dialogue. He argued that the idea that the church is only one of many ways to salvation is contrary to the Gospel and to the church's very nature. He rejected as well the principle of sharing one's faith with another person in the hope of deepening the other's faith within his or her own religious tradition.[38]

The pope's position toward other religions is clearly and emphatically argued in an encyclical which he issued shortly after the Gulf War.[39] Although this important document says nothing about Islam in particular, the pope may have had Muslims, and particularly the Arabs, in mind when he called on people in the latter category everywhere to "open the doors to Christ."[40] In traditional fashion, the pope divides humanity into two camps, Christians and those who do not know Christ. Since the number of such people in the latter category has doubled since Vatican II, he urged the entire Christian church to become a missionary church.

The thrust of the main argument of this encyclical is stated in the opening declaration of the first chapter: "Jesus Christ the only savior." The pope elaborated this point thus: "God has established Christ as the one mediator. . . ." God also established the church as the "universal sacrament of salvation." He then concluded, "To this catholic unity of the people of God, therefore, all are called."[41]

To the important question "why mission?" the pope replied that the church's faith is that true liberation can be attained only through Christ. Only in Christ can humanity be saved from slavery to sin and death. While no one can question the centrality of this doctrine to the church's faith, it is not one that Islam and Judaism accept, either as part of their own faith or as a common basis for dialogue with Christians. Nor can it serve in today's pluralistic world as a basis for dialogue with any other faith community. This is because this doctrine leaves no room for a genuine fellowship of faith, which must be the ultimate goal of interreligious dialogue.

On the eve of the twenty-first century, after the development and dissemination of the scientific study of religion and the steady advance of global communication, meaningful dialogue is possible only on the basis of religious and cultural pluralism. This means that Christians and Muslims must accept the fact that God did not speak only Hebrew, Greek, or Arabic, but rather he speaks to every people in their own tongue and to their own cultural and spiritual situation. Furthermore, the universality of divine revelation is attested in both the New Testament and the Qur'an (see Acts 14:17; Heb 1:1; and Q. 35:27).

While the pope admits that God mysteriously guides all nations to know him, he insists that true knowledge of God can be attained only through Christ and the church "which is the instrument of salvation." He further asserts, "the Holy Spirit offers everyone the possibility of sharing in the Paschal mystery in a manner known to God."[42] But this only means the possibility for everyone to be a Christian, and that should be the church's universal mission. On this principle of the inner *preparatio evangelica* of every human being, the papal encyclical calls for "mission to the nations." The objective of this mission is to found Christian communities everywhere and to develop mature and fully functioning churches in areas where Christianity has not taken root.[43]

On the basis of this encyclical and other papal statements of the 1990s, it may be concluded that Pope John Paul II is clearly committed to the old doctrine *extra Ecclesiam nulla salus*. But inasmuch as he advocates interreligious dialogue, he may be considered a neo-exclusivist. He is more aware of the diversity and richness of religious traditions than the ancient church fathers who first advocated this exclusivist doctrine. But like them, he cannot accept genuine religious pluralism, because it compromises the church's mission to the nations. He therefore views dialogue as simply an instrument of mission. "Interreligious dialogue," the pope wrote, "is a part of the Church's evangelizing mission." Dialogue, he further argued, should be based on the conviction that the church "alone possesses the fullness of the means of salvation."[44]

## Conclusion

The theme of the universality of divine guidance to all human beings to the knowledge of God is taken up by His Holiness at some length in his book *Crossing the Threshold of Hope*.[45] Here, however, he does not take seriously such phenomena as animism and ancestor worship as legitimate religious practices, but wishes to use them as openings for introducing the Christian faith to the followers of these traditions. In the veneration of ancestors, the pope sees some sort of preparation for the Christian concept of the church as the communion of saints, "in which all believers, whether living or dead, form a single community, a single body."[46] Therefore, missionaries, the pope observes, find it easier to speak a common language with these people than with the followers of the higher religions.

The pope's position toward Islam in this book is especially significant, because here he speaks not as the pope but as a private person. I must therefore conclude that what he says about Islam in this book represents his own convictions. He calls Muslims "believers in Allah,"[47] forgetting that Allah is only the Arabic name for God, which was used also by Arab Jews and Christians long before Islam. Anyone who knows the Old and New Testaments, the pope avers, can clearly see how the Qur'an "completely reduces divine revelation." The Qur'an, therefore, moves away from what God said about himself in the two testaments, "first through the prophets and finally . . . through his son." He concludes, "In Islam all the richness of God's revelation which continues the heritage of the Old and New Testaments has definitely been set aside."[48]

I noted earlier the pope's Qur'anic affirmation in his address to the colloquium on holiness, "Your God and ours is the same, and we are brothers and sisters in the faith of Abraham."[49] In this book he says, "Although beautiful names are given to the god of the Qur'an, he remains a god outside the world, a god who is only majesty, never Immanuel, 'God with us.'"[50] Thus we see that the "All-merciful God," of whom His Holiness so often reminded Muslims is the God of us all, is absent in his book. The major fault of Islam for His Holiness is ultimately that Islam is not Catholic Christianity.

It was argued above that the ultimate goal of true dialogue is a fellowship of faith. This existential fellowship will not be achieved between institutions, or perhaps even their official representatives. It remains the quest of sincere seekers after the truth, pious men and women of whom Christ said, "You shall know the truth and the truth shall set you free" (John 8:32).

# Notes

1. Alfred Guillaume, *Life of Muhammad: A Translation of Ibn Ishaq's Sirat Rasul Allah* (Oxford: Oxford University Press, 1955), 79-82.

2. Waraqah was the cousin of Muhammad's wife Khadijah and may have been a priest. See ibid., 107.

3. According to Islamic hagiographical tradition, the Negus (*Najashi*) of Abyssinia not only received the Muslims hospitably but he is reported to have agreed with the Qur'anic view of Jesus and finally died a Muslim. The personality of al-Najashi represents an interesting example of Muslim-Christian encounter. See ibid., 146-55; see also Montgomery Watt, *Muhammad at Mecca* (Oxford: Clarendon, 1953), 109-17.

4. This ecumenical assertion occurs nearly verbatim near the beginning and end of the Prophet's Madinan career (Q. 2:62; 5:69).

5. See, for example, Q. 4:171; 5:17, 72-73, and 77.

6. This essay was written in the mid-1990s and first published in 1997.

7. Quoted by His Holiness Pope John Paul II in his *'Id al-fitr* (end of the fasting month of Ramadan, April 3, 1991). For the correspondence between the sultan and Pope Gregory VII, see Thomas Michel, S.J., and Michael Fitzgerald, M. Afr., *Recognize the Spiritual Bonds Which Unite Us: 16 Years of Muslim-Christian Dialogue* (Vatican City: Pontifical Institute for Interreligious Dialogue, 1994), 3-4.

8. Edward Peters, ed., *The First Crusade: The Chronicle of Fulcher of Chartres and Other Source Materials* (Philadelphia: University of Pennsylvania Press, 1971), 2; see also 2-5.

9. Between 1978, when he took office, and 1994, Pope John Paul II made 60 trips to 109 countries. See Michel and Fitzgerald, *Spiritual Bonds*, 14.

10. *Origins* 9, no. 26 (December 13, 1979): 420.

11. Q. 4:48 states, "God will not forgive that associates be ascribed to Him, but other than this, he forgives whomsoever he will."

12. *Origins* 10, no. 2 (May 29, 1980): 20.

13. *Origins* 10, no. 37 (February 26, 1981): 592.

14. For a Muslim appreciation of the life and work of this remarkable man, see Zoe Hersov, "A Muslim's View of Charles de Foucauld. Some Lessons for the Christian-Muslim Dialogue," *The Muslim World* 85, nos. 3-4 (July-October 1995): 295-316.

15. *Bulletin: Secretariatus pro Non Christianis* 48 (1981): 182-83.

16. Ibid., 187.

17. *Origins* 11, no. 37 (February 25, 1982): 588.

18. Ibid.

19. *Bulletin* 55 (1984): 25-26.

20. Ibid., 26.

21. *"Redemptionis Anno,"* *Origins* 14, no. 20 (May 24, 1980): 31-32.

22. Ibid., 32.

23. I had the honor of being one of the participants in that colloquium, which included visits to Assisi and other holy sites in Italy. It was a memorable experience.

24. The pope here paraphrased part of Q. 29:46 and alluded to Q. 3:64, which invites all the people of the Book to unity of faith in the One God.

25. For the pope's address and all the proceedings of that colloquium, see *Islamochristiana* 11 (1985): 201-8.

26. See *Bulletin* 60 (1985): 233-37. A few days earlier, on August 12, the pope delivered the same message to the multireligious society of Cameroon. See Michel and Fitzgerald, *Spiritual Bonds*, 42, 44.

27. Michel and Fitzgerald, *Spiritual Bonds*, 65.

28. Ibid., 65.

29. Ibid., 66.

30. *Bulletin* 62 (1986): 147.

31. *Bulletin* 64 (1987): 29.

32. Ibid., 30.

33. This was his message to the bishops of Mali in March 1988, the bicentenary year of mission. See *Bulletin* 70 (1988):14-15.

34. The colloquium was organized in Rome jointly by the Pontifical Council for Interreligious Dialogue and the Royal Jordanian Ahl al-Bayt Foundation, December 6-8, 1989. *Bulletin* 73 (1990): 14.

35. Ibid., 14-15.

36. Quoted by the pope in *Bulletin* 75 (1990): 229.

37. Ibid., 230.

38. Ibid., 231.

39. *Redemptoris Missio*, January 1991 (hereafter, *RM*).

40. *RM* 3.

41. *RM* 4.

42. *RM* 21.

43. *RM* 48.

44. *RM* 55.

45. John Paul II, *Crossing the Threshold of Hope*, ed. Vittorio Messori (New York: Alfred A. Knopf, 1994), 77ff.

46. Ibid., 82.

47. Ibid., 91.

48. Ibid., 92.

49. See note 24 above.

50. John Paul II, *Crossing the Threshold of Hope*, 92.

# Selected Bibliography of the Works of Mahmoud Ayoub

## Books

1978. *Redemptive Suffering in Islam: A Study of the Devotional Aspects of 'Ashura in Twelver Shi'ism*. The Hague: Mouton.

1979. *The Revealer, the Messenger and the Message*. Tehran: World Organization for Islamic Services. A translation of *al-Mursil wa-al-Rasul wa-al-Risalah of Muhammad Baqir al-Sadr*.

1983. *The Great Tiding: An Annotated Translation of the Thirtieth Part of the Qur'an*. Tripoli: The Islamic Call Society.

1984. *The Qur'an and Its Interpreters*. Vol. 1. Albany: State University of New York Press.

1986. (Appeared in 1992) *Beacons of Light: Muhammad the Prophet and Fatimah the Radiant*. Co-authored with L. Clarke. Tehran: World Organization for Islamic Services. A partial translation of *I'lam al-wara bi-a'lam al-huda* by Abu Ali al-Fadl bin al-Hasan al-Tabarsi.

1987. *Islam and the Third Universal Theory: The Religious Thought of Mu'ammar al-Qadhdhafi*. London: Routledge & Kegan Paul.

1989. *Islam: Faith and Practice*. Ontario: Open Press.

1992. *The Qur'an and Its Interpreters*. Vol. 2. Albany: State University of New York Press.

1997. *Nahwa al-jidal al-ahsan* (Arabic) (Toward a Fairest Dialogue: Lectures on Muslim-Christian Theological Understanding) Beirut: Markaz al-Dirasat al-Masihiyyah al-Islamiyyah—Balamand University.

1997. *The Awesome News: Interpretation of Juz' 'Amma*. 2nd ed. n.p.: World Islamic Call Society (revised edition of *The Great Tiding*).

2001. *Mengurai konflik Muslim-Kristen dalam perspektif Islam* (Indonesian) (Muslim-Christian Conflict Resolution in Islamic Perspective). Yogyakarta: Fajar Pustaka Baru.

2000, 2001. *Dirasat fi al-'alaqat al-Masihiyyah al-Islamiyyah* (Arabic) (Studies in Christian-Muslim Relations) 2 vols. Beirut: Markaz al-Dirasat al-Masihiyyah al-Islamiyyah.

2003. *The Crisis of Muslim History: Religion and Politics in Early Islam*. Oxford: Oneworld.

2004. *Islam: Faith and History*. Oxford: Oneworld.

2004. *Akar-akar krisis politik dalam sejarah Muslim* (The Roots of Crisis in Muslim History). Translated by Munir A. Mu'in and Abd Syakur DJ. Bandung. Indonesia: Mizan.

# Articles and Chapters in Books

1974. "Islam and Christianity: A Study of Muhammad Abduh's Views of the Two Religions." *Humanoria Islamica* 2:121-37.

1977. "The Problem of Suffering in Islam." *Journal of Dharma* 267-94.

1979. "The Prayer of Islam [on *Surat al-Fatihah*]." *Journal of the American Academy of Religion* 47:635-47.

1985. "The Word of God and the Voices of Humanity." In *The Experience of Religious Diversity*. Edited by John Hick and Hassan Askari. Elder, England: Gower Publishing Co.

1986. "Auf dem Weg zu einer islamischen Christologie." In *Lust an der Erkenntnis: Die Theologie des 20. Jahrhunderts*. Edited by Karl-Josef Küschel. Munich: Piper.

1986. "Excellences of Imam Husayn in Sunni Hadith Tradition." In *Imam Husayn in Muslim Tradition*. London: Routledge & Keagan Paul.

1986. "The Word of God in Islam." In *Orthodox Christians and Muslims*. Edited by N. M. Vaporis. Brookline, Mass.: Holy Cross Orthodox Press.

1986. "'Uzayr in the Qur'an and Muslim Tradition." In *Studies in Islamic and Judaic Traditions*. Edited by William M. Brinner and Stephen D. Ricks. Atlanta: Scholars' Press.

1986. "Divine Preordination and Human Hope: A Study of the Concept of *Bada'* in Imami Shi'i Tradition." *Journal of the American Oriental Society* 106, no. 4:623-32.

1987. "Islam between Ideals and Ideologies: Toward a Theology of Islamic History." In *The Islamic Impulse*. Edited by B. Freyer-Stoewasser. London: Croom-Helm.

1987. "Revelation and Salvation: Towards an Islamic View of History" (delivered at Kennedy Institute Trialogue, April 1983). *Alserat* 13:10-25.

1988. "The Speaking Qur'an and the Silent Qur'an: A Study of the Principles and Development of Imami Shi'i Tafsir." In *Approaches to the History of the Interpretation of the Qur'an*. Edited by Andrew Rippin. Oxford: Clarendon; New York: Oxford University Press.

1988. "Divine Preordination and Human Hope: A Study of the Concept of Bada' in Imami Shi'i Tradition." (Persian translation) *Mishkat* (Meshhad, Iran) 20:36-52.

1989. "Interview." In *Neighbors: Muslims in North America*. Edited by Elias Mallon. New York: Free Press.

1989. "One God, Many Faiths: Islam and the Challenge of Inter-religious Dialogue." *The Drew Gateway* 58, no. 3:52-57.

1989. "Thanksgiving and Praise in the Qur'an and in Muslim Piety." *Islamochristiana* 15:1-10.

1990. "Law and Grace in Islam: Sufi Attitudes Towards the Shari'a." In *Religion and Law: Biblical-Judaic and Islamic Perspectives*. Edited by Edwin B. Firmage et al. Winona Lake, Ind.: Eisenbrauns.

1990. "Divine Revelation and the Person of Jesus Christ." In *Newsletter of the Office of Christian-Muslim Relations of the National Council of Churches*. New York: National Council of Churches of Christ.

1992. "Methodological Approaches to Islamic Thought and History." In *Research in Islamic Civilization: Outlook for the Coming Decade*. Edited by Ekmeleddin Ihsanoglu. Istanbul: IRCICA.

1992. "The Word and the Way: The Human Quest for God in Islamic Mysticism" (*Das Wort und der Weg: Des Menschen Suche nach Gott in der islamischen Mystik*). In *Horen auf sein Wort*. Mödling, Austria: Verlag St. Gabriel.

1992. "Jihad: A Source of Power and Framework of Authority in Islam." *Bulletin of the Institute of Middle Eastern Studies* (Japan) 6:205-32.

1993. "The Qur'an Recited." *Middle East Studies Association Bulletin* 27, no. 2:169-71.

1994. "The Muslim Ummah and the Islamic State." In *The Role and Influence of Religion in Society*. Edited by Syed Othman Alhabshi and Syed Omar Syed Agil. Malaysia: Institute of Islamic Understanding.

1994. "Religious Freedom and the Law of Apostasy in Islam." *Islamochristiana* 20:75-91.

1994. "Traditional Western Analysis: A Response." *Ecumenism* 116:16-17.

1995. "The Five Pillars of Islam"; "Qur'an: History of the Text"; and "Husayn Ibn 'Ali." In *The Encyclopedia of the Modern Islamic World*. New York: Oxford University Press.

1995. "And the Earth Shall Shine Forth: Fall and Restoration in Judaism, Christianity and Islam." *Conservative Judaism* 47, no. 2:17-36.

1995. "The Qur'an in Muslim Life and Practice." In *The Muslim Almanac: A Reference Work on the History, Faith, Culture, and Peoples of Islam*. Edited by Azim A. Nanji. New York: Gale Research.

1996. "The Islamic Tradition." In *World Religions: Western Traditions*. Edited by Willard G. Oxtoby. Toronto and New York: Oxford University Press.

1997. "Das Mystische im Koran: Muhammads Mystische Vision." In *Hermeneutik in Islam und Christentum: Beitrage zum interreligiosen Dialog*. Edited by Hans-Martin Barth and Christoph Elsas. Hamburg: E. B.-Verlag.

1997. "Repentance in the Islamic Tradition." In *Repentance: A Comparative Perspective*. Edited by Amitai Etzioni and David E. Carney. New York: Rowman & Littlefield.

1997. "The Word and the Way: The Human Quest for God in Islamic Mysticism" (Arabic). In *al-Isgha' ila Kalam Allah fi al-Masihiyyah wa al-Islam*. Lebanon: al-Maktabah al-Bulusiyyah.

1997. "Islam and Pluralism." *Encounters* 3, no. 2:103-18.

1998. "The Numinous in the Qur'an: An Assessment of Rudolf Otto's View of Islam." *The Muslim World* 88, nos. 3-4:256-67.

1999. "Al-Qawniyyah wa al-shumuliyyah wa al-ta'addudiyyah fi al-Masihiyyah wa al-Islam" (Universalism, Inclusivism, and Pluralism in Christianity and Islam). In *Summer Symposium*. Published by the Center for Christian-Muslim Studies, University of Balamand, Koura, Lebanon.

1999. "Cult and Culture: Common Saints and Shrines in Middle Eastern Popular Piety." In *Religion and Culture in Medieval Islam*. Edited by Richard G. Hovannisian and Georges Sabagh. Cambridge: Cambridge University Press.

2000. "Islam and the Challenge of Religious Pluralism." *Global Dialogue* 2, no. 1:53-64.

2000. "Literary Exegesis of the Qur'an: The Case of al-Sharif al-Radi." In *Literary Structures of Religious Meaning in the Qur'an*. Edited by Issa J. Boulatta. Richmond, Va.: Curzon Press.

2001. "al-Islam fi Amerika" (Islam in America) (Arabic). *Al-Minhaj* 21:145-74.

2002. "Religious Pluralism and the Challenges of Inclusivism, Exclusivism and Globalism: An Islamic Perspective." In *Commitment of Faiths: Identity, Plurality and Gender*. Edited by Th. Sumartana et al. Yogjakarta: Institute of DIAN/Interfidei.

2005. "Isa and Jesus: Christ in Islamic Christology." In *Bearing the Word: Prophecy in Biblical and Quranic Perspective*. Edited by Michael Ipgragve. London: Church House Publications.

2005. "The Children of Abraham: A Muslim Perspective." In *Heirs of Abraham: The Future of Muslim, Jewish and Christian Relations*. Edited by Bradford E. Hinze and Irfan A. Omar. Maryknoll, N.Y.: Orbis Books.

2005. "Muhammad." In a volume on "Arabic Literary Culture, c. 500-925." *Dictionary of Literary Biography*. Detroit: Thomson Gale.

2005. "Creation or Evolution: The Reception of Darwinism in Modern Arab Thought." In *Science and Religion in a Post Colonial World: Interfaith Perspectives*. Edited by Zainal Abidin Bagir. Adelaide, Australia: ATF Press.

# Glossary

*'abd*. Servant (of God)

*ahl al-dhimmah*. Non-Muslims in an Islamic state under the protection or covenant (*dhimmah*) of God, the Prophet Muhammad, and the Muslims as mandated by the Qur'an and prophetic tradition

*amān*. Protection, or safe conduct

*amānah*. Primordial trust or covenant between human beings and God

*amr*. Divine fiat or command

*'aqd*. Bond or contract

*a'rāb*. Nomadic Arab tribesmen, as distinct from city dwellers

*awliyā'* (sing. *walī*). Friends of God; Sufis; saints

*āyah*. Sign or a single verse of the Qur'an

*barakah*. Divine blessing or grace transmitted through a holy person or place

*dahr*. Pre-Islamic notion of time; fate, over which no one has any control

*Dajjāl*. "Anti-Christ"; "the one who lies"; he will appear toward the end of time only to be defeated and killed by Jesus Christ, who will descend from heaven for that purpose

*dār al-Islām*. "Abode of peace," refers to places under Muslim rule and where Islamic law is enforceable

*da'wah*. Mission; Qu'ranic reference for a call to invite people to Islam

*fiqh*. Islamic jurisprudence

*fiṭrah*. Original state of creation of all human beings

*ghuluw*. Extremism in religion

*ḥadīth qudsī*. Divine saying, related by the Prophet

*ḥajj*. Annual pilgrimage to Makkah, obligatory for every Muslim at least once in his or her life, if they are able to make their way there

*al-ḥaqq*. Truth, also one of the names of God

*ḥarbī*. One with whom a state of war exists

*hawā*. Inclination or desire

*hijrah*. Migration; also refers to the migration of the Prophet Muhammad and his followers from Makkah to Madinah in 622 C.E., which marks the start of the Muslim era

*ḥulūl*. In mystical terms it refers to an indwelling of the divine in human; divine incarnation

*ḥunafā'* (sing. *ḥanīf* ). Refers to pre-Islamic "generic" monotheists who were neither Christians nor Jews

*'Īd al-Fiṭr*. Muslim holiday celebrating the end of Ramadan, the month of fasting

*iḥsān*. Righteousness or goodness, embodying the higher stages of faith

*ilhām*. Inspiration from God; often received by those believers who are "closer" to God

*īmān*. Faith

*inbithāq.* Procession or emanation

*ittiḥād.* Union; in mysticism, union of creature with the creator

*al-jidāl al-aḥsan.* Fairest debate (Q. 16:125)

*jizyah.* Poll tax, an obligation on non-Muslims living in Muslim lands in exchange for protection and military exemption

*khalīl.* Intimate friend of God; a Qu'ranic attribute for Abraham

*kharaj.* Tax on agricultural land

*kuffār* (sing. *kāfir*). Those who reject or conceal the truth; also translated as "unbelievers"

*kufr.* Rejection of faith

*Mahdi.* "The one who guides aright"; a reference to the future messianic ruler of the world before the end of time who will restore the true religion of Islam

*Majūs.* Reference to Zoroastrians

*Masīḥ.* Messiah, the Christ

*mi'rāj.* Prophet Muhammad's celestial journey

*mujtahid.* Islamic scholar who engages in *ijtihad*—the exercise of personal judgment in interpreting the law in matters not clearly defined in the Qur'an and the hadith

*mulk.* Dominion and authority

*mu'minūn* (sing. *mu'min*). Believers; those who have faith

*mushrikūn.* (sing. *mushrik*). Those who "associate" another authority/god with the One God (Arabic, *Allah*)

*muwaḥḥid.* Unitarian; one who believes in the One God

*naṣrānī* (pl. *naṣārā*). Christian man or woman

*qiblah.* Direction toward Makkah, which a Muslim worshiper faces in prayer

*qidam.* Beginning-less eternity of God

*qirā'ah.* Reading of the Qur'an; recitation

*Quraysh.* Tribe to which Muhammad belonged and which led the Makkan opposition to Muhammad's new faith

*quṭb.* Sufi term referring to a person around whom the universe revolves; every age is said to have its *quṭb*

*raḥmah.* God's infinite mercy; appears numerous times in the Qur'an

*ṣadaqah.* Charity

*ṣalāh.* Formal worship done five times a day by practicing Muslims

*ṣamad.* Meaning eternal refuge; also one of the names of God

*shahādah.* Muslim declaration of faith; the first pillar of Islam: "There is no god but God and Muhammad is the Messenger of God"

*shahīd.* Witness; martyr

*sharī'ah.* Islamic sacred law

*shaykh.* Spiritual leader, a learned person/scholar of Islamic religious sciences

*shirk.* Major sin in Islam; the association of any thing or creature with God; idol worship

*sunnah.* Example of Prophet Muhammad known through his sayings, actions, and silent approbation

*surah.* Roughly equivalent to a chapter in the Qur'an

*tafsīr.* Interpretation or exegesis of the Qur'an

*ṭāghūt.* False gods; idols

*takfīr.* Expiation of sin; also the controversial practice of declaring someone to be a *kāfir*, or rejecter of faith

*taklīf.* Divine charge or obligation for rational men and women *tanzīh*. God's transcendence

*taqiyyah*. Dissimulation; in Shi'ah tradition, a practice of concealing one's faith to escape persecution

*taqwā*. Righteousness; piety; God consciousness

*tawḥīd*. Oneness of God; part of the first pillar of Islam is belief in the unity of the divine being

*ummah*. Global Muslim community

*waḥdat al-wujūd*. Unity of being; concept that permeates the writings of the well-known Sufi Ibn 'Arabi and his school

*waḥy*. Revelation, or the coming of revelation

*walad*. Offspring; child

*wiḥdāniyyah*. Unicity of God

*wilādah*. To engender

*zakāh*. Obligatory tax for all Muslims mandated by the Qur'an

*zunnar*. Belt or sash that non-Muslim subjects of a Muslim state wore as a mark of distinction from Muslims

# Index

## Other Titles in the Faith Meets Faith Series

*Subverting Hatred: The Challenge of Nonviolence in Religious Traditions*, Daniel L. Smith-Christopher, editor

*Christianity and Buddhism: A Multi-Cultural History of Their Dialogue*, Whalen Lai and Michael von Brück

*Islam, Christianity, and the West: A Troubled History*, Rollin Armour, Sr.

*Many Mansions? Multiple Religious Belonging*, Catherine Cornille, editor

*No God But God: A Path to Muslim-Christian Dialogue on the Nature of God*, A. Christian van Gorder

*Understanding Other Religious Worlds: A Guide for Interreligious Education*, Judith Berling

*Buddhists and Christians: Toward Solidarity through Comparative Theology*, James L. Fredericks

*Christophany: The Fullness of Man*, Raimon Panikkar

*Experiencing Buddhism: Ways of Wisdom and Compassion*, Ruben L. F. Habito

*Gandhi's Hope: Learning from Others as a Way to Peace*, Jay B. McDaniel

*Still Believing: Muslim, Christian, and Jewish Women Affirm Their Faith*, Victoria Erickson and Susan A. Farrell, editors

*The Concept of God in Global Dialogue*, Werner G. Jeanrond and Aasulv Lande, editors

*The Myth of Religious Superiority: A Multifaith Exploration*, Paul F. Knitter, editor.